THE

ANDY COHEN

DIARIES

THE
ANDY COHEN
DIARIES

**A DEEP
LOOK
AT A
SHALLOW
YEAR**

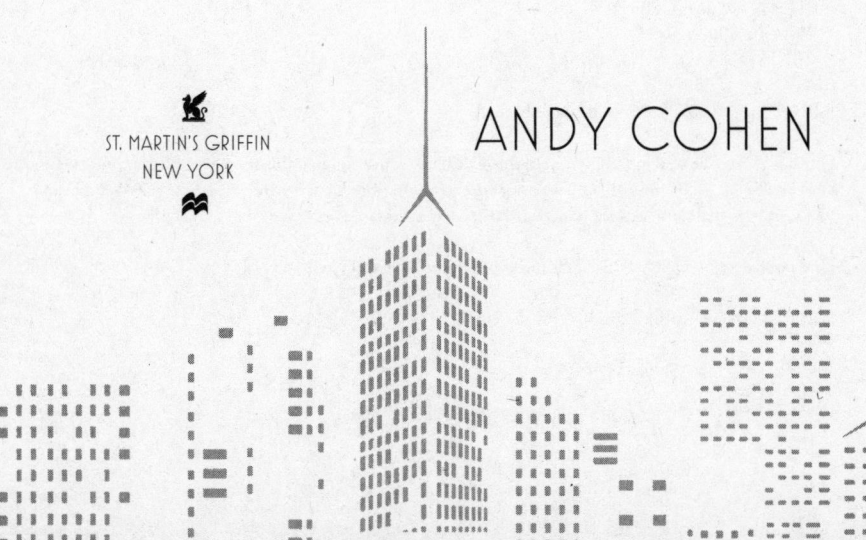

ST. MARTIN'S GRIFFIN
NEW YORK

ANDY COHEN

www.stmartins.com

Lincoln Center photograph (insert page 7) © Kevin Mazur/Getty Images for Lincoln Center

Designed by Meryl Sussman Levavi

The Library of Congress has cataloged the Henry Holt edition as follows:

Cohen, Andy, 1968–
    The Andy Cohen diaries : a deep look at a shallow year / Andy Cohen. — First edition.
        p. cm.
    ISBN 978-1-62779-228-8 (hardcover)
    ISBN 978-1-62779-229-5 (e-book)
    1. Cohen, Andy, 1968—Diaries.   2. Television personalities—United States—Diaries.
3. Television broadcasting—United States—Diaries.   4. Executives—United States—Diaries.
I. Title.
    PN1992.4.C66A3 2014
    791.4502'8092—dc23
    [B]   2014030710

ISBN 978-1-250-07850-6 (trade paperback)

Our books may be purchased in bulk for promotional, educational, or business use. Please contact your local bookseller or the Macmillan Corporate and Premium Sales Department at (800) 221-7945, extension 5442, or by e-mail at MacmillanSpecialMarkets@macmillan.com.

First published by Henry Holt, an imprint of Henry Holt and Company, LLC

First St. Martin's Griffin Edition: November 2015

10   9   8   7   6   5   4

I HAVE SOCIAL DISEASE.

I HAVE TO GO OUT EVERY NIGHT.

IF I STAY HOME ONE NIGHT

I START SPREADING RUMORS

TO MY DOGS.

—ANDY WARHOL

INTRODUCTION

In July of 1989, I was a wide-eyed twenty-one-year-old intern at CBS News in week three of a love affair with New York City that rages on to this day. A pop culture obsessive, I got deeply sucked into the summer media firestorm surrounding the publication of *The Andy Warhol Diaries*. I couldn't wait to get my hands on a copy, which reportedly was full of dish about everybody in New York City, and when I did, carried it around everywhere (it was big and heavy) until I'd devoured the whole thing.

I was already a big fan of Warhol's art, but through the book I was completely drawn into his incredibly glamorous world. I grew up in St. Louis and Warhol took me places I'd only fantasized about: inside the White House, downstairs at Studio 54 with Bianca and Halston, under the tent at Madonna and Sean Penn's wedding, traveling by helicopter with Diana Ross to see Sinatra in Atlantic City—eleven years of this stuff! I felt like I was reading a history of exactly the things I cared about—music, art, Manhattan, and all things pop.

The Andy Warhol Diaries came out two years after his death and were a record of over a decade of his daily conversations with his secretary Pat Hackett about what he did the night before, who he saw, and what he thought. His narration is sometimes passive, but on the page he comes off droll and funny, and if you read it closely, there are clear hints of exactly who he was, what he valued, and how he lived his life. The *Diaries* got slammed by some critics as being nothing more than a vapid assortment of name-dropping and celebrity bashing, but to me it read like a pop culture time capsule with an overlay of commentary from a man fascinated by all facets of celebrity.

I'm obviously no Andy Warhol, but I too am intrigued by celebrity and spend most of my nights out in NYC. Twenty-six years after Warhol's *Diaries* ended, I'm now a TV producer and host with my own front-row seat to a world not many get to see, in a city that I love. Now I'm going through today's versions of the doors that I fantasized about opening when I was reading the *Diaries* all those years ago. The city has changed a lot since the days when he was on the scene; it seems to me less glamorous and debauched, but no less fun. For years I have told my stories to friends, and wished I kept a diary. Time and motivation were always an issue, and I needed a Pat Hackett to help me launch and record my own pop diary. I found her in my friend Liza Persky, a seasoned talk-show producer who is used to culling stories from celebrities on the phone, and a friend who got this project off the ground with me by recording the first season (Fall) of this book.

This book is my own take on Warhol's fun concept: a year in my life, in my own words. It's a life in Manhattan, behind the scenes of a late-night talk show, out on the town, with some stops around the world. It's also a love story about a man and his dog.

I wrote this as I would any diary, so there are a lot of first names. Some you'll recognize from my first book (if you read it), some won't need any explanation, a few you might have to figure out on your own. I tried to make that as easy as possible without losing the tone of a real diary. Also I've left the identities of a few people opaque because I don't want to embarrass anyone *too* much—or be sued or fired.

Going back and reading your own diary can be painful—and in doing so, I feel the need for some disclaimers. Sometimes—like life itself—these chronicles are funny, sometimes dishy, and sometimes even a little sad. And sometimes they are really, really shallow. Because sometimes life *is* shallow. I understand that and have accepted it. I hope you will too. Oh, and I drop a ton of names. More names than you can imagine. I literally almost called this book *Diary of a Name-Dropper*. So if you want to play a drinking game while reading this book—and that's not a great idea and only gonna last for so long—take a swig every time you read a name you recognize.

I've often been asked if I would ever turn the cameras on myself and star in my own reality show—this book is about as close as I'll get.

Oh, and one other thing. In my previous book, I wrote about my first visit to New York City in the winter of 1986 with my friend Jackie, and it bears repeating here. We'd been in the city for all of two hours and decided to take an evening stroll. Around every corner, it seemed, was a place I'd seen in a movie. My eyes were wide and lit up as bright as the city before me. Then I saw, coming toward us on Madison Avenue, a thin man dressed all in black topped with a wild white wig. It was Andy Warhol. We screamed. I took seeing Andy that night as a good omen, a sign that I had found home.

FALL 2013

IN WHICH . . .

- ❋ I AM FALSELY ENGAGED,

- ❋ BECOME ADDICTED TO MASSAGE,

- ❋ OPEN MY LIFE UP TO A DOG,

- ❋ AM CAUGHT WITH A FINGER UP MY NOSE,

- ❋ AND REALIZE I AM FAT.

So my parents are in town for the weekend—my bright idea because I knew I could get them great U.S. Open tickets and tennis is their thing. And I thought it would be a hoot to take them to their first fashion show. (I always go to DVF because Diane von Fürstenberg is a friend. And a legend. Not in that order. And, yes, I said "a hoot.") I wound up spending much of the day (and weekend) haggling with my (seventy-six-year-old) mom about what she would wear to an event to which I invited her, thinking it would be fun, but instead awoke some sort of inner fashion angst in my incredible shrinking mother. "But what am I going to WEAR to this DVF FASHION SHOW!??!" Over and over and over again all weekend I heard this refrain.

I explained to her that it simply did not matter what the hell she wore. "Wear *black*. Wear anything. Not to be mean, Mom, but nobody's looking at you."

OK, that did come out mean, and dinner last night at the Palm turned into an official fight, my dad on the sidelines enjoying his Gigi salad. He'd already weighed in multiple times and his opinion was indeed moot at this point.

Today we were brought through the backstage area of the fashion show and suddenly I was being interviewed on a live stream about what an icon DVF is (a big one, I say) and asked about fashion (if you ever want to see me completely bullshit my way through an interview, watch me respond when someone asks about fashion) while my dad ogled Diane Sawyer (I have no clue why she looks how she looks at whatever age she is but everyone should do exactly what she's doing) and Mom fidgeted with her top. (She did find the perfect DVF top, which unfortunately no one seemed to notice, as I predicted, but she looked really cute.)

I went into the show prepared to respond to these ridiculous rumors that Sean Avery (who is straight) and I are engaged. The truth is that I didn't mind them at first, because the idea that I could get a hot former pro hockey player (the bad boy of hockey, to be exact) to switch teams for my forty-five-year-old Jewish ass was ultimately quite flattering to me. But this "story" won't die and the guy is straight with a girlfriend. It seems to be based on some shirtless pics we've tweeted over the years.

I guess the media has to assume a gay dude and straight guy can't frolic together on vacation without having anal sex? And I guess that anyone will print anything based on nothing. I showed up all prepared to go off on the topic, but not one reporter asked me anything about the "engagement," so the joke was on me.

The show itself was great. I was seated by André Balazs and Sheryl Crow, who is also from Missouri and was lovely. But all I could think as I talked to her was, "Lance Armstrong was *in* you?" (Thoughts are best sometimes when they remain in your head.) Graydon Carter was two seats away and I told him I like the new *VF* masthead and he seemed impressed that I noticed, which may be an indication of how stupid he thinks I am. Naomi closed the show and, I mean, what else do you want to happen at a fashion show but see *that* lady strut? My parents were seated three rows up across from me and they loved it, but couldn't get over the length. "It was so FAST! I mean all THAT for THAT?"

That night my mom bartended on the show and the guest was former *Real Housewives of New Jersey* star Danielle Staub. The energy was off—it was a weird show, punctuated by my mother standing over my guest's shoulder at the bar, looking like she'd rather be in her hotel bed. We should've had Danielle on tape as a one-on-one Barbara Walters–type thing, but she said no and wanted to do it live. So she took the opportunity of not being edited to confront me about why, when she left the show, I released a statement saying I had fired her. The problem is I never released any statement, but I told her I was sorry if I offended her. Sometimes, the only option is to say you're sorry, even if you have no idea what someone is talking about.

▦ MONDAY, SEPTEMBER 9, 2013

Today I had the best date with my dad maybe ever. I took him to the men's finals of the U.S. Open and it was just perfect. We were in the "President's Box" and there were actual heads of state everywhere. Former Mayor Dinkins was intermittently dozing off a few rows over, and the queen of Spain was in front of us. Looking around, I was reminded that my dad resembles an ex-President—seriously, there's an oft-repeated

Cohen family fable about my dad getting stopped at *two* gas stations in the early sixties by people who thought he was JFK—so I felt like we totally blended in. Martha Stewart was right behind us and told me I was lucky to be with my dad. I kind of put my foot in it and said, "It's too bad he's not single, Martha." She glared at me. And then it got really weird because I realized if he was single and she started dating him, she would be my stepmother and that would be not just awkward but probably awful, but then I looked at her and it didn't seem like she was into him that way, which in turn upset me. Why was Martha rejecting my father who looks like a head of state? It's easy to get lost in a hypothetical. Anyway, I said, "That would be awkward. . . ." And that hung there for a second and she just looked at me. It's fine if maybe she's not into him. She kind of made a face. She and Ralph Lauren and Anna Wintour were behind us, and Sean Connery and the Matchbox Twenty guy were next to us. Kevin Spacey was in front of us with what looked like a face full of makeup and three male companions who were definitely not raising any questions.

It was a heavy scene and very adult and quiet and during breaks in play they showed über-famous people on the screen and my dad kept saying *loudly* (for him—he is soft-spoken), "I wonder when they are going to show you. You are as famous as these people." And I was telling him, *"Shhhhh. Don't say that."* And they didn't show me and so there was injustice in his mind, and if your dad can't stand behind you and say you're more famous than Justin Timberlake, I mean, who is going to do it? So bless him. But I am pretty sure Rob Thomas heard every time he said it and so did President Spacey. Nadal won. He could not be hotter. He is so hot that you forgive him for picking his shorts out of his butt crack after every single shot.

We went straight from the tennis to my show, where both my parents were bartenders, and for the game we had them read dirty phrases in Spanish, to which my mom protested, "But we don't SPEAK Spanish!!" I told her that was exactly the point.

Parents left today. Had to go to this *Us Magazine* Stylish New Yorkers party. It's a racket. They put you on the list and then you go to their party. A guy on the press line asked about my engagement and I told him Sean is straight and to get a grip.

The place was teeming with Housewives—first I walked right into four from *The Real Housewives of Miami*, who had all been at my show the night before. Those Miami women are not afraid of a jumpsuit or a cameltoe—which I will add to the list of reasons I love them. I feel so codependent in Housewife-heavy public situations, like I need to spend quality time with all of them. I don't want anyone feeling like I dissed them, because, trust me, I will wind up hearing about it later one way or another.

I found Jenny McCarthy, who was one person at the party whom I actually wanted to talk to. We had an incredibly filthy conversation in which she explained to me how women masturbate (she said to picture them trying to rub a stain out of a garment) and I boldly tried to negotiate a three-way with her and Donnie Wahlberg. They met when they were on my show last October and I encouraged them to date. They're still together and I feel kind of proud, and that maybe I have the *right* to a three-way given my role in their situation. Jenny played along with the ménage concept but I'm not sure how Donnie would feel about it. To be honest, I'm not sure how I feel about it. Fine, I admit it, I absolutely would be too freaked out to have an actual three-way with them, so I don't know why I put in the effort.

On the way out, I saw Melissa and Joe from *RHONJ* and Jacqueline. And I felt bad for not spending more time with them.

This was the day of the ExtravaGaganza, starring Lady Gaga on *Watch What Happens Live*. I wasn't nervous at all. So far I have been more buzzed than anything when one of my LadyIdols comes on. For Cher I was excited but with Oprah I was nervous, actually shaking for an hour before the show, but the minute she came dancing into the Clubhouse (to

"Blurred Lines") and our audience gave her our first ever standing O (not meant to be a pun but go ahead and take it as one), I got right in the zone.

With Gaga, I couldn't wait to see what she was going to wear, and to hear what she had to say for herself. Her publicist told us that I was not allowed to ask about Madonna or Perez Hilton. I pushed back on the Madonna thing because anyone who watches my show knows how much I love Madonna and would expect her name to come up. They said no.

She arrived in costume, wearing eighteen pounds of hair on her head and the seashell boob covers, which I love. She couldn't have been nicer backstage and I was struck by her widdle-baby voice. Has she always had that?

When she entered the Clubhouse, with three or four incredibly big and incredibly hot (and incredibly straight) bodyguards, the seashells were covered by a jacket. Now she asks her team if she can take the jacket off so she's just wearing the seashell bikini-toppy thing, and her team says no. She begs in her baby voice and they say no again. Dave Stanley—our handsome audio guy—comes up and puts the mic on her jacket and she gets him to put it on the strap of the seashell thing, which is covered by her jacket. I say, "I don't think we can hear your mic well if it's covered by that jacket," and she says, "Oh no, I guess I have to take my jacket off!" and that was *that*. This is a smart lady I am dealing with.

I was pussyfooting around during "Plead the Fifth" and allowed her to answer a question without naming names, and during a commercial break Gaga said to me, "Don't beat around the bush. You can ask whatever you want and name names." So I asked myself that age-old question: Do I go for it and piss off the publicist? After the years I spent behind the scenes negotiating with publicists about what topics are off-limits, it is surreal for me to find myself doing it as a host, engaging in this face-to-face trust-dance in which future bookings are at stake. Gaga was already so great, talking about things I'd not heard her discuss (like stripping, doing molly), so I didn't need more. I didn't do it. I focused on getting a great interview without pissing her people off. (Her people, I should add, include her publicist who also reps Rihanna.) By the way, Ralph Fiennes was in the audience with a friend who was wearing flip-flops and Gaga chose flip-flops as her Jackhole. So that was awkward.

After the show she went back into her dressing room and billows of smoke started emerging from under the door. When she came out she theatrically announced, "Oh my God. What's the smell?" I said, "I have a feeling you're not the first person to smoke here," and she responded, "But am I the first person to pee in the garbage can?" I surmised that she was. "I just couldn't hold it in and I couldn't go through all those people to go to the bathrooms." The baby voice! Very sweet, though. We kissed and said goodbye. The second she walked out, I ran over to the PAs and said, "You need to put Lady Gaga's pee in a container so we can put it in the Clubhouse. It's the ultimate pop culture artifact."

Later that night I went to Benjamin's bar opening, Atlas Social Club, in Hell's Kitchen. It's great. Kelly and Barkin had just left when I arrived, and Anderson and I got there at the same time. (And I was thinking, there's no way Sanjay Gupta peed in Anderson's trash can after *his* show.) A reporter from the *Wall Street Journal* was desperately trying to get me to spill anything about Anderson and Ben's personal life. "This bar, I am told, looks just like their home. So it is really personal for both of them, right?" I almost felt bad for him. What did he want me to say? "Yes, it looks just like their bedroom and I will now tell you all about what goes on there. . . ." I didn't fall into the trap, partly because I used to be a journalist and did the same thing—hell, I basically still do the same thing on my show. But I didn't give him anything he could use.

THURSDAY, SEPTEMBER 12, 2013

Tonight was our five hundredth episode—with guests Gloria Estefan and Sean Kingston—but it was no cause for celebration for me. This is gross, but here's what happened: I never poo at Bravo HQ or at *WWHL*. I don't poop at work, case closed. Tonight, unfortunately, I completely mistimed my daily expulsion and by the time I got to the show, I kept hearing Whoopi Goldberg in my head saying, "You in danger, girl." I had to go. To make matters worse, catering was serving "breakfast for dinner." Breakfast for dinner always generates a ton of excitement among the kids who work at my show. (Obviously—who *doesn't* love breakfast for dinner?) But these kids really are nuts about it. Predictably, I got caught up in the buzz, and after that meal, I had *that feeling.*

The bathroom on our floor is not only shared with our entire staff but the community college down the hall (long story/don't ask) and our audience. So I was a lot concerned about giving one unlucky audience member something memorable for my five hundredth episode. I mean, can you imagine going to a talk show and seeing the host come out of a stall? That would forever taint my viewing experience of the show. And possibly make me feel revolted by the host and never, ever watch his smelly show again. I was determined not to do it.

Adding another layer to the shituation, we were doing a "Teach Me Your Talent" as one of our "Here's What's" and Gloria Estefan was going to teach me a sexy Latin dance move that a shart would have rendered unsexy. To cap it off, we were ending the episode with a conga line with the *WWHL* gay shark that I was sure would end in disaster. John Hill was the only one who knew what was going on with me, and when the show was over he pointed out that I had my feet raised off the ground for most of it, in what I assume was a clench mechanism. I raced home afterwards faster than I ever have in five hundred shows. No cake for me!

Nobody picked up my comments from the *Us* party about Sean being straight and now there's something in the *Enquirer* about us being engaged. And my buddy Jim Ackerman who lives in New Jersey was leaving his house the other day and his plumber asked him if it was true. *A plumber in New Jersey heard about it.* People in St. Louis are even starting to ask my parents about it. My mom keeps saying, "It's so STUPID!"

▦ FRIDAY, SEPTEMBER 13, 2013

Turns out we counted wrong and last night was actually show number 480 or so. *Ruh-roh.* That's just funny. We made a huge deal about the anniversary on the air; I really carried on about it. I guess we lied, is all. Also, Ryan King, our renaissance production assistant, says he read online that Lady Gaga's urine will become toxic shortly—not because it is Lady Gaga's but because urine belonging to any mammal (including lady singers) becomes toxic. But he strangely found a recipe somewhere to turn it into perfume. So Ryan is trying to make perfume out of Lady Gaga's pee, which is even more arty than just saving it on its own as a pop culture artifact.

I feel morose, or grossly opportunistic, even bringing this up, but my doorman Surfin told me a couple months ago that my upstairs neighbor, an old man who has the exact same floor plan as mine, is very, very sick. Like bedridden with twenty-four-hour care up there. And the super made it seem like making a duplex in the building is a possibility. So I mean . . . I don't wish for this man to pass away but I have been coveting his apartment and every morning when I leave I give Surfin a look wondering if he has seen the neighbor and he gives me one back saying he hasn't. I feel filthy every time I think these evil thoughts, but I can't stop. New York City turns us all into killers.

▦ SATURDAY, SEPTEMBER 14, 2013

Today was Yom Kippur and I went to the gay temple and once again I did not find a boyfriend. Cruising the Jewish Boys during the long service is certainly a wonderful diversion but I wonder if it is what the Lord would've wanted on the holiest day of the year. Like maybe it's contradictory to the repenting? At this moment it's been almost a decade since John Hill and I broke up and he was my last serious relationship. "How can that be?!" I am asked by others and often ask myself. Pick one or two: I am shut off, I am happy as I am, I am selfish and set in my ways, I put my job first, I meet people that I'm more attracted to physically than mentally, I use my friends and job to replace a relationship, I see my ex every day at work and that gives me enough something or other to tide me over. Or maybe, just maybe, *I haven't met the right guy?* It's gotta be some combination of all of them, but I have been in love exactly two and a half times and I am sure I will be again. In the meantime I will cruise guys at my gay temple whilst repenting. And I am entertaining the notion of getting a dog.

Just like every fall since freshman year in college, I broke the fast at Dave Ansel's—breakfast for dinner without any emergencies! Dave's daughters are obsessed with *Girls Just Want to Have Fun* (who isn't?), so when SJP picked me up for Jessica Seinfeld's birthday party wearing sparkly shoes, they lost their minds. It was a cute post-nosh moment. I guess you would classify Jessica's birthday event as a house party with a twist—seated dinner, hot waiters, and dancing. We arrived at the same time as Sean Avery, who said that if we *were* engaged he never would've let me out of the house with the sport coat I was wearing, which was kind of irritating given that it's a brand-new Ovadia and Sons white jacket with black trim on the lapel. I could've pretended Sean and I were indeed engaged, because I was seated between him and SJP, but his girl-friend, Hilary, was to his left, so that would've been awkward. And Sean said his dad called him wanting to know if they were going to have *the conversation*. His dad said, "We need to talk. Whatever you need to say to me, it will be OK." He was trying to say that he was ready for Sean to come out—his voice was catching and everything. Which is insane, but weirdly sweet. Sean said, "No, Dad, no. No. I'm not gay. I'm not."

Hugh Jackman was there—he's huge. There was a DJ on the terrace and it was decadent and thumping. It was my first encounter with a DJ on a residential terrace. If anyone needed to dance in Central Park, we gave them a reason. I made up for fasting all day by eating like a pig all night.

MONDAY, SEPTEMBER 16, 2013

Went to a party at the Boom Boom Room for NBC's new schedule (though not sure there is much to celebrate there) and told *ET Canada* and *Extra* that Sean is straight and this is a stupid rumor. I am pretty sure that will do it. I only stayed forty-five minutes because I had to get to the show. It is *very* weird being at the Boom Boom Room sober. I won't ever attempt that again. Talked to a bunch of the girls from *SNL*, including Vanessa Bayer. Love her. Obsessed with Jacob the Bar Mitz-vah Boy.

TUESDAY, SEPTEMBER 17, 2013

I apparently did *not* kill the engagement thing last night and tonight went to a party for the launch of Esquire TV thinking that I had to definitively put the kibosh on the rumors. TMZ asked me about it when I was coming into the party and I did my spiel and then said, "So no,

I am not banging Sean Avery, but I would like to." I can't imagine that's not running.

Major *Housewives* drama offscreen this week. We are replacing several women in two cities. So far it's been sad and energizing all at once. Hopefully we are adding life to both series by shaking things up. I spent forty-five minutes on the phone today with one of their husbands who was begging for his wife's job back, saying they have no backup plan, and I was telling him he never should have banked on this as his career. I had this same conversation a couple years ago with a (crying, literally) husband from another city and it is not pleasant. I feel horrible for these guys who had careers before the show and then went all-in on their wives' reality TV stardom. Let me say this once and for all: bad idea. Reality TV careers aren't forever. Then Ramona called upset because I had invited Jill back to play tennis for a scene. Apparently a cast revolt was brewing about her coming back for even one scene. I completely understood her point of view, actually, and we killed the shoot (which necessitated a long follow-up call with Jill). And then last night NeNe was on with Paula Patton (she brought me a gorgeous bottle of whiskey that she said Robin Thicke jacked from their hotel room for me) and I did something to piss Linnethia off and I can't figure out what it was, but she shut down on the air. Drama in four cities. I kind of love it.

WEDNESDAY, SEPTEMBER 18, 2013

I saw the Irish chef last night. He slept over. Fun, but I had three hours of insomnia in the middle of the night. My mind was churning and in the light of day I'm not sure about what.

I went to the City Clerk's office at the crack of dawn to get my marriage officiate license because I'll be officiating a live wedding on *WWHL* soon. Daryn filled out the paperwork online and then I just had to show up at City Hall to make it official. Couples who were there to get married were recognizing me and I was handing out tickets to *WWHL* as wedding presents left and right. But I was in such a bad mood, so tired. I gave tickets to Melinda, the lady behind the counter, and the sick thing is when these people all do come to the show I will have forgotten who they are but have to take pictures with them after the show and I won't want to do it because I'll be irritable and want to get out the door. I'm setting myself up to be irritated.

My mood improved at work. I got a nice email from Jacqueline, very Zen about not coming back to *Jersey*, and we let go of a couple Wives on *Real Housewives of Orange County*. One said she was too busy to take the call from the head of the production company and put him on with her intern. Her man later called back and was shocked to hear why the EP was calling. Then the weirdest cake arrived from Lady Gaga, red velvet cheesecake with white chocolate on top with Lady Gaga Art Pop written on it . . . the note said "Love, Gaga" in teeny little capitals. It looked like—I don't know what actually–robot writing? Speaking of weird handwriting, our renaissance PA, Ryan, who was making the Gaga pee-fume, writes down what I'm wearing every night for Bravotv.com. I noticed he has really unique handwriting, and he holds the pen in an odd manner. He told me he learned to paint before he learned to write, so he holds the pen like a paintbrush. I just had to hug him. I was like, "When do I find out something bad about you?" I'm borderline inappropriate with our PAs.

That TMZ thing ran all over the place and of course the headline was "Andy Cohen: I'm not banging Sean Avery but I would like to!" At least the story is dead and I haven't misrepresented myself. I have to say the comments on gay websites—I talked to Anderson about this—you just can't read them. They are the meanest. Gay people will eat other gay people alive. After all these years putting myself out there, I am pretty thick skinned, but the shit gay people say about me is, wow. I am apparently a lecherous, disgusting, old, crazy, cliché, star-fucking, ladylike, bossy bottom. That's it in a nutshell. (They without fail add the "bottom" moniker at the end. As punctuation.)

A perfect dinner with John Hill at Pastis, where I had the French onion soup and branzino. We sat at the same corner table I sat at the night before 9/11 with Natasha Richardson and Hickey after the Michael Jackson concert. We'd come late-night after the concert and SJP coincidentally had walked in from a big fashion event and sat with us. Walking out, we saw the towers and all commented what a perfect night it was. Towers are gone. Natasha is gone. Michael Jackson is gone.

Today's Housewife psychodrama involved me on the phone with someone in the throes of being demoted from full Housewife to recurring role. She wanted to be in the opening titles and I had to tell her no. She wanted to be in every episode, and I couldn't guarantee that either. Her husband was on the call, of course. At one point he said, "We pay our taxes, unlike some of your other non-tax-paying Housewives." Good for you! And apparently there's a former OC Wife in tears fighting her dismissal and I'm expecting a call from her any minute.

Glamour magazine asked me to interview Lady Gaga for their Women of the Year cover story. Allegedly her people asked for me, which if true is flattering. But the reality of the situation is I don't want to offend Madonna by being up Lady Gaga's ass. I want to interview Madonna!

Went to the launch party of the new *FourTwoNine* magazine. Walking in, I saw a huge poster of the cover, which is of SJP and me, and it's pretty gorgeous, I have to admit. You'd think that if there was ever a huge blown-up poster of yourself you would want it. And indeed someone asked me, "Do you want that poster?" and I immediately thought, "Where in the hell are you going to put a billboard of yourself?" This has happened before at Bravo and I've figured that my mom would want the posters. And of course she says, "What the hell am I going to do with THAT!? I don't want to STARE AT YOU all day!" So the truth of the situation is, nobody wants your blown-up poster of yourself—not you and not even your mother. Bruce (wearing a T-shirt that said "I Love Madonna" in rhinestones) and Liza came to the party, so that was a godsend. The Irish chef was there too.

When I got home I was doing whatever the hell I do in my apartment and I walked into the bathroom and saw a huge insect—an enormous waterbug—on the soap tray next to the sink. You would've thought there was a lion in the tub by the way I screamed bloody murder. It was like the fucking Hunger Games! I raced to the intercom and breathlessly, urgently called the doorman. *"Are there any porters in the building who can come up and kill this huge bug in my apartment?"* (This has happened before—roughly quarterly.) They were all gone, so I gave the doorman my best offer: I would give him twenty bucks if he left his post and came to kill the intruder. He said he couldn't leave his post. I told him that I would watch the front door if he came up and killed the bug. He said fine, but that it would be a few minutes. I went to close the bathroom door and peered in to look at the bear, I mean bug, and it was gone. Nowhere to be found. I called off the dogs, closed the door, sealed the perimeter by putting a towel under the door, and slept (fitfully) in the extra room.

I really need a dog. I'm lonely and I need something to care about, take care of, and think about other than myself or my job. I've been tossing this around all year, but tonight sealed the deal. Can dogs kill bugs? At least we could go through the terror together. I'm going to start browsing.

FRIDAY, SEPTEMBER 20, 2013

Today I filmed the *Queer Eye* reunion and it was a blast. *QE* had already premiered when I joined Bravo but I was an EP on close to one hundred episodes over the next few years. Now here I was hosting the reunion, on the couch with those guys. I had forgotten how groundbreaking that show was in its moment. Funny to think what a big deal it was ten years ago, seeing gay guys making straight guys' lives better, but it was. I'm proud to have been a little part of it. We had to shoot at the crack of dawn because Ted had to catch a flight to Miami for work and we were all giving him a lot of shit. Those guys haven't missed a beat. But I mean, you can't get a word in edgewise with them.

The good news about starting so early was ending early with a boozy lunch outside at Rosemary's with John Jude, John Hill, and Deirdre. We laughed a lot.

Tonight—Friday night—two Housewives kept sending me "urgent" texts. I was getting all bent out of shape because I knew they weren't "urgent" and do we not live in a society where there are appropriate times to have work conversations, or do business hours not apply in 2013? Or is it a Housewives thing? Do business hours not apply to Housewives? I don't know why I was getting my panties in a bundle but I was Mr. Standing On Principle and told them we would speak Monday morning.

One of the porters came by and did a walk-through of the bathroom, sprayed it down, and declared it safe for use. He said to keep the drain closed in the sink. How that monster fit through the *drain* is beyond me. I never found it, by the way, which means that it's still out there.

▦ SATURDAY, SEPTEMBER 21, 2013

John Hill and I went to look for a dog at the North Shore Animal League on Long Island. I met a few dogs but there were so many and it was overwhelming. I think I want a Havanese (they're small and hypoallergenic) but I didn't connect with any there. Oh, and when I arrived at the shelter I threw my car keys out with my coffee cup, so I spent twenty panicked minutes retracing my steps and found them in the dog-shit-filled trash can. Nice. Then I drove all the way out to Exit 70 to meet this Havapoo named Hemingway I'd found online. It was a long schlep in the reverse direction and I really didn't want to do it, but my Aunt Judy, who is a mega dog lady (some might say *crazy* dog lady), had blown up Hemingway's photo and was using it as her screensaver, so she was convinced I was messing with fate and guilted me into driving to Exit 70 to meet him. I spent an hour trying to figure out if I was in love. I decided I probably wasn't, so I left.

Went to a dinner party at Bruce's tonight and stared at pictures of Hemingway, trying to figure out if I was in love with the dog. The consensus in the room—John Hill, Liza, Amanda, and Lynn—was that I'm not, so the search continues. Bruce burned himself on a pan, so the painkillers came out and then we played "Heads Up!" It got sloppy at the end.

▦ SUNDAY, SEPTEMBER 22, 2013

Today I interviewed Teresa and Joe for a special about the thirty-nine federal counts against them and it was like pulling teeth. They are either very un-introspective or in complete denial. Or both. Another challenging layer was that their lawyers were there and didn't want them revealing certain details. I said, "*So* . . . you guys are facing fifty years in prison," and they were like, "Is it fifty years? We thought it was a hundred. Is it fifty years both or just one or . . ." And I said, "Is it a hundred?" And they said, "I think it's a hundred." So that's something they are going to want to clarify with their attorneys.

▦ MONDAY, SEPTEMBER 23, 2013

I spoke to one of the recently laid-off Housewives today. She is—to put it mildly—not pleased about not being asked back to the show, and she wanted me to know that she is a businesswoman and that everything she does is through a business perspective and that she is being punished for being the *realist (real-est) Housewife.* This from a woman with a generous amount of dye and Botox and fillers and all the rest. Apparently everyone tells her that her Q score is very high. I told her that I was working with different data. (People are always telling me about their high Q scores, but I guess if people tell you they love you all day everywhere you go, why wouldn't you believe your Q scores would be through the roof?) She's shocked we don't want to do a spinoff series with her. I told her we need to freshen up the show, and that we have two great new girls ready to come on. And she goes, "Well, that went so wrong for you with New York." And I told her it actually didn't, and that I would do that again, the season was a success because we refreshed the show. And then she asked why we are keeping Vicki on *OC* and I said that everyone is separate and I wasn't going to go through each woman and debate their worthiness.

This morning Surfin said the upstairs neighbor has taken a turn for the worse. The son is visiting and the son never visits. Lord strike me down.

▦ TUESDAY, SEPTEMBER 24, 2013

I've decided that, no matter what, the thing that you always say to a woman is "You're too thin. Everyone is worried about you." Who doesn't want to hear that? I said it today on *Wendy Williams*, but I actually meant it with her. She's so thin that she seemed kind of shaky. You don't realize how good her body is because she's really top-heavy, and you can tell she's a TV star because her head is huge. (People on TV have huge heads. It's true.) She is so fun; I could talk to her for a long time. Then I went to the "world's largest picnic" on Pier 84, sponsored by Hellmann's. It was, no surprise, a paid appearance. Katie Holmes and Mario Batali were there and it just made me realize everyone's on the dole.

There was this guy, Zach, who was my handler at the picnic. He was cute and there was some kind of energy between us—after half an hour I knew that I either had slept with him, met him at a gym, or almost gone on a date with him. I knew we had interacted over text in some way, so when I left I looked in my contacts and thought, "Oh great, he's in my phone." I texted him and said, "I'm so sorry it took me so long to figure out who you were," and then I got a text back saying, "Who is this?" And I said, "This is Andy," and he flipped back, "Andy who?" "Andy Cohen," I said. And he said, "Oh, I haven't seen you in forever," and I said, "Hahah haha I deserve that," and he said, "I don't get it." Turns out I was texting my former massage therapist in the Hamptons, Zach. So then I took advantage of the situation and made an appointment. He was a good masseur! Then I got a text a few hours later from Zach from the event. He *did* have my phone number but I still haven't figured out why. I've decided we didn't sleep together. I would've remembered.

Nick Carter and Suzanne Somers were on the show tonight. Nick Carter is doing this book about his struggles with drug and alcohol dependence, and some might argue that my show promotes alcoholism, so I took him aside before we went on and said I would be mellow with all the booze talk, but it turned out he still drinks occasionally. He said just don't worry about it. I felt funny interviewing him about his struggles with sobriety knowing that he wasn't completely sober. I loved him, though. Suzanne Somers said she relates to me as a businesswoman, which I don't know what to do with. Women do love to tell me they are businesswomen, especially Housewives. Should Suzanne be a Housewife? A grand doyenne of *The Real Housewives of Beverly Hills*? And the bartender was Steve Grand, this gay country singer who is pretty hot. The dynamic of my ex-boyfriend John standing next to the camera watching me flirt with this gay country singer who looked like a triple banana split made for an amusing show—for me at least.

Ryan finished the Lady Gaga perfume and I can't decide whether it smells floral or like dressed-up pee. He put it in an old-fashioned snifter-y bottle with one of those puffs to spray it. The truth of the matter is you're spraying some form of urine on yourself and whether it belonged to a pop priestess or not, whether it smells good or not, it's pee. Maybe I like the idea of it better than the reality. Not the first time.

WEDNESDAY, SEPTEMBER 25, 2013

I had Lucy Liu on the show and I got her to spank me (which seems to be happening with great frequency lately) and her Lorraine Schwartz diamond bracelet broke on my ass. What is the protocol after asking someone to spank you and then breaking their bracelet? Am I supposed to pay for this? Does Bravo pay? After the show, my mother sent a furious flurry of texts saying that my pants were too tight ("You are PRESENTING your CROTCH to people who DON'T WANT TO SEE IT!!!"); however, I also got two random emails on Facebook complimenting my bountiful basket. That's a wardrobe catch-22. By the way, it was a made-to-measure Seize sur Vingt suit. Oh, and I got a vile email from a viewer saying I looked like a "fool in a child's suit" and to "stop trying to make my hair look hip." Everybody needs to be heard.

THURSDAY, SEPTEMBER 26–SUNDAY, SEPTEMBER 29, 2013— LAKE POWELL, UTAH

Our whole group that always travels together—a group that *occasionally* could be considered jogging on the perimeter of jaded—reunited again, this time for a trip to Lake Powell, where we were completely gobsmacked by the beauty and scope of the American West. It was me, Barry, Bruce and Bryan, Jason and Lauren Blum, Ricky Van Veen and Allison Williams, Hamilton and Manuel, and Michael and Wes. (Anderson's doing a story for *60* somewhere.) I paddleboarded, kayaked, and rappelled, and got my rock-climbing teacher to tell me his sex stories. (In essence, it's hard to come by out here even though he's hot.) We played this great

Spanish card game called Pumba, which brought out the nasty bitch in us all and provided endless laughs. We stayed at the Amangiri for part of the time and on a houseboat for the rest. Imagine fifteen New Yorkers on a houseboat on Lake Powell with a weak Wi-Fi signal. (I thought for an hour that someone was going to get their throat slit over this Wi-Fi signal.) On the other end of the spectrum, I can't believe this terrain is in America. It's colossal, *incredible*. The shapes, colors, size, and patterns are mind-blowing.

Allison and Ricky played an amazing prank on the rest of us—they got the Amangiri to leave letters in each of our rooms saying we were being inducted into a select group of "Spirit Guests," which entitled us to all sorts of special privileges at Aman hotels. "Spirit Guest" merchandise accompanied the letter and it set us all reeling. There is no other hotel group that I would want to get free nights at more than from Aman, so I was personally a little high from the letter. But when you reread it really closely, it actually made no sense (i.e., the resort bragged about playing host to dictators and random celebrities, and they were a touch condescending to Allison, who by my read they referred to as a know-it-all), so we broke it down at dinner and finally realized it was an elaborate prank—which made me maybe even happier than the privileges would have.

I was the only single person on the trip. I enjoyed myself and did not give it a second thought until last night. I was Skypeing with my parents and Mom asked me who was on the vacation and I started naming all these people and three names in she got this look on her face, getting really sad on my behalf—she was almost getting misty—and I was like, "No, no, no, it's fine." Her reaction made me sad. Did it take my mom being sad on my behalf for me to feel lonely? It was interesting. So then I hashed it out in my mind—I was with a group of great friends and didn't have a moment of isolation on the trip. That being said, I do love to cuddle and it was cold at night. I really need a dog, is the thing. Baby steps . . .

Last night my Barbara Walters/Teresa moment aired and I woke up to a flood of tweets from Teresa lovers—they call themselves "Tree Huggers"—who were furious at me for asking her questions about the thirty-nine federal counts against her. They either don't think it is a big deal or think that it's not my business to be asking. So I did what I do in the face of a zillion nasty tweets, which is start tweeting about my cab ride. And I will say, my cab driver and I were magically, fully in sync today—this makes me happy. We crossed Twenty-fourth Street to go up Sixth Avenue, and it was perfect. I tipped him $4 on a $10.50 fare and gave him my *Times* and *Post*. I love it when my cab drivers enthusiastically accept my newspapers.

At 30 Rock I interviewed Lady Gaga on the phone for *Glamour*. She was in LA, snuggly and baby-voiced. I asked her which of her songs represented her or her career and she said "Born This Way" and I wondered if her experience of that song had been tainted by Madonna calling it "reductive." She thought long and hard and was very careful in answering, but we wound up speaking about their relationship for several minutes and I know it's going to generate a ton of press for the magazine. In a nutshell, what she was saying is that Madonna's true persona was revealed during the whole squabble. And I inferred that her version of that persona is a beeyotch. I, of course, am torn about being the one to generate this information, because in no way do I want to be associated with anything negative relating to Camp Madonna.

Also I asked her if she liked Katy Perry and there was a long pause and she said she would rather not answer that. "No comment" is often the most revealing answer, so I was titillated at the idea that there actually might be some tension between these two superstars who've been pitted against each other in the press.

But about fifteen minutes into the conversation, I found myself deeply engrossed in the Star Tracks section of *People* magazine and checking my Twitter feed and literally had to slap some sense into myself to pay attention to *Glamour*'s Woman of the Freaking *Year* on the other end of the telephone. What the hell is wrong with me? Am I *that* easily distracted? Can I possibly be bored talking to a major pop diva? Would I rather look at paparazzi pics of Gaga than actually talk to her? Is it ADD? Is this gonna be my golden ticket to an Adderall prescription? I can always find an upside.

I recorded the interview with only one tape recorder and was paranoid the entire time that it wasn't recording. Also, when it was over I told her I kept her pee, and she loved it and, oddly enough, thought that I might have. Maybe she's done this before? I wouldn't tell her what I did with the pee. I kind of have to get my head around the whole peefume idea before I go wide with it.

I stayed up till two in the morning looking at dogs online. I have become obsessed. It's as much fun as Manhunt was in 2006. I fell in love with a beagle-hound mix named Ron Swanson. I should've been looking at beagles all along, given my Snoopy fixation, but everyone says they're horrible animals. He looks perfect—he's white and brownish red. Preppy. Kinda like a Ralph Lauren Snoopy. And he would go in my apartment—he literally *goes* with the furniture! I'm stalking the agency, See Spot Rescued—I sent them two emails—so I can meet this Ron Swanson. By the way, "Ron Swanson" is clearly a great name for a beagle but it's also the name of a character on *Parks and Rec* (which I don't watch), and what would be worse than getting the dog and having to explain to everyone that I don't really watch the show? I would have to change that name.

I feel like a dog is going to give me some love. I need a companion; it's time. Plus if this new deal at Bravo/*WWHL* works out, I'm going to have a lot more time at home. Basically, if I have to think about only myself for another minute, I am going to rip my skin off.

▦ TUESDAY, OCTOBER 1, 2013

The government is shut down and all I can do is think about Rachel Zoe saying, "The government. Shut. It. Down!" I spent a couple hours with the *Housewives of New York City* production team, who had blocked out twenty episodes based on what we shot all summer. It's going to be an amazing season. Absurd drama and laughs in every episode. I'm excited.

Over the last couple weeks I have slowly come to the realization that I'm completely fat. It's all I see when I look down or in the mirror. I can't believe how fat I am, which for some reason makes my transition into dog owner all the more meaningful. You have to be a little chubby to be a dog owner, right? Just a little belly? I'm obsessed with Ron Swanson the Ralph Lauren Snoopy, and I heard back from the lady at See Spot Rescued. She said Ron is still available—he's in West Virginia and they are flying him up here. He was in a kill shelter there and now is in a foster home. She needs to come do a home visit and she needs three references. She means business, this adoption lady. And she said they give all their dogs pop culture names. I looked at her site and there's a Slade Smiley(!), and also a Roxie Hart. There's Marc Jacobs, he's kind of cute. Christie Brinkley was just adopted. I mean, there's even a Mila Kunis. I keep picturing Mila Kunis the dog whenever her name comes up (which has oddly happened a couple times this week). And there's a Cat Deeley. A dog named Cat. Then of course on my way to the gym I saw a Havanese and I got Havanese crazy again. But I think I am meant to have a beagle. (I know, Ron Swanson is actually a beagle-foxhound mix, but close enough.)

Alexia Echevarria and Meghan McCain were on my show. I kind of thought that I was going to make Alexia cry talking about her son, but she didn't. It may have been additive to see her cry. I like her, though, tears or not.

All night I was in a slow rage. I couldn't figure out what I was mad about. Something. I couldn't remember, which was frustrating for everyone of course. And I gave the finger to the government on the air and in my ear Deirdre wondered if you can give the finger on Bravo. After the show my trusty EP found out that yes, you can, if it's done as a joke. What do I know about the government? I'm fat. Maybe that's why I'm mad?

WEDNESDAY, OCTOBER 2, 2013

Everything came together at the last minute tonight and we had a great show. Around 6 p.m. I decided it would be hilarious to do Rachel Zoe commenting on the government shutdown, so we got Amy Phillips to get in costume and do that whole "Washington is shutting it down" thing. And then right before air, someone tweeted me that the San Diego Zoo Panda Cam was still up, so we kept cutting to that. I can't handle pandas. I mean, they look like people in panda costumes eating twigs. There is nothing cuter. And so now I think we're going to do a webcam of the night. It's very Letterman, like what he used to do, but whatever. I like it. I love David Arquette, he's got a great spirit. I said to him before we went on that it must be hard to own a bar and manage his sobriety and he goes, "I'm not sober anymore." (This seems to be a trend.) Everyone in the control room heard, and Deirdre was in my ear immediately, making fun of the awkward moment. I recovered and asked him what he was drinking and then I toasted him. The truth is he was a whole lot looser on the sauce, which is not exactly headline news.

David was with this lady who was carrying on about the Dodgers and how they may be playing the Cardinals in the playoffs. She said to me that they were gonna kick our asses. I hate smack talk. I'm not cut out for it. I told her that the proper thing to say is "It's going to be a great series." That's what you say to be sportsmanlike. You don't act like a child and talk shit. After the show she gave me her card and said, "If you need tickets to any of the games, I am one of the owners of the team." And then I realized, I almost had a fight with one of the owners of the Dodgers. *I* was telling *her* how to be sportsmanlike. I hope I didn't screw up a coin toss or a trade.

I got home around 12:30 a.m. and got a two-hour massage. It was amazing. From a new guy, Adam. He was really tough. This is going to become a weekly thing. Though I tend to give notes after a massage to the poor therapist, I had very few for him. (There *was* one thing about my shoulders.) I asked him to carry me to my bed when it was done, and said that I was joking, but I think I was serious. The whole time I was lying there I was thinking, "What if Ron Swanson was here, what would he be doing? Would he be looking at me the whole time?"

And I continue to be fat. Correction—I continue to be *very* fat. I was lying on the table like a slab of meat, wondering what I look like splayed out. I should add that I had a shot of Jägermeister on my way out of the show. Literally as I was walking out the door to get the massage after filming a response to the Britney "Work Bitch" video, someone hands me a shot and I just did it and left. So I have become this splayed-out bloated person with Jäger breath thinking about pandas. When do I start being an adult? When Ron Swanson arrives?

I woke up to a bunch of tweets saying *Good Morning America* is ripping off your Panda Cam gag. So that put me in a foul mood, although I don't know if we were the first anyway. It does seem like someone at *GMA* is watching our show, because I get tweets all the time from people saying they're ripping off our bits. It's one thing for my show to be as stupid as it is, but that show (produced by ABC News) has turned into a dumber version of *Entertainment Tonight*. And people love it, so the joke is on America. Ha!

Zarena, the lady from See Spot Rescued, came by and interviewed me and did an "apartment inspection." Oh, and did I mention she needs *three* references? Halfway through I thought maybe she misinterpreted me and thought I was adopting a *kid*, but no, it's all about a dog. We talked a lot about dog psychology, where to put his crate, and on and on. And I have to feed it. Oh Lord. I hope he likes takeout. But I decided that I am just meeting him, I don't have to walk out with him. I made that very clear to her, too.

In the cab to work, we were stuck on the left side of Sixth Avenue and the traffic seemed to be moving well in the right two lanes, which was making me crazy. I couldn't contain myself. I finally said to the guy, "Can you get in the right lane?" And he started going off on how *broken* America is and *nothing* could fix it, and then he wouldn't get in the right lane. I was sitting there wondering if somehow in his mind the right wing, or the right side of the government, was screwing things up, which he was correlating to changing into the right lane. Whatever the reason was, he would not change lanes. I was beside myself. When we pulled up to 30 Rock, I said, "Not for nothing, America may be broken but I do think we would've gotten here faster in the right lane."

I had a frustrating conference call with our *WWHL* bookers today. There is a mind-numbing pecking order among talk shows, meaning that each has a rule about which others they will and will not "follow." You can't book a guest on us, for example, before that person goes on *Letterman*. *Letterman* won't allow it. But shows that used to be fine following us will no longer, and are making publicists cancel appearances on us in order to preserve bookings on bigger shows. And these bookers are trashing us. On the one hand they are saying we're an inconsequential little show, and on the other they're upset about us going first. It's ultimately a symptom of the show doing well, but booking is a maddening process.

Tonight I had dinner with Bruce and Bryan and little Ava. Bruce said the lady from the rescue place was intensely thorough on his reference interview. I wanna make my goddaughter my dog's godmother—does that work? Ava seems into it. Then we went to that FroYo place where you weigh your yogurt. I don't usually go to FroYo but I might need to start: FroYo is fun! Plus it was a celebration, because with Bryan's (and CAA's) help, my deal closed today, so after almost two years of running development at Bravo and simultaneously hosting *WWHL* five nights a week, and nine months of negotiation, this is finally happening. It's a new deal for my show with a two-year pickup, and also I'm starting a production company with a first-look deal with Bravo/NBCUniversal. Plus I'm staying as an EP of all the *Housewives* and continuing to host specials on Bravo. In three months, I'll no longer be an executive at Bravo. Now watch me become the low-rent, Jewish, now-fat-and-old, almost-past-his-prime, with-a-more-nasty-personality version of Ryan Seacrest.

Maybe out of frustration or anxiety, I keep going to YouTube and binge-watching Britney Spears videos. Tonight I ate maybe two pounds of candy in bed and watched pieces of the "Femme Fatal" tour. It's an eighty-something-minute study on how to create the illusion that Brit is dancing. It's so funny. They are all dancing *around* her, and she's someplace else. She walks like a hologram. I just want Britney to be Britney. Our idea of Britney. But the truth is, I think Britney has left the building. After watching all of her videos, I can tell you she doesn't dance. She just walks, flips her hair, cracks a whip. It's crazy. I ate so much candy. It's like I'm trying to bulk up.

▦ FRIDAY, OCTOBER 4, 2013

I FaceTimed with Anderson today—his first FaceTime ever. He was in a chatty mood, which doesn't always happen, and we had a good, gossipy session. I wish it could have been televised. He and I broke it down, then reverted to a common refrain, how bored we both are. Both of us lead pretty exciting lives, but on any given day you'll find one of us texting the other that we are bored out of our minds. I still have that childhood affliction characterized by walking into the kitchen when my mom was cooking dinner and telling her, "I'm *bored.*" I guess it happens to the best of us. Maybe that's why we do the jobs we do. I watched the afternoon Cardinals game with Matthew Broderick at the bar at Riviera on Seventh Avenue. We won. I have playoff fever. That's a good place to watch a game.

I buried the headline. The big news is I killed a bug tonight. The booze helped give me strength. I started the night at Kelly's birthday at Indochine. After dinner we went to Club 8 and the ten of us were the only ones there. It ended up filling up and we danced. We stumbled toward home and into that new Sultan's Pizza joint around the corner from me at two in the morning. Bruce was giving advice to the owner about how to run a restaurant. Everything he told him was right, too. They are doing everything wrong at this place—the lighting is bad, the prices are too cheap (a buck per slice), and they have a bad attitude. Oh, and the pizza isn't so great unless you're drunk or desperate. This joint is not going to make it, mark my words. That guy should've listened to the King of the Palm Restaurant, but he didn't know whom he was talking to.

Back to the bug. In the haze of the night, I discovered a beetle was on my soap tray. It wasn't lion sized, but still. So I got the Raid, tiptoed into the bathroom, aimed my shaking but incredibly masculine and brave hands at the bear cub, and sprayed and killed it. I threw the soap out and the bug is still under my sink, dead. There is no way in hell I'm picking it up. I'm gonna leave it till Wednesday, when my housekeeper comes. I'm not alone on an island with the bug thing, right?

SATURDAY, OCTOBER 5, 2013

I didn't leave my house all day. I did absolutely nothing until I went out to see *The Secret Life of Walter Mitty* at the New York Film Festival with Bruce, Bryan, and John Hill; I went with the movie and thoroughly enjoyed it. I talked to Kristen Wiig a little bit at the after party. It was one of those times when I love someone so much and am such a fan that I am too nervous to think of anything to say. My personality erases itself. Richard LaGravenese, the great screenwriter, came over to me, said he loves my show, and was very nice, but we got interrupted. Ten minutes later I turned to him and asked where he lives and he said Tribeca and I said, "Oh, that's where my studio is," and he replied, "What's your studio for? What do you do?" And I tell him, "My show," and I realized I wasn't speaking to LaGravanese anymore. I'd resumed the conversation with a stranger who had the same kind of glasses. The same guy came up to me fifteen minutes later and says, "I am so embarrassed. I know who you are." And I go, "Well, I am embarrassed. I don't know who you are and I thought I was talking to someone else." So we were even. We split the Hudson and went to Atlas, where some guy came up to me and said, "I'm not coming up to you because of *who* you are, I'm coming up to you because of *what* you are, which is sexy." That's a pretty good line but that was as far as that went.

▦ SUNDAY, OCTOBER 6, 2013

The dog Ron Swanson has some kind of ringworm, so I didn't get to meet him this weekend. Gross. He'll be here in a week or two. I keep walking around my house wondering what it will be like to have a little doggy following me around. Will he follow me around? What is a dog going to do in this apartment to occupy his time all day anyway? I saw Kathy and Rich Wakile tonight at the show and Rich kept making jokes about me throwing them away in the trash, because Kathy isn't going to be a "full" Housewife this season. I explained to Kathy that I couldn't put her in the show open because it would cause big problems with other Housewives. Everybody wants to be in the show open.

▦ MONDAY, OCTOBER 7, 2013

Apropos of last night, today I had a long phone conversation with Countess LuAnn, who had hoped to be in the opening titles on *RHONY*. In fairness to her she is an original Housewife, but she is a "recurring" character this season. I had to tell her that although she's all over the show, she doesn't have her own storyline. She's not a happy Countess. So that was a fun conversation to have. Not. (Yes, I am now quoting *Truth or Dare*–era Madonna.) The upside of all this is that it's the Countess's best season. Meanwhile Carole Radziwill sent a long list of intro lines for herself that all break the fourth wall, like "Last year I was the fan favorite; I can't wait to see how you fuck me over this year." Or, "I used to think this show was fiction. . . ." But you can't say "this show" in the intro.

I had dinner at Grac's with Neal and both of her kids. I haven't seen her in forever and I was so happy to be able to hang with Marley and Sam, which is like being in the middle of a fun tornado. (A fun-nado? Could that become a thing?) After twenty-five years, Grac and I have the ability to click into a groove for whatever time we are together and just reconnect, fast. Neal says dinner at their place is like being inside a popcorn maker. They're crazy-hilarious. Marley can play guitar. I can't play anything.

The Cardinals game was amazing, of course. With their backs against the wall they rallied. Winning the World Series this season is their destiny.

Another two-hour massage after the show. Total luxury. Again I lay there wondering what the fuck that dog is going to do while I get a massage. Sleep? Watch? Bark?

TUESDAY, OCTOBER 8, 2013

Before the show I had dinner with Amanda at Waverly. Seeing her was just what I needed, a quick therapy session. The guy sitting at the table next to us was a total douchebag, an older guy with a ponytail and young girls kind of giggling at his awful stories. He was disgusting. Carter Oosterhouse was there. He's so handsome, he looks just like Superman. We told each other that the other was "killing it" like three times, which I think is what you're supposed to say to straight famous people. (Seacrest says that every time I see him.) There's a waiter there who's really hot who's straight and married but he flirts with every gay guy and makes them think they have a chance with him, but since I found out that I'm not the only one he flirts with I decided I'm done. I mean, I've been through such a roller coaster in my mind with this guy, so now I ignore him. But tonight he ignored *me*! I got furious. *I* would rather be doing the ignoring.

Connie Britton is everything you want her to be. Perfect. She was on the show with Zach Quinto. And I got to act out a scene from *Friday Night Lights* with her, which was *amazing*. I actually think I was pretty good as Coach Eric Taylor. I committed. She seemed impressed. Elisabeth Moss came with her and walked onto the show to give the gifts. She was our Vanna White. She is so sweet. And a Bravo fanatic. Zach wanted to go out, so we all went to Industry after. I had way too many Maker's-and-gingers. On my way (stumbling?) out, some guy came up to me and wanted to give me his number but I was only half committed to taking it, so I flippantly said, "Just tell it to me and I'll remember it." And he goes, "Are you sure you'll remember?" And I promised, "Yes. I'm *really* good at that. I will *totally* remember." And now all I can remember is it was a 914 number. So that narrows it down.

▦ WEDNESDAY, OCTOBER 9, 2013

Will is so sick of me looking at my hair while he tries to train me. Liza and I have this thing where we feel like our hair always looks extra great on airplanes (because the air is so dry)—and now the same phenomenon keeps happening to me when I go to the gym. I keep looking at myself in the mirror and I can't get over it, and I'm upset that I have to destroy the hair in the shower when I get home. Sometimes I think Will's going to hit me.

Went to JFK to get my Global Entry. The "security interview" was all of about two minutes and began with the most pressing threat to our nation's safety: "Tell me about Teresa." That's a broad question. I told him I love her. The TSA guy told me what he felt I needed to know about *Jersey Housewives* and now I can go in the fast lane at security and customs worldwide. Unless this guy starts hating Teresa—then I bet he could go into my account and fuck with it.

All day I was a kid before Christmas waiting for the playoff game to start, and of course I had a shoot before the show with the woman whose wedding I'm going to officiate tomorrow on *Watch What Happens Live* and it was me driving her around in this Fiat she will win as part of the wedding contest. It was two hours in a car with this girl I never met, with cars in front of me and beside me shooting us driving through the city, all while I'm losing my mind about not being able to see the game. She's an aesthetician in Atlantic City and a huge Bravo fan. She kept asking, of all my *WWHL* guests, whom I hated. That's all she cared about. I felt like nothing I was saying could satisfy her. I would say a name and she would say, "But who else do you hate?" And I was like, "Well, can I tell you who I like? Does it have to be all about who I hate?" People want to hear the nasty stuff; that includes me, so I don't know why I'm even surprised. But I don't actually *hate* too many people, which seemed to disappoint her. I said Jillian Michaels because she yelled at my staff, but the bride doesn't watch *Biggest Loser*, so she didn't really care about her. Then I said maybe Scott Baio, but he was before her time. I asked her, "Don't you want to know anything about the Housewives? You love Bravo!" I just couldn't impress her with any of my stories. This girl is supposed to be the biggest Bravo fan ever! People kept waving at us, because they put lights in the car so we were very noticeable. She thought everyone was waving at her because they know she's getting married on the show. My brow was furrowed. Her fiancé is very sweet. I made him say his vows to me, and they were very flowery, and he was saying he will try not to cry, and I was like, "No. Try *to* cry." The whole time I was driving and simultaneously trying to check my Twitter for the game score, so hopefully you won't see that danger on TV.

I got to the show and had so much shit to do beforehand—voice-overs, rehearsals, taping birthday greetings to randoms—all while the game was going on. I was going mental. As detached as I felt about the show, Rachel Maddow and Michael Strahan were great. It was so fun having two professional talk-show hosts on, so easy. I really like her. And I really liked him. In fact I was very surprised how much I liked him. Eli was at the show, which always feels like a celebration these days since he was our original Bravo exec on *WWHL* and we've been *through it* together. To celebrate, he and I went out afterwards like old times to the Cubbyhole and then had a burger at Corner Bistro at 2 a.m. I swore I wasn't going to eat the whole burger. I told myself I was just gonna have a piece. I ate the whole thing and was ready to order another one. I went home and watched Cardinals highlights (we won) and decided to go see the games in St. Louis this weekend. I didn't go to bed until three-thirty.

THURSDAY, OCTOBER 10, 2013

Neicy was here yesterday. I forgot that I'd left the dead bug under my sink for the last four days but I checked and she removed it. Phew. What's the etiquette around leaving insects for the housekeeper?

I taped *Bethenny* and it was kind of surreal to be a guest on her big new talk show. She was asking me about my love life, which I'm more comfortable asking others about than revealing myself, and she asked me how many times I had been in love and I said two and a half. I said how many times do you think you fall in love in a life and she said, "Two and a half times." Oh well, I guess my goose is cooked after my college love, John Hill, and the one-half time in 1999. Maybe I still have the 50 percent I didn't use ahead of me. *Please, Lord. Give me 50 percent of love.*

We married the couple in the Clubhouse tonight. They both had been so excited for so long that I think they somehow blew their wads before the actual show, so it didn't have a ton of energy. It was Giggy's second wedding in the Clubhouse. He was ring bearer. We all decided that the bride wanted a reality show out of it. There were tons of people there, which meant smiling and posing for numerous combinations of photos, so that was a lil irritating. It was also John Jude's birthday, so afterwards I got Sonja Morgan to do an improvised burlesque number singing "Happy Birthday" like Marilyn Monroe a capella, in an insane perfor-mance with a cake with twenty candles on it, which made the entire night worth it, and then we partied in the Clubhouse until really late.

"Delta shuttle. Miss Field?" This morning I woke up and got in the wrong car to go to the airport. I realized it's a car for Sally Field, who is my neighbor, who I guess also had a noon flight but hers was the Delta shuttle. I was on American to St. Louis. The driver was not amused by my desire for him to deliver a simple "hello" message to Miss Sally Field, who I have never once seen in the building. I got in my real car with my driver, a non-English-speaking gentleman of the Asian persuasion. We immediately fell into that inevitable negotiation over which route to take to the airport. The guy said—in broken English—"Midtown Tunnel" and I got the sense he was going to cross at Thirty-fourth Street, which is not the route I prefer. So I said, "You're going to cross downtown, right? Twenty-sixth or Twenty-second?" Frankly, my preference is to cross on Twelfth Street but he had already missed that. I could tell he was just yessing me, saying, "Traffic, traffic. Crossing Midtown." We crossed at Thirty-sixth Street, so that didn't work out for me. I did a lot of angry muttering under my breath and he did a lot of happily ignoring me.

During my backseat driving, my contact from *Glamour* magazine called to say they had hit some "stumbling blocks" regarding the interview. I said, "Are you calling to tell me you are cutting the Madonna section out of the article?" and he goes, "Well, we did hit some stumbling blocks, but I'm representing the writer, which is you." And I said, "How do *you* feel? It's your magazine." He said there was just so much strong material that it was hard to choose from and since it is the Woman of the Year issue it had to have a certain tone. My read of the situation—and I only *think* I know what goes on inside a magazine—is that Gaga's publicist didn't want to include that stuff, or that *Glamour* didn't even want to jeopardize their relationship by asking her. I wasn't surprised, but I wanted the interview to generate some buzz. Then I told him the great thing is that I bet the publicist doesn't even realize we have this stuff about Katy Perry—the "no comment" about her feelings toward her rival. More hemming and hawing and then he said, "Right now that's not in the piece. *I'm representing you, though.* You're the writer. It's challenging. There are space issues and I really want to get her stuff in about artistic freedom and her Bullying Foundation." I cut him off. "What you're saying to me is that this is a positive article and you need to protect your long-term relationship, so you are telling me this is all out." He finally capitulated and said, "Yes. None of this stuff is currently in the piece. But I will still fight for it." I ended it cordially, "OK, then we're done." So that's that.

My plane was delayed and I passed the time by studying this straight gay man at the gate—with two kids and a wife—who was wearing basically hot pants and a tight polo shirt. He was very built. I would've done it with this guy. I am consistently transfixed by straight gay guys. What is going on in their heads, or anywhere else in their bodies, for that matter? So I was switching between watching him and *Headline News*, where the lady anchor had this big chunky side braid. I felt like that lady was sending me a message. The problem was that I couldn't figure out what she could be trying to say.

I got to St. Louis and had a nice hangout with Blouse, who is always a happy sight. I love coming home on a day when Blouse will be at the house so we can catch up about any number of local (what's going on at my Aunt Judy's) and national (Beyoncé) current events. Blouse didn't like the Clubhouse wedding at all. She thought—among other things—that the guy's tuxedo looked funny, and she was kind of right. Then I told her that I was licensed to marry and I would marry her and Eddie, her boyfriend. She didn't really like that idea and it kind of drove her from the room. Or maybe it was when we were saying my mom should be the bridesmaid at Blouse's wedding. I should've asked her take on leaving that bug for Neicy. I don't think I could leave a bug for Blouse. She's family.

At the game, the Cardinals put us in this suite with Jim Edmonds—a Cardinal legend—and it was so cool being with him. My mom very sweetly—and a little too loudly—whispered to me with half-pursed lips, "Maybe he's on YOUR TEAM!" I knew he wasn't because his last wife tried out to be an OC Housewife. And I doubly knew he wasn't because he was with a hot girl who happens to be the sister of a hot guy I know in NYC. (Hot siblings are the best.) We were seated like twenty-five rows behind Em and Rob, and my mom spent much of the time riding the way that her son-in-law was ineffectively waving his homer hankie. My mom kept saying, "He's PUSHING the RALLY TOWEL. He's not

WAVING it. Look at your sister! She doesn't even HAVE a rally towel. WHO DOESN'T TAKE A RALLY TOWEL when they go into the stadium? They're FREE! It's the PLAYOFFS!" Incidentally, I was waving my homer hankie like my life depended on it.

Everybody in St. Louis, all they talk about is how great St. Louis is. The hostess lady in the suite asked me if I lived in LA and I said no, I live in New York, and she said to me very earnestly, "Why, may I ask, would you *ever leave St. Louis*?" She was completely baffled at the idea that someone would leave St. Louis, just stumped. If she didn't get immediately why I might leave St. Louis to live in New York, I wasn't going to be able to explain it to her. I bowed and slowly walked backwards.

With great flourish the dessert cart arrived. I was too into the game to indulge, but my mom was in the suite taking photos of every angle of the damn cart to show me, or whomever. She kept saying, "You can't BELIEVE this thing! You MISSED IT!" When I was ready for dessert a few innings later, they went and got it for me. (I reluctantly conceded to my mother that it actually *was* an amazing dessert cart.) The game was tied back and forth and went into extra innings. My dad hit the wall at the top of the thirteenth—around midnight—when it somehow dawned on him that it could go on forever. He was like, "What's the end game here? When are we going to leave?" and my mom enthused, "When someone CROSSES HOME PLATE, that's when we leave! We are waiting for A RUN TO BE SCORED on either side." I told her to lay off him; the man is eighty-one and made it to midnight. I asked my father if the conversation could be deferred until the Cardinals batted, and, thankfully, they won the game. I promised Cardinal legend Jim Edmonds he could bartend on *WWHL* in November.

I was supposed to meet reliever Jason Motte for a whiskey but it was 1:00 a.m. and we decided not to. He is a Twitter buddy. The truth is I just want to be friends with baseball players. I am 100 percent in awe of them. Consuelos once told me that baseball player starfuckers are called "green flies"—so I guess I'm one of them. (Maybe I'm a fruit fly?) I was also DMing Motte, who has a beard, asking if he was upset about this guy on the Dodgers who I thought was stealing his look, and he was so nice about it. He said, "Oh, he is a great guy" or something, and here I was trying to instigate a fight with this Dodger.

I realized this morning that the moral of the *Glamour* magazine story is not that they cut all the juicy material for fear of hurting their relationship and promoting positivity, it's that I am a nasty bottom-feeding shit stirrer. Here I am thinking the worthy parts of this article are the parts where she is trash-talking Madonna and dismissing Katy Perry. Am I, in fact, a promoter of negativity among women (an accusation I've heard before) as well as between baseball-playing men? Is this the person I have become? *No!* I'm an enthusiast! I swear I am. A drama-loving enthusiast.

At Game 2 this afternoon, cousin Josh and I were back in Suite 6 with Jim Edmonds. Tony La Russa threw out the first pitch and I texted him and said great job and he said "Oh, are you here? There's something I need to speak to you about and it's a matter of national significance." I was like whoa, OK . . . this sounds big, so I replied, "I'm with Jim Edmonds in Suite 6." He texted back, "I'm on my way." Wow. *The former GM of the Cardinals needs to speak to me about a matter of national importance at Game 2?* So in walks Tony, past the St. Louis–loving hostess and her bountiful dessert cart, and starts telling me that the issue is that he "and many other people" feel that I should give the Mazel on Sunday to his buddy Howard Schultz, who runs Starbucks. *He and many other people* have an opinion about who gets the Mazel? They are doing a petition to register people's outrage over the government shutdown. And in the middle of showing me the petition, and my wondering when the "national significance" part comes in, he says, "Oh, lemme pause right now because David Freese is about to do something big," and I turn to the diamond and just like that David Freese hits a double!!! I couldn't believe it. And his response to my bewilderment? "If I know one thing about something, it's baseball." *How did he know that was about to happen?* It made me feel very inside, but also like the whole thing was fixed. I'm still flummoxed about it. He left and Jim Edmonds started going on a rant about how people should stay out of politics. He's probably right. I won't be giving the Mazel to Howard Schultz—it seems like a total shill for Starbucks. If Howard Schultz actually *ended* the freaking shutdown, I would give him the Mazel. Meanwhile, we won that game and it was a glorious day.

That night I went to Em and Rob's and my folks went to the symphony. I was giving my brother-in-law shit about the way he was pushing the homer hankie, and Em said the reason *she* didn't take a homer hankie was because she knew we were sitting behind her and that Mom would be analyzing her handling of the homer hankie. How smart is that? And so this entire homer-hankie thing reaffirms why I don't live in St. Louis. I would buckle under the pressure.

At the end of the night, I lay at the foot of my parent's bed telling them about my day and the game, like I was ten years old. It was really sweet.

▦ SUNDAY, OCTOBER 13, 2013—ST. LOUIS–NYC

"I beg you to NEVER GO ON BILL MAHER!" My mother was *pleading* with me at breakfast to never, ever go on Bill Maher's HBO show, which is a curious, bimonthly refrain from her. She thinks I wouldn't be able to keep up and it's her way of being protective, but she's not getting that it's a non-issue because *they ain't asking.*

Guess who was on my flight home? The effeminate dad and his wife and kids. Actually, he was really butching it up. I think he knew I was onto him. We had a *Lord of the Rings* reunion on my show with Ian McKellen and Orlando Bloom that aired directly after the *RHONJ* reunion. Everybody wanted me to talk about the reunion but I had these two huge stars on and I had nothing more to say about *RHONJ*. We need to shake that show up, but I wasn't going to say that publicly. I'm sure our ratings stunk. I don't know that I gave the people what they wanted tonight.

▦ MONDAY, OCTOBER 14, 2013

I'm going to call what happened today Playing-Card-Gate. Bravo made playing cards for clients, with each face card featuring a different Bravolebrity (I was the Joker, Lisa Vanderpump was Queen of Diamonds), and the person who designed them (who is young and not American) made NeNe the Queen of Spades. He had no idea that "spade" had any bad connotation. We had them all destroyed, but discovered that they'd been sent out to the talent a couple days before, so they'd arrived in Atlanta. I was the lucky guy who got to call NeNe and let her know what had happened. I felt totally rotten. NeNe was incredibly cool. She said Gregg had noticed, but she was just happy to be a queen. And she is one. Potentially disastrous situation diverted!

I got an email from the guy at *Glamour*. "We put some stuff back in; I think you'll be happy," which intrigued me.

They put the Cardinals game on the big screen in the Clubhouse before the show. I had my hat on and had a blast watching with my crew. We won. The same four camera guys—Carlos, Rich, Mark, and Nick—have been with us for the entire run of the show, and I love them. Besides being my man behind Camera 2, Rich has worked for Rachael Ray for five years. He told us that yesterday she said, "Hey, camera guy. Get out of my way." She is on my show Wednesday night. I'm going to try to test her, because two of my other camera operators also work for her and don't think she knows their names. I am the worst with names, so it was a rocky first year (Deirdre constantly in my ear mocking me) trying to get those guys' names right. You gotta know your crew! Ja Rule was on the show. He was singing to the audience during commercial breaks.

▦ TUESDAY, OCTOBER 15, 2013

I worked out and thought I was going to puke. I felt whiskey coming out of my pores. I did a run-through at Grand Central Station for this American Made Awards thing that I somehow agreed to co-host tonight with Martha Stewart. There were people everywhere who were overly enthusiastic and seemed in various states of terror of Martha. She would say, "This teleprompter is horrible. Can you see it, Andy?" and I'd say, "If you can't read it, I can't read it!" And then she'd say, "The lighting is terrible. Is it hurting your eyes?" And I'd say, "Whatever is going on with your eyes it's doing to my eyes." Then, "God, the audio is terrible. You should have been here last year. It was *so* bad. I was so mad, I literally think the audio guy is dead. He's dead. I think I killed him." And she was laughing, saying, "You wouldn't believe what I did to him." It's obviously so much more fun being on Martha's side than not. And I was the worst; I just agreed with everything because I didn't have a stake in the fight. I was the guy saying, "No, you get on the train to Dachau. I'm going to stay with Martha. I'm Christian." Martha tried to teach me to knit backstage with these huge needles and alpaca wool and I was terrified. I felt like I was having sex and I couldn't get hard. Except that knitting is *not* like sex and even the Queen of Crafting couldn't teach me how to do it.

The awards went fine. Martha is trying to do something important, which is promote American small businesses. I ran into Bethenny and Thom Filicia. And I don't know what Christie Brinkley has done to her face, but she still looks like "Uptown Girl" from the video. Perfection. She should win some kind of crafting award for it. I saw Sean Avery there and I made a joke onstage about he and I buying two pairs of matching chaps. Martha didn't know what I was talking about.

Went right from the awards to the show and Sanjay Gupta was on. He was really nervous. His publicist said, "You can be funny with him but don't be silly. He doesn't want to play a silly game." And we told the publicist that this is quite a silly show, so it was going to be hard to avoid that. She goes, "Just don't make him put a boa on or anything." So we didn't make him put a boa on, which was disappointing. My director Sarah wore a Dodgers shirt, so I considered sending her directly to the *Rachael Ray* show.

▦ WEDNESDAY, OCTOBER 16, 2013

More Martha today. We were on the *Today* show to promote her awards. It was unclear how I got roped into the appearance, or what exactly I was doing there, so I decided to just try to be funny. I made my erectile-dysfunction knitting joke and it landed with a thud. Matt looked at me like I was nuts. (I don't think he could figure out what I was doing with Martha either.) I said I checked the wrong box on Match.com and Martha and I have been dating for six weeks. That got a laugh. It's the first time I've seen the *Today* show in a long time. It was upsetting because they're clearly trying to imitate *Good Morning America*, which is so bad, but number one. The *Today* show is the *Today* show for God's sake! (And I have the right to opine since I gave seven years of my life to the number three morning show.) NBC should just be doing what they do best. Before the segment Martha said to Matt, "Oh, I like the new studio. Orange is the new black." And he said, "I prefer black."

I went to this "Giants of Broadcasting" luncheon honoring, among other people, Barry. At the next table were Dan Rather and Bill O'Reilly, so I went over to Dan and he was so sweet. "I'm so proud of you," he said. Of course hearing him say that made me want to cry, and then he said, "You know, I would love to get coffee with you and just get together and talk and share ideas sometime. *No agenda* on my part." I couldn't believe this was happening: Dan Rather wants to "share ideas" with me. And I was like, "Oh wow. OK. I think a whiskey would be even better," and he said, "I would like that." And I love that he said "*no agenda*." Hamilton, Michael, Bruce, and I all showed up to see Barry and realized that it was a distinct possibility that maybe he had something more important to do. Hammy was calling his office to get intel. When he did show, his speech was great—he got up and made a joke about how all the people in the room were trying to sue him. Dick Cavett told a great Groucho Marx joke: Marx was once at a terrible dinner party and he said to the hostess, "I've had a wonderful time, but tonight wasn't it." We kind of all snuck out after Dick Cavett, which was a good thing because I hear it went on for two more hours.

The Cardinals' march to the World Series continues and I'm being tortured by my cable box. The only channel I don't get at Bravo or at home is TBS. I have no clue why. I watched the game at Bravo on my computer, and I've been watching it on my iPad at home, where it's four minutes behind the rest of the world. I'm convinced there's a TBS conspiracy against me. The playoffs is exactly the only time I ever watch that channel.

I went from the morning with Martha to an evening with Rachael Ray, who brought panini for the entire *WWHL* staff, carried by her acolytes/slaves. (Sidenote: Why do all the empresses of cooking have acolytes/slaves around them?) She also brought me a sandwich press/griddle, which is something I didn't even realize I needed, but obviously do. She seemed pretty drunk on red wine and was a total bundle of fun (stained red-wine teeth and all—she's the *real* version of Martha, see?).

During a commercial break, I tested her to see if she knew Mark and Rich's names and she did. My faith is restored. I really liked her, actually. For my Jackhole I was going to go off on the government shutdown and I specifically told the guy who bleeps our show (literally there is a guy with a button in a back room) that I would be mouthing the words "fuck" and "shit" so they didn't need to drop sound, and I mouthed the word "fuck" but I got so carried away that I said "shit" aloud. Luckily they caught it. I called Boehner and Obama "queens" and said that they just needed to go scissor it out. That was my big idea. (Maybe I *am* ready to go on Bill Maher. Lemme check w/ Mom on that.)

I have such dog fever. I keep staring at Ron Swanson's picture; I'm meeting him on Friday and can't wait! On the other hand tomorrow's *Miami Housewives* reunion is looming like a storm cloud.

▦ THURSDAY, OCTOBER 17, 2013

Adriana freaked out before the reunion taping today because she wasn't sitting next to me. She told the producers, "Just fire me now if I'm not next to Andy." I love her. Every time I see her she brings me something from Tom Ford. Usually a tie. Today it was a Tom Ford scarf. It makes me so uncomfortable that she's spending her money on me. The women were out of control, as out of control as they could possibly be. And there was so much "evidence"—which I do typically enjoy. Marysol pulled out her computer with a video message from her father in the hospital making a testimonial proving Lea didn't send Elsa flowers. Hmmm. Not sure what that proved.

We finished early and I went to Cafe Cluny to get dinner but walked up to find a crowd in front and lights and a waiter coming out with a plate of food. They were filming *Annie* the movie, and I thought the waiter was feeding Sandy (because now I have dog fever), but it was "Annie" herself the waiter was feeding, that little girl who was nominated for an Oscar. I'm all for boosting Quvenzhané Wallis's career, but does the world need a reboot of *Annie*?

Lisa Marie Presley and CeeLo were on the show, and Lisa Marie Presley was adamant that I not ask about Michael Jackson. I knew it at the time she was booked but I kept thinking, "I'll figure out a way to do it," and before the show she apparently said to the booker herself, *no* Michael Jackson questions, but somehow the message that she had personally reiterated that didn't get to me. The celebrity doesn't usually say something's off-limits themselves, usually they leave that to a handler. And so the whole show I was ramping up to say something innocuous like "I know that you've talked about the deep stuff with Oprah. I just want to know, do you have a happy memory about Michael Jackson?" But she had this look on her face that was so vulnerable and nervous and she kind of broke my heart, she was hard and soft all at once. She told me right before we went on that mine was the only show she was doing. As the interview went on I started to feel like I couldn't do it, I couldn't ask the question. I was so glad my better self thwarted the heartless shit stirrer because I only found out later that she had specifically said not to. It is eerie looking at her. She is Elvis with a long wig. She is also very Priscilla. I mean, they're her parents. It's not headline news.

I got a two-hour massage after the show, listening to the noise in my apartment and wondering how a dog would feel about it. He's from West Virginia and I'm pretty sure it's not noisy there.

▦ FRIDAY, OCTOBER 18, 2013

This morning Fredrik Eklund took me to see models of the new apartments in the building where St. Vincent's Hospital was. I consider myself pretty rich and I can't afford these places. They are four thousand dollars a square foot. Ridiculous. And they're erecting this building on the spot where thousands of people died of AIDS. Perhaps this is a bad idea all around. I felt rage towards the sales rep blithering about how fast everything was selling. They are characterless, I should add, and won't be available till 2016, when the guy said everything will be five thousand a square foot. I told him I wanted to go home to my already nice apartment and open the window and jump out. In a nutshell, this is why New York City is going down the drain. In the meantime I have heard not one word about my neighbor upstairs, which is certainly good news for him. I do not want this man to pass away. I want to make that clear. I would like to duplex my apartment but a *man's life* is not worth it.

I went to Jersey City with John Hill, who has been the driving force behind me opening my heart up to an animal (and given our past, it's ironic), and spent two hours with Ron Swanson, who apparently has been going by the name "Norman Reedus" in his foster home. This is very confusing because Reedus is an actor on *The Walking Dead*, which I also do not watch. (Given how much TV I *do* watch, how is it possible that he was named after characters in two shows I don't?)

The experience was out of body for me—it was too deep almost from the minute I met him. I felt like I was going to poop my pants. Being with Norman/Ron brought up every commitment issue I ever had and I was glad I had my asthma inhaler because I was huffing and puffing on it. I was looking at the animal thinking I was going to spend the *rest of my life* with it. My first reaction was that it was *too much dog*, so much bigger than I thought it was going to be, and it was licking my face like crazy (which I didn't like) and shedding all over (which I definitely didn't like or expect). The dog has a penis that gets hard and pink randomly (like my own, I guess?) and that was very jarring. After ninety minutes in this room just staring at the dog, my face flushed with emotion, John suggested we take him out for a walk around the neighborhood. I should mention that the dog is crate trained, didn't bark once, and was designated "the perfect dog" by John and Zarena, who runs See Spot Rescued.

I told John on the walk that there was no way I could take the dog home. He was just too big and *too much*, basically. John told me we were not leaving New Jersey without the dog. He said he knew *exactly* what I was doing (running away from commitment), and that he was forcing me to take it. As my intended played with other dogs (quite well and cutely) at the dog run, it gave me this *look* that made me feel a little pang of something, I don't know what. So I took him. I'm fostering him, that's the deal I made with Zarena. For two weeks. We will see.

He jumped in my car, went in the backseat, and fell right to sleep. A good sign, I thought. But I also couldn't get over that I had an actual living, breathing *dog* in my new car. I got him home and followed him around my apartment for an hour. I picked up his shit on the sidewalk. I did it all. This was a really big day for me. I've never picked up dog shit. Speaking of which, I DM'd with some Cardinals about today's game and I feel like Miranda waiting for a text message from a guy she saw at the gym, waiting for these guys, and I said to Joe Kelly Jr., "You're killing it." Because I do think that's what bros say to each other. (See: Seacrest.)

By the end of the night, I decided that this dog without a name is the smartest dog in the world. He's going to make this easy for me. We were sitting down to watch the Cardinals game with the Irish chef and the dog brought me his leash, to tell me he had to pee, and I took him out and he did. It was incredible. I sat there watching packed Busch Stadium cheering for the pitcher Michael Wacha—"WACHA! WACHA! WACHA!" my hometown cheered, and trending on Twitter was "Wacha"—and I realized that my dog had just been named for me by the city of St. Louis. So that's that. He is Wacha. And it kinda sounds like a dog's name, although I can imagine a future explaining that he's not named after Waka Flocka Flame. I can't imagine not keeping him. (Unclear what will happen with the Irish chef.) Did I mention the pooch looks *great* on my couch?

The Cardinals killed the Dodgers 9 to 0 and are heading to the World Series. Oh, and during the whole drama of staring at Wacha in Jersey, I found out that Thomas Roberts accepted the job I turned down, hosting Miss Universe in Russia, which I had boycotted months ago on the grounds that it would be hypocritical for a gay man to pimp a travelogue for a country that discriminates against him. So NBC got another gay guy to host the show, which was pretty smart on their part. He says he's going to prove to the Russians that there's hope, but I don't know how he's going to do that since they aren't going to let him say he's gay on the show. Instead he's going to be talking about how beautiful Moscow is. There was something irritating about this news but I was too preoccupied with the canine to focus. See—the dog is already teaching me not to sweat the small stuff.

▦ SATURDAY, OCTOBER 19, 2013

I woke up and Wacha had to pee really bad. He was running around like a maniac, so I took him out for a long walk and saw two long-lens paparazzi guys a block away. When I saw the cameras I thought, "Wow— I'm going to be photographed with this super cute dog," I was *proud* of *my* dog. And then one of the photographers came over to me and said, "My girlfriend is a huge fan, can I have a picture?" Is this how it works with the paparazzi? So I said to him, "Yes, I will, but only if you release good pictures of me," and he said, "Yes," so we just looked into space two blocks away where I guess another photog was taking pictures of us, and we'll see how the pics turn out.

The whole day was just dog dog dog. I had a rough midafternoon when Bruce met him and had the same first reaction that I did yesterday in Jersey—he's big and licky and gets boners. My best friend's reaction was a total setback for me; I got a pit in my stomach again. Then I took him to the dog run with Liza (a dog cheerleader) and he got scared when we were going in and buried his face between my legs and it broke my heart and I was back in again. He was mine. And looking around in the dog run, I'm seeing ugly dogs everywhere that drool, yelp, jump, growl, and are just generally disgusting, so I'm feeling luckier and luckier every minute with this dog. I had dinner with Liza, Bruce, the Perskys, and the Consueloses and then I went home after to have a date night with Wacha and learned that red wine at the end of a date with a dog works the same way as red wine at the end of a date with a guy. I came very close to sleeping with the dog. I was just petting and petting and loving and feeling very connected to him. He is my own Ralph Lauren Snoopy!

ⵜ SUNDAY, OCTOBER 20, 2013

Got coffee with Jake Shears and the dog. I am trying to not only get used to calling him Wacha but also not refer to him as "it," which Amanda keeps pointing out that I am doing. (It takes my friend the shrink to bring this to my attention, and she's right as usual.) After two days of being with this animal, what I have come to realize is that this city is a toilet and everything is shit- and piss-stained. I've been walking around in Ferragamo shoes like a dandy for twenty-three years and little did I know that I basically have been contracting worms the whole time. Meanwhile, Wacha is very consumed with sniffing asses. Yes, he is very smart.

I co-hosted an event with Cynthia Nixon for Bill de Blasio tonight at a fancy gay guy's house on the Upper East Side. De Blasio is super nice and super tall and super liberal. (Maybe too liberal?) I did not ask the future mayor how he plans to clean the toilet that is our city. We are beyond that. I was asked to say a few words and, sandwiched between Nixon and de Blasio, I could only think of how short I looked. Even though my mind was on how nervous I was about leaving the dog, I eeked something out. I went to *WWHL* and was just thinking of it/him the whole time. I didn't even drink on the show because I wanted to stay sober for the dog. Jenna Jameson's plane was delayed. She wasn't landing at Newark till 10:15 and had checked her luggage and makeup. We booked Bevy Smith to join Jennifer Tilly, and the broadcast became a big "waiting for the porn star to show up on live TV" kind of thing. And this begs the age-old question: Has there ever been a reliable porn star? Jenna arrived right at the end, but waiting for the porn star was maybe more fun than interviewing the porn star.

▦ MONDAY, OCTOBER 21, 2013

It turns out maybe there is no such thing as a nice paparazzo. There are photos of me with Wacha all over the Internet and I am aggressively picking my nose. I mean I am *digging*. The headline on Perez Hilton was "Andy Cohen Embarrasses His Dog As He Digs for Gold on the Streets of NY"! Wacha was *embarrassed*!? How does Perez know!? How about that *I* was embarrassed by having to pick up my dog's shit? AOL, BuzzFeed, and TMZ simply said I was "Digging for Gold!" so that's a little more respectable. *No one* was mentioning how cute my new dog is, which killed me.

I worked out with Will today. I told him he should release a CD called "Jews Working Out" that is just me sighing, groaning, and grunting, usually in response to what I have to do and not what I'm actually doing. All day everybody was tweeting me the picture of me picking my nose. People want to make damn sure I've seen it. I wanted to tweet, "I saw it, motherfuckers." But I thought better of it.

We had Amy Sedaris on tonight. She went through Lea Black's purse. It took at least a minute but it was hilarious. Doing this show has made me think of everything in terms of how long it takes. I walk around all day hearing Deirdre's calm voice in my ear counting down the time. I'm ordering my tea thinking "Can I get this done in :45?" Amy is so funny—the funniest person I've ever met. And yet all I could think about was my dog. I made the Internet the Jackhole for not noticing how cute my dog is.

TUESDAY, OCTOBER 22, 2013

Today was commitment D-day. I've been getting tweets from people saying, "What's the deal? Post a photo of your dog!" But I realized that the minute I sent out a tweet with the picture, there was no turning back. I sat there looking at Wacha all morning, trying to decide whether to tweet his picture. I knew I wasn't going to give him back, but this final act would make it so *official*. I decided I had to take the perfect picture of the dog to Instagram; in front of Bonsignour, I became the Scavullo of dog photographers, working almost an hour on the perfect picture. I got the picture and then freaked out about the tweet—no turning back, connected for life—and I waited till the end of the day. With a pit in my stomach, I did it.

It turns out I have a very popular dog. I posted his photo on Instagram and got thirty-six thousand responses. And then it really sunk in that he had been in a kill shelter. This dog, *my dog*, was in line to be *killed*. That kills *me*. I love him so much already. The idea that this dog is one day going to die made me teary on the way to the gym yesterday. Now today I'm getting teary thinking of him in a kill shelter. (I also could cry thinking of him in West Virginia, but that's me being a snob.) And I will never, ever get over how good he looks on my couch. Some celebrity dog trainer emailed Daryn wondering if "Andy wants my services?" He's coming over for free.

I was thinking about when am I going to get him groomed and about his new vet, dog walker, and his food and toys and the mechanics of it all, and it reaffirmed that if I had to spend one more day only thinking about nothing but myself, I would have set myself on fire. I am at the tipping point of boring myself by thinking about myself. Thank God this dog is here.

I *think* I had a nice photo session with Wacha and five paparazzi this morning as I was waiting for Joe Mantello in front of Starbucks. They actually asked if they could take pictures with Wacha. I said, "Yes, but only nice photos, guys." Meanwhile, I'm in glasses and my hair looks crazy, so I know how this is gonna play out. Someone on the street said his paws are really big, and that he's gonna grow huge, and now I'm terrified. I don't want him to grow any bigger. By the way, yesterday I get a tweet from @WachaCohen—a stranger has started tweeting as Wacha—and it said, "You forgot to leave the TV on. I wanted to watch your show." And then this morning I got one that said, "Wake up and get in here and take me out. I have to pee," which played into me thinking I always need to take him out and was kind of freaky. Who is tweeting as my dog and where is this person hiding?

I was at 30 Rock all day. When I left my house Wacha gave me *a look* that was so earnest, and melancholy. A look that actually, it was so emo, could have meant so many things but made me shaky and gloomy all day at 30 Rock. I was off, because of a look from a pooch! I had lunch with my agents at the Palm and then I met with my money guy. (I'm doing just fine, he says.) We are going back and forth haggling w/ Aviva over her opening line on *RHONY*. She doesn't want "The only thing fake about me is my prosthetic leg . . . [beat] and my boobs." Because she has four kids and thinks it's trashy. She is OK with "When people tell me I'm fake, I know they're just pulling my leg," which seems on the edge to me but I like it. Hilariously, Sonja is fine with saying "Things would go a lot smoother in this town if more women went commando." Bless her!

The Cardinals got totally blown out tonight. It was so upsetting. I can't get over how gross the Red Sox beards are. I taped two shows but I was so distracted by the shittiness of the Cardinals all night, I was not mentally into either one. And two turns of phrase that I had gotten wrong in the first run-through, I got wrong in the show itself, which got me thinking: What's the point of a run-through if I'm going to get this stuff wrong? Oh, and I think we may need an applause sign at the show. Josh Flagg recommended it, but is that too conventional?

When I got home Wacha was so playful and I just wanted to lie on my bed with him and watch *Primary Colors*, which I found on TV. He just kept licking my face. He would lick my face for five hours if I let him. It's like I'm a salt lick. But as I mentioned, I'm not a fan of the face-licking, and so then I was pushing him away and he was misunderstanding, thinking I was playing with him. Then he was bugging the shit out of me.

▦ THURSDAY, OCTOBER 24, 2013

I took Wacha to get cleaned and I love him very clean. I wish I could groom him twice a week, actually. But, like most fine clothes, you are not supposed to overdo it at the dry cleaner. Apparently his skin will get dry. After I took him out to pee this morning, he took a little nap with me in my bed. I fell asleep for twenty minutes. I dreamt I was lying in the middle of Time Square hugging Wacha as hard as I could in my arms. I was so happy.

Today I read an interview with Thomas Roberts about hosting the Miss Universe pageant, which I passed on. The Trump people are saying I was never actually offered it, so that's what he repeated in the interview and now it's like I am a Real Housewife of Orange County who is claiming to the other wives that I was offered a role on *Malibu Country* (see season 7). I don't want to get involved, but I decided I needed to email Roberts or he is going to keep telling people that I'm Gretchen. So I emailed him and said, "Listen, I don't want to get into a public thing with you but I just want you to have the facts and contrary to what anyone is telling you I was offered that job. Thanks." I think that tactic could've worked for Gretchen and Heather, too.

Now Sonja doesn't like the "commando" line about women in NYC. She says it's bad for her brand. She wants to change it to "Sometimes I just have to go commando." Seems like the same thing. But I want her to add the word "Sonja" to it because I think it's funny when she refers to herself in the third person (i.e., "Sometimes *Sonja* has to go commando"). I have been asking the *Real Housewives of Atlanta* producer to have NeNe add the word "Bloop" to the end of her intro, which is, "Success is in my DNA; when one door closes, another one opens." To me the line is funnier if she says "Bloop" after it. I may be the only one who likes it. Nonetheless I am trying to get NeNe to do it. She is in Mexico and I can't get an answer. I spent twenty minutes on the phone with Heather Dubrow trying to get her to agree to the deal we're offering her. Hopefully that will happen. I love her on the show and wouldn't want to lose her.

Tonight I had four loud, straight guys over to watch the game: Fred Walsh, Dave Ansel, Sean Avery, and Jason Blum—with Chinese food and beers. Wacha was totally well behaved and all I wanted was for everyone to notice the amazing brilliant things my dog was doing. Turns out that people don't really want to endlessly talk about your dog. Everybody *liked* the dog, but after a point, there was general indifference. This was tough for me to adjust to. Maybe if they were gay they would've mustered a little more enthusiasm. (Straight men are prone to indifference.) I could be happy just talking about the dog and the game. In fact I could be happy listening to someone do play-by-play on the dog. It was interesting being with this group of my straight friends, a group of people who never hang out together, and watching them essentially—in dog terms—sniffing each other's asses for three hours. I've seen this dance before. I think gay guys have fewer walls, they just go *in*. For the record, we all ate multitudes of Chinese food in front of and around the dog and he didn't beg once. And the Cardinals won, with the dog's namesake pitching.

▦ FRIDAY, OCTOBER 25, 2013

So it's official today. Zarena came over and I signed the adoption papers. I'm really excited. He's really sweet of course and I just can't believe it's been seven days. I have grown a lot in a week. The interesting thing is my sex drive has been nowhere. It's like I'm satisfying myself with the dog. I'm not fucking the dog, of course, but I think I'm being fulfilled in other ways. Between the dog and the World Series, my libido is at an all-time low. The Cardinals are going to win the Series and I feel like I'm in a really good place.

Ramona changed her opening line from "Get out the Pinot, here I come," to "It's Turtle Time." I actually texted her, "I can't believe one tag line could make me so happy." She texted back that it was Mario's idea.

This afternoon I did Regis's new sports show, *Crowd Goes Wild*, which Michael produces as well as mine, and I think everyone should be impressed that I could be on a sports show talking about baseball and making sense for seven minutes. I played "Plead the Fifth" with Regis. I was terrified he wouldn't understand the rules, so I explained them during the commercial break, and then someone came over to me and said, "Did you explain the rules to Regis?" When I told them I already did, they were like, "He understood it?" So that made me even more nervous, but it went well.

Had dinner with Grac and John Hill at Morandi. Grac was like a bird who had been let out of a cage, an untethered Upper East Side wife. She was a wild animal! I love seeing Grac that way because it takes me right back to the girl I fell in love with in London during our junior year abroad. Then I took Wacha out for a walk at two in the morning and everyone was dressed up for Halloween, and this drunk pack of girls accosted him. Maybe they were dressed as sluts, maybe they were sluts going out for the night. He was terrified. I was glad I wasn't the only one.

SATURDAY, OCTOBER 26, 2013—NYC—ST. LOUIS

Wacha and I had our first fight this morning. He chewed up my earphones. I told him NO and then he wouldn't look me in the eye. He felt bad. And then I felt bad. He was looking at me like he knew he did something wrong, following me around the apartment as I was packing for St. Louis. I put him in the crate and left. Anthony from the show is staying the night with him.

I landed in St. Louis and we basically went straight to Busch Stadium, where I shot some jokey thing for MLB Network before the game. It was really cool being on the field with my parents. Unfortunately for me, the Red Sox were on the field warming up and those beards look as not-hot in person as they do on TV. The *Boston Herald* interviewed me and I said I was not crazy about the beards, that baseball players are so hot and these beards are gross. My mom was giving me these looks like she was going to erupt. The minute the reporter walked away, she did: "You shouldn't be MOUTHING OFF to the PEOPLE OF BOSTON about these BEARDS," and I gave her my most petulant *"What do you care?"* She was probably right, though. I have a hard time muzzling myself sometimes. I wonder where I get that from?

Right before the game, I was shooting one more thing for the MLB and they took me in the tunnel, where we saw David Eckstein, Lou Brock, Ozzie Smith, Tony La Russa, and Carlos Beltrán in his uniform, looking like Superman. He looked seven feet tall, like a cartoon. I was speechless. Erin Andrews was there and she said, "Everyone says we should have a show together, but you would be too dirty for everybody," and I was like, *"Would I?"* Am I dirty? And who is *everybody*?

It was very cold. My father had earmuffs on, and for some reason, I don't know if it was for real or if he was using them as an excuse, he couldn't hear a word my mother was saying all night. It was brilliant. My mother goes, "He doesn't SPEAK to me at games. I'M ON MY OWN! I have to MAKE FRIENDS with the FANS AROUND US." Halfway through the game, the Cards bring in this guy Kolten Wong, who has never done anything, so my mother starts yelling, heckling actually, her own team. "Oh NO! HE can't do ANYTHING! He is just NO GOOD. He's never done A THING," and as she's shit-talking this guy, sure enough he gets a hit. Then he keeps trying to steal the base, and she's discouraging him. "Don't STEAL! You CAN'T!" She just has no faith in this guy, and then he steals the base! The guy in front of us goes, "Lady, what are you *doing*?"

Then *the call* happened, the obstruction call. It was so hard for everyone to understand, all of a sudden, that we had won the game. It didn't make any sense. I was texting Eli and Seinfeld asking them to tell us what the announcers on TV were saying. And then after the game we were in the car home and it was midnight and my mom was all charged up and ready to party—"Lets go get a BURGER!" Though I never turn down a burger, my dad was done—"I don't feel like it. I don't want a hamburger"—and she started to just ride him until I made her concede that the man is eighty-one and just watched a full baseball game in the freezing cold. When we got home I had a Popsicle that, upon closer inspection, I discovered was from 2010. Three years that Popsicle had been in there! (It tasted three years old, too.)

Sometimes I walk into events and realize I didn't think and got it all wrong. Today was one of those days. I went straight from the airport to a brunch for Jason and Lauren Blum's wedding. Mark and Kelly were dressed so well and I felt completely filthy in my day-after-the-game airplane clothes. DVF told me they're doing a huge exhibit celebrating the wrap dress and that I need to go to LA for it in January. I'm all for a dress exhibit, I said. I was so excited to see Wacha after a night apart, but when I got home he would barely look at me for the first half hour. He was not giving it up. Was he still feeling bad about chewing up the headphones? He remembered? Or was he mad at me for leaving? I felt terrible. I saw a cool apartment with Fredrik Eklund this afternoon, at 24 Fifth Avenue. I would have to redo the whole thing. There's great outdoor space. Wacha and I could be very happy. According to my cousin Jodi, there are a lot of dogs running around St. Louis with the name Yadi (Molina). I'm glad I have the first Wacha.

Reverend Al and Cynthia Bailey were on the show. I couldn't tell if Rev. Al was into it or not. I guess he was fine but I felt really codependent for the whole show, wanting him to be OK. He's so compact! After the show I went to a party at Bruce and Bryan's for the opening night of *Betrayal* and Daniel Craig was all seventies and super sweet. He has a mustache for the play that is just seconds away from looking very porny. I have zero issue with a porny mustache. Bruce offered some woman a blanket because she was sitting outside and he said her legs must be cold and she yelled at him, "I'm not eighty, you fucking *asshole*!" She ended up being the wife of someone famous; I guess she didn't realize he was the host. Carole Radziwill and I were going to go pick a fight with this woman, but Bruce ended up being nice to her at the end. (He takes the high road; I hold a grudge.)

Radzi told me I've gained a lot of weight, and Bruce got upset with her on my behalf and she said, "I'm a Housewife. I'm supposed to be inappropriate and say what I think." I thought it was funny. Oh, and she's right on both counts.

When I got home it was my first time taking the dog out really drunk. I let him lick all the booze off my face. So we both got laid.

This morning I screened two episodes of *NY Housewives* and a *Miami Housewives* reunion at home—barely any notes on NY and Miami is almost too nuts to give notes on at all—and then had two development meetings.

Watched the game in the Clubhouse and it was very frustrating—once again it came down to the bitter end. There were men in scoring position and at 10:55 I walked into the studio with Nancy Grace and Marysol Patton *kicking and screaming*. I did not want to be ripped away from the end of that game. I was commanding Deirdre to do play-by-play of the game for me in my ear. I wanted every pitch and every moment in my ear during the show. People can say as much as they want to me in my ear during the show, but I have no problem focusing on being a host. Maybe this is my ADD paying it forward. Deirdre, it turns out, knows nothing about baseball, so she is clueless with play-by-play. At 10:59 she's telling me, "There's two outs," and as they are counting down to air, 10, 9, 8, 7, 6, 5 . . . right when they got to 1, Deirdre goes, "Three outs, they lost." Just as she said that, my face appeared on the monitor. *That's* when I went on the air. *Live*. I lost it. I was cracking up. That has never happened to me before. The timing was so brilliant that I had to laugh at the loss.

By the way, guess who lost the game for the Cardinals? *Kolten Wong* lost the whole damn game for us. The guy my mom was heckling. Of course I got a text from my mom saying, "WHAT DID I TELL YOU ABOUT KOLTEN WONG?"

TUESDAY, OCTOBER 29, 2013

It's a good thing there are only two games left in the World Series. I actually don't know how much I can take. You would think I've been *playing* this game by how exhausted I am. I can't take the stress anymore. And Kolten Wong got really emo in a series of tweets today, saying, "All I want to say is I'm sorry. I go out every day playing this game as hard as I can and leaving everything on the field. I'm so sorry I let you down,

Cardinal Nation. I try to do my best for you every time I get put into the game." It was heartbreaking. I emailed it to my mom and she said, "It's sad but this isn't junior high school, ya know?" Man! Tough love! And then later she said, "But if he doesn't get put in again, it's gonna be some long winter for him." And she's right. Poor guy. I sent him a tweet of support to make up for the bad Cohen juju coming his way.

Glamour magazine came out today, with my Lady Gaga interview. It turned out fine. They kept a little bit of the Madonna stuff in (there was much better stuff that they left out) and they took out the Katy Perry thing. I mean, I get it. Why would *Glamour* magazine pick a fight with these people? At the same time, the interview would have been way better if they'd left that stuff in. Let's put it this way: this article has been out for four hours and it's not exactly burning up the Internet. Maybe that's only me keeping score because I often walk away from interviews wondering what was said that will get picked up by other outlets.

Jenny McCarthy and Donnie Wahlberg were on tonight celebrating their Andy-versary. They met on my show almost a year before and were so sweet. The publicist said not to talk about the relationship too much; meanwhile, it was all we talked about. They brought Donnie's dog, who was really cute. I ran into the bathroom before the show to pee and the dog was in there and Donnie Wahlberg's bodyguard was in front, so I walk in and Donnie is in the stall. I go, "Donnie, is that you? Are you pooing in here?" and he goes, "Yeah." So I said, "Are you one of those people who can poo anywhere?" And he was like, "When you gotta go . . ." I told him I haven't gone number two here once in four and a half years. Right before air he said to Jenny, "Babe, Andy busted me pooing." Here I am worrying about someone walking in on me and I walked in on the guest.

▦ WEDNESDAY, OCTOBER 30, 2013

The Cardinals lost the World Series. It was horrible, so upsetting. They played so shitty tonight, they deserved to lose. Halfway through I turned the sound off and turned music on. It was actually a perfect way to passively watch my hopes and dreams go down the drain. I'm just glad it's over, because I am frankly exhausted by the entire process and I have so much other stuff going on. Again, I know that I did not *play* in the World Series and I know it seems like I *think* I did. This is just one less thing to worry about and I am putting my upset into a little lockbox and I will throw away the key. Hopefully my buried feelings won't come out some wrong way at an inappropriate time.

While I'll never regret going public as a Cardinals fan, outing my adoration of Snoopy may have been a mistake. People keep sending me Snoopy *everything* and I do love him but I'm in my forties and it's getting weird. I could open a warehouse with all the stuff I've amassed. It reminds me of when Em announced she loved penguins when she was five and that's all she got for twenty years. Part of my punishment for going public is that I was asked to write a foreword to the reissue of the *Peanuts Guide to Life* book and, while adorable, it has become this albatross. The publisher asks for the foreword every day and I have been looking to Wacha to tell me something profound, but he's busy licking his ass. I hate writer's block.

I saw the dog trainer and he told me that for a dog five minutes of mental exercise is like two hours at a dog run. I thought that was interesting.

Christina Hendricks and Dylan McDermott were on the show and I kept forgetting Dylan McDermott's name, with the whole Dermot Mulroney/Dean McDermott/Dylan McDermott trilogy playing in my head. I forgot his name on air five times. And between Dylan McDermott's tight pants, which looked loaded up, and Christina Hendricks's overstuffed bosom, the atmosphere was so sexualized, but I felt like I was firing blanks. I wasn't connecting and I felt like they were looking at me funny; nothing was landing as a host. It's a form of erectile dysfunction. Everyone in the control room thought it went well but I didn't believe them.

▦ THURSDAY, OCTOBER 31, 2013

Saw the morning news show Halloween costumes and I love it that CBS did not dress up. They're going for Halloween as *news anchors*. What a novel concept! I did not get *GMA*'s costumes. It was like Halloween on a budget. Josh Elliot was Abe Lincoln with a synthetic beard. It just looked bad. Abe Lincoln?

We did a hilarious Halloween pageant with Neil Patrick Harris, with trick-or-treaters coming throughout the show. Neil and I were in suits. Neil didn't want to dress up, which made me realize, I'm a forty-five-year-old man and maybe I shouldn't dress up either. (My last costume on the show was Giggy and in the rearview mirror it was humiliating.) At this point I have to be *reminded* that I don't need to be a child; it doesn't come naturally. The costumes of our trick-or-treaters were: Teresa and Joe, drag queen Mona Lisa, Mr. Sheffield and the Nanny, drag queen Britney on the "Circus" tour, Endora from *Bewitched,* Slutty Tin Man, and John Hill's dog Colonel was dressed as Mark Cohen from the West Coast production of *Rent.* The drag queen Mona Lisa won. NPH and I had a quick meal after the show and talked about a lot of gay stuff, including debating Kevin Spacey; I still get enraged when I think about him talking about being in love with that woman on *60 Minutes.* Come out, sir.

FRIDAY, NOVEMBER 1, 2013—NYC–LOS ANGELES

The Village was a shitshow last night. I was in bed early so I could wake up at the crack of dawn for my flight to LA to do Leno. All night there were throngs of people under my window doing God knows what. It sounded like gang warfare, the Crips and Bloods duking it out over cupcakes in the West Village. I wanted to throw eggs out my window. I can't believe it now but I actually used to do that in the early nineties— throw eggs out my window at the hookers on Horatio and Washington, before it was gentrified. They were some noisy-ass hookers and it was the only thing I could think of to get them to get off my corner. Now I kind of miss that New York. I also miss having eggs in my refrigerator. And hookers on the street!

I've been negotiating with Leno's producers because I want to play "Plead the Fifth" with him backstage for our YouTube channel during his pre-show dressing-room visit. I sent all these questions for him to approve, since his people asked to see them beforehand. After going back and forth for a few days, I got an email late yesterday that they are not into it.

I got a "ride" to LA, which was lucky, because there was a tragic shooting at LAX and traveling was chaos. (Don't get me started on guns.) On the flight I read the Carson biography, the one written by his lawyer who is now spilling all his intimate secrets after Carson's long gone. Riveting.

On the way to Leno I found out they do want him to play "Plead the Fifth"—not backstage, but on the show. I was glad. Leno came in pre-show to visit in the dressing room and I asked him how he felt about leaving and he said he feels totally fine about it. He said that Conan and he are not that far apart in age, ten or fifteen years, and when he watches Jimmy Fallon's show he sees that Jimmy does stuff he can't do, like sing with Justin Timberlake. He said he gets it because it's going to be a different show. Hearing his POV made me even happier for Jimmy because I want it to go well for him. I asked Leno if he was reading the Carson book and he said no. He thought it was so shitty of this lawyer to write it. Meanwhile, I couldn't put it down on the plane, but I kept that to myself.

The show went well but he really is looking over your shoulder at cue cards and time cues for at least half the interview. It's jarring. I got him talking about Letterman and Carson during "Plead the Fifth," which doesn't happen much. During the break I asked him if Letterman was going to come on his show before he leaves, and he said no, because Letterman never comes to LA. I didn't buy that as an excuse. If he wanted to do the show, he'd come to LA. He went off on Jimmy Kimmel a little bit, saying that Jimmy has been really mean to him. He said Letterman is funny when he's mean, but Kimmel is just mean. Leno asked me who was on my show next week and I could not remember a single person, which is kind of embarrassing. I was on with Melissa McCarthy and the band Empire of the Sun, who are really good but there was some significant body odor happening there. Maybe it was their costumes. Went to dinner at Sunset Tower afterwards and we were molested by Dmtiri the maître d', who the New York Times—on their front page—called "the Most Discreet Man in Hollywood," but who actually tells you everyone who is in the restaurant and in the hotel, so the press got that one wrong.

I finished the Carson book on the plane. It was revealing, but at the end this lawyer has the *gall* to say, "You know, I would like to think that Johnny would have loved this book." Yeah, he certainly would have loved an entire book telling all his secrets and portraying him as a raging asshole. Simon Baker (*The Mentalist*) was sitting across from me on the flight and I spent a fair amount of time trying to figure out if he dyes his (gorgeous) hair. I think he has to, but I just can't picture him reading *People* with foils in his hair. I dunno. I noticed a cute guy across the other aisle, and when I got home that same guy was standing in the lobby of my building talking to Surfin. Turns out he's Sally Field's son. Weird. (No update from Surfin on neighbor upstairs.)

I went to dinner at the Beatrice Inn with Mark and Kelly and turns out that when Mark was leaving for dinner he saw Simon Baker walking into the Crosby Street Hotel. Essentially, we live in Mayberry. With a twist, because Lindsay Lohan was sitting across from us at dinner with a friend and they were both texting the whole time. Unclear if they were texting each other.

I went out with Bill Curtin afterwards on a Hell's Kitchen gay-bar crawl that ended at this place Viva at Forty-eighth and Eleventh. It was so fun and packed and I had three very good guy prospects I was flirting with and I chose instead to go home and fool around with my dog. Leaving three balls in the air for a dog, that's a first. On daylight savings night yet! In my mind I gained an hour of Wacha time.

Before I went to dinner the dog walker showed up with this gorgeous pooch, Neville, who apparently Wacha has been walking with. He came into my apartment looking just like the Target dog. Turns out it's Marc Jacobs's dog, so I kinda feel like Marc Jacobs has been in my apartment. Unclear what he thought of the décor. Basically, Wacha is always either with Neville Jacobs or Kissy Broderick. He has a social life and is running with a glamourpack of dogs! It's a fast crowd, though. I hope they don't get him into drugs or anything. Or worse, what if he gives one of them worms? Something new to worry about.

▦ SUNDAY, NOVEMBER 3, 2013

Wacha can't hang out only with famous dogs—he needs to have some values and learn about real life. So today was all about him and we started at the Union Square dog park, which I discovered is like a massive box of kitty litter. I feel like *I* have kennel cough now, although I really wore him out, so it was half-worth it. Except this woman with a mean dog named Eddie came over to me and wanted to run some "marketing ideas" past me. I was like Lindsay Lohan on her phone, just saying, "I really don't know!" Back at home I gave Wacha his first bath, during which a horrifying quantity of dirt accumulated in the tub. Is there that much dirt spread everywhere in my apartment? It's like that *Dateline* when they come over and expose the filth in your own home.

It was *Atlanta* premiere night and I was so engaged with Kandi and Kenya that it made me wonder if I had been asleep for other episodes. *WWHL* is bursting with extra fun when *Atlanta* is on. Wacha was so exhausted when I got home from the show, he didn't even want to come out of his little house. It's very satisfying when he's worn out.

▦ MONDAY, NOVEMBER 4, 2013

Tonight Lisa Vanderpump and Whitney Cummings were on and Cardinal legend Jim Edmonds was bartending. After the show, I took Lisa and Jim and posse to the Cubbyhole, which was really fun and not too packed with ladies. Now I literally can talk dogs endlessly with Lisa, so that's good. Though it was amusing watching La Vanderpump holding court in the middle of my neighborhood lesbian dive bar. I put her in her car around 1 a.m. and the rest of us stayed. Somehow Jim Edmonds was controlling the jukebox from his phone and kept playing country music. I need to get that app.

At around two-thirty in the morning I went around the corner and got Wacha and brought him to the Cubbyhole. So now Wacha has been to a gay bar. Suffice to say he was very popular.

⬛ TUESDAY, NOVEMBER 5, 2013

Tonight I had two guests who didn't know who the other was, and did not particularly care to, Reza from *Shahs of Sunset* and the actor Zachary Levi. I felt very codependent trying to make sure both of them were OK, because frankly, I got the feeling they each thought the other was a loser and would've rather been on with anyone else. After the show I met Jim Edmonds and his group at 675 Bar for a quick tequila. Once a month I'll get approached at a club or a party by someone overweight who's involved in a NetJets-type operation, trying to sell me a share in a private plane, and it happened again tonight. No sure what that's about. They all were disappointed that Wacha wasn't there. Now I'm no good unless I bring the dog.

⬛ WEDNESDAY, NOVEMBER 6, 2013

Wacha threw up and ate it. So that's great. After all the agonizing about the intro lines for *NY Housewives*, I finally heard them all together in the intro and I think they are funny, but Shari Levine said it looks to her like an *SNL* sketch. So now I'm second-guessing myself. De Blasio was elected mayor and I think Cynthia Nixon deserves a lot of the credit. (And I'm starting to second-guess myself on him too.)

I had fights with two TVs in two different cabs. As much as I love TV, I do not want to watch it in a cab. Ever. Even if I'm on it.

After nine years of twice-yearly offsites sitting in hotel suites brainstorming and planning the future of the network, today was my last Bravo offsite. Nobody knew about my new deal, so I sat there feeling bittersweet all day.

LinkedIn is doing some "Take your parents to work day" promotion, and they sent me this huge blowup of my parents. The first thing I thought was, "How am I going to throw this out? How do I throw out my parents?" So I sent a picture of it to my mother and she goes, "How are you going to throw THAT out? THAT'S THROWING OUT YOUR PARENTS!" And I said, "I had the exact same thought." But she's thrown away plenty of blowups of me. By the way, LinkedIn bugs the fuck out of me.

I had Katey Sagal and Giada De Laurentiis on the show. Katey Sagal has Bitchy Resting Face, so I kept thinking she was mad or not having a good time, but she just has a severe case of BRF and once I figured that out, I loved her. I asked Katey to give me one word to describe Christina Applegate and she's thinking and then this woman in the front row goes, "Spiritual," and her equally mouthy friend next to her yells out, "Strong," and I looked at them and said, "You don't know Christina Applegate and I'm pretty sure Katey Sagal will be able to find the answer. And you're not *in* the show." OK, I just thought it. But I wish I'd said it out loud. People are nuts.

⠿ THURSDAY, NOVEMBER 7, 2013

SJP joined Twitter and I've been coaching her, which has been funny. She's been concerned about appearing to be shilling (which she is not) and was gun-shy to jump off the cliff and just start, but she's doing well. But now she's having guilt about not responding to everybody, which I am trying to explain is essentially impossible. But she's as sparkly in a tweet as she is in life, sprinkling them with "xx sj" at the end. Who doesn't love that?

I went to see the B-52s at the Brooklyn Bowl with Grac and Neal and Jeanne and Fred. You bowl and a band plays, but we stopped bowling when they went on, because who *actually* wants to bowl while the band is on? Before the show I was thinking, "I don't know if I have it in me tonight. I'm so old." And then I was looking around at the crowd, which felt equally old—the B's are like the greatest party band ever, and they're all now hovering around sixty and the audience has aged with them but the music hasn't aged at all.

They sounded perfect but Kate's face resembles that of a Real Housewife of, I don't even know where, outer space? A space-aged Real Housewife. Cindy has sort of let herself go but the two of them sound so tight and harmonious and they did some songs I wasn't expecting, like "Legal Tender" and "Girl from Ipanema Goes to Greenland." It filled me with joy and love to dance with Grac and Jeanne and let go. And I *did* have it in me.

Afterwards we said hi to Fred Schneider and he said, "You danced on the risers for us?" I was glad he remembered Grac and my memorable stint as go-go dancers. "Yes, I did!" And I met Kate again and I've got a whole Susan Lucci thing with her. I don't know what to say to these women. I'm like jelly. Mercifully none of them seem to know what Bravo is or who I am, which in my mind is how it should be.

When they walked offstage I was thinking to myself, "I wonder if I'll ever see them again, because as good as they sound, they are getting older. How much longer will they perform?" And then, sure enough, Fred says they have five more performances in the area and then he thinks they're done. After years of shows in countless cities, that may have been the last time that I see the B-52s. I was standing by Cindy, waiting for her to end a conversation so I could just be a fan, but the convo was not ending and these guys were coming up to me to get their photo taken with me. I left without talking to her. Cindy renders me powerless.

Then we had The Wanted on my show and I felt like a perv asking them about their sexploits. After that, I got a two-hour massage and Wacha barked when he heard someone coming down the hall. I was bragging to my masseur about what a good protector he is and the masseuse goes, "Yeah. You wouldn't want to live in a building like this without any protection." Everyone's a comedian.

▦ FRIDAY, NOVEMBER 8, 2013

In August I did a favor for Cynthia Rowley and she was wearing a denim jumpsuit at the time and when she said, "I owe you," I told her she didn't, but she kept saying it. So I told her to get me a denim jumpsuit like she was wearing. And she declared, "I will make you one." For the longest time I really didn't think she was going to make me that jumpsuit and I started to really want one. I was wondering where the hell I was going to get a denim jumpsuit. Then a few days ago I got this call: "Your jumpsuit is ready for a fitting." So today I had a denim jumpsuit fitting. Glorious.

I talked to Bill Carter from the *New York Times* about my deal. I started to tell people at Bravo. This is feeling very real and I am feeling scared and excited; I am officially cutting the cord from the security of a day job.

Glamour editor Cindi Leive called to see if I would marry a lesbian couple onstage at their Women of the Year Awards on Monday night. I pointed out that with Gaga and Streisand as witnesses, this will be the gayest wedding on the planet. So that's happening next week. They just have to find a couple now. (Idea first, execution later—exactly how we do it at *WWHL*!)

Lynn's in town from San Francisco and tonight I took her to see Kathy Griffin at Carnegie Hall. The people sitting next to us talked the *entire time*. At one point the guy was on his *phone*, in *Carnegie Hall*, and Lynn, my protector since our days at CBS News, would not let me say anything. She was trying to save me from making a messy public scene. It took all my strength to follow her orders but I did. After the show, Anderson hosted a little party for Kathy downstairs at Trattoria Dell'Arte. I was at the bar and this woman turns to me and said, "I thought I recognized your voice. You were sitting next to me." It was the chatty couple!

And I said, "Were you forced to come tonight? Are you a relative of Kathy's? Do you work with her?" They said no, no, and no; and I said, "You seemed like you didn't like it, because you talked through the whole show." She said, "*That's what we do*. We talk during movies and we talk during shows." I said, "Oh, *that's what you do*." And then turned away. That's what they *do*!?!?! Here's what *I do*: turn away from people who talk at Carnegie Hall.

Kathy was grateful Kathy (versus any other kind of Kathy you might come across). She was very thankful to me for all the Bravo comedy specials she's done, because now she's done more comedy specials than any other female comedian (grateful and proud Kathy). Truthfully I had little to do with it but I said, "You're welcome," because I have *manners*. Gloria Steinem was there looking Santa Fe chic and ageless.

After the party Liza and I dropped Lynn at her hotel and meandered down Fifty-seventh Street looking at Christmas decorations. I found an incredible tree in the window of Lee's Art Shop that simulates snow falling. We need it for the Clubhouse. On the way home I sent a drunk tweet in the back of a speeding cab, referencing a parallel Dodi/Diana situation, which people were quickly and loudly offended by. Sixteen years later it's too soon, huh? I deleted it, which I never do. Deleting a tweet is an admission of guilt, but I wasn't going to endure a shitstorm of abuse for a Dodi and Diana tweet. As far as I was concerned, the biggest crime of the night was not my tweet, but that rude couple at Carnegie Hall. I got home and watched Wacha chew on a bone in my lap for forty-five minutes. By candlelight, listening to music. Very romantic.

SATURDAY, NOVEMBER 9, 2013

I'm in love with my dog. We had the best nap ever today. It turns out that I have a better chance of having a long-term relationship with him than with a person, because everything I say goes. The dog trainer came. Wacha is so receptive to learning, but I had to stop myself from tuning out a few times. I'm sitting there telling myself, "This guy's here to *help me*, don't tune him out." This tuning out of people who are trying to help me is an ongoing problem.

Went to James Wilkie Broderick's eleventh birthday party, which featured one of those ladies in a high ponytail whose job it is to hype up the kids and completely freak out the parents' friends. She was a pro. A nutbag, but a pro. SJP was too busy taking photos to notice. Any comparison that I had begun to make in the last month between having a dog and having a kid was erased after five minutes in the party. Lots of energy in every direction. There were no cabs, since it suddenly gets dark and crazy at 3 p.m., so I took a pedicab home. I negotiated him down to forty bucks from Fifty-fifth and Seventh. Even though that's an obscene amount, I felt victorious. I did tell him to stop singing at one point because it was impeding my enjoyment of the ride. I had a coffee date with this guy who I'd met on Fire Island who is alternately amazing looking and then, when he smiles, a psychopath. Probably not going anywhere.

I went with Bruce to a dinner for Giancarlo Giammetti at Sotheby's. I think he and Valentino have been honored at dinners every night for the last nine years, and I'm all for taking part. I sat next to Charlene

Shorto de Ganay, who I am *obsessed* with and immediately started following on Instagram at the table—she's chic, gorgeous, sweet, and super jet set—and across from Mike Ovitz, who was on and off his phone all night. I'd eaten pot candy on the way to the dinner and it really improved the quality of the night, as it always does. I had a nice chat with Marc Jacobs about Neville. Marc said there's a private dog run somewhere in the West Village that's run by a nutbag (of course it would be run by a nutbag) and that the application process is brutal. A private dog run in my neighborhood!? I need to find out more. At one point during the meal I went to the bathroom and one of the model waiters was in there just loitering by the mirror and he told me he was "taking a break," which I loved. So I took a break with him. We took selfies in the mirror. It was like an episode of *Vanderpump Rules*.

SUNDAY, NOVEMBER 10, 2013

I took John Hill to the Knicks day game and we did the celeb thing where beforehand you go up to the owner's dining room and it's an endless buffet. John correctly compared the experience to being in Panem in *Hunger Games*. We saw the Grubmans and the Azoffs. I tried to get some good Diana Ross stories out of the Azoffs. We sat behind Nelly and Larry David, who were not together. They put me on the Jumbotron and wrote "Actor" under my name and I was welcomed with a smattering of boos. The Knicks lost.

I had dinner with Jimmy and Nancy Fallon at some Japanese place called Hane, which reminds me of the way Roseanne Roseannadanna said Jane Curtin's name when she was on "Weekend Update." There was a lot of late-night-TV talk, which at the end of the day is my fave kinda talk.

On my show I had Porsha Stewart and Nelly. I love Nelly. I feel like Nelly could run for President. He's smiley and approachable and lovable. And he lets me wear his jewelry. I was trying to set Porsha up with him. He ended up inviting her to some party he was doing after the show. I don't know what happened there but it made me happy to think there was a possibility.

I found out Nelly has a serious girlfriend, so my match wasn't a match. Tonight was the *Glamour* Women of the Year Awards. I'd hosted last year and my parents came and loved it. So we repeated this year, which coincidentally fell on Dad's birthday. When we sat down, a debate erupted about whether our seats were crappy or not. We were in the fourth row, by the way. Then Streisand got seated across the aisle, which of course made them the best seats ever. I just wanted to watch Barbra watch the show. She looks great. And weirdly, her ass looks great. Gaga I think was dressed as "the dead." Speaking of which, my dad was wearing a suit I bought him last year that my mom refers to as "the Box Suit" because she is assuming that it will be the suit he will be wearing in his casket, which of course is incredibly upsetting to me, but they seem to think is hilarious. Happy Birthday, Dad!

The awards were very uplifting—sometimes things like this can actually be inspiring. Melinda Gates, Malala, a teacher from Sandy Hook (incredibly upsetting), and Streisand were honored. Hillary Clinton spoke. They nixed the onstage wedding in favor of me doing a tribute to women who had been responsible for the legalization of gay marriage, and it was lovely. I talked to Seth Meyers backstage about his show and about Gaga hosting *SNL* this weekend. Katie Couric was backstage getting pictures with everybody. Oh, and the kids from PS 22 performed—the kids' choir who I mistakenly gave my real opinion of on *Morning Joe* and was subsequently lynched by the media. I feel like their goal in life is to terrorize me, and guess what? I'll say it again. *I didn't think they were great.* Sue me. Hang me.

We stopped by the party at the Oak Room and I wanted to tell Gaga that we made perfume out of her pee, and I wound up in a three-way convo with her and Malala. And watching those two try to communicate was to me funnier than anything I bet I'll see her do on *SNL*, Malala in her drag and Gaga looking like the undead. Malala asked Gaga who made her clothes and then Gaga, in her baby voice, did a ten-minute soliloquy about her little monsters and the youth, which I think was lost on both Malala and me (maybe I am too old?), and I was getting very impatient because I had a live show and *really* wanted to tell her about the pee-fume before I left. I was waiting and waiting for an opening but finally I just interrupted her and told her. Gaga loved it. And Malala *definitely* was confused. I took a quick selfie with Gaga and then ran to the show.

Brandi Glanville and Mark Consuelos were on. Brandi had her tits out, flirting with my father, in front of my mother, who kept tooting her horn from behind the bar. On the after show, Brandi said, in front of my parents and the world, that she heard that Miami Housewife Joanna Krupa's pussy smells horrible. Mark fell off his chair, my mom blew her horn, my dad was agog, and I couldn't stop laughing. My poor parents.

TUESDAY, NOVEMBER 12, 2013

Wacha pooped inside. It was very traumatic. He had been sitting in front of the door, which meant he had to go. I made the executive decision to give him a bath instead of taking him out. He made the executive decision an hour later to poop on the bath mat.

Today Gaga tweeted, "So @Andy told me they made perfume out of my pee from the trash in *WWHL* dressing room (long story) U HAVE BEEN WARNED IF HE TRIES TO SPRITZ U." And the Brandi allegation about Joanna Krupa's pussy is getting picked up everywhere. This is the world we live in and I am feeding the beast.

WEDNESDAY, NOVEMBER 13, 2013

I woke up early. I "listened" to Wacha's cues—he sat in front of the door three times, and I took him out each time and he went each time. I need to listen to this dog!

Today the *Times* ran their piece about my deal, and I was expecting more from it. You always expect more when something is being written about you, because to you it's a big deal and you overthink what a big deal it will appear to be to others. And I've been working on it for months and months. But it's not a big deal. Maybe if you're Ryan Seacrest, the news comes out and it's a big deal. I'm not Ryan Seacrest and maybe I'm just not a big deal!

After the announcement went out I realized, "OMG, I have this company now," so I called Daryn in and told her it was her and me against the world, and we need to get @MostTalkative and Mosttalkative.com. Idiot me had not even given this production company plan any detailed thought. Mosttalkative.com is owned by Holt, all about my book, which is fine, and then the Twitter is some girl in Palampur. So I told Daryn, you need to make a list of everything you would do if you were starting a company, OK? And I named her Chief Creative Officer. She's twenty-five years old. I know how to produce TV shows like I know how to talk, but I am backing into running this production company and learning as I go.

I hosted the Emery Awards for the Hetrick-Martin Institute at Cipriani tonight. Doing an event like that is tricky. The charity really needs someone to get up there and MC the night, but on the other hand it's a thankless job. Two thousand people talking and you have to be the guy who reads every item in the gift bag to fulfill sponsor obligations. But I saw a lot of friends and talked to even more people with bad breath. The amount of people who don't maintain their breath is staggering. It makes me think they have a belly full of raw fish and spoiled meat. I saw Chelsea Clinton, so that's two Clintons in one week. Didn't smell her breath.

I got a haircut in my dressing room before my show, and as I sat there, out of nowhere felt this huge weight had lifted because of the deal being announced. I let out a literal deep sigh of relief. My parents came to the show. They had been representing me at opening night of *Stars of David*. It's a new off-Broadway musical where each song is the story of a famous person's relationship with Judaism. I put them in matching Mazel hoodies and they did a shotski with me. I was full of gratitude for them tonight, how lucky am I to have parents who can share in this weird existence with me—not all parents are like them. After the show, Hickey, back from LA, came over and finally met Wacha and loved him. We got very drunk and watched Madonna concert videos.

Today I had lunch at Rosemary's with my parents after they met Wacha. My mom stresses people out inadvertently. And animals. She puts out a lot of energy and made my non-hyper dog a little hyper. She had him on high alert, which then had her on high alert.

Then Carole Radziwill texted me saying she would love some doggy time and she came over and got Wacha and they went to SoHo, which he needed after his visit with my mom.

Someone leaked a story to Radar Online that I was actually fired or pushed out. I'm pretty sure it was a former Househusband. Radar will print anything.

I had two-hour drinks with Bonnie Hammer at the Monkey Bar. We talked about business mainly, but then got deep about animals and love.

Terrence Howard was on my show with Nia Long. They told us not to give him any liquor. When I walked into the Clubhouse, he was drinking out of a bottle of Jameson. We had the following conversation during the break:

TERRENCE: How many dimensions are you?
ANDY: What?
T: How many dimensions are you?
A: You mean, how many personalities do I have?
T: No . . . how many dimensions do you see through?
A: Uh . . .
T: How many dimensions do you see through?
A: A few—I'm very multidimensional.
T: I don't meet many people like you. I really don't.
A: Really?
T: No, I don't. You're boundless. You have *no bounds*.
A: Wow—thank you!
T: It's true.

I talked to Padma about my deal and she said, "Good. It's been hard to talk to you as my boss. I'd rather speak to you as my friend." I went to the bank to open an account for Most Talkative and this beautiful teller came up and gave Wacha a treat. He was sitting there like a good doggy and all of a sudden that pink tube of lipstick came out between his legs and I said to the teller, "Oh, you're giving him a boner!" I guess that was really not appropriate. Neither she nor her colleagues found it humorous. So you don't say that, I learned.

Went to Waverly Inn for dinner with Liza, Ricki Lake, Bruce, and a friend of Ricki's. Ashley Merriman, from *Top Chef*, is the chef and sent over some truffle mac and cheese. I picked up the check and gave the guy my credit card to pay, and then flashed back to the last four times I picked up the check and got the bill—the Waverly is always really expensive. It was almost six hundred dollars. (The flirty waiter wasn't there. I wonder what happened to him.) Then we hung out at my apartment with Wacha. Liza said Wacha is the dog version of Hugh Grant. I agree. Hugh Grant is very cute, a little withholding, and he looks like he's a bit of a cad, just like Wacha. The dog and I walked Bruce home and stopped for FroYo. It had just closed but there was this couple sitting there in front on the bench and the husband got me high. Who says New Yorkers aren't neighborly?

I went to bed staring at a picture of Marie Osmond that she tweeted of herself with Olivia Newton-John, which raised a lot of questions for me.

I went to the toilet, I mean the dog run, immediately followed by a bath, and then to Sascha Seinfeld's bat mitzvah and I think the rabbi was trying to be a little bit of a comedian because of Jerry. Sascha was amazing. Ali Wentworth and I were cutting up a lot. Great nosh from Barney Greengrass in the lobby after. I ate like a pig. I'm eating as though I'm trying to *put on* weight. Like I'm aggressively trying to add pounds.

I met up with this boy who I have seen around here and there for the last couple years and we have always talked about having a drink. I met him for a coffee fully thinking it would lead to something. Turns out he is twenty-one!! Oy. *Redirect!* Then I went to Sascha's party, which was at the Boom Boom Room. Suffice to say I think this was the first bat mitzvah party held at the Boom Boom Room. I sat between Kelly and Ali and I talked to George Stephanopoulos about *GMA* and how he didn't want to dress in a Halloween costume. They had hired those dancers to hype the kids, and I started to inappropriately flirt with one of them. This is as low as you can get. I nipped that in the bud.

SUNDAY, NOVEMBER 17, 2013

Today I went to Ellen Barkin's mother's funeral and it was a killer. She was loved by a lot of people and I couldn't stop crying.

They are filming *The Normal Heart* on my block, so I decided to bring Wacha to Joe Mantello's trailer. Said hi to Ryan Murphy and saw Taylor Kitsch but was too freaked out to move. Even with a bad blond dye job he is so hot. Clear Eyes, Full Hearts, Dye Job, Still Hot.

I went to Barkin's for shiva and then went and did my show (with Pheadra and the preachers from *Thicker Than Water*). And then afterwards I brought Wacha to the shiva at 1:00 a.m. to pay *his* respects. The vibe of the shiva had definitely changed for the drunker.

MONDAY, NOVEMBER 18, 2013

I was woken by two jackhammers, a tow truck, an electric saw, and what sounded like a pack of wild dogs below my window. Good morning, New York.

I had a dud Fallon pre-interview for my appearance tomorrow. I told them the story about the Gaga perfume but the producer said that Jimmy doesn't like bathroom talk. We'll see.

Britney Spears's people asked me to interview her onstage at her album release event this Thursday in LA, which I am trying to leverage for her coming on my show. They said it will really help me get the booking if I get to know her a little. She wants to feel comfortable and build a rapport, which makes sense. I would miss SJ's opening night if I go. I emailed her and she said it's fine. "Come to the show anytime but don't tell me in advance when you're coming," and I said, "But I want to be there to support you," which is a line said at least once by every Housewife in every city. She's not a Housewife, so she ain't gonna hold it against me if I go to LA.

I had dinner with Ralph Fiennes at Barbuto. Saw Jonathan Waxman, who is always really nice. That chicken of his is so damn good. I was trying to explain the show *Vanderpump Rules* to Ralph and it was not translating. I wanted to give up but he really wanted to know what it was all about. It was like trying to fit a circle into a square.

I went home to change for my show and ran into Wacha, who was on his walk. He freaked out when he saw me on the street. He knows I'm his master. I loved it.

Stassi and Jax were on the show. They hate each other. And it was a dead audience. Maybe we do need an applause sign. I can't decide. It seems so conventional.

▦ TUESDAY, NOVEMBER 19, 2013

I did Jimmy's show this afternoon. They were OK with talking about the Gaga thing but wanted to let Jimmy decide if he wanted me to bring the perfume out. Ryan brought the Lady Gaga urine bottle uptown so I could show them how funny—rather than gross—it looked. Jimmy came in to say hi and he loved it, but was worried the audience would say to spray it on him, so I didn't bring it on, but we talked about it. It was great. The Roots played my theme song when I came out, which was a cause for celebration (for me).

Jimmy has the whole "say hi to the guest" thing before the show down pat. He gets you all excited and pumped up. He is in there for a minute and then some girl comes and says, "I have to pull you out." I'm trying to imitate how he does it with my guests, but I always wind up staying longer. (Leno pulls up a chair and it's a whole conversation. Letterman you don't see at all before you go out.)

After that I went straight to co-host the unveiling of the Bergdorf Goodman Christmas windows. We couldn't find the car outside 30 Rock, of course (#FirstWorldProblems), so we took a cab and then yelled at the car company, which happens constantly and is rarely as satisfying as it should be. I never dress for the weather and it was 30 degrees and I was in a suit with no jacket, so the Bergdorf Creative Director Linda Fargo grabbed a plum Loro Piana scarf from the store and styled me, which I kind of loved. They had these people climbing down the wall outside of Bergdorf's and dropping glitter. So I was wearing a plum lady's scarf and I had glitter all over me. That wasn't gay. I gave the scarf back.

Then I went to my show. Meredith Vieira was really loose and my Hebrew teacher Yitz was the bartender. Turns out his dad circumcised me, and so Yitz busted out that old chestnut: "I was going to bring a wallet that you could rub and it turns into luggage." The prompter went out right before I had to do a really complicated Mazel and Jackhole and then it came back on like the last second. I don't know what happened, but Dave my normal prompter guy wasn't there. The temporary lady froze the prompter and I was frozen myself for a second. It must have looked crazy on air. I'm still a little shaken from it.

After hemming and hawing all day, I decided to do the Britney thing. We'll see.

WEDNESDAY, NOVEMBER 20, 2013

All the entertainment blogs are talking about what a disgusting pee fetishist I am for making perfume out of Gaga's pee. Yes, I love pee. That's my thing. (It is so not, to be clear.)

I had a conference call with Britney's people. This is the audition to get her on my show, so I did my homework, which consisted of actually trying to find a message in fourteen new Britney Spears songs. I felt very smart when I correctly guessed the song that is about her sons, Jayden James and Sean Preston. I talked to her manager, who said they were on a shoot in the desert, and I wanted to ask him, "How many things can Britney shoot in the desert??" but I refrained. That's Britney's go-to place. (Britney in the desert in a crop top . . . Britney in the desert with a whip . . . with a motorcycle . . . with a guy.) I told them I want it to be positive and ran through everything I was going to talk about. I said she sounds great on the album and how usually her voice gets lost but this time it is front and center. I said I wanted to talk to Britney about the misconception that she's not in control, but how she *is* really in control of Britney, Inc., and it seems like that was the only problem area. He will get back to me tomorrow about that, which means she is maybe *not* actually in control.

I went to the *Hunger Games: Catching Fire* premiere. I thought the first one was so cheap it looked like they shot it in the Clubhouse. This one was the complete opposite. I loved it, especially on the IMAX at the AMC Lincoln Square theater, which is allegedly the biggest movie screen in the country. Patti Smith was sitting behind me. I kept wondering what she was doing there and what the great Patti Smith could possibly think of this movie. I was trying to see it through Patti Smith's eyes. Was there some kind of a poetic allegory playing out for her way beyond the suppression of the Capitol? I left for my show at 10:27, missing the last ten minutes of the movie, and got there at 10:50. Went on at 11. No run-through. No nothing. And it was a great show. There was so much cocaine talk with Gina Gershon. I can't imagine that our sponsor was thrilled but what can you do?

▦ THURSDAY, NOVEMBER 21, 2013—NYC–LOS ANGELES

If someone told me five years ago I would be bitching about getting on a plane to go interview Britney Spears, I would think they were high. But I didn't feel great when I woke up, and I certainly didn't feel like getting on a plane. It is what it is.

I got to Newark in no time and headed to the United lounge, where this woman told me, "Your platinum Amex does not get you into the United lounge and *hasn't for two years*." So I went and sat in a Coffee Bean and Tea Leaf (I like that United terminal at Newark, FYI) and five minutes later they start paging me, "Andy Cohen, please come to the United lounge immediately for an important message." I thought, "Oh great, somebody loves NeNe Leakes up there and saw that beeyotch at the counter turn me away." And here's what I said to myself: "I'm not going." They paged me three more times and it was embarrassing pretending I wasn't hearing my name.

I stepped on the plane and came face-to-face with a flight attendant who looks just like Baby Jane Hudson (the old lady, Bette Davis version) but with the complete opposite energy. She was insidiously upbeat and in my face trying to help me get situated, "Let's get you *settled*!!! Should we put your magazines *here*??" "Can I help you with your computer??" I couldn't handle her energy. I am not a man who needs help *settling*. After I navigated her away from me, this woman comes in from the United lounge saying, "Even though your card doesn't get you in, we are such fans of yours we wanted to present you with these," and she hands me a bunch of free passes to the United lounge. Very sweet but her soul sister back at the counter already kinda ruined it for me.

Then we take off and I'm getting *settled* in (without the help of #Baby JaneFlightAttendant) and I pick up my *New York* magazine and turn to the last page, The Approval Matrix, which is my favorite, and on the heels of the love from the flight attendants I am smacked in the face by the bile of the editors of my go-to section, who put a revolting photo of me in the depths of the Lowbrow/Despicable corner and it says: "Bravo extends Andy Cohen's talk show, and the *Real Housewives* **circus** rolls on." My heart sank. Sometimes these things do get under your skin. I was upset! Then I watched a marathon of *Vanderpump Rules* and you know what I thought? "Fuck The Approval Matrix." I know good TV.

The rest of the flight was a dance between me and #BabyJaneFlight Attendant that involved me responding to her cacophonous service with one-word answers so I could get her out of my face quicker. *So many words!*

I got to LA for the Britney thing and for an hour and a half people kept finding me to tell me that they are going to bring me to Britney for an introduction, and I'm like, "OK. No problem. No stress. I'm fine." I ran into Ryan Seacrest and we gossiped about *Shahs of Sunset* and talked about the idea of making people famous and what happens after, which is one of my favorite conversations, and he was claiming he can't afford a yacht, which I don't believe, and I was hoping he'd tell me I was "killing it" or "crushing it" but instead he said, "Keep up the hustle, buddy. You're doing great." You always want Ryan Seacrest to be a dick but he isn't.

Then they took me to meet Britney and it was awkward. I walked over to her and her mob of handlers and yelled, "It's Britney, bitch!" and she said, "OMG!" And there was a big cake. I asked if it was her birthday and she said, "Well, the radio stations are celebrating my birthday today but it's in ten days." And I just thought, "It's so weird to be Britney." She asked me if I wanted a piece of cake and I said yes. The cake was shaped like her, so she said, "Which part of me do you want?" I said, naturally, "I think a boob." So she cut me a piece with her boob on it and a heart. And she said, "Here's a boob and a heart," and I said, "Well, if that doesn't represent Britney Jean, a boob and a heart."

I told her I saw a picture of her kissing a guy in her new video and she said she thought he was gay, and I said, "Throw your scraps to Daddy," which didn't get the reaction I was hoping for. Then I said, "Or just send me some background dancers." It was all very stilted. They brought me in to "connect" with her but how do you do that when there are twenty people around? She seemed shy and somewhere else, which made me a little sad about the whole situation. And then they said Britney was going to get touched up. I walked out and was in the hall and they kept trying to introduce me to Will.i.am, like three times, and he wanted nothing to do with me. I thought, "Oh my God. What have I said about Will.i.am or the Black Eyed Peas on my show or in life that has made this guy hate me?"

Finally we did the Q and A and that was even more awkward. She's simple and shy, and doesn't give you much, and what she does give is pretty short answers. I would ask a couple questions and then we'd sit and listen to a song in front of an audience that was standing there watching us listen. I became obsessed with the dynamic between Brit and one of her handlers, an older woman who has welded herself to Brit's hip, whispering in her ear at every opportunity. While the songs were playing she would come up to the stage and whisper something "important" to her. I think she's there to help but it's clear to my novice eyes that she is doing the opposite. I started thinking that maybe Brit wouldn't be so good on *WWHL*. You really have to be sharp and on top of your game. After schlepping to LA for eighteen hours, I came to that conclusion.

I took a picture with Britney and I felt almost ashamed. Then I had dinner with Hickey and Jeffrey and Brad Goreski and Gary at Madeo. Mood improved.

FRIDAY, NOVEMBER 22, 2013—LOS ANGELES—NYC

Halfway through the morning ride to LAX it became clear to me that my driver was high on crystal meth. Literally. When we got to the airport he goes, "Are you sure you don't want to come party with me?" He wasn't talking about a cocktail. He's a good driver and I've had him before, but he was definitely high. I didn't tattle on him. He needs the job to support his meth habit!

On the plane it dawned on me that I had sent a bunch of nasty tweets about the Black Eyed Peas during the Super Bowl halftime show a couple years ago, but Will.i.am would never have seen that. Then I remembered that when Eve was on my show once, she said she heard that Britney didn't record the tracks on "Scream and Shout." Maybe he was pissed at that? Maybe he just thinks I'm a loser. Maybe he thinks nothing about me! We are all just stuck with our head up our own ass, that's the net net here.

I read on the plane that Patti Smith has a song on the *Hunger Games* soundtrack, so now I know why she was at the movie. And I saw a picture of myself in front of Bergdorf's with that plum Loro Piana scarf. I look like I am mid–gender transition. Not my best look.

When I got home Wacha burrowed his face in my legs. I think he's really scared that I'm gonna leave him. And maybe he's wondering if this is a part-time love affair or what. If I could tell him anything (that he would understand), it would be that he is not going anywhere and neither am I. He is home.

SATURDAY, NOVEMBER 23, 2013—NYC–SAG HARBOR

I took Wacha to Ava's birthday party and I might've enjoyed the pottery party as much as my goddaughter. I made Wacha a dog bowl with his name on it, then we drove out to the Hamptons for his first trip and what was essentially a tour of the East End's best houses. We spent the afternoon at Marci Klein's and he had a good explore on the beach. After lounging at my house, we went to Albert Bianchini's and Mark and Kelly compared him favorably to Albert's codependent dog, Rufus, which made me a proud daddy.

At the end of the day, I noticed that something was wrong with the way he was standing up. He seemed to be in pain.

SUNDAY, NOVEMBER 24, 2013—SAG HARBOR–NYC

Today Wacha visited Sandy Gallin's and the Seinfelds'. I kept looking at him, saying, "You stepped in shit. You were in a kill shelter in West Virginia and now you're at Jerry Seinfeld's in the Hamptons."

Sandy told me that I'm fat and that I need to lose weight because I'm on TV, and he's right. And as much as I've been thinking it myself, hearing it from a friend who managed talent for as long as he did really hit home. He was being a friend and he should know. So I decided then and there, amid a sea of white furniture and dark wood floors, that I'm going to be sober for the month of January and I'm going to lose ten pounds. Besides discussing my emerging obesity, we all noticed that Wacha was having major trouble getting up and even walking. He was really tentative—this after playing in the yard with a bunch of other dogs. It was freaking me out.

On the drive back to the city, I took Wacha to the animal hospital in Riverhead. The vet says he thinks his hip is sprained. He popped a boner. Wacha, not the vet.

I got a message from Teresa saying congrats on my new deal. She said she wanted to wait until it was final to call me. I mean, did she know that I've been working on this deal for nine months? Was she aware? Then she said, "I think we should partner together. I'm going to make you millions. I'm going to make you richer than Ryan Seacrest." Intriguing!

I went to Bruce's and watched the AMAs, and once again his doorman acted like he'd never seen me before. I have been going over there for years and it's always like the first time with this doorman. This guy could not pick me out of a lineup.

⊞ MONDAY, NOVEMBER 25, 2013

I took Wacha to the vet, who said "Oh my *God*!" when she saw the X-ray. Apparently his hips are fucked up, I mean really fucked up. He's gonna have to get surgery, she says. I have to take him to the animal hospital uptown. I feel so bad for the little guy. Surgery??

Ricky Van Veen and Allison Williams came over and we ordered in and basically had a four-way with my poor handi-capable dog.

⊞ TUESDAY, NOVEMBER 26–SATURDAY, NOVEMBER 30, 2013— NYC–ST. LOUIS

My annual Thanksgiving pilgrimage to St. Louis. At the airport my Dopp kit was inspected by the TSA agent but she failed to clock the big fat joint I'd mistakenly left in there that was staring her in the face. And I saw the winner of *Battle of the Network Reality Stars* going through security but I can't remember his name. Maybe Joe Schmo? I wonder what was in *his* Dopp kit.

I'm shooting something on *Sesame Street* right after Thanksgiving, and when I got to my parents' I had a call with the wardrobe guy about how not to get lost shooting w/ Elmo and the Muppets. (Don't wear red seems to be the answer.) He was taking me through potential colors on the phone and my mom was in the background screaming, "YEL-LOW!!!" Wear YELLOW!" After a few minutes the guy said, "Do you want to wear yellow but don't want to mention it for some reason?" I told him my mom was being nosy.

All weekend, all over St. Louis, I saw lesbians. You cannot throw a can of Budweiser without hitting a lesbian and they all drive Subaru Outbacks. Besides seeing lesbians, I didn't do a hell of a lot. I basically ate like a champ and wandered aimlessly around town. Every time I brought up going to the Galleria, Em told me it was going to be a *zoo* and to avoid it at *all costs*. Well, I went twice and it was fine. She likes hype. I got my rings cleaned, which tells you how busy I am here. I ate some Provel cheese on a pizza. Oh my God, that stuff is so good. Actually it's disgusting and so am I.

I went to a benefit called "Guns and Hoses" for families of fallen cops and firefighters during which cops and firefighters box each other. I went with Kari and met Jim Edmonds there, and they set us up ringside. It's a huge event—thousands of people at the place where the St. Louis Blues play. I was looking through the program of cops and firefighters like it was a husband catalog. I was literally circling my picks, waiting for my fights. The announcer brought me into the ring to introduce me in front of those thousands of people and said, "Actually, we could really use you to kill some time between fights," and just handed me a microphone. WTF. So I just wished everyone Happy Hanukkah, which I thought was hilarious, but may have been lost on the crowd. I took pictures with a lot of (lesbian) cops and firefighters but unfortunately didn't meet my match. Afterwards we went to Jim Edmonds's new bar. It was full of fuzz and firefighters—lots of beards—but none on my team. I've always loved going out the night before Thanksgiving.

I spent all Thanksgiving morning watching the Macy's Thanksgiving Day Parade while my dad hammered me with questions about specifics of the parade, such as "How much does it cost to put on this parade, Andy? How many people are there?" "HE DOESN'T KNOW THE STATS, LOU!" Mom chimed in. She had other things on her mind, primarily to RAGE at the mustaches and beards that Al and Matt were sporting for Movember. My dad loooves Savannah but any attempt to talk about her was interrupted with "Well, she's NOT HAPPY sitting next to that HAIR!"

I sent a tweet—"@Andy: This Thanksgiving I am grateful that *Spider-Man the Musical* is finally closing!" And that upset tweeps because it means a lot of people are losing their jobs. Calm down, people. Jesus, you can't say one word about anything these days without offending someone. (And that show was the worst!) I wanted to tweet more but no one has a sense of humor anymore and half of what I'd say was slamming the parade and the promotion and I don't want to get fired from NBCUniversal. We also watched the dog show for the first time ever. I miss Wacha. When have I ever watched a dog show?

Em invited her neighbors to our family Thanksgiving and everyone was on their best behavior. We all realized we should always invite strangers. Nobody chewed each other's face off.

I ate so much starch and fatty foods all weekend and have now reaffirmed my vow to go alcohol-free in January. I even texted Will and told him, which makes me accountable.

Now I can spend all of December eating and drinking!

WINTER

IN WHICH . . .

» I BOMB ON *LETTERMAN*,

» CAVORT IN BRAZIL,

» TRY TO NOT DRINK AND TO NOT BE FAT,

» OFFEND BARBARA WALTERS ON LIVE TV,

» AND SHOOT A LADY GAGA VIDEO.

SUNDAY, DECEMBER 1, 2013—ST. LOUIS—NYC

The whole time I was away I was thinking about how much I missed Wacha and I couldn't wait to be reunited with him. But after all the buildup, it was a quietly emo reunion. We had a long, dramatic hug but it wasn't a jumping and freaking-out moment. Then later on I let him lick my face for what felt like half an hour. I took him out and he did something to piss me off and we had a fight. So that was a lot to come home to.

Liza Instagrammed a picture from that Madonna exhibit downtown, and now I'm hoping she didn't buy Bruce and me that book of photos from the show for Christmas. It's Madonna in the early eighties. I have one here for Bruce and one for Grac. I have a feeling we're all going to be giving it to each other.

Cynthia Bailey and Sandra Bernhard were on tonight. Sandra caught me in a big yawn during the show. Is it normal for a talk-show host to yawn during his own show? My suit was too tight and it constricted my breathing. I am fatter than ever! One month more of drinking.

MONDAY, DECEMBER 2, 2013

Everything and nothing is going on today: Wacha's hips are hurting him, I almost puked at the gym, and Mama Joyce has been trending on Twitter for eighteen hours.

I was emailing with Sandra Bernhard, encouraging her to reach out to David Letterman because she seems to be banned from his show again and so I told her to just email him or send him a note and say you miss him. So we'll see how that works out. I want to see them together again, as a fan.

Took a cab to the Upper East Side to have Hanukkah with Grac and her kids. It was a half hour each way in the cab and fifty dollars when it was all said and done. So that's insane and maybe de Blasio is right. Who the hell can afford this mess? Grac got me the Madonna book(!) and purple toilet paper. I never considered purple toilet paper a contender for a gift, but now that I have it, I'm wondering why we're not all giving *that* to each other.

Lisa Whelchel and Kim Richards were on the show. All day on Twitter people were saying that Lisa hates gay people and is very Christian, so I decided to in turn be Christian and forgive her with open, celebratory arms. She looks great. Blair!

There was a drunk woman at the show who kept screaming at me, "Don't you remember me?" And somehow she got past "security" (our PA Mike) and was getting her picture taken with me after the show. (I take pictures every night with folks who buy tickets in charity auctions. So far we've raised over $700,000!) She rather belligerently asked why I didn't remember her from the *Sex and the City* movie premiere (I looked it up, that happened in *2008*), when apparently she had told me that if I ever do a *Housewives of Greenwich, CT* she should be in it, so I said, "Oh *yes*!!! I *totally* remember you." That shut her up for a half second. Then she reappeared because she didn't like her picture (it's the nutbags who always demand a retake) and I said—I thought under my breath—"Oh, the drunk lady wants another picture." She slurred, "I'm not *that* drunk," and I'm like, "OK."

The poll question was: Who's the top dog in Beverly Hills? And both Giggy and Rumpy Pumpy lost because Kim was there and campaigning for Kingsley, so I will be hearing from Lisa. (If Wacha lost such a contest I would never leave my apartment.) And in the meantime Patti Stanger is on Wednesday with Robin Quivers and Patti is saying that she *has* to sit next to me. (There are exactly five Bravo stars who have a thing about sitting next to me.) We told her no because Robin has never been on and we usually like someone with a very strong personality in the far seat so they don't get lost. I'm sure we haven't heard the end of this.

TUESDAY, DECEMBER 3, 2013

I had a sleepless night and woke up Wacha early and he was alternately like, "Why the fuck *are* you up?" and really gentle and huggy. We had quiet morning time. I'm extra in love with him knowing there's something wrong with him and he may soon be wearing a cone, which is to me worse than having surgery.

I put toothpaste on a massive zit last night before bed (does that work or not?) and took Wacha out at 7 a.m. and ran right into Cameron Diaz, whose trailer is in front of my building. She is shooting *Annie*, and it seems Annie lives on my block in the new movie, because you just can't walk anywhere without running into that crew. Anyway, I talked to Cameron for a minute, asked her an inappropriate question about Naomi Campbell which I immediately regretted, and went upstairs to realize I had a clump of toothpaste on my face the whole time. Lovely. At least Wacha looked cute, and she noticed.

It turns out if you wanna know the way to *Sesame Street* you just take the Fifty-ninth Street Bridge. Why is it kinda perfect that *Sesame Street* exists in Queens? Wait—is *Sesame Street* actually set in Queens? Am I just figuring this out? My gentle morning put me in a sweet headspace for my early call. They had written a cute sketch involving me teaching Elmo the word of the day, which was "popular." There were also a bunch of Muppets that were takeoffs of reality characters. During breaks all the Muppets stayed in character and at one point I called one of the Real Houseplants of Atlanta a bitch as a joke and quickly learned that you don't curse at the Muppets. I loved doing the scene with them. I felt upbeat and sincere. I never got the appeal of Elmo until I met him (him, right?) in person. He is very charming and cuddly and almost as cute as Wacha. Almost. It was so cheery doing something with dolls for kids. I asked when it airs and they said September 2014. Um. I hope I make it till then. Seriously. Jeez.

I had a Friends In Deed board meeting. We're planning a photography auction in the spring and our dinner later in the year. I'm trying to dose Wacha with doggy dolls until his doctor's appointment on Thursday because I'm now overly worried he's in pain. Robin Quivers canceled and I think Patti took out a hit on her.

WEDNESDAY, DECEMBER 4, 2013

Started the morning with Cameron Diaz again. This time Wacha raced right up the stairs of her trailer, and just as he got to the top, the door opened and out she came. At least I got to tell her that the toothpaste all over my face yesterday was to clear up a zit. She certainly did not seem to care or remember. Appropriately. But she hugged and kissed Wacha for a good five minutes. Meanwhile I don't remember a time in my life when *Annie* was not being shot in the West Village.

Had a massive blowout with my driver about crossing Fourteenth Street to get to the West Side Highway on the way to the dentist. In his rant to me he called Bloomberg a "Jewish Nazi," so that didn't go over well and I let him know it. Then I stopped speaking to him and then he clearly felt bad and he gave me two hot stock tips to make up for it. Now I can retire.

At the dentist my hygienist told me she is positive that I should be a blond, which is insane.

I spent all day at 30 Rock, where it's mayhem because of the tree lighting. As I was leaving I said to a cop, "Who would want to come to this?" And he pointed to all these people and said, "Them. But if you ask me, they're all retarded." Can a cop say "retarded"?

I went to Bruce's and had to reintroduce myself to that fucking doorman. "Who may I say is here?" he says.

Mariah Carey was performing at the tree lighting and I emailed Cindi Berger begging her to bring Mariah on *WWHL*. I got a reply immediately, saying "Great idea!" and now I think it's going to happen, as our Christmas finale! Would that not be a great way to end the year? Am I not the luckiest person?

Patti Stanger was on my show. Somehow she started talking about how Jewish people start developing Jewish jaws and chins and I wondered if I had one and she said, "You don't look Jewish," and started describing Jewish features, like a big nose, and I stopped her before the Anti-Defamation League killed us all. Then on the after show a blind woman called and said she had a boyfriend and started to say that she "had a hard time—" and Patti interrupted her, saying, "Seeing him?"

So today I had an un-PC cab driver, cop, and guest. What kind of trifecta is that?

I dropped off shirts at the cleaners on Eighth between Horatio and Jane quite possibly for the last time. I'm done with them. This lovely old couple used to run it, they were there for years—in rain or shine—and now, somehow, they have disappeared. And every time I go in and ask about the old couple, the young people behind the counter suddenly can't speak English and pretend they don't know what I'm talking about. Are they tied up in the back? Are they dead? I'm trying to rally the neighborhood to look for them. Unfortunately, the alternative is that mean tailor on the corner of Jane. I am about to be a man without a cleaners.

I took Wacha on his first cab ride, which he loved, to the doggy hospital, which he tolerated. The waiting room is a trip—all dog and cat people (obviously) but they are in various stages of freak-out about their animals, to which they are extremely attached. Some disaster was sitting next to me carrying on so, *so* loud about her little dog's heart condition or something. She said, to no one, she has to come in three times a week. She was a river of words but *nobody was listening*! The doctor said Wacha does have hip dysplasia and needs hip replacement surgery. They are so nonchalant about it (99 percent success rate) that I am choosing to be too, but my heart is breaking for the pup because he doesn't know what's coming to him. And the doctor was coy about whether he'll have to wear a cone, which I know means he will. A dog in a cone, nothing sadder. Sigh. He has another appointment with the surgeon next week. I had a mini Shirley MacLaine moment waiting for his drugs at the checkout counter—probably not my last.

Bruce came by in the afternoon. He saw the Madonna book that Grac had given me and said that he bought it for me, so now there's officially a surplus and we're all frozen. Do we keep what we have or go through with the exchange? (By the way, the book isn't even so amazing, just photographs of her from her early days.)

Went to Laura Linney's baby shower. I brought a huge Snoopy, which always kills at a shower. She is beaming with her big miracle baby inside! I am so happy for her.

Whoopi Goldberg was on my show and not only brought me a vape pen as a gift(!), she taught me how to do something (on air) that I still haven't gotten the hang of: roll a joint (with oregano). Then I got a massage for two hours, and I always fall asleep when he does my legs, and then wake up when he says we're done. So I ask, "Did you do my legs?" He says yes and then, I don't know . . . it's a whole trust fall. I *guess* I believe him. *Did* he do my legs? Does it matter?

ⵘ FRIDAY, DECEMBER 6, 2013

I got paparazzi'd walking Wacha wearing mismatched everything and no underwear under sweats and unfortunately I looked down after the guy left and my dick looked like a thimble. Basically, like an outie belly button. So I'm convinced I'm going to be on a "talk-show hosts with small dicks" website. I would prefer a week of nose-picking photos. For the record I'm quite pleased with my dick.

GMA ripped off the vault again. They didn't even get their own graphics. It's our vault and it says *GMA* on it!

I brought Wacha to the gym. He loved it. He watched me box but got very upset when some lady was doing crunches. Unclear what the issue was there.

I was interviewed for this year-end NBC special all about everything that happened in 2013. They wanted funny opinions about everything "big" that happened. Unfortunately, I didn't care about anything that they considered "big." I don't care about Miley twerking. I don't care about North West. Or selfies. I was not as enthusiastic as they needed me to be. Like, "I love that Kim Kardashian!" I started wondering what I *do* care about from the year. Basically Wacha and what's going on in my neighborhood. I guess I'm all about me and the little box around me, just like our apathetic country. Then again, caring about twerking would not make me a better person.

I continued cleaning out my office at 30 Rock and put together boxes of stuff Daryn's gonna throw in a conference room and see if anybody wants. It was bittersweet going through everything, but mainly a pain in the ass figuring out what to do with all the *shit* I've accumulated.

Through pouring rain and Christmas hell, I met Amy Sedaris in front of Sarah Jessica's play. Amy is carrying around this little phone that looks like an old Nokia phone, but it's wood, and she's screaming into it. She's doing the annoying-lady-on-her-cell-phone routine and people don't realize it's a piece of wood. And when they announced before the play for people to turn off their cell phones, she was making a big production, saying, "I'm going to leave it on vibrate. My husband's supposed to text me." The play was great and Sarah Jessica blew me away. So good to see her onstage again and she gave a performance with velocity. She has a full-on breakdown ninety minutes into the play. It was like a happy slap in the face, seeing her do that. As instructed, we hadn't told her we were coming, and after the show we had dinner at Orso with her and Ron and Iva Rifkin. While the waiter was taking our order, Amy was screaming into "her phone" talking to "her husband." For some reason I have a vodka trigger at Orso, and I can't think of anywhere else it exists. But I digress. Amy wound up coming over after dinner until 2 a.m. We talked about Wacha and smoked her electronic hash cigarette. Then she left and I lay nose-to-nose with Wacha, desperately trying to communicate with him with my eyes. At one point he put his paw on my face very gently. (I was trying to tell him I am crazy about him and I'm not going to give him up.) It was a more intimate moment than I have had with a human in some time.

SATURDAY, DECEMBER 7, 2013

Who cares that—besides the Madonna books—I haven't bought one Christmas present? Who cares that my Christmas party is in one week and I leave for Brazil in ten days? I pretended it was January and watched *Gosford Park* under a blanket with Wacha and we took a two-hour nap. Took Josh and his daughter Molly to the Lambs Club, where I have never dined and nonetheless was flooded by "Good to see you again" and "Welcome back," which in turn led me to pretend that I owned the place. The meal was very fair. I was pulling out all the stops for my cousin and his daughter, so we went to *SNL*, which was a blockbuster show. Paul Rudd hosted, with musical guests One Direction and cameos by Kristen Wiig and the *Anchorman* dudes, plus my current favorite character, Jacob the Bar Mitzvah Boy.

▦ SUNDAY, DECEMBER 8, 2013

Another lazy day when I should've been doing everything but did nothing. I watched the entirety of *The Parent Trap*. And started crying the second Natasha entered. Took Josh and Molly to see P!nk at the Barclays Center. I'm interviewing her Tuesday at the Billboard Awards and they wanted me to see the show. They set it up so Ray the Driver could go in the back entrance and down a huge elevator big enough for tour buses and trucks—it felt like we were in the trash compactor scene in *Star Wars*.

The woman couldn't have been better onstage (the "So What" finale knocked me out) and nicer off. And she's a huge *Top Chef* fan. I took pictures with some of her backup dancers' abs. Went deep with her tour manager about the B-52s. He worked on the "Cosmic Thing!" tour and I drilled him with questions. That was their huge breakout success and it happened right after Ricky Wilson died of AIDS. He said Cindy was heartbroken the entire tour because her brother had not lived to see them become massive. So sad.

Kandi and Fantasia were on the show and the entire audience seemed to be made up of white auction winners from St. Louis. It was the wrong audience for a killer show. I bet we raised a lot of money, though.

▦ MONDAY, DECEMBER 9, 2013

I woke up and took Wacha downstairs for his walk and was greeted by a heavy vibe coming off Surfin and the super, who were giving me the stinkeye. I asked what was up and they solemnly reported that the man who lived above me had passed away in the night. I swear Surfin and the super were looking at me like I had gone up there and killed him myself. I said I was very sorry and that I felt terrible. I reiterated to them both that I did not *wish for* this gentleman to die, and that it was a tragedy.

I then walked the dog and, because we live in a dog-eat-dog world, on the way in asked the super when the appropriate time to contact the building would be, as they, not the family, own the apartment. He said to wait a few days. I gave it a few hours, then emailed the building and said, "The timing is awful but I know how NY real estate works, and I would be remiss if I didn't say I hope you consider me first when you resell this apartment." Then I took Wacha to the gym and he was so good, but while I was working out I had a flash-forward to the year 2043 when there's a gay guy with a dog living next door to me willing me to death. So, this will haunt me.

Some vaporizer company saw me rolling joints with Whoopi Goldberg and now the folks at VapeXhale want to send me a complimentary Cloud EVO, whatever the hell that is. (What it is is a perk I never expected.)

Before my show I saw *Times Square Angel* with SJ, Matthew, Hickey, Scott Wittman, Victor, Rainer, and the whole gang. A yearly ritual that never disappoints! Joan Rivers was the stand-in narrator for Julie Halston and there's something so beautiful and heartbreaking at the end when Charles Busch (in drag) sings "Have Yourself a Merry Little Christmas" to the audience. Maybe I'm overly emo about Wacha, but I shed a tear.

At my show Magic Johnson's son came with Kyle Richards and he's, like, a six-foot-eight flamboyant gay dude in high heels, which is incredible. Abigail Breslin was on and though she is so lovely, I now think that seventeen-year-olds should not be allowed on the show. I was censoring myself.

I got booked on *Letterman* for Wednesday and I have nothing to talk about and I'm completely freaked out.

▦ TUESDAY, DECEMBER 10, 2013

It was snowing, to which Wacha seemed indifferent. I interviewed P!nk at this Billboard Awards luncheon. Tamron Hall was onstage before me, interviewing Janelle Monáe, and she said that she had emailed Prince to find out what he thought of Janelle and then she pulled out her phone and read the email to Janelle. So when I was onstage with P!nk I said I texted Madonna to see what she thought of P!nk and I just got a text back. Then I picked up my phone and fake-read, "Never fucking text me again." It was pretty funny. (I actually *do* have Madonna's cell phone number but she is too much of an idol to me to fuck it up by over-texting her.) We played "Plead the Fifth" and for someone with an exclamation point in their name, it turns out P!nk is indeed really cool. And even cooler, Debbie Harry was at my table. I wasn't prepared to see Debbie Harry at a lunch, though. I don't even think about Debbie Harry *existing* during the day, much less sitting down to lunch. Debbie eating lunch? One of these things is not like the other. . . .

I'm really anxious about *Letterman*. I feel like I'm talk-showed out. I am searching my brain for a witty anecdote and there's nothing there.

I had dinner with Bruce, Grac, and Amanda at Añejo. Angelo Sosa sent over a ton of stuff and on the way to the show I was stuffed and tired. I'd had tequila at dinner, and even though I was so excited about the *Downton Abbey* cast (Mrs. Patmore, Branson, Thomas, and Lady Edith), I was spent and wanted to go home. I got there and I was sitting in my dressing room reading the research at 10:53 and all of a sudden I thought, "I'm gonna puke," and I ran into bathroom and puked. It was a fluke puke. Out of nowhere! I walked back into the control room at 10:56 and said, "I need makeup. I just threw up my guts." No one believed me. They thought I was kidding or lying or I don't know what. They didn't really react, like I was the boy who cried wolf. Meanwhile my eyes were watering and I was pukey.

We got all these tweets during the show saying my eyes looked glassy, and asking if I was I stoned. I wanted to say, "I just *puked*, people!" And the disgusting thing was that indeed I was sipping a Fresquila during the show. I didn't want to freak people out by not imbibing. (I am making up for my imminent long month of sobriety now.)

The show, barfing aside, was great. My favorite thing of the night was the actress who plays Mrs. Patmore being impressed by my promo for Susan Sarandon and Ralph Fiennes (they're on tomorrow) and then watching her find out that Meryl Streep had done the show. She turned to one of her co-stars and said, "He's really going low with us lowly cast members. Those high-and-mightys who wouldn't do it probably regret it now. Bloody Susan Sarandon." I guess Lady Mary and Lord Grantham weren't into doing the show.

It was a classic win for the help.

Went to the doggy hospital for Wacha's pre-surgery follow-up. Saw the same loud annoying woman in the waiting room who made such a spectacle of herself last time. She was back because her dachshund gets a weekly EKG, and she literally was acting like *she's* the one getting the EKG. Two weeks straight I moved seats.

Then a nurse brought a blind man over and seated him next to me. The nurse said to him, "I'm *so sorry*." After she left, he made a phone call, voice-activated, to someone to explain that his guide dog had just died and he needed a ride. I was just sitting there, frozen. It was a situation that I had never considered, and so overwhelmingly sad that tears were streaming down my face. I told him how sorry I was. He said this was his guide dog of twelve years and that he got a tumor out of nowhere. They'd just put him down. He said it could be June before he gets another dog. The place he called for a ride phoned him back and said they couldn't get to him until 1 p.m. (this was 10 a.m.), and he kindly asked if they could please try to get him sooner, that he had just lost his dog. The whole situation was heartbreaking, and through it all this man was so calm. He was Indian, in his forties. What a gentle man. They called back and said they could be there in a half hour. He asked me to help get him to the elevator and I did and said goodbye.

I met with the surgeon and they had sedated Wacha a little bit and he was so cute when he was high that I considered asking for sedation juice for home use. We scheduled his surgery and I led Wacha outside, where I ran into the blind man waiting for his ride. He was standing in front of the hospital and his bus was there idling but the driver wasn't inside. It was confusing. I told him the bus was there and waited with him. It was a weird few minutes of limbo. His driver returned and off he went. I hope someone nice was waiting for him at home.

In the cab downtown I had my *Letterman* pre-interview and I felt better about the segment. I tucked Wacha in and went to the cleaners, where the people who killed that old couple now have a tip jar. Why is there a *tip jar* at a cleaners?

I went to work and had my last EP and development meeting, which should have been weird but was uneventful. I spent half an hour looking for my car to *Letterman* at Rock Center amidst the tree gridlock, couldn't find it, asked Daryn to yell at the car company, and ultimately walked in the tundra, which took only seven minutes, so that was all a huge waste of time. The *Letterman* producer told me that Dave had said, "Why has it been so long since he was here? We loved him." I tried to point out that I had been attempting to get back on the show for the last two and a half years but they had been saying no, but since Dave "loved me" I guess we're pretending that didn't happen.

Before I went on I ran into Josh Groban in the hallway and thought he was a PA I worked with once. I totally didn't place him. I have to address this problem I have of not placing people's faces. He's been on my show.

My segment was completely surreal. Even though I'd been on once before, I felt out-of-body sitting with *him*. I'd been briefed a few times about everything Dave was going to say and then he went out of order and off script, which I liked. We talked about me taking pitches, yawning at Charlize Theron, and then we started talking about my show and he opened up about his alcoholism and what a bad drunk he was and I made the parallel between him and Carson in that regard. Then I made a comment that I was going to give him a chip when I left, referencing his years of sobriety. It wasn't a joke, just a comment. A comment that landed with a thud. His response was, "Are we done? Is the interview over?" *Very awkward*. Then he asked Paul if *he* had anything else to say. He kind of threw it to Paul, vamped, and I was out. After the segment I tried to save face, thanking him and asking him what he thought of the Carson book, and he said it was horrible that that guy wrote it.

From the moment I got out of the chair, the segment producer started talking me off the ledge about the thud that ended the segment. I'd been *kind of* freaked out, but this guy's urgency made me totally paranoid. He kept repeating, "I know you think that was weird but it wasn't. I think Dave loved it." And all I heard was the word "think." On the walk back to 30 Rock, I called a friend of mine in AA to see if I had said something wrong. He said it was fine to mention the chip but that he didn't think Letterman was in AA. What the hell did I say that for?

Next it was straight to the NBC Christmas party, where I was starstruck by Chuck Scarborough and had a nice chat with Matt Lauer. I think I made a comment about his goatee, but he pointed out that he actually has a full beard. So I think he thought I was making fun of his gray facial hair or the growth pattern or something. I wasn't. All the NBC News stars were there, but I gravitated to the local news stars, as I always do, and it turns out Shiba Russell is a huge *Housewives* fan. I kissed Savannah Guthrie and ran out to meet Bruce at the Waverly. The flirty "straight" waiter wasn't there again. I wonder if he flirted too much and got canned.

On my show Susan Sarandon compared me on air to Jerry Lewis at a telethon, which I have to assume was a read. She and Ralph were hilarious and perfect together. It was a lightning-in-a-bottle kind of night. Ralph said he was flying off his martinis.

Wacha was really hyper when I got home and I'm terrified that I'm gonna give him new hips and he's going to turn into a wild dog. What if I prefer him as a cripple?

THURSDAY, DECEMBER 12, 2013

I watched the *Letterman* interview and it looked to me that he was dissing me at the end. And I looked fat and fifty. Random people on Instagram (the People's Court) thought he was mean to me and I think I am assuredly, permanently off his list.

I was also upset all day because I'm giving Wacha to the dog walker for the weekend because of my Christmas party, and I was carrying on to Bruce about it and he reminded me that he is, after all, a dog. That reframed it for me.

I co-hosted the NY Women in TV and Film lunch with Wendy Williams. I loved that Frances was one of the honorees (easy for me to honor my boss). The others were Barkin (another easy one), Connie Britton, Robin Wright, and Sonia Manzano from *Sesame Street*. I loved gossiping with Wendy and the lunch was concurrently incredibly unorganized, long, and fun.

I was on the red carpet doing interviews with Wendy and behind me these two women were getting their picture taken. One of them, I thought, was either Sharon Gless or Candice Bergen. If it *was* Candice

Bergen, I didn't think she would be happy that I was thinking that she was Sharon Gless. It turned out to be none other than Cagney *and* Lacey. That story was not good for anybody.

Sharon Osbourne and Tyler Perry were on my show and we may as well have had two heads of state with the amount of security they had. It was Orange Alert in the Clubhouse. Tyler had like twenty people in front of his green room and then I went in and it was just him alone, which was fascinating. He's a really nice guy.

I got home and I had one of those endless massages and I lay there thinking and churning and at the end I felt like I'd solved all my problems. The first revelation was that I remembered reading recently that dogs essentially have the comprehension of a two-year-old human. As much as I want this dog to understand me, I have to think of him as a two-year-old. For some reason that struck me as a big relief. I also decided to buy a MacBook Air, which during the massage seemed revolutionary.

My screeners have started coming for Oscar movies but I'm only getting bad ones so far. Oh, and I almost forgot, Cynthia Rowley's jean jumpsuit arrived and it's kinda like a denim Mao suit, very cool!

FRIDAY, DECEMBER 13, 2013

I texted Madonna inviting her to my Christmas party and she texted back, "Yes. I need to have fun," and now that Madonna is coming to my apartment I am a complete and total wreck. I worked out and was a total pain in the ass at the gym. If I were my trainer, I would have kicked me out. Wacha left for the weekend and he was quite fine about it. He didn't look back.

I ran around doing errands for the party. After all these years of throwing what I boastfully view as one of the great annual apartment parties in NYC, I have the prep down to a science. I stayed home to chill out, and at 11:30 p.m. Harry Smith and Andrea Joyce showed up, thinking the party was tonight. I forced them to stay to have a drink, which turned into several, and we hung out till one-thirty. Andrea told me about this charity where you take your dog to visit terminally ill kids. I want to do it.

It was a huge snowstorm, and I did everything for my party yesterday, so I just mellowed out all day. Madonna texted me saying the music better not be as bad as it was at Anderson's and my joint birthday party in June, which sent me into a tailspin. I asked her what she wanted to drink and she said either Krug Rosé Champagne ("Everything else is for losers") or a cosmo.

The party was a smash. It's essentially the same list every year, with old friends and new, and no work people allowed. (I think I'm actually self-conscious about getting wasted in front of them.) The quadruple killer was that Bruce was sick, Bryan in LA, Amanda out of town, and Jeanne doing something with her kid, but a great hodgepodge collage did show up in the snowstorm. Troy Roberts, Grac, John Hill, Liza, Jackie, Anderson and Ben, Hickey, Mark and Kelly, Sean Avery, Amy Sedaris, Shea, Jason and Lauren, Susan Sarandon, Barkin, Monica Lewinsky, Ralph, Scott Wittman, Ricky and Allison, and on and on. Jessica Seinfeld brought Cameron Diaz. Madonna came and stayed for at least ninety minutes. I ejected Billy Eichner from his prime seat (there aren't that many seats btw, it's more of a standing affair) on the red loungy thing in the corner, saying, "You don't mind making room for Madonna, *right*?" Given that he had a Madonna-themed bar mitzvah, he absolutely did not mind making room for the Lady. I was predominantly too freaked out to talk to her most of the night, and just happy she was there. When I finally did go in for a quick chat, she asked me when my birthday was and said to get myself a better sound system as a gift to myself. Thoughtful! I handed her my phone and told her she could DJ on Spotify. She didn't care to. She wanted the password for my Wi-Fi. Which is "Andrew Cohen," in case I ever forget. She was mouthing the words to "Hung Up" when it came on. That moment alone was enough to last me till the next party. The last guests—Fred, Ralph, Bridget Everett, Hickey, Chris and Bill—left sometime after 4 a.m. I used to take pictures at my Christmas party and now I don't. Nothing's special anymore?

⊞ SUNDAY, DECEMBER 15, 2013

Recovery day. I ordered a cheeseburger deluxe from Village Den, which was like candy. I realized I should've offered Madonna one of those books last night since I have a surplus. Or maybe not.

I took Liza to the *Anchorman 2* premiere at the Beacon Theatre. Sat in front of Hoda Kotb and Willie Geist. John McEnroe brought Patty Smyth over—she wanted to say hi apparently and to get a picture to Instagram, and she made McEnroe take about ten, none of which satisfied her, so Hoda wound up taking the shot. I reminded McEnroe that I'd met him at Janie Buffett's in the spring and had a funny conversation in which he revealed that he was wearing Björn Borg underwear (as was Will Arnett), and he said he had it on again and that it's great underwear. The idea of McEnroe wearing Björn Borg underwear blows my mind. The movie was funny. I'm having Will Ferrell and Steve Carell on Tuesday night. I'm nervous and trying to pinpoint exactly why. It may be because they're huge, funny movie stars with whom I don't have a natural connection, and I don't know if I have the confidence to be funny around them. And Sue Simmons is bartending, which is making me even more freaked because she is a local TV legend, and we all know my feelings on that front.

Apparently I carried on too much about Kenya's boobs tonight. My mom thinks I'm demeaning women with my boob obsession.

⊞ MONDAY, DECEMBER 16, 2013

Wacha is at a photo shoot with Heather Thomson. She needed a cute dog and asked for him, so he went from the dog walker in Brooklyn to the shoot and then he's coming back to the West Village. He's officially a city dog. Who came from a kill shelter in West Virginia.

I went to Bergdorf's and got a ton of shopping done. I was at Bravo all day doing Christmas stuff and they came to me at five and said I was needed in the conference room and I realized as I was going over there that there was gonna be a champagne thing for me because it was my official last day at Bravo and I just felt like I didn't want it. I was not feeling like being celebrated. It was weird. I'm like half in and half out, half leaving but half not. Then when Frances said it's been an amazing nine and a half years I started to get emotional. And it was really fast and then it was over—the party and the nine and a half years.

My show was so irritating. Brandi made an inadvertently racist comment about blacks not being able to swim on *RHOBH* last week. I have been dealing with a lot of shit coming my way.

▦ TUESDAY, DECEMBER 17, 2013

I worked out with Will and I hated everything I had to do. It was awful. I feel like my legs are perfect and I don't want to do one more freaking squat. I must be a real joy to train. To think I have to actually amp this up after the New Year.

We taped the Will Ferrell, Steve Carell, and James Marsden show early because of their schedules. I narrowed down my nervousness to a severe inferiority complex, which is rare for me. Sue Simmons told me before the show that she'd seen an episode and noticed that the bartender doesn't do much. I assured her it would be special, but ended up being codependent with her on the show because I didn't want her to feel un-special. Dave came to sit in the audience and was not only moral support for me tonight, but when I told him about my no-booze January he joined the wagon with me. If we both pull this off, there may wind up being a whiskey surplus in the Northeast.

The moment we started taping, I felt, among other things, like I should not have worn a glen plaid wool suit, because I was sweating like a whore in church. I was self-conscious trying to be funny in front of these really funny huge movie stars. Like, the funniest movie stars in the country. Some of the funniest in the world. The sweating aggravated my nerves, which then made me sweat more. I wanted to reference the sweating, but then I thought that would sound self-conscious, which in my mind I already felt. And Sue Simmons is over their shoulder activating the whole codependency thing. By the way, her hair has gone natural and she is full Afro queen. The show turned around for me when we played a game with funny clips of local anchormen. (Also the prizes were robes and Sue said she had been in the market for a nice robe.) Will

Ferrell was so nice during the breaks and took a real interest in the evolution of the show and all that we're doing, which was very flattering, yet it didn't stop me from sweating. Caroline raced into the studio during commercial breaks and was telling me how bad my sweating was, which of course made me sweat more. Dave didn't think I was as bad as I did.

After the show I went with Hickey and a group to the Barclays Center to see John Mayer and his band. I've known him a few years but never seen him perform onstage. The set details were amazing. I don't know why I was so surprised but he is Mr. Showbiz onstage—major charisma—and he shreds the guitar to the point that the band becomes a jam band in the classic sense. I was *loving* it. And as if all that wasn't enough, halfway through the show he spotted me in the audience and scrapped the song he was about to sing and said, "I have to sing this next song for my friend Andy," and he sang "Whiskey, Whiskey, Whiskey," which is my favorite. I was floating. After, we all stayed in Brooklyn for a dinner at Rucola. I talked to Karlie Kloss about St. Louis stuff (she's from there too). I was starstruck by John after seeing what he could do onstage, which was a new feeling with him. I also chatted with Katy Perry for a long time. She's lovely. We talked about Beyoncé. We talked about Mariah and I told her she's coming on *WWHL* tomorrow. She was asking about that, and I alluded to the challenges associated with some bookings. (What I didn't mention was the Do Not Mention list, which basically boils down to not discussing any other lady singer.) What I should've done was ask Katy about Gaga. At one point at the end of the night, she told me to stop screaming at her and I tried to explain that modulation issues run in my family but that fell on ears that I had probably already rendered deaf.

▦ WEDNESDAY, DECEMBER 18, 2013

Today was a major TCB day so I could get all my shit done to leave for Brazil tomorrow night. Am I really ditching Christmas in NYC to go to Brazil? Tomorrow? Christmas to me is synonymous with New York and I always stay in the city for the holiday with friends and ditch town on the twenty-sixth with Bruce or some amalgamation of people. This doesn't seem real. I basically ran around like an idiot getting a few final Christmas presents, and I brought Wacha with me, so we both looked spastic on the streets of the Village. I bought Dad a Double RL sweatery-coat thing that on second thought I don't think he is gonna dig. I wish Ralph Lauren hadn't converted the West Village stores into Double RL—it's too costume-y for me, as I tell the poor people who work there every time I go in.

We were meant to tape our Winter Finale with Mariah at 6 p.m. and I had to get there at 4 for a shoot with DVF and Coco Rocha to promote this live-stream thing I am doing in January for her big dress exhibit. Shooting a promo for something in January before you leave for Christmas break just makes you wonder if the world will end before the show you're shooting the promo for sees the light of day. Am I the only one who thinks that way?

Mariah's people pushed the taping a half an hour three or four times. Her lighting guy was on time, I'll tell you that. She finally was in the chair around 8 p.m. (The audience had to have been extra-hammered.) I went over the Do Not Mention list with her people before the show, to show them that she was safe and I wasn't going to fuck anything up. What was *not* on that list was *Glitter* and Whitney Houston, two things that were on my list of things *to* talk about. I was worried about her reaction to *Glitter*, as it was not exactly a high point in her career.

She was lovely and seemed up for the show. We had a little toast in her dressing room; she'd brought her own goblet (See: Patti LaBelle, who also travels with a personal goblet) and she suggested two little bits to me (her makeup guy touching her up while she was mid-convo with me, and a bunch of guys helping her take her coat off at the top of the show), to which I said, "OMG, that sounds great!" without ever actually intending to do them. While she and I were talking, *Access Hollywood* was on in the back playing Christina and Gaga's duet from *The Voice* and someone hurriedly turned the tube off. Hmmm.

On the show we talked a lot about *Glitter* and Whitney, and during the break she brought up *Idol* and said I could ask about it. And I did exactly the opposite of what I did with Gaga when she gave me permission to "name names" during her commercial break: I went there. Mariah is a rambler, the lady really talks and talks, and she kept telling me to interrupt, that it's my show, but I felt bad doing so. She is clearly a handful but she knows her shit and I enjoyed her. I surrendered my seat to her—or I should say I surrendered my seat to her "better side"—and it was weird doing the show from the left. And I was schvitzing again, so Deirdre was saying "Lip!" into my ear every time I needed to wipe mine, which was a lot. Mariah seemed to have a blast. I gave her a Mazel robe and she stayed in her room for a couple hours afterwards doing who knows what. I want her to come back.

The live show, our last real show of the year, was with SJP, and as tired as I was, I was just pumped that it was her and that it would feel like a vacation sitting there on TV with her. And it did.

We had a good catch-up in her dressing room beforehand—she in her bra looking very hot. Hickey was a surprise guest for the shotski, and I made her do a cosmo shot but it was way too strong for her and she spit it out just as we were going to break. I did this thing at the end of the show where I acted like I was going to fuck her when we got off the air. I must've been drunk. Me, SJ, and Hickey hung out in the Clubhouse after the show for about an hour and had cocktails.

I was zonked out. We all were. Oh, and Anderson texted at some point in the night saying our flight to Rio was canceled. He rebooked us through São Paulo. Oh, Brazil!

▦ THURSDAY, DECEMBER 19, 2013

In the midst of trying to get the hell out of town, Wacha *bit* me today when I was cleaning his paws off. Like, it broke through my skin. I was so pissed. I called the trainer, who said it may be that he has salt on his feet from the street and his paws are hurting. So we had a rough few hours, and when Sherman the dog walker came to take him to Brooklyn, he was incredibly excited, which made me simultaneously pissed and happy. I wouldn't want him to go somewhere he wasn't happy to go but what the hell does Sherman have that I don't? And by the way, I have been calling Sherman "Stanford" for the last three months. And he hasn't been correcting me! And he was even in my phone as Sherman. On the way to the airport, I realized that I forgot my asthma inhaler.

FRIDAY, DECEMBER 20–MONDAY, DECEMBER 23, 2013— NYC–RIO DE JANEIRO, BRAZIL

Slept like a champion on the plane, with help from white wine and Ambien. I found my inhaler. I feel like an escapee from the thunder of friends and parties in Christmastown; suddenly I'm anonymous (with Anderson, Benjamin, and Pablo) in Rio. It feels great here, quiet—high clouds and hot. Not a crazy amount of people on the beach like you see in February. The people who go to the pool at the Fasano are the same type that go to the Delano in Miami—obnoxious liars and frauds and the people who love to hate them, but on an international level. I talked with a handsome guy from Prague who was with a much older girlfriend and was blathering on to me about his friends "Elton and David"—so I mean . . . Some other lonely dude is a "trader" insinuating himself on everyone, feverishly desperate to make a plan. I think he's here alone. It's a weird group of people. And yet the men are more beautiful in Rio than anywhere else. It's like living in a candy store. They are all available too, even the straight ones.

How's this for a joke in search of a punch line: Me, Anderson, and Sam Champion are in a bar in Rio. That actually happened. We ran into him one night.

TUESDAY, DECEMBER 24–SATURDAY, DECEMBER 28, 2013—TRANCOSO, BRAZIL

A super chilled-out clump of days. It started out a little dicey because I'd been in charge of Anderson's and my bag and had only checked them through halfway (we changed planes), so I fucked up the baggage of Mr. International Traveler. I lost them. I don't think AC's bags get waylaid that often. Anyway, we got them the next day. I read—and loved—*The Goldfinch*, and either because the book was so vivid or I wasn't used to getting so much quality sleep, I dreamed more than I can remember in a long time. Big, active, dramatic, vivid dreams . . . all of which I've now forgotten but they were great in the moment. Even though we were in the land of Portuguese, I was strutting my high school Spanish and it seemed to translate: Gracias, Señora Walter. I remain fat, but the people here don't seem to care. These Brazilian men are incredible. And available. And friendly. There is no greater pleasure for me than zoning out for hours walking on the beach listening to music. And of course I am happier with a tan, which I have now. The town, built around a square (the Quadrado), feels like Brigadoon, a perfect place with bright colors and twinkly lights and romantic Brazilian songs with strumming guitars. We had excellent meals even though the service in Brazil is so bad it's funny. It's like they're trying to figure out ways to fuck up or slow down your order. And who cares, because they don't and they're so damn cute. The Winklevoss twins were staying at our hotel, and I'm pretty sure they were with their own security, which felt weird. We all figured out which *Sex and the City* character we'd be; I was Samantha and Anderson was Miranda. He wasn't pleased. I was.

SUNDAY, DECEMBER 29, 2013—SÃO PAULO, BRAZIL

Not sure which of us decided it would be fun to have a party night in São Paulo before we left, but I was kind of wishing I was still on the beach in Trancoso. I am in the middle of *The Book Thief*, which my mom implored me to read. She writes her name in all her books, which I found cute when I saw the "Evelyn Cohen" in cursive on page 1. I watched three movies in my hotel room—it was too hot to go out—*Dallas Buyers Club, Her,* and *Inside Llewyn Davis*—I was snoozed out by all of them in different ways. Sometimes movies on DVDs don't translate at all. We went out big and it was fun. I grew a beard on this trip.

MONDAY, DECEMBER 30, 2013—SÃO PAULO—NYC

Landed at 6 a.m., got a full eight and a half hours on the plane and was ready to go. So happy to see Wacha, who seemed like he had a great time at his dog walker's in Brooklyn. But I mean, what the hell do I know about it? We had a sweet reunion and cuddled all day together. Literally. I dropped him at the groomer and ran up to ABC Carpet and picked out a rug for my living room in about five minutes because it seemed like Wacha wasn't digging the wood floors. It was speed-shopping and it worked—I found a great white rug on sale that he will destroy by February but should help him through his hip surgery recovery in January. My tan and beard are on fire and so I am dreading the moment in the next couple days when the tan fades and the beard looks stupid. Went with John Hill to see Sandra Bernhard's late show at Joe's Pub. She was fresh and dark and funny. I especially loved her de Blasio stuff, about how NYC can look forward to Slam Poetry sessions on the streets (due to our new poetess first lady), and how maybe dressage down Fifth Avenue *wasn't* such a bad thing after all. Now that we voted him in, everybody's scared he's too liberal. I am. And Sandra said she hates Halloween so much that she preferred the hurricane (Sandy) to Halloween last year. We went back and said hi after. It's sad that her "Sandrology" segment didn't work on *WWHL*. My goal was for her to be my Andy Rooney.

⠿ TUESDAY, DECEMBER 31, 2013

I think you're supposed to spend the last day of the year reflecting or meditating or something, but I basically played with Wacha for most of the day, and man, did I have a great time. We walked, and I marveled at his cuteness. On cue, he started ripping up the new rug. So that plan is working. I celebrated my last day of drinking for a month with a ton of wine and laughs at lunch with all the Perskys at Morandi. As predicted, Dad didn't care for the Ralph Lauren sweater-coat I got him, so he sent it back to me and I gave it to my East Coast dad, Bill Persky. He loved it. Took a long nap with Wacha. Went to a New Year's Eve dinner party at Scott Wittman's with John Hill and it was lovely. It was Hickey and Jeff, SJP and Matthew, Nathan Lane, Victor Garber and Rainer, John Slattery, Brooks Ashmanskas, and a bunch more. Apparently Seacrest was taking credit on ABC for introducing Donnie Wahlberg and Jenny McCarthy. Didn't I do that? I got a zillion tweets asking. I walked Wacha around 2 a.m. and let a lot of sloppy drunk people pet him. I thought one girl was just going to hurl all over him, but I let her keep drooling on him because her boyfriend was so hot. I have been half wondering all day if I could start not drinking on the 2nd because hanging out drinking a chalky red wine on New Year's Day seems very appealing. It was a good year. On with 2014 already.

⊞ WEDNESDAY, JANUARY 1, 2014

First day of not drinking and I chilled out all day inside. Did absolutely nothing. Oh, I did think a lot about wanting a red wine. I didn't have one. Watched *The Wolf of Wall Street*. Loved it. And I took an amazing nap with the dog. Loved that too.

⊞ THURSDAY, JANUARY 2, 2014

Snowmageddon. Took Wacha over to Joe Mantello's for a visit. He and Hickey and I had lunch at the Village Den, then I spent my afternoon thinking of red wine and watching five *Housewives* cuts (two *RHOBH*, one *RHOA*, two *RHONY*) on which I have notes due by Monday. I was so happy to finish my homework early, and it was all good TV. I got an endless massage in front of my fire during the monstrous snowstorm. Wacha spent three hours watching the fire as if it were a movie. I'm pretty sure he enjoyed it more than *The Wolf of Wall Street*.

⊞ FRIDAY, JANUARY 3, 2014

Woke up to eight inches . . . of snow today. (That was filthy. And dumb.) My big news is that Wacha loves snow. I took him into the former-den-of-homeless-junkies-but-recently-gentrified-with-free-Wi-Fi Jackson Square Park, where it was all fresh untouched snow. And the park is teeny, so this lady and I closed all three gates and took the leashes off our dogs and let them go wild. It was tremendous watching him, but I ran him around too much and his hips were hurting all day. He was limping around, poor fella. And little does he know he's having surgery in a week.

So he is just perpetually blissfully ignorant. It was intensely cold tonight but I ventured a full two blocks for dinner with Bruce and Bryan at Monument Lane, where we went over the (fantasy) floor plan of my combined apartment that I do not yet own. (On that note, I spoke to Mr. Liebowitz from the building, who is not the easiest person to get ahold of, and he said to follow up with him at the end of the month.) After dinner they came to my house and I couldn't resist a little red wine. So I slipped. And it wasn't just a little red wine—it was like bottles and bottles between all of us. My teeth might be red for days. But that was just a slip for one day and let me put my rationalization into print so that I can be clear that there was a great excuse: the fact is that I missed Christmas *and* New Year's with Bruce, so he and I deserved *and earned* one drunk-y night together to celebrate. That excuse is infallible. And I'm done now. No more booze. I swear. Watch me fly.

SATURDAY, JANUARY 4, 2014

I lied to Amanda—and anyone else who asked—about drinking last night. I am going to pretend it never happened. (A very healthy way to start my massive health kick.) I watched *12 Years a Slave* while Wacha slept with his head on my leg. It was hilarious! Just kidding. But it was excellent. It was eighties night for Amanda's birthday dinner, meaning we ate at Gotham, which is a total throwback. The décor is untouched and the tall food is still tall, and delicious I might add. I was picturing people doing blow at their tables thirty years ago. Speaking of which, Fred said people were vaporizing on his flight to San Fran. So pot may be officially no big deal. I ate pot candy before dinner. So I can't say I am sober. I'm not *drinking*, but I'm not sober.

I FaceTimed w/ my parents and got an EARFUL about how hard *American Hustle* was to understand for them and their friends, but the big sermon was about my intentions to wear this beard on TV in a couple days. "You look OLD and it's TWO-TONED! You see that the chin part is GRAY, right?" Mom howled. "Do you SEE that?"

▦ SUNDAY, JANUARY 5, 2014

My new fitness regime started today, as did *WWHL*. I kept my beard and knew that for better or worse I would have instant feedback on Twitter, which turned out to be pretty good. Got an email from Frances during the show saying the beard looked "Clooneyesque." And is there a *better* email to get from the head of Bravo while you're on air? Josh Groban caught me yawning twice during the after show. What am I going to do about this? I have a problem. There were two very energetic ladies in the front row who were screaming at me that they wanted to invite me to their Shabbat dinner on Long Island. I kept saying, *"Great!"* and when I left they were furious and screaming that I didn't stay to take a picture with them. I took the freight elevator out and before I turned the corner into the lobby, I listened to them first hammering the doorman for information about which exit I use and then lamenting that I hadn't paid them enough attention. "You know what—I get it if you have a bad day but he's an *asshole. We were inviting him to Shabbat!"* Finally the woman said that she had spent hours making me some collage and when I heard that I felt terrible and walked out like I hadn't heard a word ("*Hey!* You're the girls from the audience!"), took pictures (she asked if she could feel my ass, I didn't respond, and she grabbed it), took my collage and left. I ain't going to that Shabbat. The collage is really nice and I'm amazed at the idea of someone sitting down and gluing and cutting and *collaging* on my behalf. What would it take to get *me* to collage for someone? I wonder. *And for whom would I collage?* I got a text from Evelyn after the show: "love josh groban, hate the beard," which was great because I was wondering how she was feeling about my beard.

▦ MONDAY, JANUARY 6, 2014

I am a free man! I woke up today and it was the first day in twenty-four years that I have had no boss. It's not what I would categorize as complete freedom, because I can still get fired from my jobs, but still, it feels different. Like I am a real mobile unit, truly my *own* boss. I don't have to tell anybody where I am, or get pulled into a meeting. Come to think of it, I might really miss testing the limits of NBCUniversal's HR department with intensely inappropriate remarks during the middle of development meetings, or killing an hour loitering around other people's offices looking for stray gossip. But my big plan for my new schedule is to double down on training, to work out as many days as I can at noon with my Ninja at Will's gym. The Ninj boxes and does crazy core work with me; this along with the not drinking is phase one of transforming my body this year. Because I'm fat.

The guests tonight were Sophia Bush and Carlton from *RHOBH*. Before the show this friend of Sophia's told me my beard looks "religious." So I said, "Thank you?" and asked her if that was a good thing. She said it looked Jewish and that was a good thing. And I said it was a good thing unless you happen to hate Jewish people. So that was odd. As a reminder, I was sober for that interaction. (It might not have seemed so weird on whiskey.) We taped a Skype piece with my parents RAILING on my beard. They asked my mom for three words to describe it: "OLD, DISHEVELED, and UNATTRACTIVE," she said. "If it was all ONE COLOR it might look OK, but the GRAY!!!! I don't like the WHITE with the DARK!" "To me it looks a little dirty," Dad chimed in. I hopped in the elevator after the show and this lady from the audience raced over to get in and I yelled, "Close it!" instead of "Open it!" so now *she* thinks I am a dick. I guess it was a Freudian slip, but I swear I did not mean to close the door on her. *I swear.*

TUESDAY, JANUARY 7, 2014

I had a pitch meeting at True. We're trying to think of some shows to pitch Bravo, for instance a docuseries either with the Williams sisters, LL Cool J, or Dwyane Wade. They're all long shots but worth pursuing. Asa and GG from *Shahs of Sunset* were on the show. GG is kind of deaf, so you have to repeat to her what the callers are saying without anyone at home realizing you are repeating what just happened. The unspoken taking care of her is sweet. She revealed she slept with Jax from *Vanderpump Rules* (I love a crossover!) and I turned very pervy asking questions about Jax in bed. I frankly could've gone on and on but forced myself to stop. I ran out right after the show—even before the audience left—so I didn't wind up offending any strangers at the exit tonight. I was home by 11:50. A first. I watched *Nebraska* and absolutely loved it. Wacha slept through it. I got booked to co-host *The View* next Monday. Hope they like dog talk.

▦ WEDNESDAY, JANUARY 8, 2014

My first alcohol-free shotski night. I faked it with iced tea with Will Forte and Dan Rather. Dan was lovely—so gentle and complimentary and sweet; I regretted not taking him up on that coffee date last month. I get codependent around him, wanting to take care of him and for everybody to give him a lot of respect. They did. Will Forte was enraptured by him too. I asked him about doing heroin for a story in the sixties, and his description was comical ("It made my head hurt") and he told a story about his relationship with Cronkite that seemed heavily revised from what I think really happened. I asked him before the show about all the drama going on at *60 Minutes* and he said, "I think you'll agree with me, Andy, that the show was better with five regular correspondents. They were the stars." And I do agree and I also agree that I love when people use my name in the middle of a sentence. After the show, Ryan always asks all the guests what designers they are wearing so we can put the information on our site. He gave Dan a piece of paper to write down the designers and I guess Dan thought he wanted an autograph and he signed his name and handed it back. Adorable. (And we still don't know who he wore because we didn't have the heart to ask again. But the autograph is up on Ryan's bulletin board.) Earlier in the evening we taped George Stephanopoulos and Ali Wentworth. George was clearly uncomfortable not being in control but had a great time and kept marveling at all our bits. I wanted to tell him to watch his show closer because they like to poach our shit. I really like them both.

Wacha is getting feisty and hyper and clingy to me. He is slowly destroying the rug in teeny ways before my eyes, and is growly and mean when his three-thirty dog walker comes to get him. So he's gonna miss her when he's recovering from this hip surgery soon. Poor Wacha.

Who greeted me as I walked on board my flight to LA this morning but #BabyJaneFlightAttendant. "*Well, there you are again!* Can I help you get *settled*?!" What is it with this woman helping me get *settled*? And what does she think that entails? I figured out that the more words you give her, the more she comes back with, so I became a robot for five hours. For instance, when she said, "The beef is *so good today*!!! *And I'm not a meat eater!* So then, is that what you want, the beef???" I replied, "No." I drowned my sorrows with four episodes of *Vanderpump Rules* on the plane in preparation for the reunion. It's so good it's criminal. And I don't condone violence but Jax had that punch coming! I no longer find him attractive after his inability to feel remorse for sleeping with the girlfriend of his best friend *of ten years*! I stopped into Bravo and then went to the Tower and for ninety minutes sat and contemplated going to the gym, and ultimately decided to take a bath instead. With my phone. (My phone loves a hot bath.) I had dinner at this Moroccan restaurant, Acabar, with Bryan, Bruce, Hamilton, and Kevin Huvane. At the table next to us was the one Moroccan person on the planet who I have had sex with. I guess now I know where to find him. After dinner I had ice-cream sundaes at the Tower with Allison, Ricky, John Mayer, and B. J. Novak, who I had never met but who seemed nice. Man, those sundaes would've gone down a whole lot better with some whiskey. I am still sobes, though—or *not drinking*, as Bruce keeps pointing out. Dave began his month of sobriety today and we're going to be sober buddies. (Well, *not-drinking* buddies, I guess.) Dmitri, who remains *not* the most discreet maître d' in Hollywood, was trying to bring over a relative of Camilla Parker Bowles to meet John. The truth is that I barely want to meet Camilla Parker Bowles herself, so the idea of meeting her *relative* was a nonstarter and I surmised couldn't have been that appealing to John or anybody else. I shut that down.

Wall-to-wall tears and wild absurdity all day long at the *Vanderpump Rules* reunion. This group of servers (they are *servers*!) is a crazy combination of ego, emotion, beauty, ugly, stupidity, humor, and fearlessness that makes for perfect reality TV. Jax continues to have no remorse about sleeping with his best friend's girlfriend, which baffles me. During lunch Lisa and I walked up to the construction site of her new gay bar, Pump. She knows what she's doing. We started filming the reunion at ten and ended around five-thirty, so it was a ton of drama and talk, and by the time I got back to the Tower to change for the night I was totally spent.

I ran into Seth Meyers in the lobby and the convo was about whether he should have a band for his new show or a DJ or what. He says he hasn't decided and he better get cracking because he's got like five weeks. Walking away, I felt better about all the decisions I haven't made.

I had to hustle it to the opening of the "DVF: Journey of a Dress" exhibit at LACMA—I was co-hosting the live stream with Coco Rocha. DVF took me through the exhibit as they were about to open the doors and it blew me away—wrap dresses on mannequins everywhere, DVF colors and patterns on the floors and ceilings, and a Studio 54 Room and a room of all art of DVF. Insane. The live stream was not my favorite thing in the world to do. They were bringing people over to me who I hadn't a clue about and I was interviewing them trying to act like I did; it was awks, as Ja'mie would say. Robin Wright came with her daughter and introduced her by name, which I forgot by the time Coco threw the live stream back to me (a total of seven seconds), and I said, "I'm here with Robin Wright and her daughter." So I am sure they both hate me. I also interviewed Seth and Allison and Rachel Zoe. Every single woman there was wearing DVF, so it was an army of wrap dresses. And Kathy Hilton brought Paris over and she did her demure paparazzi stance even in person, in a DVF long dress, and I loved it. And speaking of paparazzi, I tried to give serious beard-face in the photo line but I am sure I will wind up looking constipated. Everyone was there—fifteen hundred people to be exact—Uma, Demi, Gwyneth, lots of one-named women.

We had dinner with a big group at Tortilla Republic (next to Sur) and then all wound up at Revolver. Anderson and I were last to leave. He and

I were waiting for his car at the restaurant valet when these drunk girls came up asking to take a picture with us. One of them kept yelling at us, "I don't know who you are! *Who are you?* Tell me!" It went on and on until she was begging us to tell her who we are, which is essentially the number-one-with-a-bullet irritating thing to say to someone. Who cares then? If you don't know who we are, and we don't know who you are, then let's all call it a draw and move on. Anyway, we took a pic with the friends of the girl who didn't know us and then the drunk girl herself loudly demanded a photo. "Why do you want a picture if you don't know who we are?" I asked, using reason on someone who had none. She got indignant and the friend said, "Are you really not gonna take a picture with her?" at which point I was ready to just do it, but now the vexing one was all over Anderson, yelling in his face. So he told her to leave. And she did. Joy! (Anyone who is excited to take a picture with me because they like something about me is exempt from this rant.)

▦ SATURDAY, JANUARY 11, 2014—LOS ANGELES—NYC

Where has the Chili's gone at the American terminal in LAX? It's all "fancy" food now! They used to have a great chicken sandwich at that Chili's. Damn, if it's not stuff closing in the West Village it's the gentrification of LAX. I can't blame Bloomberg for the Chili's closing, though. By the way, that paper store on Eighth and Horatio is closing next week. I actually don't know how it's stayed open so long. They may still have "Typewriter" in the name of the store. Anyway, it's a final sale and the other day I bought some cheap wrapping paper that I'll never use and got really emo with the storekeeper; I acted like we had a deep neighborly relationship, but in actuality I had potentially never met him. Still, I don't like seeing local stores closing. And so now the Chili's is gone, which is my way of saying I flew back at the crack of dawn this morning. I could've stayed in LA to hang out and go to parties but I wanted to see Wacha. And on that note, I was supposed to have dinner with Mark and Kelly but wound up staying home with the doggy, who has five weeks of recovery looming after surgery Monday. We watched the *Downton Abbey* premiere finally and I just want to know if the dude who plays Molesley has nekkid pics of Julian Fellowes, because *nobody cares about Molesley*, and there was a whole lot of him. So that was a little exhausting. I'd rather watch Mrs. Patmore wrestle with that electric mixer for an hour than endure another minute with Poor Mr. Molesley. Oh, and somebody tweeted me that all the restaurants at LAX are now from California-based companies, so I get it and that's cool. Plus you can't really compare Chili's to a mom-and-pop store anyway. I just miss that pre-flight chicken sandwich is all.

▦ SUNDAY, JANUARY 12, 2014

Wacha woke up unaware that he is being cut open tomorrow, and I felt so bad for the oblivious pooch that I decided to pretend it was his birthday and go balls to the wall. We went on a really long walk around the West Village, then went over to Hickey's and hung out, then to my gym, where he watched the Ninj and me box for six rounds, then got doggy treats at Marc Jacobs *and* Jack Spade, and then I gave him a bath that he did not hate. I conditioned his hair with this Kiehl's doggy potion that my mom gave me and his coat is silky and shiny. During his bath I realized I haven't had one of those fucking chicken sandwiches at LAX for like five years, so why am I even romanticizing it?

Watched the Globes at Joe's with Hickey and Wacha. It was fun for the first twenty minutes, then boring. Which is essentially every awards show there is. Oh, and watching an awards show sober is an experience I hope never to repeat. NeNe was on *WWHL*, so I kind of felt like I had the night off. She was great.

▦ MONDAY, JANUARY 13, 2014

I felt like a daddy and got a little emo when I dropped Wacha off at the hospital for his hip surgery. I thought I had time to kill before going to co-host *The View*, so I stopped by 30 Rock to putter around my office and go through a mound of stuff that had accumulated over the holidays. Turns out I puttered too long and wound up being late to the hosts' meeting before the show. This is the famous (in my world) meeting where the ladies sit around the makeup room and decide what the Hot Topics for the day are going to be; it's a hotbed of emotion and sometimes pre-show bitching. Though I had co-hosted a couple times before, I certainly did *not* want to miss today, because it was my first time on the show with Barbara Walters, aka the High Priestess of TV Journalism and someone who has set the agenda for my TV news viewing for my entire bloody life.

I walked into the makeup room and the meeting was already in progress. I took a seat and Sherri very sweetly asked how my dog was and I explained what was going on, at which point a half-made-up Barbara Walters (*this* was also one of the things I didn't want to miss) asked what hospital he was at and then informed me that she is on the board of that hospital should I need anything. How nice!

Hot Topics were debated and opinions were bandied about. BW said she didn't have a clue about A-Rod so someone would have to fill her in if we discussed it; Whoopi said she'd skipped the Golden Globes the night before, and turned to me and said under her breath, "Why should I kill a good high?"; Jenny wanted to talk about my complaint about Seacrest taking credit for introducing her and Donnie; and everyone agreed we had to talk about Woody Allen and the tweets about him during the show from Mia Farrow and Ronan.

After the meeting Whoopi and I were talking about *The Butler* and it seemed like BW was trying to get in on the conversation. I told her that Dan was on the show recently and spoke well of her. She said she was one of only a few people to defend him at the end of his run with CBS. Then she pulled me close and asked if she could speak with me pwivately, and as she did, she leaned back and I realized she was about to get her hair washed and I was about to see her with wet hair, which was really amazing. I saw the whole thing: the hair getting wet and then her looking back up at me, a wet Barbara Walters asking in a hushed tone if I had heard anything about Tom Brokaw having cancer. I told her I knew nothing but would research it. She said she was concerned and please do. I was trying to figure out why she thought I knew anything about Brokaw and I realized she probably assumed I knew him since I was being a bragasaurus about being friends with Dan.

I then spent a half hour with Whoopi—in my room and then hers—talking about innovations in pot (vapes and candy and e-cigs) and her telling me what life was like at the show. Suffice to say that the Oscar-winning lady does not appear to be the happiest camper at that table every day. I loved every second of it.

Hot Topics was going pretty well until *American Hustle* came up and Barbara said she didn't understand it. Suddenly I heard my mom in my head saying that she and her friends hadn't understood it, and I suggested to Barbara Walters on live TV that perhaps it was a "generational thing" that she hadn't understood this movie. As the words came out of my mouth and I turned to look at Barbara, who was next to Sherri Shepherd (I was in the middle of the henpack), I knew that this was *exactly the most wrong thing to say on live television to Barbara Walters.* The conversation moved on and the very *second* the camera started swooping to the applauding audience and the announcer teased what was coming up later in the show, a furious Barbara Walters turned to me and screamed, "Thank you for INSULTING me on MY OWN SHOW! THANK YOU!"

As the steadicam swooped back around the Hot Topics table to get a final cutaway of the group before cutting to commercial, it picked up me *pleading,* "I am sorry I'm sorry I'm sorry!!!!" But I was apologizing to her fucking *hand,* which was raised to my face. Jenny's hand squeezed my leg as I, terrified, tried to explain about my mother, and how much I respected BW and how I would never insult her on her own show. She yelled at me some more. I turned to Jenny and asked her what the fuck to do. Did I need to apologize when we came back from commercial break? She said to hang tight and it would roll off Barbara's back quickly. Sherri said, "Welcome to *The View.*" Whoopi looked at me, nodded, and did her eye-bulgey/forehead move.

I felt like I was drowning. Someone with a headset came over to me and grabbed my shoulder: "You're doing great. Forget that. It never happened. *We need you back.* Energy high. Get back in the game. *That didn't happen.*" Good advice. I took it.

We were back and talking about Jacqueline Bisset and I said I loved that she was aging naturally and hadn't touched her face. I blanched for a second wondering if Barbara was going to call the hospital on the air and have them pull the plug on Wacha. She has connections there! But she didn't seem to care. We moved on. I felt like I was in the clear.

During the next commercial break, she was back in my face. "I *created* this show to be about people from different *generations* with different points of *view*. Understand? Different *generations*!"

"I know! And it is the most brilliant format!!! But everyone wants to know: *Who is going to replace Joy!?!?!* You still have an open spot! *Who will it be!?!?*" I was desperately trying to change the topic.

"Well, I think we will try a man." It worked! I deflected a legend and we were on a new subject.

"But your show is about *women*!" I said, a little too enthusiastically. The conversation went on and she later focused her mood on Queen Latifah, with whom she had some kind of weird misunderstanding/ tussle. I was out of the hot seat, poor Dana Owens had taken my spot, and over at the end Whoopi was bugging her eyes out. During the next commercial break an audience member asked if BW would do my show. "Not after what he said earlier," she sniffed. I thought Jenny said she was going to let it go?

As I walked out, Whoopi said, "We gotta *talk*." I left the studio and called my mom, who was fiercely on my side. "Maybe it WAS a genera- tional thing! You said exactly a FINE THING and by the way isn't that show supposed to be about sharing points of VIEW?"

This afternoon we pretaped Queen Latifah for our Thursday show. She walked in and said, "*You* got her real mad and then she took it out on ME!!" which she kinda had.

I made myself the Jackhole tonight so I could show the clip of me groveling at Barbara Walters as we went to commercial break. (The clip is simultaneously funny and pathetic.) And by the way, I had a bad taste in my mouth about it all day. I don't like insulting old ladies and I espe- cially don't like insulting legends, especially lady legends. I'll send her flowers tomorrow.

TUESDAY, JANUARY 14, 2014

I felt like shit today and just stayed home under a blanket chilling out. I tried to start *The Interestings* AGAIN and couldn't get into it. It'll happen, I know it. The surgeon called and said Wacha is doing great and bearing weight on his new hip, which is a good sign. They won't let me visit him in the doggy hospital because they don't want to rile him up, or perhaps Barbara Walters has him sequestered as she decides how to torture him. In any case, it feels really empty and boring in my house without him.

I don't know what I would be doing with myself if I never got him. Looking at myself in the mirror? Having an orgy with a Dominican baseball team? Volunteer work? I could've gone in any direction.

Whoopi emailed and said, "You are a class act." Then I got an email from Barbara Walters: "Dear Andy, All is forgiven. You were wonderful on *The View*. Not to worry and the flowers are beautiful. Hugs, Barbara." *Hugs!!!* (And I loved that she italicized the name of her show, which is absolutely correct but I was hearing Cheri Oteri saying it.) I forwarded it to my mom, who said that she is acting her age. I don't know what that means but I think it's a read. *Hugs!*

Cheri Oteri and Zach Gilford were on the show and it was a great one. We taped something where Cheri yelled at me as Barbara Walters. And I was totally sober. Again.

WEDNESDAY, JANUARY 15, 2014

I have the phone number for the Bus Stop Cafe written down on a piece of paper in a kitchen cabinet and the way it's written apparently it looks exactly like the *Forbes* magazine switchboard number, so I keep calling *Forbes* magazine when I order out. This has been happening for about three years. Will I ever rewrite the number, or will I continue torturing myself and the *Forbes* operator? It's a standoff.

The water-main break on Fourteenth Street and Fifth Avenue fucked me up three different times today—what are the chances? It's like I kept forgetting and drove *into* the scene over and over. En route to pick up Wacha from the hospital, my cab driver *loved* my red sweatpants. Was he coming on to me? I mean he really wouldn't shut up about the sweat-pants. It was notable.

Wacha was a total champ despite the fact that he has a shaved patch and stitches and is wearing the dreaded cone and also a T-shirt that says, "I had surgery at Animal Medical Center," which combined with the cone created a look that was simultaneously adorable and sad. *Sadorable.*

John Cena and Natasha Lyonne were on the show tonight—weird combo but a fun show. Oh, and I sexted my sister by accident today. I was having a back-and-forth with the Italian and sent "I want a piece of you" to her and she sent back "?" and I said I was texting Grac Britney Spears lyrics. I don't know if she bought it. Awkie!

▦ THURSDAY, JANUARY 16, 2014

Today Jimmy Kimmel announced he's taking his show on the road to SXSW in Texas in March. The thing is that we're going back again this year too, so now we are all freaked out that he's going to swoop in and we're going to look like losers and won't be able to get anyone to come on. I don't know whether to cancel or what. Michael (sagely as always) wants to stay the course and do our thing.

To make matters worse, I can't shake this cold. I worked out and it was shitty. I weighed myself and was the same as I was a week ago. I plateaued because I ate like shit in LA, I think. So now I have to grind it out. Met NeNe for tea at the Trump SoHo. She wants to do any variety of talk show. I told her to talk to Lisa before she agrees to go on *DWTS*. Had dinner with Sean Avery at the Waverly and he was late and I spent twenty minutes at the booth trying unsuccessfully not to stare at my phone, but guess who was back to keep me company: the flirty "straight" waiter. He was friendly again and beaming because he just became a new dad. So this proves that he's absolutely straight. It was actually sweet seeing him gushing about the wife and kid, but it reframed everything. (My relationship with this waiter has now been reframed four times in my mind. I need a hobby.)

SJP came over after her play. She ordered Thai food, I watched her eat, and we talked for hours about everything. Wacha had pooped in the guest room but neither of us smelled it, which was a relief because SJ is not a dog person at all (even though they have one). I don't want to give her ammo against Wacha; I want her to love him as much as I do even though she's not predisposed. I don't know what's up with the poop; I think he's constipated from the hip medication and it's fucking everything up. And the cone is just as sad as can be!

FRIDAY, JANUARY 17, 2014

I went to 30 Rock and Martha Stewart had sent me this piece of wood shaped like the United States as a gift for hosting the American Made Awards . . . in *October*! Not to be a dick or look a gift domestic diva in the mouth, but aren't we well beyond the "proper" window of thank-you gift, or do you have a year to thank someone for co-hosting your awards show? She did write a nice note. Anyway, it's a cool piece of wood with which I have no clue what to do.

After ten years on the other side of the table, I had my first pitch meeting at Bravo where *I* was doing the pitching. It was a funny dynamic and since I'm such a know-it-all I was telling them where to schedule the show I was pitching. After the meeting I sat down to catch up with Frances, who asked me how long I plan on keeping the beard. The question seemed innocuous until I told her I'd probably get rid of it in a few weeks. "What are you waiting for?" she quizzed right back. *Was there something I wasn't getting about the hair on my face?* Apparently there was and what at first was giving off a George Clooney vibe was now making me look like George Clooney's elderly uncle, and it was time for a shave. I (blissfully) get barely any notes from Frances about the editorial of *WWHL*—she really lets us do our thing—so I was weirdly energized by her strong point of view (albeit negative) about the beard. I'm shaving Sunday. Looks like Mom was right? Ugh.

Spooned with Wacha in bed for a two-hour nap—I still have this cold. But I had to get out of bed to go to Ralph's movie, which has been out a few weeks. I'm going to see him this weekend and won't be able to hold my head up if I don't see the movie first. It was good, he was great, but I am pretty sure Charles Dickens was a dick.

SATURDAY, JANUARY 18, 2014

The mean tailor on the corner of Jane has been there for as long as I have and I go to him only when forced (for instance, now that the nice old couple has been done away with). He hates his customers, is the problem. So this morning I was taking Wacha on a walk and saw the tailor for the first time out of his habitat, and he was super*nice* and dare I say *cheerful*. It was weird. I would think he would be mean on the street and nice in the store. People are nuts. Wasted a Saturday night home sick again. Being sick is certainly helping me not drink, though. It could be worse, I could have a cone around my face preventing me from licking myself, like Wacha.

Ralph came over for tea and we had a long talk and then made dinner plans for tomorrow. I think I offended him by asking if we would have anything to talk about at dinner since we'd just spent ninety minutes together.

SUNDAY, JANUARY 19, 2014

Good workout today. When was the last time I worked out on a Sunday?? I've been eating great too. I might see a little bone structure on my face or I might just be going crazy from lack of alcohol.

Had dinner with Ralph at Barbuto. That chicken is never bad. We had plenty to talk about.

It was the men of *RHOA* on *WWHL* tonight—a perfect example of a time where a whiskey would've really helped. By the way, Dave is white-knuckling, whiskey-less in Harrison.

MONDAY, JANUARY 20, 2014

After a great workout I had lunch with Kandi at Morandi. We both ate so healthy: salad and grilled fish. After lunch I contemplated getting a burger. I didn't.

People on the street laugh at Wacha's cone the way I used to laugh at dogs with cones, uproariously. It doesn't feel great with the cone on the other foot. He pooped in the extra room again—very confusing. I can only assume that he's backed up or fucked up or upset or something. (I'm a veritable Cesar Millan with my uncanny abilities to read his mind.)

After the show I watched *Downton Abbey*—thankfully Mr. Molesley was not on. I just couldn't take it if he was. Mrs. Hughes was extra comforting to all tonight and Lord Grantham is still a dick.

▦ TUESDAY, JANUARY 21, 2014

I was a guy who went to an office every day for twenty-four years, and suddenly these last few weeks I'm realizing the life I didn't have. There are all these *people* downtown. I don't know what the hell they're doing. Even today, in a blizzard that never stopped, there were people eating, shopping, working out, and carousing. Doesn't anyone have a job? The snow didn't stop me from an amazing workout; my Ninj and I did core work on the floor and five rounds of boxing and the good news is I am down to 171.5. I must've been 177 when I started. At least. I'm in a zone.

Met Bruce for a cozy lunch at Cafe Cluny. We ordered salad with double the chicken, and the chicken paillard was as thin as bologna, so it was expensive and completely unsatisfying. Like frisée and airy meat. Saw Andy Samberg and Seth Meyers there. So it was man-date day at Cluny. I'll never understand why they have that big roach sculpture thing on the ceiling; I don't get it. Every time I see it I get panicked that there's going to be a big-ass roach on the soap tray when I get home. Wacha definitely couldn't kill a roach with that cone around his face.

Gaga's people emailed asking for Housewives to be in her new video. We went through each cast and sent back two suggestions from each. She also asked me to play Zeus in the video; I said yes, although for some reason I can't see it happening, nor do I know what playing Zeus entails. I did a bunch of scheduling with Daryn today and I just don't know when I'm going to be able to do it, or if I believe Gaga really wants me in the first place.

Because of the blizzard we taped our show at seven so the crew could get home, which was a godsend. Neither rain nor snow nor dead of night can keep Adam from me, so I got a two-and-a-half-hour massage at nine-thirty with the fire blazing. It was heaven.

WEDNESDAY, JANUARY 22, 2014

Wacha got freed by Abe Lincoln Cohen last night. I took the cone off *and* let him sleep with me through the night for the first time. It was pretty great. He was so quiet and sweet. No snoring. Just shnoogled up against my leg. It was cold as shit today. Worked out and then took Wacha to get his stitches removed. He is doing great. I remain proud of my dog, as if I had something to do with his resilience after surgery. The *Today* show called at 5 to see if I would co-host the 9 a.m. hour tomorrow with Natalie Morales. I am happy they thought of me, and said yes. I've got Matt and Savannah on tomorrow night, so it'll almost seem like it's a planned tie-in, when I actually think Roker just has a case of the sharts. I actually may develop the same condition because I'm nervous about interviewing Lauer tomorrow. He's one of my favorite broadcasters and I guess I always thought he was too big or too cool to do my show; I don't want to fuck this up.

On my show we had Melissa Gilbert, Nick Kroll, and a gigolo from *Gigolos* behind the bar, so that was an insane conversation. Melissa Gilbert was very nice and Spanxed into a Herve Leger dress (which I can spot a mile away because it is an OC Housewife favorite). Apparently that gigolo makes 4k for an overnight. His ass was great but we looked at naked pics of him after the show and I don't know if he looks like he's worth 4k. I did a fake shot (iced tea) and weigh 171.

THURSDAY, JANUARY 23, 2014—NYC–LOS ANGELES

I let the dog sleep with me again because I'm ditching him today for LA. And it was more like a nap because I was up at six-thirty to do the *Today* show. I had some early-morning nako-time in front of the mirror and it was horrifying. I've been feeling thin but I gotta lose the gut. It was so

129

cold and I was so tired that I drank three teas before the show. Sweet David Lauren was there "unveiling" the new Ralph Lauren U.S. Olympic team sweaters they're wearing for opening ceremonies, and he gave me one. It looks like a Christmas sweater threw up in Washington, DC. But I Instagrammed it anyway. I was surprised by the lack of pre-show preparation; the producers really do just throw you into the ring and let you go, which is kind of an amazing trust fall. During the host chat we played a clip of this tennis reporter asking the winner of the Australian Open what guy she'd like to date—there's a controversy about whether the question was sexist. I referred to "the poor lesbian reporter who asked it" and I guess either outed the lady or offended someone or speculated when you're not allowed to speculate. She was a bull dyke and you wouldn't have to be a rocket scientist to figure it out. The crew all busted up. The segments were really simple—car-buying tips, animal adoption, some uplifting Olympics piece . . . And at the end of the show the producer said that they'd put something in the prompter that I needed to read, clarifying that I don't *know* whether she's a lesbian and I was just *speculating* about something I don't know. At that point Hoda said, "You're already apologizing???" I left the studio thinking it was funny and hoping it will go away. Everything becomes a "controversy" these days.

I went straight to *WWHL* for the Matt and Savannah pre-tape. It was perfect scheduling because I had to go to LA and they needed to tape early. As nervous as I was, Matt was lovely, really came to play, and I didn't sweat. The two of them were almost better on my show than they are in the morning.

I ran home, packed, changed, had quality time with Wacha for an hour, and hit the airport. Imagine my surprise when on a packed United flight the chatty flight attendant (blissfully *not* #BabyJaneFlightAttendant) came over to tell me she loves my show, never talks to people, and that she was more excited about my being on board than Madonna. *"Madonna is on this plane?"* I could barely get the sentence out of my mouth. She told me that the Material Girl was in seat 1A and I think that I actually pushed this poor woman out of the way as I bolted over like a flash. "I know her! I can say hi!" I protested—or justified—to her, but really to myself. The idea that Madonna was flying commercial, with *the people*, blew my mind. And there she was, small, in black, with glasses, tiny in her window seat. I asked her what the hell she was doing, and instead of answering she proceeded to make fun of my (yellow flannel) Gant shirt, which I love. "Are you *trying* to be noticed?" she said. (Hello, pot, this is kettle. . . .) She asked if I was "in front" and said she would visit me later. I said that actually she *wouldn't* come visit and she agreed that she wouldn't, but asked me to come visit her. I didn't know if I would be able to muster up another burst of blind courage to make the trip to her seat twice, and I returned to mine grateful for our moment. The plane was a little delayed for mechanical difficulties, so I texted her and said she looked great and tan, and she said tanning is for sinners. When I marveled that she was on a commercial plane, she texted that she does it all the time. She said she is "everyday people." Uh-huh.

I went to the bathroom several times during the flight and stayed away from her but did notice a very handsome man seated a few rows ahead of me. Every time I went by, his eyes were on me and we gave each other many half smiles and nods. I pulled the flight attendant aside and asked her if she could find out his name, and while she was at it, if I could see how Madonna was listed on the manifest. Back she came in a jif with the documentation that I am sure is illegal to show passengers and there, in black and white, was "Madonna Louise Ciccone." I had goose bumps. I mean I know that's her name but I didn't expect it all written out like that. The whole thing? I wanted to keep the manifest or take a pic of it but didn't want to push my luck. The flight attendant asked if I had a crush on the dude in the fifth row and I said I just thought he looked familiar (I am discreet, see) and wanted to remember his name. She read it aloud and I'd never heard it before, and by the time she left I'd completely forgotten it, so there went my chances of finding him on Facebook.

I did go speak to The Lady again right before we landed, and she was as nice and normal as could be. She said it's too expensive flying private all the time and that you can feed a lot of people with the amount it costs to fly back and forth from LA. (Madonna feeds people, people!) She said she was going to LA to do something small on the Grammys and I said nothing she does is small and she said she would take that as a compliment. We talked about Lola and her new boyfriend, and about my need for a new sound system in my apartment. I skedaddled back to my seat and on the way back saw a wedding ring on Row 5's finger. Figures.

He left the plane before me but gave me a few lingery looks on the way out before completely disappearing into LAX. He was husband material: professional, handsome, big and tall. He looked like a man. I didn't look for Madonna once we landed—I was grateful for the time we had. I'm a fanboy, but I only act that way 50 percent of the time.

▦ FRIDAY, JANUARY 24, 2014—LOS ANGELES

I had a nice email exchange with Matt Lauer about last night. Frankly, I remain amazed that he even knows my name. That show is getting picked up everywhere because he told a hilarious "embarrassing moment" story in which he commented to Vince Gill about some girl's boobs and she turned out to be Gill's daughter, and Savannah discussed how awful Kate Gosselin is.

Shot the *Shahs of Sunset* reunion today and it was quite engaging and along with the usual histrionics there was a long and interesting conversation about Iran, the Middle East, Islam, and how it all related back to these kids—taking place around a feast of Persian food complete with an Iranian waiter named Farbat who I flirted with the entire day (and he back) until the very end when he told me he is married. This "married" thing is cockblocking me all over the place lately.

During my break, Diane Ronnau met me for lunch on her break from the *CBS Evening News*. (I guess she and I are the center of the Venn diagram of CBS News and the *Shahs*.) I miss working with her—she has the best spirit and the best energy. Very Elaine Benes. Got back to the Sunset Tower just in time for dinner with the Blums and Sandy and Brian. I felt triumphant showing Sandy that I had lost seven pounds based on his unfavorable weight assessment of me last November in the Hamptons. Lily Tomlin came to the table to say hi to Sandy and he introduced us all and asked if she knew me. She said she knew "of me" and an hour later I figured out that she knows "of me" because I am sure Dmitri blabbed to her who was at our table. Aunt Blabby. I hated not drinking at the Tower, which is like being on the inside of a whiskey bottle, but I feel thin!

SATURDAY, JANUARY 25, 2014—LOS ANGELES–NYC

I screened two episodes of *RHONY* on the plane and they were hilarious in that absurd *RHONY* way, so I had very few notes. It was hard not eating the nuts on the plane. (Or the cookie in the hotel room both nights. Well, I confess I picked at the edges of the cookie but didn't eat it all.) I went straight to Michael Rourke's birthday dinner so I didn't flip Wacha out by coming home and leaving right away. I felt like a dry drunk at dinner, aggressively boring and tired. So I was scintillating company.

SUNDAY, JANUARY 26, 2014

I weigh 170.5. How the hell I was able to lose half a pound over the last forty-eight hours of no exercise is beyond me. And how am I going to keep weight off when I start drinking again? I heard from Dave, who is in Vermont and going mental he can't have a post-ski whiskey. I'm actually in a zone and enjoying not drinking, I decided today.

I shot intros for two Bravo countdown shows, then did m'show and raced out of there to watch *Downton Abbey*.

My gift to myself (as I am my own lover and long-term companion, I like to treat myself special every so often) last night was sleeping with Wacha. At one point both our heads were on my pillow facing each other. Disturbingly, I may be isolating myself from human contact by getting satisfaction from this dog. I ate all protein and quinoa today. There is some potential that I will go mental one way or another before this month is over.

MONDAY, JANUARY 27, 2014

I was at the courthouse at the crack of dawn this morning because I'd deferred jury duty three times and had no choice. I brought my boarding pass for my flight tomorrow and discovered that I was scheduled to a *two-week federal case*. I had no clue what I was dealing with. I was at the front of the room negotiating for dates to come back in late April when the woman looked at me and said she just realized who I was. "I am gonna mark you as time served, Mr. Cohen; we will see you in four years." I almost came in my pants. This is exactly the kind of illegal, totally unfair celebrity perk I have been waiting for all my life. I gave her tickets to my show and skipped out of the courthouse.

To make the day even better, I weighed myself and had lost a half pound, which is a good thing since I essentially starved myself yesterday. Also, I spoke to Mr. Liebowitz at the building management company, who reported that I can see the upstairs apartment in late February. And I walked the dog while wearing the Ralph Lauren Olympic Christmas Sweater—it's so insane it's starting to grow on me.

We did a live show and taped one so I can be in Miami tomorrow night.

Wacha shit in the extra bedroom. He knew he fucked up. It's really hard to stay mad at a dog. Especially *this* dog, with *those* eyes.

TUESDAY, JANUARY 28, 2014—NYC–MIAMI

How on God's green earth is it possible that I had the *same* driver to LaGuardia that I had a few months ago and we had the *same* interaction about how to get there in which I told him to cross town on Twelfth Street and go up Third Avenue, he pretended to not speak English so good, and we wound up going up Sixth Avenue and crossing on Thirty-sixth Street, which was exactly the way I *did not want to go*. Sometimes I feel like I'm talking to myself because ain't nobody listening.

Meanwhile it is cold as balls.

The flight attendant went on and on about my rings and asked what my wife does. I should've made up a story. "*My wife* is a realtor! But she has amazing taste in jewelry. I just do what she says. . . ." Why *didn't* I say that? Instead I told her I don't have a wife, which made me feel lonely. Maybe I want a wife?

I landed and got a brilliant forty-five minutes of sun and a salad (no rosé, ugh) at the pool of the Delano before heading to NATPE at the Fontainebleau. I did a session with a reporter from *TV Guide* that I thought went pretty well. I managed to successfully avoid saying anything stupid about the *Duck Dynasty* scandal or the upcoming Olympics. (I don't want to piss off my employer, thank you—although I would've *liked* to say that, as a gay man, I would rather go to hell than to Sochi.)

I presented Lauren with a Brandon Tartikoff Legacy Award tonight in front of a heady crowd. The other honorees included James L. Brooks, an idol of mine and anyone who loves TV. There was a dinner after and LZ let me off the hook after cocktails and told me to go back to the Delano if I felt like it, which was much appreciated given that I felt like a white-knuckling dry drunk. I was tired and boring, and I probably would've been more upbeat with a whiskey. Sad but true.

Oh, and today I wore what I thought was the perfect Todd Snyder suit—olive and cottony and kinda summery but all-weather—but I forgot that when I tried it on initially Todd himself offhandedly shared that they use some strain of stainless steel, or metal, in the fabric. I didn't think twice about it but after walking through two airports and the perimeter of the Fontainebleau I realized that the metal was chafing the back of my legs and my ass. By the time cocktails began at the last event, I was trying to pull the suit away from my backside, making it seem that I was picking it out of my ass, which is disgusting. Some guy who runs production at Macy's *came up to me* and said that he wasn't even gonna ask me what I was doing with my pants, which seems rather forward from a stranger but indeed I explained the whole story to him.

I had a Gay Sophie's Choice moment at the end of the night choosing between two Miami locals who've regularly provided me sweet South Florida hospitality: one a gingy, the other a black man. I am confident that I made the right choice. Once you go black . . .

WEDNESDAY, JANUARY 29, 2014—MIAMI—NYC

I was so proud of myself yesterday for just packing a backpack to go to Miami for the night and then I was chafing and hobbling my way to the last gate in the American terminal in this fucking suit. What kind of *metal* is in this fabric? I couldn't wait to take it off! My suit hurts!

Sonja wants to change her intro line about going commando because she's a businesswoman and she doesn't want to lose deals, but the shows are locked and loaded, so we can't.

Sarah Silverman was hilarious tonight. She doesn't drink either, so we just had sober fun. I did a shot of iced tea in the shotski. And Cher called in. Two more days of sobriety.

▦ THURSDAY, JANUARY 30, 2014

We heard from Todd's people, who said it's impossible I got chafed from the suit because it's only 6 percent stainless steel. I want to bring him the pants so he can see that that 6 percent was basically up my ass.

Today we had three-city *Housewives* drama. Spent a fair amount of time on the phone with Lisa Vanderpump, who is not thrilled with something coming up on *RHOBH*, then I was trying to get Phaedra to come on *WWHL*—she doesn't want to at this moment because of the charges against Apollo—and all day I was feeling bad for Ramona, who has filed for divorce. Had lunch with the World of Wonder guys and came up with two ideas—one is a documentary on the Supremes, which I've been wanting to do forever, and the other is a live-action scripted show about celebrity dogs, like a fake reality show. I am Kate Gosselin and Wacha is Mady, that's what's happening apparently.

I lost another pound, so I'm 169. It's falling off now.

The *Full House* guys reunited on the show and they'd been doing press all day, so John Stamos was a lil drunk and repeating himself but so sweet. What he was repeating were all compliments about me and the show, so I wanted him to just keep going. And he called me handsome, so what do I care about repetition.

I had an endless late-night massage. Fell asleep a few times on the table. Didn't actually get to bed until almost three.

The day was good but the night was epic, and not because I was able to break my drinking hymen. (That's a thing.)

Whoopi Goldberg had given me this portable pot pen/vape thing that I took on a test run right before going to Howard Stern's sixtieth birthday party, which was a live radio show from the Hammerstein Ballroom and as close to Oprah's Legends Ball as I'm ever going to get. The pen worked, and I was totally overwhelmed by the event—it was exactly what I love. Really random stars everywhere. I brought Eli; he is a huge Howard fan. I was gleeful to find Sandra Bernhard and Sarah seated at my table. Also Dr. Drew and his wife were there. We were directly below the box where they put the Wack Pack, so it was High Pitch Eric and Mariann from Brooklyn and the rest. A fight broke out between them at one point. And Mariann from Brooklyn passed me her number—she wants to bartend.

The tables around us were packed with the eclectic group of stars who love Howard . . . Steven Tyler, Dave Grohl, Robert Downey Jr., Barbara Walters (I stayed away), Johnny Knoxville, John Stamos, Larry King, Harvey Weinstein, and on and on. Lena Dunham was at the table next to me with her cute boyfriend, who gave me fruity gum. She said she's about to adopt a dog from the same place as me, but hers is deaf and blind. So I guess she is going to heaven. (I wonder if Wacha's bum hips will get me in?) Ryan Phillippe was at Lena's table and I spent a lot of time just looking at his back (and by back I mean ass). He was puffing on the exact same pot pen thing that Whoopi had given me. I didn't puff mine inside for fear of getting written up somewhere and fired. (I really, really don't want to get fired.)

Jimmy Kimmel hosted and it was the greatest variety radio show ever. Performances from John Mayer (he killed "Like a Rolling Stone"), Adam Levine ("Purple Rain"), John Fogerty ("Fortunate Son"), Jon Bon Jovi ("Wanted Dead or Alive"—all I need to hear ever), plus Letterman, Fallon, Rosie, Joan Rivers, Whoopi, Sarah Silverman, Chris Christie, Tan Mom, Bryan Cranston, and Louis C.K. spoke.

I love Sandra's commentary of award shows on Twitter, and view her as a supreme celebrity snarkologist, so to have her across from me even to look at during the show was heaven on earth.

As I sat there watching this often inappropriate yet perfect marriage of high and low culture, it dawned on me for sure that *WWHL* is closer to *The Howard Stern Show* than it is to any other show, which made me happy. And the Housewives are my own Wack Pack.

I grabbed a "VIP Gift Bag" at the exit and Eli and I gave Sandra, who somehow missed the gifting area, a ride home; I made her announce each item from the bag and we all divided them up in the backseat. It was, as all gift bags are, sundry pieces of crap, but I would've paid good money to hear Sandra announce them ("a power bar, full of toxins!" "Female lubricant"). I gave her the big-ticket item, a Kindle Fire. I wasn't sure whether I would've used it, and she deserved it.

Eli and I made a pit stop to smoke the pen and walk Wacha and saw a car fully on fire across Eighth Avenue from my apartment. The NYFD got there before it could blow up, but it was engulfed and pretty exciting. Wacha was not too impressed. Then we went to the *GQ* party at the Top of the Standard. On the way in, someone was screaming at me that he was with Kyle Richards in the bar and the lady with the list said, "We can*not* open up the list," so immediately I am codependent not wanting to leave a Housewife in peril. But I went upstairs anyway, where sure enough ten minutes later Kyle materialized. (Housewives are resilient!) I had a lovely chat with her and Mauricio, who kept mentioning how hot his wife is. Good for them. Also Michael Voltaggio showed up looking as cute as ever. He is very straight but somehow I wind up very handsy with his hair when I see him.

Eli and I toasted over my first whiskey in a month. For two hours I sipped two of them, and, man, did they taste great. I impressed my own damn self with my pacing and strength in not guzzling. Cardinal legend Jim Edmonds joined us with his fiancée Meghan and that was a fun hang. The crowd was a weird mix of sports and fashion. And Macklemore was at the table next to us. (No sign of Lewis.)

Although there was no reason to leave, I impressively called it a night around two. (I am glad I was able to impress myself so many times today, because I'm pretty sure I didn't impress anybody else.) I forgot how fun it is to be with Wacha when I'm a little drunk.

There's a disturbing article in the *NY Post* about a young Puerto Rican boxer who was killed and his family honored his dying wish by propping up his corpse in a fake boxing ring they'd constructed in the corner of the rec center of his housing complex. There are photos of this embalmed boxer propped up, and of his family posing for pictures with the corpse, which is wearing boxing gear and sunglasses. It's called "Dearly Begloved." I ripped it out of the paper.

I took Wacha on a long walk through the Village. I wore the Ralph Lauren Olympics Opening Ceremony Sweater, which I need to reiterate looks like a bomb exploded somewhere between SantaLand and Washington, DC. People were *agape*. We stopped by Bruce's and his doorman, *of course*, gave me "And your name is???" He looked right through the Christmas Olympics Sweater too. What *does* he notice?

On the way home a homeless lady sitting by the subway complimented the sweater. So it turns out the homeless are wild for Ralph's Olympic gear. I walked two blocks, turned around, and brought her five dollars, the least I could do for the only person to compliment my ugly sweater. Frankly, she seemed more pleased with the sweater than the five bucks. The sweater does fit great.

Oh, and somehow I wound up with the female lube from that gift bag last night. Usually I give leftover gift bag stuff to my housekeeper, but this would seem weird, right?

Went with Bruce to *Buyer & Cellar*, which was hilarious. Had dinner at Morandi. I had invitations to a bunch of Super Bowl parties all over town, each with a different great musical act (Robin Thicke at ESPN, Nelly at Playboy, etc.)—so we had to make a decision and went with the DirecTV bash, where Jay Z was performing, and rumor had it that Bey was going to as well. Mistake! Ten thousand people in an airport-hangar-y type of tent by the river. I am sure there was a fun roped-off area, but we didn't see it. Convinced it was a shitshow and there was no way Bey was going to show her perfect face, we left after about three minutes and saw Kyle Richards coming in on our way out. We had a nightcap at Waverly. Over the course of the entire evening I had a tequila and a red wine; slow and steady wins the race, is my new philosophy.

Gayle King emailed that it was an incredible party we missed. So, shit. Apparently, McCartney and Leonardo DiCaprio were there and Beyoncé did perform and Jay Z sang all his hits.

I brought the article about the dead boxer to the gym. I feel like I need to discuss it with people because it's so nuts. Will was disturbed, but not disturbed enough for my taste. I gained a pound and I blame Equinox. I have no clue why I still have a membership there since I get trained at Willspace, and in my first visit in more than a year yesterday I drank a fucking sugary protein shake after I worked out, under the false pretense that it was perhaps healthy, but Will broke down the ingredients for me. I hate eating right. I was happily swilling SpaghettiOs over Christmas and now I'm eating only protein, not snacking, and white-knuckling over shakes.

I guess a few months have elapsed since my mom's last breakdown about my going on Bill Maher's show, because we again spent a few minutes Skypeing about this *hypothetical* non-issue. It is amusing to me how upset she gets by just the notion of me having to keep up with Bill Maher. "I really DON'T think you're dumb," she tried to reassure me. I think I found my April Fools joke.

Tonight I spent twenty minutes searching the couch for my right contact lens, which I was very sanitarily cleaning in my mouth when I somehow dropped it. Wacha was incredibly confused by what I was doing. I gave up and went to the spare pair. Went to Marci Klein's for the Super Bowl, and she served the best brick chicken I have ever eaten. Ever. Mark and Kelly were there as well as Tina Fey, who is exactly the person you would want to watch watching the Super Bowl, which I did as much as I possibly could. She said she'd seen and liked the *Anchorman* episode of *WWHL*, which made me nervous in retrospect. I never imagine anyone specific actually watching the show, which is probably a good thing. I wonder if she noticed how bad I was sweating. Kelly had seen the *NY Post* article about the boxer and also was very freaked out, so that was oddly satisfying.

I went home and watched *Downton Abbey* and *Looking*, which were better than the shitty football game. I went to bed at twelve-thirty, which is maybe the earliest my bed has seen me in years. I'm sure it appreciated that.

MONDAY, FEBRUARY 3, 2014

One of my ten happiest moments of every day occurs the moment Wacha squats down to poo. It's a win for the universe every time Wacha shits. And today it was snowing, so I was glad he took a big quick one so we could get back inside. He still has the cone and it's too much to bear. For me. He walks into walls with it and is constantly misjudging distances. But he's a trouper. It's me who is feeling the brunt of how sad it is.

I found the contact lens between the cushions of the couch. It seems fine and is currently resting comfortably in saline solution.

TUESDAY, FEBRUARY 4, 2014

Bravo is moving (my fourth move since working there) to the fourteenth floor and my new office is way smaller than my current (blessedly big, I would actually say huge) corner suite. Since I'm no longer an exec there, it's pretty cool they're giving me a place to hang my hat when I'm at Rock Center; regardless, I have a ton of stuff to get rid of and that's what I did today. I have so many papers that I would like to consider a part of TV History that I fear may just be trash: casting for every season of *Top Chef*, *Housewives*, and *Project Runway*, research on shows that worked (*Flipping Out*) and ones that didn't hit (*NYC Prep*), and early development of everything in the past ten years. I threw out a bunch of *Housewives* casting but now I'm regretting it.

It seems like the Gaga video is actually happening on Saturday morning in LA. I think it's just me in front of a green screen in a little room. I gotta download that song.

Tonight Jonathan Groff was on the show and he is so cute; I tried not to flirt.

WEDNESDAY, FEBRUARY 5, 2014

Every year the big black-tie amfAR event happens on the day of a major winter storm, and so, like clockwork, this morning ice *and* sleet began falling at once from the sky. Mother Nature is mixing the shit up! Wacha tried to frolic but quickly realized that it sucked, and wanted to go inside. I always wonder whether they'll cancel amfAR and they never do and everyone shows up, including me. I went as Natasha's date for years before she died, and tonight they were honoring Joely and Vanessa and this storm wasn't going to keep me from that. It was a heavy-hitting crowd—it always is at those things—and the person I was most excited to hear speak was Harry Belafonte.

I was supposed to begin the tribute by introing a video and then Jessie Eisenberg was due up, but his flight got canceled and Liam stepped in to do it last-minute as a surprise to Vanessa and Joely, who was trying to guess who the presenter could be. I would only tell her that it was someone she loved and someone I loved, so she was sure it was Hickey. The boys came and it was incredibly touching having them there, grown up. Natasha would've loved it. I think about her—and miss her—every day.

Also at our table was Dr. Mathilde Krim (holla!) and Ethan Hawke and Ryan Shawhughes. Ethan had been paying his respects to Philip Seymour Hoffman earlier in the day (who is all anyone is talking about this week). I'd felt bad about missing *Macbeth* but Ethan was so cool about it; I wish everyone was as cool as he was about missing a show. Some people I'd classify as only casual pals have been really offended that I've not shown up to see them onstage recently, so I worry.

Liam was in great form. He has movies stacked up like planes at JFK waiting to take off—eight of them. Joely and Vanessa, expecting Jessie Eisenberg, seemed touched and emo about him speaking on their and Natasha's behalf.

I had to run out early to do the show and missed Chic and Grace Jones, but on the way out shook hands with Chelsea Clinton, who is very unlike both musical acts. I left thinking there's gonna be a cure for AIDS in the next ten years.

We had the *Top Chef* winner and finalist on, which is always fun. I drank two tequilas and was feeling no pain by the time I got home. After a drunky walk with Wacha (the best kind, if I haven't made that clear), I stepped into my elevator and walked smack into a handsome man with whom I immediately started flirting. It was a light flirt, a smiley

"How was your night?" He'd been working late. I told him mine was "great!" He told me he'd actually been on an airplane with me a couple weeks ago and it took me exactly two floors to realize this was the handsome stranger with the wedding ring from the Madonna flight to LA. *OMFG.* The door opened on ten and before I could muster anything he told me that's his floor and hesitantly started stepping out. "Wait—what's your name?" I asked, though I had looked at it on the manifest two weeks before. It's Brendan. Brendan! How'd I forget that? We would've talked longer but in came the sweet Italian man who loves Wacha.

The airplane guy lives on the tenth floor! Who is his husband?

THURSDAY, FEBRUARY 6, 2014—NYC–LOS ANGELES

Before my walk this morning I made Surfin spill the tea on my tenth-floor future lover. He is *not* married, says Surfin, and he is barely in NYC. He mainly lives in LA, and he rents. He's a renter. I am beside myself about the whole thing. I will say, he's not as tall as I remember from the plane. I remember thinking he was huge. I need to see him again when I am sober.

I am back at 169 even though I drunkenly ate a fistful of gummies after the show last night. My Ninj made me do a zillion squats today. All the fuck I do is squats. My ass should be a cantaloupe by now.

A thousand years ago, a woman gave a boatload of money to Hurricane Sandy relief for the (honor?) of having dinner with SJP and me. The date has changed fifteen times in the last year and a half but tonight was it. I picked up SJ and had made a list of eight essential items to discuss with her before we gave ourselves to the johns who awaited us at Blue Hill. The biggest item on the list was getting her counsel about next week's American Songbook Gala at Lincoln Center honoring Bryan, where both of us are appearing. I've been stressed and overwhelmed daily trying to find the right words, or poem to read, to pay tribute to my friend who is not only a Hollywood Superagent but a great communicator and gentleman. I want to say something that'll match and capture his grace. She had some ideas, and something for me too, which was an invitation to her table at the Met Ball—which is an OMG invite. It's better than the Oscars and harder to get into. She has room at her table and was saying, "If you could invite anyone, who would you invite? Someone that would blow you away." I said Prince Harry. She is going to see what she can do but thinks he is probably booked for the next two years. On her list was Donna Tartt. We were both so blown away by *The Goldfinch*; I'm all for it.

The dinner turned out to be lovely not only because the food was so freaking good, but the group who paid for our time were great, from Cincinnati and just the type of people you would want to do something awkward like this with. It was all really loving and fun and easy and they were big Bravo watchers. We took every combination of photo available and then I careened it to the airport to get an eight-fifteen flight to LA to reunite the Real Hens of Beverly Hills.

I am rereading *The Andy Warhol Diaries*, so I was sucked into that for the whole flight. On this date in 1982, Andy had dinner with Diana Ross, Iman, Bianca Jagger, Steve Rubell, and Barry. He said he tried to make Barry laugh "because he never does and everybody says it's impossible," which of course tickled me. I think it's gotten less impossible thirty years later but he's still not handing out laughs to just anybody. After dinner they went to see Calvin Klein's new apartment on Sixty-sixth and Central Park West and Diana Ross took a limo. Just when I started to think I was born in the wrong decade, Andy starts talking about a guy at dinner who he didn't want to get close to because he had "gay cancer." I was born at exactly the right time and I'm lucky to be alive.

FRIDAY, FEBRUARY 7, 2014—LOS ANGELES

Ugh! I woke up at six forty-five this morning and opened the shades to discover what looked like the apocalypse, but turned out to be a smoggy morning in LA. The end-of-days visual seemed an apt metaphor for what I was facing: the *RHOBH* reunion. I suspected it was going to be long and brutal and it was. Two of the Housewives refused to sit next to Carlton because they believed that she had put *spells* on them, or that somehow she would *put* a spell on them. So there was last-minute seat juggling. They'd all watched the last five episodes (which haven't aired yet) yesterday, so they were lathered up, especially Lisa, who gets a little ganged up on in the finale. She apparently watched them with Tyler Perry—TV watching à deux I really would have liked to witness.

I went into the day with the hunch that this was going to be the first and last reunion for Joyce and Carlton, and I didn't get the sense they had the same idea. Actually, I am pretty sure Carlton does know and I feel bad for her—we only showed her as a sex-starved Wiccan. In retrospect we could've fleshed out more aspects of her life. Joyce was a river of words and was bugging the shit out of Yolanda; as the two of them were going at it my mind turned the corner into morphing this into some other kind of alternate-universe version of the *Housewives*: "Joyce, you are no longer a Housewife. Please leave the reunion."

After about seven hours I tried to wrap it up and go into full conflict resolution with Lisa and Brandi, and Lisa and Kyle. ("What one thing do you want Lisa to own right now, Kyle? Can you do that, Lisa?") I don't know if it worked but I was trying to make it all better as I saw genuine tears in Brandi's and Kyle's eyes and hurt in Lisa's. During a break near the end, Lisa asked me what I thought of the day and I said, "It is clear these girls love you," but she intimated they were only acting that way because they thought they came off badly in the finale. One of the issues here is that in every city, some of the women are simultaneously living their real lives and playing to the audience's perception of them, and that always winds up biting them in the ass. It's worse in this franchise than anywhere else, maybe because it's an industry town.

We wrapped at about 9 p.m. and I met Hickey and Jeff, who were having dinner with Jeff's family somewhere on Melrose. I had a Maker's-and-ginger, which I drank too fast, but only one. I'm really trying to stick to my protein/veggie plan and I already felt victorious having barely made a dent in the reunion craft service (crafty is my kryptonite), but the booze loosened me up and I grazed on all their desserts, so that was a big cheat. Then I shame-ate a chocolate chip cookie in the hotel room. I'm powerless to a chocolate chip cookie next to my bed. Or anywhere.

I missed a great party in NYC tonight at Jimmy's, celebrating his last night on *Late Night*. I hate missing great parties. Hate.

Another early morning, this time for the Lady Gaga video shoot. I was told it was a green-screen solo shoot they were tacking onto the schedule because it was my only available day. I'd listened to the song ("G.U.Y.") a few times on the treadmill last week but otherwise didn't give it a moment's thought even though John Hill kept telling me what a big deal it was. I got there and it turns out he was right.

Here's how it went down: A cool woman leads me through a huge soundstage to my dressing room, says they added this day—at great expense—for me, and hands me the lyrics and tells me to learn them while I get made up. I thought I was just supposed to learn the chorus! "You're playing Zeus," she says, "and you're singing in front of a green screen." I've done no research on Zeus or contemplated what this might entail. "I'll tell LG you're here. She wants to come brief you."

Wait—*LG is here*? And is that what we call her? *LG*? I foolishly assumed that *she* wouldn't be at the shoot. I don't know if I thought she was too busy or what, but it turns out she is directing the video. I text John immediately (who is crazily in town for the weekend) to get his ass over there in a hurry, *LG is directing me*!

Gaga comes over and is warm and enthusiastic and blows a ton of smoke up my ass (she says something along the lines of "This is about a celebration of your success and career and women everywhere wanting to be with you, or be slaves to you") and recites parts of the song ("Touch me, touch me, don't be sweet / love me, love me, please retweet / let me be the girl under you that makes you cry") to me—surreal—while giving me attitude cues ("Be sexy, strong, playful, godlike"). She's wearing a do-rag, Anthrax T-shirt, leather jacket, and jeans. I ask her if she's directed other videos and she starts rattling off her hits. She says they are mixing in another song from *Artpop* and needs me to hear it, so she grabs my phone and starts looking for the album, only to find that I don't own her album. I only downloaded "G.U.Y." and "Applause" and what are the chances that the artist herself would find out? Awkward. She puts the phone down and says they are only using my head, which will be floating in the sky, so there is no wardrobe. And by "no wardrobe" she means I should just take off my shirt because they need my shoulders bare. *OK . . .*

They bring me to the set just as John is walking in with raised eyebrow—he knew it was gonna be a big deal. Never could an intense six-week workout regimen be more instantly rewarded than the moment I take my shirt off in front of Gaga and a soundstage full of people without embarrassment. Gaga cues up the track and gives me specifics on how to sing the lyrics. I fuck up the lyrics left and right but I am a music video superstar, and she is there by the monitor cheering me on, singing along with herself, whooping it up, and making me feel like a million bucks the whole time. (John's standing behind her shaking his head.) When I finally get the lyrics in my head and the right attitude, I scream at her that I am about to cum, which I hope she takes as the expression of gratitude it is meant to be. I get the take.

We shot for about forty-five minutes and it just so happens that singing along to a blasting Lady Gaga song shirtless in front of a massive crew and Lady Gaga cheering you on is *really fucking fun*!

Oh, and I couldn't resist telling her about Mariah's lighting requirements.

I was so pumped after the shoot and had time to kill before my plane, so I had to make a plan. It was only 10 a.m., so I met Hickey for breakfast at the Tower and we had a ton of laughs. Heidi Fleiss was at the next table, so that was very LA. I fucked her. Kidding.

I had a few tokes of the Whoopi vape pen and walked onto the plane feeling so Jah and happy until I heard a familiar *very cheery* voice around the corner. It was the #BabyJaneFlightAttendant! Three flights with her in three months. On top of that, Mariah's publicist, Cindi Berger, was sitting behind me and Brandi Glanville catty-corner. She was exhausted from the reunion, natch. (Aren't we all, Brandi? Aren't we all.) I had an important epiphany: The reason I am so upset by and nasty to #Baby JaneFlightAttendant is that she *lingers* two beats longer than is necessary for every interaction. "The jury's out on these new seats!!!!!" Beat. Beat. Beat. "You want more nuts? No?" Searching. For. More. Interaction. It's exhausting. #FirstWorldProblems.

The tribute to Bryan is Monday, and I had vowed to write my speech for him on the plane; Bruce had steered me in the direction of speaking about his love for theater, which was a good idea, but instead of writing I did other homework—watched three episodes of *RHOA*. So that's still hanging over me. I landed in NYC and met Bruce and Bryan for a drink.

Turns out I missed another fun party tonight—this time *in LA*—Mary McCormack's birthday. Wrong city two nights in a row.

▦ SUNDAY, FEBRUARY 9, 2014

I saw a guy at the gym today wearing tights and his ass was so round and big and perfect that I couldn't get it out of my head all day. If I had an ass like that I would wear tights too. He wanted nothing to do with me.

The show was a disaster—tons of technical fuckups. It felt like the first time we'd ever done it. I hope nobody I knew saw it. Actually, I hope no strangers did either.

▦ MONDAY, FEBRUARY 10, 2014

I woke up freaking out about speaking tonight at Bryan's tribute at Lincoln Center. I took Bruce's advice and wrote something about his love of theater and our late nights at Marie's Crisis. Hickey was on a plane to New York and we were emailing back and forth—he really helped me shape it, but still, it nagged at me all day.

We taped tonight's show with Jenny McCarthy and Brandi Glanville early. The game tested their knowledge of a U.S. citizenship test that Yolanda had taken on *RHOBH*; it turned out to be kind of hard—neither of them did so well and yours truly wouldn't have done much better. Jenny, who is simultaneously a few days into starving herself on a juice fast *and* quitting smoking, essentially lost her grip in the hallway after the show. She was really upset about the game, which she thought was built to make them look stupid, and said she was never doing the show again. We wound up subbing out a game of word association. She was really appreciative. I like her. When she's not quitting smoking and on a fast, which is clearly a deadly combination.

So then it was on to Lincoln Center. I recited my speech the entire way up Tenth Avenue until I'd memorized it. I got there just as Mantello, who was directing the night, was speaking to all the actors taking part. The concept was Barkin welcoming everyone in front of a closed curtain, saying that she knew Bryan would prefer to be at home in his living room right now, so we attempted to bring his living room to Lincoln Center, at which point the curtain comes down to reveal a group of us— Alan Cumming, Kristin Chenoweth, Mark and Kelly, Anne Hathaway, Allison Williams, Patty Clarkson, Marisa Tomei, Matt Bomer, SJP, and me—sprawled on couches with cocktails in a re-creation of Bruce and Bryan's penthouse. I was the only non-actor up there, and I was relieved to be sitting on the couch with SJ, who was nervous herself to be singing ("NYC" from *Annie*). The unspoken barnacle stuck on our nerves was that the audience was going to be filled with every fancypants power person and movie star from both coasts. The convo on the couch was whether to go up holding my piece of paper as a crutch or not. SJ said to do whatever made me comfortable. I was second up, after Chenoweth, didn't bring my paper, and immediately saw Hickey in the audience, which put me at ease. It was good, and better even, I got to sit back and enjoy the rest of the show with a cocktail in my hand.

Before SJ went up to sing she whispered, "Is that Madonna sitting in the third row?" Indeed, directly in front of us, there she was and as I breathed a sigh of relief I hadn't seen her before I spoke, SJ bravely stepped up and broke my and everybody else's hearts with her song. By the time Daniel Craig (sans porno mustache, the play closed) brought Bryan to the stage, the whole audience felt like they knew him a little better. A powerhouse crowd milled around the party—Anna Wintour, Reese Witherspoon, Barry, DVF, David Geffen, Brad Grey, Sandy, Lorne Michaels, Gwyneth Paltrow, Liam, Whoopi, and a shitload of other people who I am thrilled also not to have realized were in the audience before I spoke. Jimmy (he starts *The Tonight Show* next week!) and I laughed over our carb faces. He is so ready to go, and along with all the press he's been doing he was on the cover of *Men's Health,* which is hilarious given that I think of him as a booze-and-chips buddy. Oh, and amidst it all the Countess walked up in a white gown. And Carole was there too, not that I think of Carole as a Housewife, but she is one. A magical NYC night.

Bryan had a very happy soiree in the sky (at the Skylark), jam-packed with iconic revelers ready to light it up, surrounded by a 360-degree view of Midtown. I met a sweet guy—an actor—and we exchanged numbers and planned to get drinks. I can't tell if the guy thinks it's a friend thing or a date thing. I need to let him know I'm not looking for a new friend. Hickey, Joe, and I tried to make something happen on the dance floor but people were falling all over each other and a few gay guys were closing in on a straight hockey player; we left just as we sensed it was turning the corner into messy—about one forty-five—and went home to walk Wacha. The boys were so happy to see him—and he them—and the group of us had a drunken, laughter-filled walk around the Village in the freezing cold at 2 a.m.

TUESDAY, FEBRUARY 11, 2014

I need to marry a fireman. That's my new plan.

Tonight was Radzi's book party at her house. I re-met Kristen, the new New York Housewife, whom I hadn't seen since the night we were introduced by Brandi a year ago. She's gonna be great on the show. I tried to prep her husband, Josh, because I think it's going to be a rough season for him. We show him being tough on his wife.

After the party Bruce, Liza, Bryan, and I walked to a Mexican restaurant and that's when I had the moment with a tall fireman in front of that firehouse on Sixth Avenue and Houston. He made a point to tell me he had seen Kelly's show that morning, and we couldn't figure out exactly why he wanted me to know that—I thought he was trying to say he knew who I was because Kelly and I are friends, but the discussion as we walked away veered into the idea that he was trying to subliminally come out to me. At dinner, we debated it and decided it absolutely was the former and he was straight. That being said, I think I need to date a fireman. They have to spend a few nights a week at the firehouse, which is perfect for me. I gotta do my show while he's fighting fires and I think the distance would be good for us, although of course I'd be worried all the time about my man. Maybe I would bake cookies for the guys in the station and tell them about Teresa. I for sure would get involved with the other Firehouse Spouses. I am completely ready to embrace a new community of people.

WEDNESDAY, FEBRUARY 12, 2014

This morning Harry Smith interviewed me for *Meet the Press* about the state of gay America. I talked about Michael Sam coming out and called Putin a bastard. I hope they use that part. I didn't tell my mom beforehand; she would have been terrified. Sean is doing *Dancing with the Stars*. I hooked him up with Ricki Lake to give him advice. I want him to go far.

I am 168 pounds.

It was sleepover night! Dave came to the show (Seth Meyers was on) and back at my apartment we did what we spent four years perfecting in college: sipping whiskey, listening to music, talking about the imminent environmental destruction of our planet, and noshing. We lit a fire and cuddled with Wacha as we watched another big snowstorm blanket the city. At 2 a.m. we took Wacha out for a walk (with our cocktails) and it was completely still and quiet. Wacha made the cutest little paw prints in the fresh snow.

THURSDAY, FEBRUARY 13, 2014—NYC–BRITISH VIRGIN ISLANDS

Woke up very hungover after only about five hours of sleep—my first bad hangover of the year. Last night's snowstorm was still raging and meant to go on all day. I taped two shows during the day and was scheduled to fly to the British Virgin Islands at 7 p.m. to spend five days at sea with our regular group (See: Lake Powell), but needless to say, the snow was a factor.

Turns out there was a window of time between six-thirty and seven-thirty where the ten of us could take off before the icy snow started again—we made it. Careening out of Teterboro in the middle of the storm, we felt like we'd escaped. Went to bed at sea.

Five days of long morning swims in the open blue-green ocean, a rainbow of colors underwater snorkeling, afternoon hikes, tons of laughter, lots of sleep, and probably too much booze and food. I can't not indulge myself on vacation—what is the freaking point of *life*? I finished reading *Sedition*, which I enjoyed. I did no work, but managed to stress myself out about my production company. One night Wendi Murdoch came over for dinner with her party of eleven tech smarties, including Larry Page from Google, the guy who invented kitesurfing, the inventor of the Segway, and the (former?) head of YouTube, who all made us feel kinda dumb. None of them seemed to have much of a clue about pop culture; let me put it this way—they are so busy reinventing the world they didn't even know who Anderson was. We visited Page's private island off Virgin Gorda; as private islands go, it was a winner. (And by that I mean I have never been to a private island before.)

We landed Tuesday midday in another fucking snowstorm. This is torture. But Wacha was very hyper to see me, which made me happy to be home.

Robin Quivers and Patti LaBelle were on my show, and the fire alarm went off as we were close to air, meaning that Miss Patti and Quivers had to walk down six flights of stairs. The ratings for my show are growing but it remains blissfully very homemade; we made air and it was a good one.

At midnight, I had what I hoped was a date at Anfora with the actor I'd met at Bryan's party, but I had initiated getting together so earnestly I was not sure how the invitation was received. But I think it was indeed a date. There was a lot of innocent flirtation and getting-to-know-you, which, frankly, I haven't allowed myself to engage in in longer than I care to admit. The truth is I just haven't been able to get it up (figuratively) for anyone in . . . forever. But I did with him and that took me by surprise. He inadvertently walked me home, where I turned a peck on the lips under my awning into something more substantial of a goodbye. I went upstairs feeling really tingly and sweet. I sent a text affirming (and seeking his affirmation) that that was really nice and fun. Affirmation received.

What the hell was going on with the traffic all day? Wacha's hip appears to be better—he is busting out wanting to play—and he was supposed to have an X-ray on the Upper East Side at the Barbara Walters Animal Medical Center, but I spent twenty minutes going three blocks in an Uber and decided to put it off for a week.

I texted my date something innocuous and he waited ninety minutes before texting me back something equally innocuous. I responded immediately and got his reply another two hours later, so Bruce has put me on text lockdown. I am not allowed to contact him until Sunday. (I am gonna get that moved to Saturday, though Bruce doesn't realize it yet.) Whatever winds up happening there, I feel like I broke my date seal, which had been closed up for too long.

On the way home from an hour of heavy weights/low reps with the Ninj, I stopped at the bodega on Bleecker and Hudson, the one that I stop at every day and they act like they've never seen me before. I didn't have enough cash for my bread, flowers, chicken sausage, and eggs (I don't know what's more shocking—that this diet actually has me preparing food in my kitchen, or that those few items amazingly combined to total forty-something dollars), so I removed the chicken sausage but still was a dollar short. I asked if I could bring back the dollar bill tomorrow, and told them that of course I was good for it, I'm there four or five days a week after the gym. It was a little touch-and-go as they hemmed and hawed in front of all the people in line behind me, but they finally said yes. That place is always a little humiliating in some way.

The show was fun and we all stayed and drank after. I got home at 1 a.m. and Lance Bass texted that he was in a cab heading downtown, so I invited him over for a nightcap. He is sweet as ever—we talked dogs for a long time (he agreed that Wacha is perfect), and I got some good Lou Pearlman stories out of him.

Maybe because of my text lockdown with the actor, I've remembered my future husband on the tenth floor. He disappeared again! I need to tell Surfin to let me know the next time he's in town. Or at least his full name so I can find him online.

THURSDAY, FEBRUARY 20, 2014

Woke up hungover, but it was sunny and warmish for the first time this year so I took Wacha out for a long walk and we sat in the sun on a bench in front of Bonsignour for an hour. Wacha sat proudly (guarding me?) and I felt like I hadn't a care in the world. Surfin had the day off, so I will have to wait to find out about my backup husband. (The actor left for London today, incidentally.)

I spent the afternoon at Bravo cleaning out my football field full of shit. Who do I think I am, a future President who will one day have his every doodle and paper housed in a museum somewhere? And now I'm obsessed with recycling everything even though it's impossible. I just don't know where this crap (old iPod docking stations, batteries, chargers) *goes to die*??? What happened to all the beepers we carried in the nineties? Are they on a barge somewhere?

Met Amanda at *The Glass Menagerie* and it was an incredible production—intense, powerful, and exhausting. OK, it's not like I was *in* it or anything. We went backstage after to congratulate Zach Quinto and he was lovely. (Diane Lane—looking great—was back there to see Cherry Jones.) I really did wait till the last minute to see him; it closes Sunday. I hadn't seen Amanda since early January, so dinner at Joe Allen (Zach and Joe Machota were at the next table, funny!) was like an intense therapy catch-up session. At one point near the beginning she even said, "Any concerns?" which sounded like something she would say to her patient. It ended up being a good session for both of us. I love giving advice to shrinks.

FRIDAY, FEBRUARY 21, 2014—NYC–ST. LOUIS

Wacha was so cute this morning, and there's no way he did not know I was leaving him again to head to St. Louis to host the Beggin' Pet Parade at the St. Louis Mardi Gras. (I have to assume Dame Judi Dench turned them down this year, because it's a very prestigious invite, as one can imagine by the title.) He's starting to notice the luggage and figure out my packing rhythms.

*Dad and I at the US Open—
nice photobomb, Martha!*

*Nobody seems to want this huge poster
of SJP and me!*

*Jim Edmonds, Tony LaRussa, and me
at the playoffs—I'm wearing Tony's rings*

Ryan, our renaissance PA, with the Pee-fume

My huge office at Bravo, RIP

World Series with my folks

John Hill, Bruce, and me at the Walter Mitty *premiere*

clear how I got roped into posing with these
ds with Martha at the Today show

John Hill and Wacha the day
we met him—so licky!

first Instagram of Wacha

Jumpsuit fitting with Cynthia Rowley!

urry selfie with Gaga—as the undead
at the Glamour *awards*

With Britney. Awkward.

Taping Sesame Street

With the Downton Abbey cast—do I look like I just puked?

My beard and me with DVF at her "Journey of a Dress" LACMA opening

...kfast in Brazil with Anderson and Ben, ...ssed with The Goldfinch

Barbara Walters giving me "talk to the hand" as I apologized

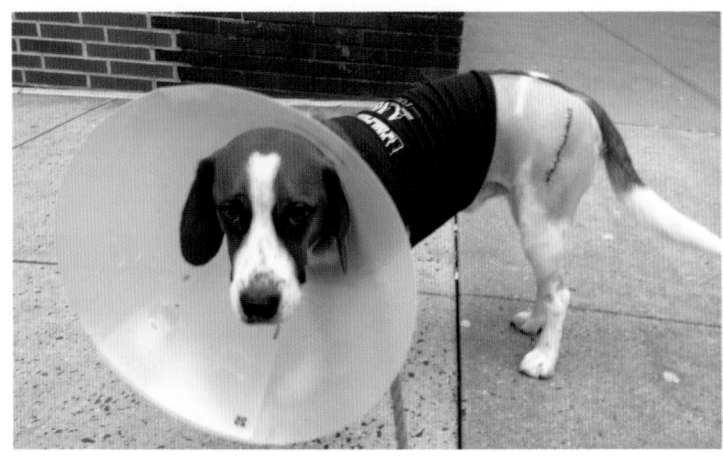

Is there anything sadder than this pic?

Ralph Lauren Olympics sweater backstage at the Today *show*

Bruce, Michael, Hamilton, Kelly, Benjamin, and me at the Vanity Fair *party*

"Cast photo" at the 2014 Lincoln Center American Songbook Gala honoring Bryan Lourd—I'm serving Angelina Jolie leg realness

BVI dive off the boat

At sea with Bruce in the British Virgin Islands

Montana bromance

It started to snow while John was recording, and he took me out for a quick photo session.

With the groom, Dave Serwatka, in Nola

Wacha's TV debut!

Shaq picked me up? I don't even remember.

Gaga and Grac backstage at Roseland

Wacha with St. Louis Cardinals Shelby Miller, Jon Jay, and Daniel Descalso

I am obsessed with Gaga's hot bodyguard— backstage at Roseland

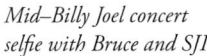

Mid–Billy Joel concert selfie with Bruce and SJP

Jerry, me, and Mark at Jerry's birthday

Cohosting Revlon Run/Walk with Emma Stone

On the Met Ball red carpet

In SJP's bathroom before the Met Ball

Me, Abby, and Em at Rock Center

Housewives crossover at dinner!

Shooting The Comeback
*with Val and Mickey
(Lisa Kudrow and
Robert Michael Morris)!*

Fighting with my Ninja!

Liza and Surfin backstage at WWHL

Rejected pic to send Cher from Italy

Feeling fit and strong!

th of France with Liam, Jason, Ralph, and Tom Hollander

Jason Blum and I re-create Hockney

After the game with January Jones

Shot from the control room of Dave, me, and Padma shooting Top Chef

Nancy Fallon, Kelly, and Marci K

From a West Virginia kill shelter to helicopters to the Hamptons!

My parents and Jimmy in my dressing room backstage at The Tonight Show...

... while I beg Julia Roberts to come on WWHL

Two great dames: Mom and Joan

Bruce, Liza, and me at her wedding

Kim Kardashian ass selfie

It's always magic hour wi[th] these two—Hickey and S[...] in the Pines

Ending the summer on Fire Island with Amanda[,] Graciela, and Bill

I got to my parents' and immediately worked out with a trainer I use when I'm home, who charges so little (sixty bucks) that I almost feel like *I'm* ripping *him* off. I am used to getting raped up the ass by New York City trainers, I guess. We went to Pastoria for dinner. But not before a chorus of hysterical "We will never GET INTO Pastoria! It WON'T HAPPEN!" from my folks. We are in Clayton, Missouri, I tried to tell them. Getting into a restaurant is, in my mind, well within the realm of attainability. Shockingly, *we got in*. And the place was empty by eight forty-five. I hired a driver (so I could drink) and met Kari at a new place called Planter's House, which we loved. As we were sitting there I said, "Man, would it be great if Jake's Leg was playing tonight in St. Louis," so I Googled them and sure enough they were playing in Ballwin, which is all the way in West County but I was at that point a man on a mission to hear my favorite Grateful Dead cover band from high school with my classic friend from high school. The driver had no idea where he was going, I don't know where the hell he was from but it was not St. Louis, so it was us telling him how to get there. Jake's Leg were so great and it felt free and easy, dancing to Dead music. I felt hashtag blessed.

SATURDAY, FEBRUARY 22, 2014—ST. LOUIS

I boxed through a hangover this morning at this gym next door to where my parents live. The day's dominant conversation (there always is one topic a day in my family) revolved around the Joe's Stone Crab Dinner we were going to *en famille* at Westwood, which is my brother-in-law's country club that apparently does not allow jeans in their main dining room. All I brought home were jeans, so this became a lightning rod, made worse by my not-so-secret desire to get kicked out of the club—in front of all the fancy St. Louis Jews—for wearing said jeans. Rob, whose membership I would be putting in peril, did not wish for me to get kicked out of his club, and texted asking how dark the jeans were and for as many details as I could provide. As we were getting ready, my outfit was under a new layer of intense scrutiny, this time from my mother, who deemed my Ralph Lauren Olympic Skiing Sweater (my friends at Ralph Lauren had sent a turtleneck, alternate version of the Christmas sweater) "too loud" for the venue and demanded a costume change. (She was wrong, but I crumbled under the pressure and complied.) I sadly did not get kicked out of the club, but we ate buckets of stone crabs flown in from Joe's with the hoi polloi of St. Louis County, half of whom are somehow my relatives. The evening could also be viewed as an informative exploration of innovations in midwestern plastic surgery techniques.

After dinner I went with the cute guard at the St. Louis Zoo Penguin House I met a few years ago to some gay bar that was fairly empty but seemed like it would be fun if it ever filled up, which it didn't.

▦ SUNDAY, FEBRUARY 23, 2014—ST. LOUIS–NYC

The taxing responsibilities of Grand Marshal of the Beggin' Pet Parade at the St. Louis Mardi Gras consisted of waving at thousands of dogs forced to wear beads and costumes by their (drunk?) owners. It was a scream. If I could ride at the front of a pet parade once a month, I wouldn't be unhappy. Em, Rob, and Abby came and had a ball. Having Abby there kicked it up a few notches in the fun department. She's seven, so probably the bull's-eye age for the event.

After being forced by Bruce to wait five days, I texted the actor today. It was not completely satisfying but I did get a text right back, so maybe the plan worked. I am allowed to ask for another date tomorrow, per Bruce. In the meantime, I got a Facebook message from someone I met at my show two weeks ago, talking about getting a drink. The next phase in making a plan with me is a knockout round for some people, because it's me saying, "OK, is it possible to meet me at midnight after my show?" Normal people with actual jobs don't love the idea of waiting until late night for get-to-know-you cocktails, but before my show never works and I keep leaving town on weekends, so this seems like my best option. He, though, said he's a late-night guy so he's up for it.

I flew back in time for the show. My hair looked so good on the plane I didn't want to get off. It looked less good for the show, but RuPaul's great energy made everything better. Met John Mayer for a few drinks at the Greenwich Hotel at midnight and stayed up entirely too late going deep. He and Katy Perry broke up. (Again.)

MONDAY, FEBRUARY 24, 2014

Surfin told me the airplane dude neighbor's name, and once again I'd forgotten it one minute later when I walked into my apartment. Am I intentionally pushing my future husband away?

I did text the actor in an attempt to get together and he said he was going to LA and we could connect there. But connecting in LA during Oscar weekend is totally impossible, and I'm going to Austin a couple days after I return, so I am feeling doomed here. And by the way, at this point I am pretty sure I am just romanticizing one nice evening. I'm in that phase before a second date where the possibilities are infinite.

My buddy who EPs an entertainment show on the West Coast tracked me down tonight while I was getting my makeup done to tell me it was time to consider moving on to a show that was more my own, and by that he meant his twenty-five-year-old show that has absolutely nothing to do with me. I tried to explain that I could not be doing more my own show if I was broadcasting from my bathroom every day, but he didn't really get it. I was happy to be asked, I'll say that.

Linda Gray was on looking—at seventy-three—like a million bucks. I tried to instigate some friction between her and Victoria Principal but there is none.

TUESDAY, FEBRUARY 25, 2014

I had a great time with my Ninj today and much of the discussion was that I planned to have a big indulgence at lunch. It's hard to believe that I used to eat whatever I wanted, and now the prospect of a delicious cheeseburger and cottage fries at J.G. Melon with Jerry Seinfeld suddenly is a talking point with my trainer. Jerry and I are perennially searching for the best burger in town and we keep coming back to J.G. Melon, so maybe we've found it. I can't stop thinking of the guy last night who thought his show was better for me than my show, and so we talked about how everybody thinks what they are doing is the most important thing. Who can blame anyone, anyway? Jerry's going to Puerto Rico to perform and had just been interviewed by someone from a newspaper in San Juan who only wanted to rehash the Puerto Rican Day Parade episode of *Seinfeld*. He paid, I protested, and, in reference to the hundred-dollar bill he put down, said he wanted to get rid of this anyway. . . . So we laughed about that for a while. Most people want to kill a five or a one, you know?

Took advantage of being on the UES and met Graciela for tea, which was a divine half-hour reconnect. She walked me over to Ralph Lauren, where I quickly bought two sport coats. I pretended that I need them for our shows in Austin next month but I'm pretty sure I don't.

I shook things up and had a *pre*-show ninety-minute massage because I was in so much pain from the gym, and learned that it's not that fun being lotioned up at 9 p.m. having to ponder hosting a live cocktail party two hours later. And Wacha must've been trying to tell me he really had to go while I was stressing about my show, because he just started to pee on the rug during the massage. Adam let me stay on the table and ran Wacha downstairs to finish. I tweeted on the table until he came back. And during the massage I realized I never returned that fucking dollar bill to the bodega on Bleecker and Eighth Avenue. Fuck.

I met John Mayer again at midnight and we went even deeper this time. He and Katy Perry are still broken up.

▦ WEDNESDAY, FEBRUARY 26, 2014

Surfin told me the guy next door to the vacant apartment upstairs is now asking about it, so I freaked out and called the building manager to see what was going on. Mr. Liebowitz was out of the office but I left him a long message. I am like a slave to Mr. Liebowitz at this point. He keeps putting me off thirty days. Now it's going to be a bidding war. Joy.

I returned the dollar to the bodega and it was a whole new crew behind the counter and they looked at me like I was crazy. It's never the same two people back there but they always have a bad attitude, so they're at least consistent with that.

Wacha got X-rayed at the Barbara Walters Animal Hospital today and they had to sedate him. The doctor said he was a lightweight with drugs (unlike his daddy), so they kept me waiting like an hour for him to get his shit together, during which time I fantasized about falling in love with a vet. That seems cute. Wacha is in perfect health and his hip recovery is to blame for all his new puppy energy. I have been quietly considering hitting him (gently) with a hammer on his new hip to calm him down a little, but I have an appointment with a dog trainer tomorrow instead.

Dierks Bentley was on the show tonight and a caller asked his favorite concert venue. He said Red Rocks and I talked about shrooming there at a Grateful Dead concert. I got a text from Mom after the show: "Good thing I didn't know about this shroom thing. Even tho I don't know what it means I don't like it."

After the show I had a date with the guy who'd followed up with me on Facebook last week. (The date with the actor has encouraged me even though it seems to have gone nowhere.) A few minutes into the convo I asked him what he did before meeting me (at midnight) and he said he'd been hanging out with the dog who belongs to "this guy I've been dating." So that ended that and I sat there wondering how much longer I had to stay without seeming rude. I lasted another twenty minutes. Maybe twenty-five. And I did let him know that I didn't love that he was dating someone, and he said he didn't know the *context* of our (midnight) drinks.

THURSDAY, FEBRUARY 27, 2014

Great workout and I seem to have stabilized at 167, which makes me really happy. I met with a new dog trainer, who told me kind of under her breath that she charges three hundred an hour, which at the time didn't faze me for some reason but I have been steaming and stewing about it all day. Is she training him to eat caviar? Ride in limos? I just need him to learn to do like ten more things so I can get a little of the puppy energy out. Now we both have expensive trainers, I guess. So that's kinda cute, but really not.

I recorded a country song at my apartment to promote our trip to SXSW in Austin. I absolutely can't sing but it was really fun. Like karaoke.

I had tea at Ralph's and was almost falling asleep on his couch. I don't know why I'm so beat.

John Hill and I had one last meal at Pastis, which closes this weekend. I'm sad about it closing but not as heartbroken as I was about Florent, which I am still not over. And that greedy landlord still has an empty restaurant in that space, so that didn't work out so great for her.

I am going to LA tomorrow for the Oscars and never got an invite for the *Vanity Fair* party. I lamented this to Hamilton, who emailed that he was going to get into it, and then that he had gotten into it and to stand by. But I emailed him back and said the idea that inviting me to their party is any issue at all is all I need to hear. And it's ironic because there was a period of time when all I wanted was to go to their party and either he or Barry would get me in, but the fact that I can't get an invite now that people actually might *want me* to come to their parties makes me feel exactly like the loser that they think I am. So I will be going to Madonna's party Sunday night and I think that's quite enough.

▦ FRIDAY, FEBRUARY 28, 2014—NYC–LOS ANGELES

Wacha realized I was leaving and really turned it up. I saw the super today, who told me that Mr. Liebowitz is out until Tuesday and I will hear from him then. He said not to worry because he told Mr. Liebowitz that I am famous and that money is no object. I actually gasped. He thought he was doing me a favor by helping me secure the apartment this way, but *that is exactly not the thing to say*! And he said they'd been moving stuff out and the place was empty, so I went up there and the door was open and I let myself in. It is a total gut job, but the exact footprint as mine, so I'm in. (If Mr. Liebowitz will have me and the guy next door doesn't outbid me.)

Torrential rain is forecast in LA all weekend and it's supposed to snow in NYC again (of course) on Sunday and especially Monday, so now I am wondering if I will just come back early to be sure to be back by Monday for my show. Meanwhile I got an email from Jane Sarkin saying to come to the *VF* party. Now I feel like a double loser that I made it an issue.

The headwinds were terrible, so the flight was not only very turbulent, it was so long I thought we would wind up in Greece. We eventually landed in rain-soaked Los Angeles. My driver was obese and had great difficulty with the tasks at hand, like getting to the car and driving me to Bruce and Bryan's. Poor guy.

Throughout the CAA party, as I began to talk to any given woman, I had to spend the first ten to forty seconds churning my brain to figure out to whom I was speaking. Most of them I actually knew but they have filled their faces and plumped their lips and all look like some approximation of Chelsea Handler. Although she's all-natural. Kidding. It was weird, and occasionally embarrassing because I sucked at faking it. Also there was every famous person on the planet, from Tim Tebow to Jared Leto, Will Smith to Sandra Bullock. Marcy Engelman is a big *WWHL* fan and really wanted me to meet Julia Roberts in the hope that we would connect and get her on the show. She sweetly introduced us and we had a long and lovely chat; she's an *RHOBH* and *RHONY* fan. I told her I want to make an animated show called *Lil Housewives* and she agreed that anything with "lil" in front of it works. Madonna gave Bruce her coat and he wore it over his suit all night. We mortified her by quoting "The night is young, and the show has just begun" to her face. (This is what she said every night of the "Confessions" tour before the song "Jump," not that I saw that show more than a few times.) I flirted with a very hot guy all night who ultimately turned out to be too drunk to materialize into anything. Got back to Bruce and Bryan's around three and had another cocktail and gorged. I am powerless to a big bag of Doritos.

SPRING 2014

IN WHICH . . .

- I HIT MY TARGET WEIGHT,

- JOIN THE ONLINE DATING WORLD,

- DON'T SHOOT GOPHERS IN MONTANA,

- GO TO THE MET BALL,

- AND APPEAR AS MYSELF ON MY FAVORITE TV SHOW.

SATURDAY, MARCH 1, 2014—LOS ANGELES

All day I waffled between leaving LA tomorrow morning in order to miss the potential storm and risking it by hitching a ride back privately on Monday morning. I have so much to do when I get back, and if I miss air Monday night, I am the loser who *missed air*, which is essentially the worst thing you can do as a host of your own show, made unbearably humiliating if your excuse is "because I stayed in LA to party." This is a no-win. Anderson had to leave for the Ukraine yesterday, which is making me feel all the more lame for staying. *I'm* not nominated for a fucking Academy Award, so besides trolling for guests, what the heck am I actually doing here?

Today was Barry's annual lunch for Graydon Carter—downsized because of the torrential rain from a huge party of 450 to a small one of 50, which was a cozy gathering of the earth's moguls plus Mr. Carter. The fascinating subtext was that there were a few people in the room—Wendi Murdoch, Sergey Brin from Google—who were subjects of recent mean articles in *Vanity Fair*. I do enjoy an awkward moment.

I was ogling the mac and cheese in the buffet line with Oprah and she was very sweet about being on *WWHL*. I thanked her for doing the trust fall with me and told her she couldn't have been more Oprah on the show, a comment which made a lot of sense to me. Not sure it did to her. I got Gayle all freaked out about flying on Monday, so she became a refuge where I could belabor what has become my favorite Oscar weekend topic. It was nice to be together on that island of indecision.

I sat next to Wendi Murdoch (her newly ex-husband across the room), who told me she shook Graydon's hand, which seemed big of her. We talked about the book *Crazy Rich Asians*, because I think she should make it into a movie. Julie Chen was there and told me she saw Brandi Glanville trashing her on my show the other night, which I'd totally forgotten. When a guest is bad-mouthing someone, I never put the pieces together that the person may be at home watching or will eventually find out. Between Twitter and blogs, it's impossible *not* to hear if someone's trashing you somewhere. Oy.

Bruce, Bryan, and I all got massages in the afternoon—separately—and then went to Bruce's annual pre-Oscar dinner at the West Hollywood

Palm. After dinner we went to eighties night at Revolver and it was all Pat and Cher and Go-Go's and Madonna on the video screens. Some girl came up to me and said she was Jax's girlfriend and I told her *that's a long list*, which seemed to surprise and offend her.

I said goodbye to everybody as though I was leaving in the morning, and I went to bed booked on the 9:25 a.m. flight but not really sure because it seemed like the storm was dissipating. Apparently I have turned into a cross between Sam Champion and a Jewish mother.

▦ SUNDAY, MARCH 2, 2014—LOS ANGELES

Started the day with Bruce in the kitchen at seven-fifteen, weighing whether I should leave or not. The car for the airport was waiting outside, and I had emotionally already left, so I was ready. But the forecast changed, I sent the car away, and Bruce and I met Mark, Jason, and Lauren at SoulCycle, which I hadn't done in a couple years because I always feel like if I wanted to be screamed at by lesbians, I'd go to the Cubbyhole. The same shit coming out of the mouths of these SoulCycle instructors that made me nuts years ago did again today—faux inspiration and "depth" spurted out with the passion of a McDonald's drive-through operator. I got depressed by the tribes of Lulu Lemmings in a place shallow enough to make this dime-store philosophy meaningful. That being said, I sweated out a bottle of tequila and almost puked twice, so I think the workout was a success.

We had lunch at Hedley's and took long naps. Watched the endless red carpet and awards at Bruce's with Jason, Lauren, Hamilton, Mark, Benjamin, Albert, and Kyle.

You walk into the *Vanity Fair* party (obviously I did not stay on my high horse—I wasn't going to stand on ceremony when every one of my friends was going) and see every beautiful superstar in the world dressed perfectly and it smells clean and fresh, which is something I don't say about a lot of parties. Then there are lots of hellos to people you really don't know but have hosted on the show, like Anna Kendrick and Jenna Dewan-Tatum, or meeting people you tweeted with once or maybe think you have met but never have, like LL Cool J and Mindy Kaling. I chatted with Tyler Perry, who has the same issue as me: forgetting people's names; gawked at Tim Tebow and Channing Tatum (separately); kissed Gaga (nice, engaged, and baby-voiced once again), who said the video will be done in a couple weeks; and reconnected with people like Neil Patrick Harris and Elisabeth Moss. Bruce and I saw Bette and told her she stole the show and was trending all over Twitter all night. (I forget how small she is.) Someone cut a fart while I was in a group of famous people and I am fairly certain I know exactly who it was, because she and I went to the photo booth and the smell came with us. I ran into the actor I'd gone on the sweet date with last month and we kind of avoided each other for much of the night (schmoozing and people watching are not conducive to reigniting a possible love connection), but near the end of the party we chatted for ten good minutes. It was light and flirty. I sent a text on the way out saying how great it was to see him.

Hopped a ride with Kelly, Mark, and Benjamin to Madonna's party, which was an absolute blast, lots of famous people letting loose and dancing. I danced all night and said hi to Travolta, Leo DiCaprio, and Jamie Foxx. McCartney and Miley Cyrus and Mick Jagger were there—none of whom I really know. I kissed Madonna. I can't remember much more than that. I went to bed at four forty-five just after realizing the actor never returned the text.

▦ MONDAY, MARCH 3, 2014—LOS ANGELES—NYC

The weather was fine everywhere, so that was forty-eight hours of wasted worrying. Luckily, Bruce and I got a "ride" home privately and Jane Fonda and Fran Lebowitz were also on board. Jane Fonda is the coolest— she was upset because a friend of hers was high on something dancing with Travolta all night, and she wound up bailing the party early because her foot hurt. She was pissed because she missed a great time, an emotion to which I can relate. She's seventy-six and talking like me, which made me love her even more, and then wonder if I am still going to be talking like a teenager when I am seventy-six. I sort of hope so. I don't get the sense that Fran Lebowitz likes me too much. When we landed I got a return text (eighteen hours later) from the actor, saying, "Great seeing you too! Have a good trip!" So that's over. I went straight from Teterboro to a promo shoot for NBCUniversal's upfront (happening in May), where I was made to dance and jump—that seems to be what they want you to do at these things, dance and jump, over and over. I didn't particularly feel like dancing *or* jumping after the night I'd had, but I excelled at both. Went straight to the show from the calisthenics and it was a blur but I got through it. I was asleep before I hit the pillow.

▦ TUESDAY, MARCH 4, 2014

Lord knows what kinds of chemicals I sweat out at the gym. Shot the *Blood, Sweat & Heels* reunion most of the day. It was more entertaining than I thought it'd be.

Had a hilarious chat with Mark, who said Kelly had reminded him of a bunch of conversations he'd had Oscar night that he had totally forgotten, and then he in turn reminded me who we were dancing with and around at Madonna's (apparently P!nk, Cameron Diaz, A-Rod), all of whom I'd totally forgotten. One might question the wisdom of not paying enough attention to my surroundings to be able to even drop the right names after the biggest party of the year.

Tonight we made a super DIY music video for the song I "recorded" promoting next week's trip to SXSW, which sounds terrible, and I fear I am embarrassing myself beyond the pale this time. The backup dancers (I use the term "dancer" loosely) were from Hogs & Heifers and one offered herself up to me, but she seemed very high (pills?), so maybe she thought I was somebody else. I didn't take her up on her offer, tempting as it was not. Kimmel announced his guests for next week and blissfully there's no one that's going to make us look like losers. He's doing my show, which is great for us.

Wacha and I snuggled after my show; while I watched *Downton Abbey* he was chewing on his Kong to beat hell, so I thought. Turns out he ate a big chunk of my red cashmere blanket. So I'll be seeing that coming out of his ass over the next couple days. It's important to have things to look forward to.

Insane day—two *Housewives* conference calls, a pitch meeting about a potential show for me to produce at CAA's new offices in the Chrysler Building (highlight: the bathrooms are gorgeous!). I also saw a $12 million two-bedroom apartment (I think it used to be Jennifer Aniston's?) with Fredrik Eklund for the hell of it (highlight: great outdoor space) and spent an hour with the dog trainer, trying to teach Wacha how to chill out (highlight: he can kind of "shake"). To or from one of those meetings I wound up in a supercute cab I thought was a Mini Cooper but turned out to be a Ford. (Good for America!) My driver was so sweet, from North Africa. I was asking him about how he likes living in NYC and he started to give me the cheery version but it got deep fast, talking about how hard it is to make ends meet. He feels like he's on a constant merry-go-round and he will never get ahead. I felt horrible. Gave him a ten-dollar guilt-tip.

Wacha made his TV debut tonight and I asked the audience to refrain from applause so we didn't freak him out. I had given him some over-the-counter doggy downers but they didn't seem to faze him one way or the other. He was on my lap for the last four minutes of the show and he was perfect. I felt pride. For my dog. I never re-watch the show but I watched the Wacha section twice when I got home. He couldn't have been bothered to even glance at the TV. I should mention that I did *not* feel similar pride before the show when he shit some of that red blanket out, though it was oddly satisfying.

Wacha slept with me last night and it was bliss. Saw a little more of the blanket this morning before I went to the gym. Flew to Austin. I checked into the W to find not only an abundance of tequila, Fresca, and Swedish Fish waiting for me in my room, but two framed pictures (pulled off Instagram) of Wacha. Awesome celebrity perk! I was gobsmacked that someone took the time to do this. I had dinner with LZ and we gossiped and caught up for two straight hours. At the end we were trying to determine how many names we'd mentioned cumulatively. I said sixty; she thinks less. Feels exciting to be on the road with the show.

▦ FRIDAY, MARCH 7, 2014—AUSTIN

I opened my shades this morning and I have a clear view of the massive complex where Kimmel is doing his show—with a huge banner that has his show's logo and a map of Texas. So that's what I'm gonna be looking at all week. I rethought the name count from last night and I think it's closer to one hundred. I worked out with an Austin-based trainer whom I have booked for the whole week. He seems good, if a little too into Kesha's "Timber." I sweat my ass off.

I hosted a panel today about "Super Fandom in the Digital Age" with YouTube stars Tyler Oakley, Grace Helbig, and a content producer for BuzzFeed. I was literally so bored that I struggled to keep my eyes open, much less not yawn (I let three slip). I fake-laughed *a lot.* Then I shot a cold open on a cowboy's back on Sixth Street and the cowboy face-planted—simultaneously hilarious and painful. Had dinner with my *WWHL* team, then went to meet Bryan and Billie at the opening party for *Chef,* where I saw a little of Gary Clark Jr. (amazing), then went to Maggie Mae's, where I schmoozed around at a Bravo ad-sales party and posed for funny pics with a guy who was either passed out drunk or sleeping in the corner. I think people were more entertained by him than they were by my panel today. I wound up meeting the posse of a trainer I'd met at the gym (gyms are the best place to hook right in with randoms in a foreign city) and flirted with a twenty-four-year-old yoga teacher all night who is straight but was very handsy, reaffirming my forever-belief that flirting with straight guys is just an epic waste of energy and resources, resulting in blue balls and frustration. We all wound up at Rain on 4th, where a lady who looked just like Barbra Streisand from *The Main Event* told me how disappointing it was to finally meet me in person because I didn't give her the "hello" she felt she deserved while I was midway through ordering drinks for ten people.

▦ SATURDAY, MARCH 8, 2014—AUSTIN

Feeling a little uneasy about tomorrow's show with Jimmy Kimmel—it's my normal nerves associated with a big straight comedian I've never met coming on the show (See: Will Ferrell and Steve Carell). I have changed "the creative" for his show twice since being down here and am still not sure it's right. Feeling great about the rest of the week, though, and did lots of press today to get the word out. The set is gorgeous and Steadicam Steve is back for the second year to taunt us all with his beauty behind the roving camera. Oh, and we have a whopping 150 people in the audience, which feels like Madison Square Garden to me. Ian Somerhalder came and shot a cold open with me; the guy is so sweet and touchy-feely, and now that I think about it, fairly smoochy. We kissed maybe ten times. We love each other. And I watched him do his hair, which was a flurry of tornado-like motion on top of his head—like he was jerking off his head, basically. He knows what he's doing, though. I shot a *Friday Night Lights*–themed cold open with Seth Meyers in the women's locker room of the YWCA, which kind of went against the testosterone we were projecting dressed in our matching Coach Taylor outfits. We were so excited to be in Dillon Panther outfits that it didn't particularly matter where we were. Had dinner at the Driskill, which sucked, with Jason Blum, Bryan, and Billie. Then went to NBC's party for Seth, where he and I discussed the fact that no one upon no one knows how to operate their cell phone cameras. Also several people passed gas when I was talking to them, and come to think of it the same thing happened last night. I don't know if it's all the Mexican food in Austin or people think it's so crowded at these parties that they can get away with it. They can't.

▦ SUNDAY, MARCH 9, 2014—AUSTIN

We did two shows today. Our first (for air Wednesday) was with Seth Rogen and Dave Franco. It was a great one with probably a little too much pot talk. Kimmel was on the live show and we rejiggered a bunch of stuff during run-through and I went into it finally feeling like we'd gotten it right. I went to say hi before the show and he had a roomful of people with him. (I recently discovered that late-night hosts roll deep with big posses wherever they go. Yet I keep showing up alone. Maybe I need to drag Michael, Daryn, and Ryan with me everywhere, but I don't think they'll do it, which makes me like them even more.) Kimmel couldn't have been more pleasant and I was glad he brought his wife, who is also from St. Louis. She and I did the normal St. Louis thing, which comes down to sniffing each other's butts asking where you went to high school, etc. We had a local Austin dude warming up the audience and we forgot to warm *him* up, so the show began with our "huge" audience sitting there not clapping, which was highly embarrassing and almost resulted in a half hour of intense schvitzing with Jimmy, but I got my shit together. Got an email from Nancy Fallon during the show saying that she and Jimmy were watching, which made me feel like I was cheating on Jimmy with another Jimmy. I am a little codependent. The interview went really well and Kimmel was all compliments afterwards. I felt really good about it. He looked thin and told me about his crazy eating plan; I think he said there are some days where he doesn't eat at all, or only eats one meal a day . . . ? Whatever it was, it sounded painful but seems to be working.

Went to an Irish bar with Michael and Deirdre after the show.

▦ MONDAY, MARCH 10, 2014—AUSTIN

I guess I got caught up in the "excitement" of the tech buzz around me and randomly joined Tinder. So I spent a good portion of the day swiping people's faces away in a fluid stream of rejection. I said yes to a few, though. I feel like that date with the actor last month left me wanting more; Tinder is my ticket to meeting people I wouldn't normally come across, like an architect who lives in Murray Hill, or a scientist from Williamsburg. (Welcome to my rich fantasyland.)

We had two shows again today and during run-through for the Shaq show I decided that the funniest thing would be (during "Plead the Fifth") to mention how big his shoes are (size 23) and ask him straight up how big his dick is. Before the show I went into his dressing room and was totally intimidated by not just his size but his attitude, which immediately conveyed something to the effect of "Are you gonna fuck with me out there? You gonna ask me about old girlfriends?" I told him that in fact I would be *celebrating* him and not fucking with him. I asked if he'd done Stern because I am the gentler version. "I did and I OWNED HIM." Fine, I told him, *you will own me too.* I walked out of there muttering into my mic to the control room that I couldn't possibly ask him how big his dick is. I started the show thinking I was going to bag it but he turned incredibly playful once the cameras went up and I went for it. The question itself got a huge response from the audience and he took his shoe off and put it on his leg to give me a sense of what he was dealing with. Cousin Dave was in the front row, apoplectic. It was a moment. Shaq is one of my new favorite guests.

I was meeting and greeting people after the show and a blond woman approached me. She was shaking. "I need to say something to you," she said with her voice trembling. "I am a very conservative woman. Do you understand? I am *conservative.* I want you to know that you have changed the way I think about a lot of things. I need you to know that. You changed the way I think." I gave her the biggest hug. I was so happy. She couldn't have said anything better to me.

I ate insane barbeque from Salt Lick—sausage, ribs, chicken, the whole thing.

▦ TUESDAY, MARCH 11, 2014—AUSTIN

It was a beautiful day and I ate three tacos, a piece of pizza, and ice cream. I'm training every day (lots of "Timber") but also taking advantage of Austin—that's my philosophy and we'll see what kind of a disaster it nets out to when I see the Ninj next week. Sonja performed a "Tex-burlesque" that was a minute and a half in rehearsal and like four minutes on live TV. It was endless and I didn't know how to stop it. I didn't want to offend her by walking in during the middle when I was the one who'd asked her to do it.

We had a wrap party in the front bar of Rain on 4th and a few hours in started to get sick of each other, so we sent Anthony and Chase back into the club to grab some cute people to liven up the joint. I spent a fair amount of time flirting with this really tall, muscular guy. I was on and off with him all night and near the end John Hill whispered in my ear, "Are you enjoying those heels?" at which point I looked down and realized this dude was wearing *sky-high heels*. Not even platform shoes, heels. He became a little less hot after that. (Just a hair.) We went to a smoky after-hours club and danced to early nineties music.

Made two matches on Tinder.

▦ WEDNESDAY, MARCH 12, 2014—AUSTIN

We had the day off. It was fantastic. The gang from *WWHL* who stayed behind went to see the Mowgli's, then had dinner at Paul Qui's restaurant, then to a party where Aloe Blacc ("Wake Me Up") sang and I once again walked into several farts. WTF is going on with the gas at SXSW?? John Hill and I went to see Jay Z and Kanye West—it was really powerful. I only knew 35 percent of the songs but it didn't matter.

▦ THURSDAY, MARCH 13, 2014—AUSTIN–NYC

Woke up to news that there was a bad car crash blocks from where we were last night. A drunk driver. People killed. The whole plane home I was thinking about our promoting drinking so much and I am going to start asking people to not drink and drive at the end of every episode. It's the right thing to do after getting people wasted.

Had two interesting calls in the car home from the airport. The first was a pre-interview for *Fallon*, which I'm doing tomorrow. It wasn't great. I don't feel like I have a thing to talk about and I wasn't particularly funny at all. I don't know how that is going to go my way. I'm racking my brain trying to think of funny things. I flirted with a guy in high heels? I asked Shaq his dick size? The second call was from building management—not Mr. Liebowitz—saying the apartment upstairs was on the market and they'd begun showing it. I asked the price and then I told her I wanted it. We agreed that I'd see it in a few hours, and when I hung up I realized she really didn't get that I was saying that *I want it*. I called her back and said I am buying the place and can close in thirty days and get a mortgage and all the rest. When I got home, I went upstairs to see it with her (I had to pretend I hadn't already because I'd snuck in there when I did see it). It's still a dump but I am buying the space, that's it. Absurdly, there was an item in the *Post* today saying I was looking for $12 million apartments with Fredrik. So that was possibly the worst timing ever for a stupid item to appear, on the very day I make an offer for the apartment. I was about to get my jumbo massage tonight when the phone rang and it was the broker saying they'd accepted my offer. I am so excited. And yet I still have nothing to talk about on *Fallon* tomorrow.

FRIDAY, MARCH 14, 2014—NYC–SAG HARBOR

The Shaq episode aired last night and everybody's talking about the dick question. (And by "everybody" I mean a bunch of shitty entertainment blogs.) As it turns out, I have heard from two people who claim to know that Shaq's dick actually *isn't* so big.

I got picked up at five forty-five this morning to shoot the "Summer by Bravo" spot, for which I was in a *vile* mood, obviously because of my start time. There was a time not too long ago that I could dig into my well of enthusiasm to muster up the energy for dressing as a circus barker and smiling wide in front of a green screen, but I was so tired from the week and I felt like I'd hit my breaking point. Luckily, also there were Padma, Gail, Tom, Fredrik Eklund, James Lipton, and Bevy—so it was a low-drama, mellow crowd. Fredrik referred me to his real estate lawyer, who's going to do the deal for my apartment. We shot a thing where Padma and I get our legs cut off and switched. I really don't care for the circus one bit.

Bruce came to *Fallon* with me; he wanted to be there for my first appearance on the NYC *Tonight Show* and it became something of a full-circle moment for us because Bruce more than anybody has been there for me from the very beginning of my wanting to be on air and then slowly getting on air. He (and Lynn and Liza) gave me notes on every TV interview I gave in the years leading up to *WWHL* getting picked up. His being there made it extra special and fun. The energy backstage was electric; it felt like it does backstage at *SNL*—people racing everywhere, costumes, music, crowds. Janice Huff walked by my dressing room and popped in to say hi. Hearing the Empress of NYC Weather™ tell me *personally* that it was gonna be gorgeous tomorrow but cool down Sunday and perhaps snow again Monday gave me chills (for more than one reason—this winter will not end). Questlove came in too and the three of us took pics together.

I got briefed and nonetheless turned to Bruce and said, "What the hell am I gonna talk about?" When I was finally out there, Jimmy and I just vibed off each other and vamped. He spontaneously suggested at one point that I should go on Tinder, which was hilarious given that I just did a few days ago. He kept me onstage to panel and I couldn't have been happier. His energy is infectious.

I drove out to the Hamptons feeling on top of the world: about the week in Austin, my apartment, *The Tonight Show*, and Wacha. I listened to the Grateful Dead for two hours in the car, and everything felt exactly right.

I got to the house—first time since November (the weekend I realized Wacha's hip was bad and I was fat)—and it was in great shape. Headed to Albert Bianchini's for some cocktails and when I got home watched Wacha chase his own shadow for ten minutes. He is officially dumb. How could I ever think he is smart? Literally he was chasing his shadow. It sure was cute, though.

▦ SATURDAY, MARCH 15, 2014—SAG HARBOR

Today was a new best day ever for Wacha—he keeps topping himself. We woke up and went for a run together by the water, which was great for me because he forced me to go at a good pace and kept looking up at me smiling. Then we had an epic eight-hour hangout with Jimmy and Nancy during which Wacha and Gary Fallon ran and frolicked and then ran and frolicked some more. I ate a jumbo bag of Doritos, then Jimmy made ground beef tacos, then I ate more Doritos. And I drank several Fresquilas. We laughed and listened to music and talked and talked and talked. I wonder if I overstayed my welcome. Would they have kicked me out? It was awesome and I was asleep by eleven. Maybe it was one of my best days ever too.

SUNDAY, MARCH 16, 2014—SAG HARBOR–NYC

We had a lazy drive home from the beach. I Skyped with Mom and Dad and Mom says she shrunk another half inch. She thinks it is humiliating being this height and though she has nothing against little people she is very upset that she is becoming one. Her words.

Lady Gaga's manager came by to show me the "G.U.Y." video and we shot my reaction to it for a YouTube video. The Housewives look great. I'm in two shots, so it doesn't seem like that big of a deal, but what do I know? I like being there for posterity.

MONDAY, MARCH 17, 2014

After the gym I hosted a panel for hundreds of NBCUniversal ad-sales people. I'd guzzled two bottles of water before going onstage, so the entire hour was a countdown to the bathroom. I thought I was going to pee in the chair. It was a nightmare. The rest of the day was mortgage contracts, the dog trainer, two shows, screening some stuff, and a couple conference calls. My office at *WWHL* is almost done.

I am bored of Tinder.

TUESDAY, MARCH 18, 2014

Today is the fifth anniversary of Tasha's death. I was going through old photos, sending them to mutual friends, looking at the blog I wrote the week she died, clips of her on YouTube, and got really down. I feel like she's missed so much and I miss her so much every day. I can't believe it's been five years. It just doesn't seem possible.

Before the show I took Wacha to Bruce's and of course his doorman gave me his blank stare. How is it that Surfin remembers *everyone* but every day for this man is like Groundhog Day?

When we got home, Wacha started getting out on the wrong floor. The man in the elevator turned to me and said, "He's dumb, but he sure is handsome." Let it be said that *I* am the only one allowed to call my dog dumb.

Sultan's Pizza on Greenwich Avenue went out of business and I'm not crying over that one. They were mean and stupid. And Nikki—the chattiest lady on my block, who owns Tea and Sympathy and has the 411 on everything and everyone—and I were *convinced* that place was a front for something anyway.

▦ WEDNESDAY, MARCH 19, 2014

I had Wacha dry-cleaned while I was at the gym today and his fur is so soft and shiny. I brought him to Starbucks and the manager finally busted me for bringing the dog in. I've been waiting for someone to tell me it was illegal. I had a good run there for a couple months.

My cab driver to CAA today was Bangladeshi and Adorable, which I believe makes him Bangladorable. I tweeted as much and then wondered whether it was racist in any way. I swear sometimes I do hold my breath after I tweet, wondering, "Is this the one that will get me fired?" I am almost tempted to just tweet something horribly racist or vile or anti-Comcast, just to see how quickly I can destroy my wonderful life. Is that normal? When I was a kid I would fantasize about opening the car door when we were on the highway. I guess it's kind of similar to that. I can't be alone here.

I was pitched two shows today. One is with Mike Darnell and it's based on people telling stories about sleeping with athletes and rock stars—called *I Slept with a Celebrity*. It's an idea whose sleaziness absolutely does not preclude it from becoming a big hit. Worth pursuing if we can find a way to introduce a modicum of taste. We'll develop it together, take it out to networks, and see what happens. No harm, no foul.

I had dinner with Bruce (at Good) before the show and he came and stayed after.

Miss Piggy was on. The puppeteer's arm hurt and so there was a little drama with that, an issue I can't say I've confronted before. Made two Tinder matches with people who are very age inappropriate.

⸬ THURSDAY, MARCH 20, 2014

Today was the first day of spring and it was actually finally kind of nice. Kind of.

I met with my tax guy and was on Tinder swiping away while he talked to me about my finances. When will I stop acting like a seventeen-year-old? I am waiting.

We have a week off *WWHL* coming up and I can't decide where to go or what to do. John Mayer invited me to Montana and I also want to go to Miami, but I should also go to Sag Harbor and try to get some work done. As you get older, vacation time can be a little depressing for a single guy.

Had dinner with Bruce and Liza at Catch. Hung Huynh is the chef and brought us out a lot of extra food and I gorged on lobster mac and cheese, which is as amazing as it sounds. Liza's wedding isn't until August but it's ripe for plenty of conversation, which suits me just fine. A fan sent us a round of drinks and came over to tell us she absolutely did not want to speak to us or bother us, she just really wanted to send us a round of drinks, which was so nice. We told the waiter we were all set for drinks, but maybe he did bill our last round to the woman, who then came over and wanted a long discussion about what kind of drinks we had ordered. She kept saying, "It's no big deal, I just want to know. . . ." It turned into a whole drawn-out thing, which seemed contrary to her original goal.

Enrique Iglesias was on the show and I don't think he had a very good time.

Came to New Orleans at the crack of dawn for Dave Serwatka's wedding, which I wouldn't have missed for the world. After all, Dave and I have been *through it* together working at TRIO and then Bravo for years—big life stuff and late nights all over the country on the set of *Top Chef*. My room at Soniat House wasn't ready when I arrived, so I wandered around the French Quarter, where a beautiful guy with huge blue eyes, bulges everywhere, and a southern accent came up to me and asked if I was me. He told me he was a cheerleader for Kentucky and was on his way to meet his gay dads at the gym. I stopped. Wait—*what?* I had a million questions and was intrigued (gay dads?), turned on (the eyes and the body), conflicted (I should be thinking about his dads, not him), and excited (See: the eyes and the body). There was no way I was letting this kid go without a plan to have tea after his gym—I needed some answers to my questions. (I love a backstory!)

I went back to the hotel to press my cream suit, which Bryan advised I could wear to the wedding because it's officially spring. (I am a season jumper and have worn white tuxedoes at the wrong time of year several times, including Oscar night a couple years ago, when Valentino told me I looked "very Côte d'Azur" and Graydon Carter said he confused me with a waiter. Oh, the shaaaaade, hunty.)

Suit pressed, I met the kid for tea. He answered all my questions—we talked about cheering and his ex-boyfriend and his dad coming out and the dad's boyfriend. And we took selfies. And what I really wanted to be doing, while legal, would certainly be frowned upon by his *dads that are my age*. And I had to get dressed for the wedding.

The wedding was packed with people I love from TRIO and Bravo—from Magical Elves Dan and Jane to LZ and my beloved old assistant Thierry, who now lives in Australia. It was in a beautiful old church across from Soniat House and when it was over a band led us dancing around the block and right into a perfect reception, which was more like a choose-your-own-adventure party. There were two bands and a DJ, food by John Besh, a photobooth with props, a hashtag for Instagramming pictures (it's #loridavelove—look it up!), and lots of booze. A guest insisted on going through every person with the last name Cohen that she knows in New

York City to see if I knew them or am related and would not hear my plea that there are too many Cohens for this exercise to be worthwhile. Sometimes people hear what they want to hear. Around 10 p.m. someone slipped me half an Adderall and the night was perfect. Love, love, love.

SATURDAY, MARCH 22, 2014—NEW ORLEANS–NYC

I decided to go to Montana next weekend, then Miami. I think it'll be a fun adventure.

Landed back in NYC to a gorgeous day. I can feel spring. I took Wacha on a massive shopping trek around the West Village. Every store in the neighborhood has dog treats and I was trying to get him to show off by having him lie down for a treat and he failed every time. Had a great wander around Three Lives Bookstore on Tenth Street and couldn't help but wonder how long until it gets driven out by a greedy landlord. The state of this city is really depressing. Fantastic independent neighborhood staples are closing one after the other. *Do we need another Duane Reade???* Can the human beings of Manhattan suddenly not maintain their life systems without a freaking drugstore and ATM on their block?

Dinner celebrating Aries birthdays of SJP, Amy Sedaris, and Bruce at Betony on Fifty-seventh Street—we were trying to get out of our box, so we went to Midtown. I was playing with my rings and lost one and it became a huge scene with flashlights involved. SJP, bless her, was determined to find it. At the last minute she found it under her scarf on her jacket. Weird. And phew.

The Lady Gaga video for "G.U.Y." was posted tonight and I got a flood of tweets from her Little Monsters. We posted our response video tonight too. Who knows.

SUNDAY, MARCH 23, 2014

Wacha and I had a rough day. He was nipping at me in bed last night, so I put him in his crate and this morning he was driving me completely nuts, barking at nothing, hyper, the whole nine yards. I actually think the dog trainer is making him crazy. My bed is like a dog-toy showroom. Oh, and he won't shit. Meanwhile it is a tundra again outside and I'm really dizzy. Feeling defeated by it all.

Also I had orientation in the private dog run Marc Jacobs had told me about last fall. There are many rules and I feel like one wrong move by me or the WachStar will get us kicked out. It was a little terrifying. And windy.

Bruce had a birthday thing at Atlas Social Club (wanna see gay boys lose their shit? Bring DVF to a gay bar) and then dinner at Añejo. I was showing Anderson, Hamilton, and Michael how Tinder works and Barry took my phone and started swiping "yes" to a bunch of "nos"— one of whom looks like Diana Ross but is a man (which given my love for Ms. Ross you might consider a positive for me, but is in fact not)— which then matched me with them. I felt like I was watching a runaway train. He freaking *owns Tinder*, so he knew exactly what he was doing. Lovely! I guess I can block them. I might add that everyone else thought it was hilarious. I had to leave early to go to the show.

The Gaga video got me a lot of respect from the kids at *WWHL*. They think it is a super-big deal. So now I know for sure.

▦ MONDAY, MARCH 24, 2014

Of course I woke up to a Tinder message from Male Diana Ross. Thank you, Barry Diller. I don't want to block the guy and offend him but I also don't want to engage. So I decided just to leave it hanging. Meanwhile someone I had been talking to blocked *me*, so who the hell do I think I am?

The day was cold and I'm still in a foul mood. I wasn't the only one. Walking Wacha this morning, I turned the corner from Horatio onto Greenwich and an old lady looked me up and down and snarled, "Oh, *give me a break.*" She just kept going. I didn't want to let her off the hook, though. I yelled at her as she crossed the street, "Give you a break about *what*? *What's your problem?*" She never looked back.

Sean was eliminated from *DWTS*. They kept Billy Dee Williams, who can barely walk, and got rid of him. I'm outraged! I want to start tweeting people to boycott the show, but NeNe is on it, so I won't.

I had two pitch meetings about new shows, during which Brandi called to ask if I would come buy a pie from her for a *Celebrity Apprentice* challenge. Thankfully, she and Kenya are on the same team. Otherwise I would've had to go to two different pie stores.

The show was Uma and Dominic Monaghan; Gaga called in and explained her video eloquently: "In the story, where I am beginning as the Phoenix, rising from the ashes, I go to the Hearst Castle in order to be brought back to life. As the people from the planet Venus dunk me into the Neptune pool, I am snapped back into reality by reality television. We wanted you to play Zeus or God in the sky because I feel as though reality TV and reality media really runs our lives. It's really an image of how I think pop culture is today." Smart . . .

After all the Zeus talk and my posting a throwback paparazzi pic of Uma and me on the beach in St. Tropez, I got a text from Mom saying, "Reunion was really good. They r giving it to Lisa! Ur show was good. Like Uma. Gaga good. Aftershow short. Lay off urself for a while. Getting too self-centered:). Love mom."

I spent most of the two hours of my post-show massage pondering how a talk-show host can *not* become a totally self-obsessed monster, and whether I had gone to the dark side already. People, fans of the show, keep sending in paintings of me and I asked Deirdre to put them up in the control room because I didn't know what to do with them myself. Suddenly I wondered if that was megalomaniacal of me. Is everyone laughing behind my back? While I in the meantime am a tornado of self-promotion, Instagramming endlessly, blathering on Twitter, windbagging on television, and *publishing a diary*(!) about essentially *nothing*. Is it too late for me? Can I go bartend on an island and find myself, or am I past the point of no return? The massage was *not* relaxing.

▦ TUESDAY, MARCH 25, 2014

Wacha took three shits on his morning walk. Consecutively. I marveled.

After the gym I ran over to Union Square in my sweats to support Kenya and Brandi at the *Celebrity Apprentice* challenge. I didn't give any thought to the number of cameras and press that would be there, so showing up in gym clothes might have been dumb. (Or maybe, just maybe, I was keeping it real because I am *not a monster*.) Leeza Gibbons gave me a pie. Vivica A. Fox rang me up. Apparently Kate Gosselin was there but I didn't recognize her, I guess, which is a good thing because I have talked a lot of shit on Twitter about what an awful person she is. Also I made a mean joke on camera about Brandi not being able to add and I feel bad.

The dog trainer came and told me Wacha is mouthy and easily aroused. I wanted to say, "Stop talking about *me* and tell me about my *dog*!" (I'm here all week, folks. . . .)

We taped a show with the Long Island Medium and she did a spontaneous reading on Marc, our Deadhead cameraman, that blew his and everyone's minds. I asked for a few minutes with her afterwards to see if Natasha would come through; she didn't, so it was a lot of fishing.

Bethenny and Ramona were on and Ramona texted me earlier in the day to confirm that I would not be asking about her divorce from Mario. I confirmed with her that I *would* be asking about her divorce from Mario. So we went back and forth on that a few times. And on the show of course I asked. The bartender was a zookeeper from San Diego. There was something hot about him.

I ate the *Celebrity Apprentice* chicken pie when I got home at one. It was gross.

▦ WEDNESDAY, MARCH 26, 2014—NYC–ATLANTA

Big article in the *Times* today about how all the bookstores in NYC are basically closed because of rents. So I was right to be worried the other day. Theresa Caputo's manager called Deirdre and said she feels terrible that she didn't give me a good reading and wants to do it over, a polite offer that I refused. Tash was either going to come through or not. Flew to Atlanta and went straight to a production meeting for the reunion tomorrow. There was last-minute drama involving whether Mama Joyce would come, but she's in and all else seems fine. (Which of course means we should be very worried.) Had dinner at Optimist with Lindsay Denman, who I see once a year when I come to Atlanta for a reunion, and forced him to take me to Swinging Richards, which is an amazing all-dude strip joint. Why is there no Swinging Richards in New York City? No bookstores and no strip joints, but plenty of Chipotles and Bank of Americas. It's not the city I moved to twenty-four years ago.

THURSDAY, MARCH 27, 2014—ATLANTA

The day started off great—I shared a Four Seasons elevator with four Portland Trail Blazers. I gazed up at them (while pretending not to gaze up at them) and wondered why I wasn't dating a pro basketball player, at which point I remembered that I am a forty-something-year-old short(ish) Jewish dude. *That's why I'm not dating a pro basketball player.* Also they are straight, to the best of my knowledge. So I nixed that fantasy.

I don't even know how to describe the reunion today. Messy, how's that? Kenya brought a scepter and a bullhorn (I *used to* love props because I'd viewed them as comedy) and she was waving both in Porsha's face, and Porsha just snapped. She stood up and got in Kenya's face. I stood to break them up and as soon as I did they somehow wound up on the floor with Porsha pulling Kenya's hair. It was ugly. I was upset—everybody was. My gut reaction was that we had to send Porsha home, and that she was not emotionally ready to handle going back into the verbal firing line with these women. Meanwhile she was worried she'd ended her whole "career" in the course of ten seconds. It was a bad look for the show and the women. Kenya filed a police report against Porsha, and the other women felt that Kenya had it coming because of the props.

It was just a weird, bad day. And I found out that NeNe was apparently pissed at me because I didn't seat her next to me when Paula Patton was on the show with her a few months ago. That's why she kept turning down requests to come back on. Seating is very important. This is the kind of advice I can offer the world.

John Mayer texted (during hour nine of shooting) asking if I wanna shoot guns this weekend. I said I thought so but I didn't want to shoot anything living. He said, "Not even gophers? They're terrible and we'd do a service to nature." I said we would discuss it. And I did think about guns and gophers for much of the time that the husbands (who were clearly pre-gaming backstage before they came out) were imparting their wisdom. I don't think I wanna shoot anything.

We wrapped around twelve-thirty, at which point I lunged for a cocktail.

▦ FRIDAY, MARCH 28, 2014—ATLANTA—MONTANA

I got invited to play in the MLB celebrity softball game the day before the All-Star Game in Minneapolis this summer and I am really tempted to do it. On the one hand, I am so uncoordinated and it's pinging every bad memory of the three nasty words Dad used to taunt me with after dinner ("wanna," "play," "catch") and the indignity of my horrible, sad Little League career. On the other hand, I'm stronger and older now; I *have* to be able to get through a game of softball at this point in my evolution as a human being, right? They say Jon Hamm is playing, which is alternately tempting and terrifying. He's on my show in a few weeks and I'm gonna ask him about it.

When I forwarded my parents the invitation, my dad emailed "wow" and my mom said, "This looks dumb to me." I also sent it to Consuelos to see if he wanted to do it with me. (He thinks he's gonna be shooting his show.) My flight attendant on the way to Montana was an Edie McClurg twin who was getting in my face and exaggerating everything loudly with a southern drawl steeped in kindness ("Want more IIIIICE?") but with undertones of rage and hatred. She might be worse than #BabyJaneFlightAttendant, I can't decide. I would barely look at her and didn't have lunch to spite her (but wound up being really hungry, so that backfired). As we were landing she went row by row: "It was SO NICE GETTING TO KNOW YOU!!!!!!" I gave her such side eye. "Although you didn't let me SERVE YOU ENOUGH! I hope you'll COME BACK TO DELTA and let me SERVE YOU!!!!" I swear that's what she said to me. I know it *seems* like I have a big problem with flight attendants but I really don't. It's just the ones who smother me with their big personalities.

SATURDAY, MARCH 29–MONDAY, MARCH 31, 2014— SOMEWHERE IN MONTANA

John picked me up at the airport—looking good in a big Montana truck—and immediately explained to me that gophers fuck up everything up here, they dig holes where they shouldn't and get under people's houses, and when they die, they are food for the birds. So it sounded like pretty "Circle of Life," *hakuna matata* stuff when he explained it, but I still didn't wind up killing any. I did a lot of napping, going deep with the Grateful Dead, taking walks by the Yellowstone River, and listening to John play guitar and sing. We made a few stops at the Albertsons in town—miles wide and deep with goodness—where I met a girl called Cierra ("like the mountains but with a 'C'") handing out peanut butter Pop-Tart samples. It turns out she hates Pop-Tarts and gave me many reasons why, which seems exactly contrary to how to sell Pop-Tarts but I didn't care (nor did I buy any). One thing is for sure, John Mayer cooks a mean breakfast and there's something hot about a pop star in sweats with bed head slaving over a hot skillet for his houseguest. Twice we went to Montana's Rib and Chop House, where everything was delicious and the whiskey tasted better than anywhere else. John is on a major cleanse/body-conditioning thing, so he's not drinking and looking hot as hell. He is, however, still having sober fun, which means we closed down a bar full of the entire town, men and women of all generations of mainly coal miners and cowboys, dancing together and each one a live wire who seemed to be simultaneously hugging you and picking a fight. I really had to be on my toes. They all thought I was Carson Daly, maybe because I was with John (who was convinced that they actually thought I was Carson *Kressley*). As I went to bed to the sounds of a rushing river, I realized how completely stressed I've been for the past few weeks. I took a lot of deep breaths. Which wasn't hard because the air is perfect.

I was so pumped to prank my mom today that Wacha and I got on Skype first thing and she said, "Oh, Wacha, are you sad that the Cardinals traded Michael Wacha?!?!" I was shocked. How could they trade him, and how could my mom have heard this news before I did?

"APRIL FOOLS!" she crowed.

Good one, Mom! Now it was my turn, and she teed it right up. "So who called yesterday? What's the news you couldn't tell me on email?" She was making it so easy.

"Don't be upset, but Bill Maher's people called and I got booked." She froze at my news. "Don't worry," I tacked on, "it's about *gay stuff*."

"GAY STUFF??" she howled. "Do you ever WATCH the show? Gay stuff? Well, is it POLITICAL? You're not that politically well read." She seemed weirdly mollified by the fact that the topic was gay and not political and wanted to know when it aired. She was happy to hear that I thought it would be in the next few weeks, when they're in France. Less misery for her. She told me to study up and I assured her I would.

"He does most of the talking, so just LET HIM TALK." Now she was starting with the advice. I needed to put an end to it.

"April Fools!"

"You SET ME UP for that! I was thinking all day someone had called you and COME OUT OF THE CLOSET!" Any time I call her with some kind of news she always assumes someone has come out. "That was a good one and I am just GLAD you're not doing it. Please don't tell me it's not true and you ARE doing it. ARE you doing it or NOT?"

Now she thought I was double punking her. Poor thing. I have made her so cynical. I told her it was a straight punk.

"OK, I get it. It's like the Shawnee thing but it lasted a minute, not a year."

Right! And in her defense she wound up accepting both my claims— that I was an Indian (See: *Most Talkative*) and a Bill Maher guest.

When that was over I sat on a bench in front of Bonsignour with Wacha and this neighborhood jackass that's always there was playing mind games with him to make him bark and drive him nuts, which he did. Rabbi Kleinbaum walked by on the street and I was too irritated to grab her and chat. Came home and found a jury summons in the mail! WTF! What about that celebrity free pass? I called Daryn, who has that lady's email address (because I got her tickets to my show!) and will see what's up.

At the gym I was talking to the trainers about getting ready for the MLB All-Star thing in July and they're going to take me to the batting cages. They asked what position I thought I should play. *Position?* I never gave any thought to being in the outfield in a *position* with a ball coming at me, in front of everyone. Then we pulled up the list of who played last year: Hamm and Chris Rock and Kevin James, along with a slew of former *professional* baseball players.

Who am I kidding? I can't do this.

Tonight was a command performance at a cocktail party for NBC-Universal ad-sales clients with a bunch of talent from different areas of the network, like Savannah Guthrie, Mark Feuerstein, Mika Brzezinski, and Joan Rivers. I chatted with Ronan Farrow. I don't see how he's not Sinatra's son; he's the spitting image.

Met the Perskys and Bruce at RedFarm on the Upper West Side and Bruce pointed out that there was a moment in time that Mia Farrow looked just like Sinatra too, so maybe Ronan just looks like his mom who looked like Sinatra. In any case, he looks nothing like Woody Allen, so that's something.

I had a two-hour massage and at one-fifteen I had to tell him to stop—I had to be up at six-thirty for Miami.

▦ WEDNESDAY, APRIL 2, 2014—NYC–MIAMI

Checking into the Delano in Miami makes me so happy—the smell, the vibe that is unmistakably Miami circa 1992, the Philippe Starck décor that serves drama and fun everywhere you look. I started coming here the minute it opened. Most of the times I stayed here, I was a "have-not"— waking up at 7 a.m. to save pool chairs for Bruce and me because they wouldn't reserve them for us; he and I getting kicked out of the elevator by Mr. Armani's security a month after the Versace/Andrew Cunanan mess. Now I can actually afford to be overcharged for everything from suntan oil and a salad to an ocean room with a balcony, and they'll save me chairs in exactly my favorite spot (halfway towards the bar on the bungalow side)—which is a great thing because I love hanging out at that pool for six-to-eight-hour stretches watching the scene unfold in front of me. It is mostly populated by attractive liars and fakes (and the people who love them, like me) who want to tell you their stories, like "I'm a model!" (um, no you're not) or "I'm a movie producer" (with no actual credits?). There are more fake boobs at that pool than at a *Real Housewives* open call. (Btw, we don't do open calls.)

Sitting there today—in my two designated seats for the week—I became obsessed with a gorgeous couple I have decided cannot be American. He has a great body and a lot of style; she is a beauty and half her (perfect) ass is hanging out of her bikini bottoms. They're all over each other and in their own world. They don't even seem to care about the circus playing out in front of us, which made me feel a little bit like a bottom feeder.

Tonight my friend Alex showed me his new boutique hotel and took me to a strip club. Two strip clubs in a week is pretty much my quota for the year, although I still can't get over that there aren't any like this in Manhattan. I used to blame Giuliani for shutting down all the smut, but I'm soon gonna start blaming de Blasio if he doesn't start returning a lil filth to Manhattan. I have faith.

▦ THURSDAY, APRIL 3, 2014—MIAMI

I reserved a big Aryan ginger dude to train me on the beach every day and so we met this morning at eleven. I didn't reserve a specific type of trainer, of course, but it became a happy ginger coincidence when he appeared.

I spent the rest of the day at the pool and decided the hot couple is definitely Brazilian. They're clearly very in love. I've also got my eyes on a girl who seems to live on a raft. Her spray tan is like a real-life Instagram filter. She looks like Sutra. With enormous boobs. Some dude with her had Björn Borg undies sticking out of his shorts. So now I know who (besides John McEnroe) wears Björn Borg underwear: Euros who frequent the Delano.

I had a Tinder date tonight—my first—with an Italian lawyer from New York who was in town on business. As I was waiting for him by the bar in the back of the hotel, I ran into Carson Kressley. It was great to see Car-Car, but as soon as the Italian arrived we ducked into a corner. The date was not successful—not a ton of chemistry. One plus was that he had no idea who I am, so it was all fresh and new, which I liked. He seemed confused when people kept coming up for photos.

We booked JLo for the show, which is good timing because I'm in Miami obsessed with "I Luh Ya Papi." I predict a conference call to discuss her wants and needs imminently. Daryn heard from the jury-duty lady and she said there's nothing she can do to help, she's federal court and this is another branch. Oh, and she wants to redeem the tickets I promised her when she supposedly let me go for four years. So this is payback for reveling in a celebrity loophole. I guess I deserve it.

FRIDAY, APRIL 4, 2014—MIAMI

Super hot today. Working out with the Ginger on the beach today, I was sweating my ass off and two paparazzi were in the bushes shooting the whole thing, which was awkward. Who would want those pictures?

My buddy from the Cardinals, reliever Jason Motte, was in Jupiter for extended spring training and saw on Twitter that I am in Miami. He drove down for lunch, which turned into "Fifty Questions with a Baseball Player While I Slurp Whispering Angel!" "Who is the biggest dick on the team?" ("They don't allow dicks on the team.") "Do you get nervous?" ("Not much.") "Are you competitive with other people on your own team who play your position?" ("Not really.") "What's your least favorite city to play in?" ("Philadelphia is tough.") "What kinds of hotels do you stay in? Where do you sit on the plane? What is the food/drink situation on the plane? What time do you get to the games? When do you eat? What do you eat? What do you like to do in bed?" I asked all but the last one, and more. He is a really nice guy and answered them all. I told him I was starting to feel creepy for naming the dog after Michael Wacha because I don't want the dude to think I'm a stalker or obsessed with him or something. I think he's a great pitcher but it was a spontaneous decision. He said I shouldn't worry about it. And he was as amused by the pool situation as me, so it was good to have someone to discuss it with. He is heavily involved in charities for kids with cancer. Hearing him describe the kids made me very emo and motivated to get involved with one, maybe with Wacha. I asked him about the MLB thing, but he is exactly the wrong person to ask because he can't relate to my Little League impotence.

After he left, I at last got to talking to the hot couple. Turns out he's British (in finance) and she's American (a dancer). They'd been judging the same people as me, so we mind-melded and judged together for about ninety minutes. There was a massive bachelor party going on around us, with groups of guys drinking hundreds of Corona Lights while standing around rafts talking to each other. What the Brit realized is that none of them ever left the pool, which meant they were all just pissing on each other underwater all day. Wonderful. I grilled the hot couple about every detail of their relationship. They were quite forthcoming—they live together and are probably going to get engaged; sounds like they have a healthy sex life, and he manscapes.

Sent a polite follow-up text to the Tinder guy (I like to keep everything nice) and he responded, "If you didn't have the famous side I would've fallen for you but the attention you were getting killed my ego." So I was rejected by someone for my "fame" before I had a chance to reject him because we didn't have chemistry. Joke's on me!

Met Ryan who I kind of know from NYC and his friends at the Palace, which after all these years is still serving sunset sidewalk drag performances. It was so fun, but the margaritas are not what I remembered. Went to Score with my friend Jorge and cruised Latinos.

▦ SATURDAY, APRIL 5, 2014—MIAMI

I worked out in the sweltering beach heat with the Ginger while photographers started slowly assembling like ants taking pictures they won't be able to sell. I spent fifteen minutes by the pool trying to decide if it was depressing that I was here alone, but I decided that I love spending time alone and that I'm never alone even when I go away alone. I know a lot of people here and when I don't I meet new ones.

I think I have a sixth sense for people around me who are on meth. First it was my driver in LA a couple months ago, then today I realized that my waiter at the pool had to be high. It was a day of endless Whispering Angels with the hot couple, so I had plenty of time to observe him. He was alternately highly functioning and horrendous at his job. Two people separately came up to me in the pool and said I know their sisters-in-law, and I didn't know either sister-in-law. Near the end of the day, the methy waiter overheard me complaining to the hot couple about how atrocious the service was, which made me feel like a jerk and I wound up giving him a huge tip that will ultimately fuel his meth habit, thereby continuing to make him a poor waiter.

I met Ryan and his New York posse at the Palace at the end of the day and you cannot beat their sidewalk drag show. I video'd a lot of it. When am I ever going to watch that?

▦ SUNDAY, APRIL 6, 2014—MIAMI—NYC

Tanorexic that I am, I spent an early-morning couple hours getting the last minutes of sun by the pool before heading back to NYC and a gorgeous 55-degree spring day. Sat next to a guy on the flight home who made fun of me for being pleased about the spring that awaited me. People who live in nice weather year-round are prone to being barbarians towards people who have seasons. Let me enjoy my spring! I took Wacha to the private dog run in the West Village and he ran like a motherfucker for an hour. When your dog goes to the bathroom in the run, the rule is to get the hose and spray down their waste. It's phenomenally clean in there. I am fully on board with the rules. He was exhausted at the end, which as usual made me happy.

I Skyped with parentals and it turned out that Mom *was* pissed about the April Fools thing; it apparently brought up all her residual anger from the Shawnee Indian prank years ago. So that didn't go as smoothly as it seemed and maybe I should stop pranking her. Nah.

I brought Wacha to *WWHL* and gave him a huge frozen bone marrow to keep him occupied in my—now fully decked-out—office. He loved it in there and after the show I hung out and drank with Rashida Jones for ninety minutes. She is beyond cool and fun.

The jury-duty lady was supposed to come to the show tonight and *didn't show*! I should send *her* a summons for something!

▦ MONDAY, APRIL 7, 2014

There is maybe going to be a doorman strike in NYC and they have a sign-up for residents to man the door, so I signed up for a Monday slot, three to five. I am oddly excited to be a doorman. I was a great waiter when I was in college; I think it's a similar skill set.

Took Wacha to the dog run first thing this morning and it's a godsend. He was mellow all day from having run. I had my own great workout and then we taped an early show with the cast of *Southern Charm*. Thomas Ravenel kind of announced his candidacy for Senate in the state of South Carolina. But he also kind of didn't—if Lindsey Graham is the nominee then he's gonna run, is what he said. So, OK, I still maybe don't get it, and that's probably why my mom doesn't want me going on Bill Maher.

I went with Graciela, who had a bad tummy, to see Lady Gaga perform at the final night of Roseland. We saw Gayle King, who was sitting with Gaga's mother, who told us that Gaga was running late. (You feel special getting that kind of intel straight from the mouth of the mother of the Gaga.) Graciela and I were trying to remember all the shows we had seen over the years at Roseland—I listed a few B-52's gigs, several Broadway Bares, a few premieres, and there was a Madonna thing, but I knew I was missing something really gay. It turns out Grac had been christened "Maxi Halson" (her early nineties alter ego) at the White Party at Roseland. That was monumental.

The show was pretty great, although I wanted her to talk less and sing more. She climbed right up to our balcony when she sang "Bad Romance," but Grac was in the toilet and missed the whole song. My highlight was "Applause." We went backstage and while we were waiting schmoozed with Rita Wilson and Patty Smyth. I asked Patty if her husband was still wearing the Björn Borg underwear and she said he's all over them.

Gaga took a while to come out because she was changing into a completely different Gaga look with new makeup, hair, and dress. I killed time by flirting with her huge straight bodyguard. I made her bow to me (I am Zeus, after all) and she did. I gushed about the video and she said it's something everyone will recognize as great in ten years. She may be right. Maybe it went over everyone's heads; I know when she explained it to me I realized I hadn't really gotten it at all and I was in it.

⣿ TUESDAY, APRIL 8, 2014

Good news: Angela, Rashida's friend who lives on the eleventh floor, signed up to man the lobby with me. So I dodged some bullets there.

Got a top secret phone call from Lisa Kudrow and Michael Patrick King; they want to use me on the premiere episode of *The Comeback*, which apparently involves Valerie Cherish trying to make a pilot for me. I am dying. I LOVE *The Comeback* and would've been thrilled if they were simply calling to tell me that it was coming back. They told me not to tell anyone at all, and I am busting at the seams.

I did Kathie Lee Gifford's podcast and used it as an opportunity to coax her onto her soapbox about various things. I love it when she preaches the gospel of anything, for instance, "Please don't get an animal if you can't take care of it, please don't have kids if you can't deal with it." Just life stuff.

Clay Aiken called me asking to put my name on a benefit for his congressional run. What is the appropriate response? I haven't been schooled in this particular etiquette. I know nothing of his platform or really anything about him. I said yes, but that I couldn't attend the actual event, which is the truth.

I got a two-hour afternoon massage and took calls and did work during it. It was very Sandy Gallin.

Taped a one-on-one with NeNe tonight. She said she actually wasn't mad about the Paula Patton seating. The live show was Aviva and Carol Leifer. I was off my game and made a terrible Betty Ford joke when I said the drinking word. I said that it was her birthday and if she had taken better care of herself she would've lived to play the drinking game. OK, now I think it's actually pretty funny.

I told John Hill about *The Comeback*. I had to.

▦ WEDNESDAY, APRIL 9, 2014

I have gone to the private dog run every day this week. At ten-thirty in the morning, it is full of straight men who don't seem to have jobs. Today they talked about Chris Christie, their kids' school auctions, Mike Tyson, and a TV show I'd never heard of (odd). I felt like I was in a weird club. I actually felt like a bro. They all talk about each other's dogs too. A lot. And when each new person and dog arrive they make a big thing about the dog: "Uh-oh, here comes Klondike!" Wacha is fitting in well. He is the cutest of them all. And I am being totally objective.

I did a green-screen shoot and photo shoot with Wacha for Bravo this afternoon. He was a little all over the place but they got enough stuff they can use.

Amanda and I had dinner, then saw the Carole King musical, which we loved. The people in the theater were dressed like shit. Just no effort whatsoever. The tickets are so expensive you think it might make people want to dress well, but they go the other way. I ran out during the last song, grabbed Wacha at home, and brought him to the show. The *Million Dollar Listing New York* guys were on with Wacha—they were all perfect.

▦ THURSDAY, APRIL 10, 2014

I am 166.4—spitting distance from 165, which was my goal—and now I think I wanna go for 160. I have been working out like a motherfucker and eating protein like a champ. Tomorrow night is going to set me back, though, because I'm going to Sam's in East Hampton and plan to inhale a medium pizza.

All the talk in the building is about the doorman strike. I tried to get Surfin to come to my Tracy Morgan show but he thinks Morgan mugs too much and doesn't want to come. What do you *really* think of Tracy Morgan, Surfin?

Wacha walked his first red carpet. I took him to some ASPCA fund-raiser, where I got in a fight with a photographer from Getty who was yelling at me to pose eighteen different ways. I couldn't because Wacha is a dog and sadly doesn't pose on command. Daryn came with me and took Wacha downtown so I could meet Liza at RedFarm. I walked her home and it was intensely depressing seeing what's happened to the Upper West Side—CVS, Marshalls, Starbucks, Bank of America, repeat. How do we stop the cycle of rents going up and everything unique about the city falling prey to greedy developers? And where does it end? We stopped in one of the few independent bookstores left in the city and I bought that Jim Morrison biography *No One Here Gets Out Alive*. I haven't read it since I loved it in college. I ended the night with a Tinder date with a guy who works for a magazine. Seems nice and very calm—I couldn't get a final read on him but he is handsome and smart. I want to see him again.

▦ FRIDAY, APRIL 11, 2014—NYC–SAG HARBOR

I ran at the gym and the heat was *pumping* on the top floor, so it was more like Bikram running. It was a gorgeous spring day and Wacha and I drove to the beach with the top down. I spoke to SJP on the way about the two free seats at her Met Ball table. An invitation to the Met Ball is a great one, so we were trying to think of a fantasy guest. Donna Tartt will be on a book tour in Finland and can't come. I suggested we try to invite a legend to such a legendary event, and the first legend who came to mind was Diana Ross. SJ thought that was a great idea, and we fanta-sized about Ms. Ross at our table in a dress by Mr. de la Renta. If I wind up next to Ms. Diana Ross wearing an Oscar de la Renta dress at the Met Ball, I will for sure poop my (fancy) pants. She is inviting Ms. Ross. I hope she comes; I just want to watch her all night. We don't even have to speak.

Went to Sam's Pizza with Marci and Andrew. The other night Marci saw an old acquaintance at a book party who asked her what she's doing these days and Marci said, *"Haven't I done enough?"* which is the best ever response to that question. In her case it's true, by the way. Sam's was incredible. I killed a well-done medium mushroom and onion, my regular order.

▦ SATURDAY, APRIL 12, 2014—SAG HARBOR

Today I saw the ghost of Esther Rolle. Before that, I took Wacha to brunch—then shopping—in East Hampton, then we went to the beach and just screwed around. It all went haywire when we took a run on Long Beach in the late afternoon and this woman gave me a big smile and it was unmistakably Esther Rolle, getting into a big gray van. She looked older than the *Good Times* Esther, and also a little Asian, so maybe she was the Asian Ghost of Esther Rolle. When she gave me that classic Florida Evans smile/side eye with her neck rolls bulging out, I slowed down to a gallop, my mouth hanging open. Simultaneously, closer to the ground, Wacha was transfixed by a pile of crushed matzo spread in front of him. Before I had time to process the ghost or the crushed matzo, I saw another pile, and then another pile beyond that. Horrified, I realized that I was in the middle of some Pagan anti-Passover ritual presided over by the Asian Ghost of Esther Rolle. When I turned back to see if she was torching a bottle of Manischewitz, she and the gray van were gone. Now I cannot figure out what the hell was going on, and why there were *seven* mounds of crushed matzo in the parking lot of this beach.

I had dinner at the Lobster Inn with Anderson and Benjamin—I didn't mention the matzo to them but did tell them about *The Comeback*, about which they were appropriately excited. There were a lot of talkers in the restaurant—everybody had a big personality and wanted to share it—and one dude and his wife twice pulled up chairs to our table to chat with us, which was incredibly ballsy. Jewish Long Islanders have moxie!

▦ SUNDAY, APRIL 13, 2014—SAG HARBOR—NYC

We went running this morning on a search for the Ghost of Esther Rolle but she and her gray van were nowhere. There were, however, the remnants of the matzo stacks. Went to Brooklyn for dinner at Jeanne and Fred's. Great to see the boys, who wanted to know "if celebrities get better Wi-Fi than regular people."

Mad Men premiere was sadly quite boring.

▦ MONDAY, APRIL 14, 2014

I wore shorts outside today and that needs to be noted given all the pain and suffering it took to get to this moment in the year. In said shorts, I sat in front of Bonsignour and that same jackass from last week was taunting Wacha, which makes him bark and go nuts. I told him that Wacha does not care for him at all, and he seemed awestruck, like he couldn't figure out what he could've possibly done to make this dog not like him.

I did a really stupid move at the gym where I was hanging on to a punching bag by my feet trying to pull myself into a sit-up but wound up falling with a thud right onto my back. It felt like I'd been punched. Between that and three long attempts to do a handstand, my body is going to kill tomorrow.

Had lunch with Bruce and after we went to three bodegas to find matzo, placing bets in front of each one about whether they'd have it. One lady thought I wanted juice(?) and pointed me to the cooler; the place on Bleecker and Eighth with the rotating checkers thought I wanted Wasa crackers. So it turns out you *can't* get everything at a bodega. Dave and I had a cozy lil Passover together at my house (his family is all in Florida) and he wound up bringing me a box of matzos and we had a lovely seder. I discovered there are less cals in a matzo than in a piece of whole-wheat bread, so that's my new breakfast. He turned me on to Arcade Fire and we watched a lot of their videos. Jeanne and Fred brought the boys to the show and they seemed to have a blast. I loved having them there; I felt like I had to be funny for them.

I signed Wacha up for Twitter and Instagram. He is @TheRealWacha. @WachaCohen is still taken by a stranger who is tweeting as my dog—which is not weird at all.

▦ TUESDAY, APRIL 15, 2014

There is an article in the *NY Post* today that says we're going to have the most brutal summer ever—horrible humidity and terrible rain—which put me in a foul mood all day. I don't know when I started letting weather bum me out; it may be because I view it as a sign of the planet falling apart and a precursor to the upcoming apocalypse, or maybe I'm perimenopausal.

The NeNe one-on-one that aired on Sunday night got 3.5 million viewers. We beat the MTV Movie Awards and NBC and ABC. And all I can think of is that NeNe's gonna want to raise her fee. Oy. I took Joey to J.Crew's Ludlow store in Tribeca to pick out a suit for his eighth-grade graduation today; he looked so proud when he saw himself in the mirror. It was very sweet. I bought a couple myself. (It's like they're giving suits away there.) We had a Friends In Deed board meeting and I am not feeling confident about our June fundraiser. We have a lot of work to do. I think we're going to postpone it till the fall. (I am a firm believer in postponing things if they won't be great.)

Before the show I got in a K-hole about our lead-in, which was shitty, then we got word that the temp outside had plummeted and the rain had turned to snow, and I went into a serious funk. Had another date with the Tinder/magazine guy after the show. He has a sweet temperament. We kissed in the (empty) bar at the end of the night. It wasn't an amazing kiss but I shouldn't kibosh the whole thing based on a couple bad kisses, right? And it was still snowing to beat hell when he walked me home at 2 a.m. Snowing. Again.

WEDNESDAY, APRIL 16, 2014

I have tickets to *Hedwig* Saturday and the question is whether to bring Liza or the date from last night. I would probably have a better time with Liza, but when was the last time I brought a date to a show?

Bruce and I took Barkin to Cafe Cluny for a birthday lunch. Amy Poehler was there and we awkwardly said hi.

We taped Lindsay Lohan tonight for air tomorrow. There was a bet going in the control room about what time we would start taping. It was *Price Is Right* rules, so whoever came closest to the time without going over won. Dave Stanley won the pool—seventeen bucks. He guessed 8:34 and we started at 8:37. She had a crown, which she decided she was "over" midway through the show and took off. She was incredibly nice and kind of fragile. Her *Housewives* intro line brought down the house: "I'm through with mug shots and ready for my Oscar." I kept her cigarette butt and put it on a shelf in the Clubhouse next to Patti LaBelle's half-eaten Life Saver, and as I write this I'm wondering where we put the fake joint Seth Rogen rolled on the show. I know we kept it. Hmmm.

The live show was a treat: Joan Rivers and Tracy Morgan. I fangirl over Joan every time I get a chance to be with her on TV. I go right back to watching her on *The Tonight Show* and pinch myself that she's on my show. Speaking of pinched, you think she's a little more unrecognizable every time you see her, but then she opens her mouth and whips out some Helen Keller jokes and "It is JUST . . ." and *she* is just . . . Joan! She often brings a list of topics she wants you to talk about and tonight was "death, plastic surgery, Melissa, Kanye West." It is a joy to set her up to land a joke and watch her kill, and she did. Amanda and Jim were there—he's a big Joan fan and I got him a pic during a commercial. Tracy Morgan was in awe of her and we kept the after show going for a long time. It was a purely joyous night.

THURSDAY, APRIL 17, 2014

I'm 165 pounds! I can't even think of the last time I was this weight, maybe ten years ago. Wacha played with a very barky dog named Bellini at the dog run. Bellini's mouth doesn't move when he barks, so I've decided he's a ventriloquist dog.

I hailed a cab to take me to 30 Rock and was all excited when I opened my cab door and it was a LadyDriver wearing Dior sunglasses. I thought we were going to have a breezy fun ride uptown but she was mean as fuck. Scary, actually. She wanted nothing to do with me, my newspapers, my casual convo about traffic and Taxi TV. In summary, she was nasty. Nonetheless I gave her a three-dollar tip on fourteen dollars and she didn't seem too pleased with that either. Is that actually a really bad tip? I spent the day at Bravo. It was great to be back there. I need to go more. Julia Roberts isn't doing *WWHL* for *The Normal Heart* in May, so that's a bummer. I guess that schmooze over Oscar weekend didn't do the trick. One day . . .

Went to the Waverly for dinner with Mark and Kelly. Our waiter's skin was amazing and we bet on his age—*Price Is Right* rules—and I won. He was twenty-six. I did see the flirty waiter, and after all this time I have revised my opinion of him once again; he's nice and the fact that he's a dad has mellowed me about his history of flirting.

▦ FRIDAY, APRIL 18, 2014

All I really care about is Wacha's Instagram. I constantly think about what cute photo of him I can post and when. I am obsessing. He is up to 12k followers. This from the man who couldn't believe it when @Giggy ThePom demanded attention from me on Twitter.

Billy Joel is doing a residency at Madison Square Garden—one Friday a month for two years—and tonight Bruce, SJP, and I went. It was phenomenal. I guess Billy likes to leave the second the show is over, so he sees guests before he goes on, which seems efficient but, now that I know how incredible the show is, I would've been so much more enthusiastic back there after the show than I was before. We had pre-show energy, which pales in comparison to post-show ebullience. Backstage were Paul Reiser, Barry Levinson, Rosanna Scotto (I love a local news star), and John McEnroe. True to form, McEnroe said he was wearing the Björn Borg undies but that he's running out. I said I was sure Björn would send him a case and he said Borg is actually hard to track down. I wondered if he wasn't simply reachable at bjorn@bjornborg.com Ha-ha.

I had spent a few nights with Joel around the time Katie Lee was hosting *Top Chef*, and at that time he was kinda poking me, wondering when we were gonna pick up the show because season one had been such a hit, but I knew we were likely going to let Katie go, so it was a precarious dance. I wondered if he remembered any of it—he didn't let on one way or another and couldn't have been a more gracious host. Also they had some gorgeous Barolo back there, which we brought out to our seats and it took us through the night. We were about twenty-five rows back on the floor and I really hit the loser lottery with my seat partner, who was a curly-haired Billy Joel *fanatic*, amped up to beat hell, flagrantly violating my personal space with undulating dance moves and unyielding passion, which for me begged the question "Is 'Pressure' a song worthy of going all out?"

"You gotta rush the stage with me when 'Allentown' comes on! That's when you rush it! C'mon!!" He was begging me. I laughed, although I should mention that if there was a song that would've made me rush the stage it actually might've been "Allentown," because whenever the video came on—when I was sixteen—my pants went down and it was bedlam as I watched the bare-assed coal miners showering. It was before you had the capability to pause or rewind or anything, so you just had to do it the minute it came on. (I have spoken to other gay guys of my generation who experienced the same "Allentown" phenomenon. The Internet didn't exist!) Misplaced erotic memories of the video aside, I refused the opportunity to rush the stage when the first chords of "Allentown" emerged, and he was severely disappointed in me, and then probably more so at security, who kiboshed his rush mid-song.

When a chorus of uniformed officers came onstage during "Goodnight Saigon" I started tearing up, and by "Piano Man" I even began to soften towards my neighbor when I overheard him telling the people behind us (he was talking to everybody) that he was from Seattle and it was his dream to see Joel at Madison Square Garden. By "Scenes from an Italian Restaurant," he turned around to take in the sight of the entire New York metro area singing in unison about Brenda and Eddie and sighed to himself, "We don't have this at home." At that moment I was completely smitten. This man was having his moment and why should I begrudge him that? I was happy to have shared the night with him.

After the show we were searching for SJ's car and a woman, Patti, came up to me wanting an autograph, which I gave and enjoyed because it was old school. I was so immersed in searching for our car—OK, maybe I was actually freaking out a little bit because the guy was nowhere to be found—that when I noticed she was still standing there, I kind of shunted her away with a "Goodbye, Patti!!" Turns out she was the wife of the NYPD Chief of Patrol, who had parked right in front of MSG (um . . .), and we were standing in front of their car, blocking it. Good ole Patti was waiting for *me* to get my *ass out the way*!

We went to Odeon, which was a refreshing blast from the past. I learned that Diana Ross is not available to come to the Met Ball. Why would she be? She is Diana Ross, after all. I think SJ is going to ask André Leon Talley, who is something of an approximation of Ms. Ross if you really think about it.

⊞ SATURDAY, APRIL 19, 2014

Wacha has 21k followers on Instagram. I feel like JonBenét's parents, pushing him into the spotlight. (Although I won't wind up being suspected for his murder, of course.)

Ralph Fiennes met me at the dog run and as we caught up, Wacha was having intense playtime with a huge pack of dogs. Out of nowhere, all the owners started gathering their pooches and splitting like a bomb went off. "What's going on?" I asked one of the owners, who pointed at a man in the corner who concurrently said, "Who does this beagle belong to? *He has my dog's ball.*" What I learned is that this man is notoriously obsessive about his dog's ball to the point that no one wants to deal with him and everyone splits. After two rounds of him telling me to control my dog, I did too. We ran into a couple of the displaced dog owners on the street and Ralph became a cross between Lord Voldemort and Norma Rae: "You must *stand up* to this bully and *reclaim* your dog run! He does not have *jurisdiction* over your dog grabbing a random ball." He is so right! I can't wait to do the right thing next time I see this guy.

Jerry Seinfeld's mom died. The shiva starts Monday. I met her once and she was lovely, so it's sad. And on another note, I can't imagine how gorgeous the food will be at the shiva. Is it wrong to speculate?

I went to see *Hedwig* with the Tinder date. NPH was great but it's not my show. I didn't love it fifteen years ago and I didn't love it tonight. NPH said he'd been dealing with stomach flu and I told him to stick with it because it's making him really ripped. After the show we went to the Algonquin of all places and I was at least relieved to see that that was one New York institution that hadn't been converted into a Bank of America. We had a few drinks but I felt like the gulf in our ages was somehow getting more pronounced as the night went on, and we mutually ended the date by midnight. I happily went home, but Bruce was texting me to meet him, Barkin, and Bryan at Marie's Crisis ("Come for a few songs, I'll order you something"), which I was refusing to do. Then he sent me exactly the kind of text that will automatically get me to leave my apartment: "Someday we will all be dead and you will be praying for a Saturday night at Marie's with the gang." I went and it was, predictably, a lot of fun. Messy, but fun. I wound up at Two Boots breaking my great diet, bingeing on two pieces of pizza. Bryan dragged me out of there at two before I did something I would really regret.

⠿ SUNDAY, APRIL 20, 2014

Happy Easter! Happy 420! We had a debrief at the dog run about the bully, and we agreed to stand up to him next time. In the meantime Wacha fell in love with a big German shepherd.

It was a lovely drive upstate, where Vanessa Redgrave hosted me (and the WachStar) for Easter lunch—a mainstay holiday that Natasha pulled off flawlessly up there every year. It felt sweet to be there and catch up with everyone, with a sad undercurrent of memory and longing. I visited Tash on the way home. Dinner with Bruce, Bryan, and family at Mr Chow, where everything tastes like fried sugar, and then I got hammered on Twitter all night for my behavior at the Atlanta reunion. Everyone thought that I caused the fight and was wrong to tell Porsha to apologize. How can the producers and I have had the complete opposite reaction from the viewers to what happened?

MONDAY, APRIL 21, 2014

I am back up to 168—thank you, Two Boots pizza and Mr Chow.

The Met Ball is white tie this year, which means tails, and one of the few people who carry them is Ralph Lauren, where I had a fitting for mine. I looked like the caricature that Risko did of me.

I am still being hazed on my Twitter feed from people who hold me accountable for the fight at the reunion, for allowing the props and not foreseeing trouble. Violence is not in my vocabulary, but they don't believe me.

I had dinner before the show with Sandy and Barry at that steak house in the Time Warner Center. I can't get used to eating in a mall.

TUESDAY, APRIL 22, 2014

There's not going to be a doorman strike, so I won't be volunteering for any more door shifts. I am secretly a little disappointed. I like it when strangers have to band together through tough (but not too extended) times for the greater good. Anyway, I am happy for Surfin.

Wacha walks into that dog run and makes everything great—he's everybody's best friend and he loves to play. He's good energy. (That's what I think, but maybe when we leave they all talk about him, what do I know?) It turns out that his new German shepherd bestie has brain cancer. I am speechless.

An architect came by for an interview and we talked for an hour about various options for combining the apartments. My problem is that I have no attention span and after forty minutes my mind started to move on to the next thing. Not great. It's for *my benefit*, is what I always have to remind myself in situations like these.

I had been looking forward to tonight's show for some time because we had Jon Jay and Shelby Miller from the Cardinals behind the bar, and an audience full of Cardinals wives. (They're in town playing the Mets.) Nonetheless it took me a while to conjure up things to say to them. They were so sweet, but the longer you talk to them you realize how young they are. In your mind they are heroic, almost larger than life, because you mainly see them in uniform on the field playing or talking about the game, but when you start scratching the surface, they're twenty-four. So it became like a Tinder date after the show when they stayed hanging out drinking in the Clubhouse for a few hours. I asked Shelby Miller about the MLB softball thing and he said, "You got this." I said, "No, you don't understand, I got nothing." Given that my fantasy is to be a baseball wife, I had plenty to say to the ladies. One thing I asked the wives is if they get sex when the husbands play well. They said they are men—they want it whether they hit or not. Daniel Descalso was there too, so that was a bonus. And they all played with Wacha (which was very meta) and stayed till after one.

▦ WEDNESDAY, APRIL 23, 2014

Indeed the food at the Seinfelds' shiva was to die, so to speak. I ate like a pig. No, I ate like a Jew at a shiva. There is a difference. Part of the routine of the shiva, and of mourning, is to eat and have a chat about the person who passed away. And I am typing this trying to justify the two bagels, lox, rugelach, turkey, cheese, crackers, cookies, and more bagels. *I had to because I am Jewish.*

There was a game but the Cardinals wives came back to the Clubhouse instead for the Cameron Diaz/Leslie Mann taping, so that's where their priorities are and I kind of can't blame them, although if *my husband* was playing I'd like to think I'd be at the game. But that's me. I asked Cameron the best and worst thing about dating a baseball player (I thought this was an incredibly genius way to talk about A-Rod without talking about A-Rod directly). She said, "The schedule and the schedule." The Cardinals wives nodded. *"Mmm-hmm, sister! Tell it!"* (They didn't say that.) From where I sit, the schedule would suit me, because mine is fucked too. So the time we spend together is great and the rest of it we deal with. That's how me and my slugger, or m'slugger, look at it.

Had a long chat with Kenya today; this reunion and altercation has turned into a shitstorm for all involved, including myself. Did I send the wrong person home? What is permissible and what is not? Should we have aired what we aired? It's an inundation on social media, in the press, and at work.

Brought Liza to the opening of Joe's play *Casa Valentina*, which was beautiful and funny. Saw Anna Deavere Smith and told her I'd recently learned that Wacha plays with her pooch, Memphis Deavere Smith. (Wacha likes show folk.) Valerie Harper was there looking very well, so that made me happy. Rhoda is alive and well.

▦ THURSDAY, APRIL 24, 2014

The *Southern Charm* reunion this morning was refreshing because it was a discussion—no fighting—with emotion and fun.

Bruce and I went to the Mets-Cardinals day game and had seats directly behind home plate, which gave us an opportunity to ogle the Mets catcher Anthony Recker, who we thought just had an incredible ass but then we got a look at the equally incredible face. He was a beauty. In the fifth inning the Mets wives found me. They heard that the Cardinals wives had been to my show and wanted to come. I asked them if their men want sex when they hit a home run. Two of them sighed. One said, "My husband never hits home runs—he's the pitcher." I turned to David Wright's wife. "Mine does." She said what I was thinking with a smile. Then we had them bring over the catcher's wife, who was pretty but nowhere near as pretty as the guy. (Who would be?) Man, is she lucky. I am going to start living *The Secret* and though I don't 100 percent understand what that actually entails, I will *will* this baseball wife thing to happen.

Wacha has been having issues with his afternoon walk for the past couple months. He intermittently either doesn't want to go or gets growly and potentially a little threatening (but he hasn't actually bit) with his walker, and the coterie of walker's assistants who are trying to figure out why he hates this sweet walker. So today I sent him to doggy day care at Sherman's house in Brooklyn and he loved it—played with a dog called Whiskey all day (I play with a dog called Whiskey every night but that's another story)—and he was completely crashed out all night. Amazing.

Dinner with Troy Roberts and Lynn—in town from San Fran crashing a piece for *20/20*—and Bruce. We went to Perla, where if you cancel you have to pay fifty bucks a head, and where they have wineglasses with pour lines because maybe they don't trust their bartenders or they want to completely rape you of having any casual enjoyment over a meal? The topics were the end of the world, climate change, the revolution to come, and home invasions. It was quite uplifting. I have total understanding that I am moving into this duplex and at some point in my lifetime the water will come to the building, there will be no power, and I will be an old man stuck in a once-chic West Village twelfth-floor walk-up duplex. Not hot.

FRIDAY, APRIL 25, 2014—NYC—SAG HARBOR

Drove to Sag Harbor and it took forever. Had dinner at the Palm with Sandy and Bruce. Met a very handsome dude there, a surfer/finance guy. Perfect, but has a boyfriend of three years. Still, I have more of a shot at a surfer/finance guy than at someone in the major leagues.

SATURDAY, APRIL 26, 2014—SAG HARBOR

Lunch at Sandy's, where Wacha ran like a rocket. Echoing his thoughts about me losing weight in November, today Sandy was schooling me about not letting Wacha get fat. And he's right. I do not want a fat dog. Speaking of fat, Bruce, Sandy, Joe and I had a glorious dinner at Sam's, where I killed a medium mushroom and onion.

▦ SUNDAY, APRIL 27, 2014—SAG HARBOR–NYC

There is nothing more boring than hearing someone's dreams, but last night's was a doozy—John Mayer and I were houseguests at Barbra Streisand's and she had a huge mausoleum. John seemed to know his way around and was my guide. It was *South Park*–ian.

Part 2 of the reunion aired and I said my piece on *WWHL*.

▦ MONDAY, APRIL 28, 2014

I closed on the apartment, and you want the closing to feel really great and ceremonial but it's a bunch of strangers sitting in a room signing a ton of papers that make zero sense even though the lawyer is next to you explaining each one. There was a lovely lady, very heavy, from the bank who turned out to be pregnant and I was so happy I didn't ask her when she was due before I knew for sure, because that scenario has never played out well for me. I got an email from someone with Clay Aiken telling me they wanted me to speak for thirty minutes at his benefit tomorrow and I said there's been a horrible misunderstanding, I can't go. So they weren't happy with me. What would I say for thirty minutes about anything other than Wacha?

Spent the afternoon at Bravo, where, among other things, we tried to figure out which Atlanta Housewives to bring back from *Atlanta Housewives* and what to pay them. I am so far not thrilled with the new casting, so we rejected the latest bunch and are going to dig deeper.

Ran downtown to pick up Sarah Jessica for the New York Pops tribute to Marc Shaiman and Scott Wittman. As we were pulling up to Carnegie Hall, I noticed everyone was wearing black tie and I froze. SJP said she thought that I knew but that I looked great (in my *light denim suit and plaid shirt*). I had to tell every single person we talked to before the show that I didn't know it was black tie. How boring. But I was surprisingly (given how high my threshold can be) mortified.

The show itself was wonderful and among other things reinforced how truly talented Marc and Scott are—it was Martin Short, Patti LuPone, Matt Morrison, Jane Krakowski, and more singing songs from *Smash*, *When Harry Met Sally*, *Catch Me If You Can*, and *Sleepless in*

Seattle. I was completely done in when the original cast of *Hairspray* got together at the end and sang "You Can't Stop the Beat" (they couldn't!), because it brought me back to that great time in the not-too-distant past (okay, a full twelve years ago) when I was young and madly in love and everything felt possible. Almost every night at 10:35 p.m., I would sneak in the back of the theater (with the other "*Hairspray* Husbands," as we called ourselves then) to watch that amazing cast try to stop the beat (they couldn't then either) and then I'd go backstage to get John, and he and I would go out and frolic until all hours of the night. It was complete waterworks for me watching this crew doing the same choreography—they were the happiest tears, though.

We went to the dinner at the Mandarin Oriental, me in my light denim tux in a sea of black, and sat with Marc, Andrea Martin, Martin Short, and Nathan Lane. Listening to those classics try to one-up each other further filled my heart. Everybody wound up in the thirty-fifth-floor bar and I quizzed Martin Short on every aspect of his career—well, mainly *SCTV* and *SNL*. Queen Latifah showed up randomly late in the evening wearing a tan Adidas sweat suit, and that's pretty much really what I want Queen Latifah to show up wearing whenever and wherever I run into her in the future. Ladies and gentlemen, please welcome Miss Dana Owens, wearing Adidas, to the stage of the Mandarin Oriental. . . .

▦ TUESDAY, APRIL 29, 2014

Man, was I hungover this morning. I sweated a pound of whiskey out at the gym and almost puked twice in the process.

I interviewed another architect at the apartment, which is quickly becoming my least favorite activity. I'm having dinner with Bill and Joanna tomorrow and I told them I would go uptown because it's supposed to rain but they want to try this Thai place on Spring Street. I hope I'm like that when I'm eighty-two. I hope I make it to eighty-two.

We taped Julie Andrews and Idina Menzel today. Ms. Andrews was lovely. As perfect as you would want her to be. She drank tea. I kept the tea bag and put it on the shelf next to Lohan's cigarette butt.

Before the show I stopped by a sixtieth birthday dinner for Jerry Seinfeld, who doesn't look at all sixty. Typically, Jewish men don't age well, but he's breaking that mold, which I am hoping is a good sign for me (I'm getting a lot of signs about how to be older from Jewish men today). Hugh Jackman was there with a beard. I wonder if he has a mean bone in his body. I gorged—cheese, pasta, meat. I will pay for it tomorrow.

Grumpy Cat was our bartender, there shilling Friskies, and her owner has a great backstory. She'd been a waitress at Red Lobster, her boyfriend died, she needed money, and the cat suddenly became famous on Reddit and essentially saved her life. Wacha has already kind of saved my life—not really that dramatic but he's opened me up a lot—but I am ready for him to start bringing in some *coin* like Grumpy Cat!

WEDNESDAY, APRIL 30, 2014

Pouring rain, like an apocalypse. Taped a one-on-one with Porsha. Met Bill and Joanna at the Thai place, Uncle Boons, on Spring Street. Bill was in rare form. He was explaining why he doesn't get upset when there's a tragedy in Mississippi and Texas. He couldn't read the check, so he gave it to Joanna and said, "Tip well, I'm known for it." I had a driver but they preferred to take the subway uptown. I'm forty years younger and I don't prefer to take the subway uptown. After dinner Bill and I stood waiting for Joanna under the awning, watching the monsoon, and a handsome man in a yellow raincoat got my attention. Since I was with Bill, it seemed awkward to initiate a flirt but there was a connection and many long glances as Bill and I continued our conversation. I got in my car and gave him one last look. I know we will meet again. I feel it in my bones.

The show was kinda blah tonight, but snuggling with Wacha turned my mood around. He sleeps with me every night now and is perfect in bed: quiet, compact, doesn't get up until I am ready to get up, and extra cute in the morning. Tonight he was a little scared of the apocalyptic storm outside but we made it through. He has 28k followers on Instagram; maybe that helped him fall asleep.

▦ THURSDAY, MAY 1, 2014—NYC–LOS ANGELES

Of course on the first actually beautiful, 70-degree day in Manhattan, I was on a plane to Los Angeles to enjoy their 95-degree weather. Thankfully, I haven't seen the #BabyJaneFlightAttendant in months and feel like I'm overdue, but instead I got Candice Bergen, who was neither Baby Jane–esque nor my flight attendant. She was just a passenger with dreams, like me. I was thinking on the plane that I should've given Yellow Raincoat Guy my number. Will he find me on Facebook? Then I started wondering what happened to that guy I saw on Madonna's plane who spends half his time in my building in New York. Men are slipping through my fingers.

I landed and went straight to host a panel about *Top Chef* for Emmy voters at the TV Academy with Tom, Padma, Gail, and some *TC* alums, during which I revealed that we play a game while watching the taping in video village where we count the amount of times Padma says "in my mouth" during each Judges' Table. Little did I know she, to this day, had no idea that we did this. She thought it was funny, but I felt busted. For some reason, Ron Jeremy was there and I met him at the after party. Padma had no idea who he was. Good for her. I then had what I thought was going to be a date with this guy I'd met over Oscar weekend; we had been corresponding for a few months and I'd been wondering if he was one of those extra-handsome LA gay flakes or a real person. I determined very quickly that he was the former, bailed out, and met my Bravo friends for more cocktails. I felt quietly victorious (and mildly disappointed) about figuring the guy out so quickly. I think he liked the idea that I'm on TV, but it ended there.

▦ FRIDAY, MAY 2, 2014—LOS ANGELES–NYC

On my plane home was a man with extensive plastic surgery who seemed to know me very well but I couldn't place him and still can't. It's killing me. He greeted me like a long-lost friend. He is between my age and sixty-five—I can never tell with all the face stuff because it ages you so badly. Also I saw a muscly flight attendant who used to be a staple of my

2011 Los Angeles–NYC round trips; he's on the Vegas route in coach now, he said. I don't know what he did to get demoted but he seemed a little dejected.

Had dinner with Bruce, Wes, and Michael at Rocking Horse, followed by FroYo. On the walk home Bruce and I started talking to a man on Eighth Avenue with abnormally large hands—they were like mitts—and it turns out he's an ironworker, which seemed perfect. I asked him if he had an abnormally large peen but he wouldn't say. I can't stop thinking of those mitts. He should get into massage therapy if he gets sick of ironworking.

I got a message on Tinder at the end of the day from a handsome guy I've been talking to online saying that he was on my plane today but didn't have the balls to come say hi. I guess this is one of the hazards of being "known" and on a dating app? Intriguing and odd, all at once.

SATURDAY, MAY 3, 2014

I was up at seven to co-host the Revlon run/walk for cancer with Emma Stone. My job was to announce the start of this race of thousands of women (50k? 75k? 20k? Who knows?) in Times Square. They told me to "vamp for a minute and a half and then count down from ten." I feel like every time someone tells me to vamp I wind up saying the wrong thing, but I made it through. It was inspiring to see all the cancer survivors and the women fighting the disease. Emma Stone was lovely and fresh and sweet. The positive energy kept me going all day.

It was a beautiful day and the West Village was packed with hot straight guys. Met one from Australia who just got in from Delhi and was carrying a bag full of cricket gear. He told me he's trying to make cricket the next big thing in America. I don't have the highest hopes he'll be successful but I wish him luck.

I had a long-overdue catch-up with Jackie. We clicked right back in as though we'd seen each other yesterday. The new development in our thirty-something-year-long friendship is that we now both have dogs, so we can dissect that for hours. We ate outside (with the dog) at Bubby's in the Meatpacking District, which just opened next door to where

Florent was. By the way, Florent is still empty, which still seems like karma for that landlord who drove him out.

Wacha has 34k followers on DogStagram. I thought I figured out who the plastic surgery guy was but then looked on Facebook and realized I got him confused with a different plastic surgery guy. Oy.

I stayed home and watched the White House Correspondents' Dinner. I didn't think Obama was that funny and Joel McHale wasn't at his best but he was incredibly brave to stand up and insult Chris Christie like that. While watching McHale do his thing, I had a flashback to the comedienne Pudgy, whom I discovered at age thirteen. She was an insult comic hosting a Showtime special from a male strip club. She would come out and insult the audience for five minutes, introduce a stripper, then come back and do more comedy. I taped this show on my VHS and I would watch the strip routines when I was alone and show my junior high friends the comedy, because I thought she was hilarious. I acted like I only taped it for the comedy and would zip through the strippers, but what did my friends *think* as I was fast-forwarding through these *men* stripping down to banana hammocks? What was I thinking?? I'm pretty sure I showed my parents too. And I'm pretty sure I showed everyone my hand. I am having residual embarrassment. And wondering where that VHS tape is.

⊞ SUNDAY, MAY 4, 2014

There was an Urban Bear festival happening on the same block as the dog run, so I saw lots of heavyset hairy men who perhaps subliminally inspired me, because I ate like a pig all day, starting with Bubby's, some midday rosé with Joe, and dinner at the new Il Mulino with Jimmy and Nancy Fallon. I actually ate pasta at that dinner. I couldn't help myself. Maybe I want to look like a bear at the Met Ball tomorrow. Jimmy has reached an entirely new level of fame and popularity because of the white-hotness of *The Tonight Show*. He is like the mayor, supersized, or SJP at the height of *SATC*. And he is super nice to everybody, which is a testament to him.

Met Ball Day! Dena came over to help me put on my white tie and tails, which I was initially unenthusiastic about and then changed my mind when I put them on. I felt like Thomas the evil gay footman. Actually, I felt like Matthew, or Branson even, because the downstairs folks wouldn't be wearing Ralph Lauren. I picked up SJP, who was wearing an incredible black-and-white Oscar de la Renta creation that was very much an homage to the night's honoree, Charles James, with an intricate lattice stitching on the back topped off by de la Renta's signature sewn in at the bottom, which I believe was her idea. She had an entire team of people, including Leslie Lopez, the man who'd actually built the dress, and Serge Normant, who made her hair into a double-pointed sculpture. I announced to all that I was going to make mad love to her at the end of the night, which was very not true but got a laugh. She was a co-host of the evening with Bradley Cooper and Lizzie Tisch, so we had to get there at the beginning so she could stand in the receiving line and shake every single guest's hand. I was worried I would have trouble sitting with my tails but I was free and easy compared to SJP. Between her hair and her Cadillac-sized bustle, just getting in the car was a challenge. She was sitting hunched over in the middle of the car in a huge pile of bustle. I am pretty sure we were the first ones on the massive red carpet and the hundreds of paps all went crazy for her, as they should.

After depositing her with Ms. Wintour and the receiving line (AW said I looked "very chic," which I was puffed up about), I joined Bruce and Bryan for cocktails. Only 40 percent of the crowd got the dress code dead-on. I found Nicole Richie, who seemed to be unescorted, so she and I did a couple schmoozelaps, which was fun and allowed me to awkwardly run into several women who have been guests of my show but had been erased from my memory, and to others who hadn't but with whom I still was able to be super awkward, like Leighton Meester. Buoyed by SJP's great energy, our table was really fun. I sat between SJ and André Leon Talley, and across from Bruce and Bryan, who were with Pat McGrath.

Right at the beginning of dinner I met a very handsome designer with whom I had an incredible flirt, the kind that knocks you off your feet a little bit. SJP gave me his full backstory and I was feeling bullish about continuing our conversation at the Boom Boom Room after dinner. Concurrently, a handsome young hedge fund gentleman in white dinner jacket (I still can't figure out if it counts as white tie but am pretty sure it doesn't) whom Jessica had been trying to fix me up with found me at my table and initiated a flirt. So I was feeling optimistic about the after party even before it began. Not to get ahead of myself, because the dinner itself was pop culture theater—Kanye and Beyoncé wandering by, Taylor Swift looking for Lena Dunham. Naomi came over to me three times in the course of the evening screaming, "KEEP PORSHA! DO NOT FIRE HER! I CAN'T STAND KENYA!" Valentino passed by and whispered, "I was turning the channel last night and saw you with the Black Laaaaaaadies!" Frank Ocean performed with an orchestra and was phenomenal; I heard he was supposed to sing five songs but cut a few because he was so nervous. The bathrooms are where the real party is if you are very tolerant of smoke—it's all boldface names huffing cigarettes because of course you can't smoke in the Met and God forbid someone should wait three hours for a cig. On our way out of the museum, we ran into Kylie Minogue, who said, "Boy, were you drunk the last time I was on the show!" I thought *she* was too, but learned it was more of a party for one. Ma-ha!

The Boom Boom Room was initially gorgeous and civilized, then turned into a shitshow after a couple hours, which I guess is how it always goes. I started talking to a woman who asked me if I "ran or walked the other day"—I had no clue who she was or what she was talking about and gave her a super vague answer. She introduced me to her British boyfriend, Andrew, whom I spoke with for several minutes before realizing he was *Spider-Man* and his girlfriend was *Emma Stone* with whom I had fucking co-hosted the run/walk *two days before*. I have certainly ruined any chance of her coming on my show. I don't know why I didn't recognize her. (Whiskey?) Anyway, he was lovely and is looking at an apartment in my old building on Horatio Street tomorrow. Around the time of that faux pas, SJ decided that the shitshow had boiled over and she was done for the night. Bruce and Bryan left with her but I decided to stay for one more drink, quickly gave up and started to leave myself, but ran right into the hedge fund guy, who was well into his double vodka

217

sodas and insisted I stay and drink. We had a bunch of fun and sat on the floor in the corner by the fireplace, where he let me know he would *not* be going home with me at the end of the night. I told him that was my understanding already and that it was OK. We went to the bar to get another whiskey and ran straight into the designer from earlier in the evening, who pulled me aside to let me know that he was engaged and that he had been looking for me to let me know because we had had such a nice flirt but it needed to stop. I told him I was crushed and heart-broken and we hugged four times. In the meantime I decided that was a good sign and told the hedge fund guy it was time to go. He said he would walk me home and as we walked out, Kristen Wiig grabbed me and said to pile into her party bus and go to Rihanna's after party, which was kryptonite to my plans of going to bed. She kept screaming, "It's worth it! It's worth it!"—which was very funny at the time. We all got into the packed elevator and I was jammed into a corner with Hedge Fund Guy, Wiig, and Nicole Richie, and we were stuck for about ten minutes, all of us drunkenly telling each other to get out and work the controls. We weren't moving. It was messy and drunky and we finally all got out and went down through Le Bain and wound up in Alexander Wang's party bus rumbling over cobblestone, Kristen Wiig on a stripper pole screaming, "Is this a dirt road!?" listening to dirty rap while careening through the city.

Rihanna's party was packed but no comparison to the ride over, and they were only serving cognac (whaaaa?), so I didn't last long. Hedge Fund Guy walked me home and we said goodbye in front of the building.

▦ TUESDAY, MAY 6, 2014

So, so, *so* hungover. And so glad I sent Wacha to Brooklyn yesterday, because I could barely handle myself, let alone him, this morning. I did make it to the gym at noon and sweated out a gallon of whiskey and shockingly weighed in at 166, even with the carbo load Sunday night. Had lunch with Martha Stewart at Morandi, which I had kind of been dreading, but we wound up getting inspired and coming up with a potentially great format for a show, a different version of a business reality show with Martha. I told her I thought Bethenny would make a genius yang to her yin; I pitched her how that could work and she surprisingly went for the idea. We need someone else too—P. Diddy? Wendi Murdoch? Now I have to sell Bethenny on the idea, but I think she'll dig it. I walked over to Three Lives Bookstore, where I bought SJP the new Michael Cunningham and Diane Keaton books to thank her for the night, and myself the Roz Chast as a pick-me-up. Before the show, I hosted a party for Todd Snyder celebrating his CFDA nomination at his store. I not only love his clothes, but he's a great guy. We talked about the stainless steel issue I had in Miami and he was surprised. I should send him those pants. I was quite foggy and didn't stay that long.

▦ WEDNESDAY, MAY 7, 2014

First thing this morning I was in the elevator with a man who seemed to be staring at me and I realized it was probably the airplane guy. "Are you the guy from the plane to LA?" I stammered, in front of a stranger looking on. "No, I am from Italy!" he chirped. Then I was stuck in front of the elevator explaining myself, the plane, the handsome stranger, and Madonna to both the Italian and the stranger, who were acting like they deserved an explanation.

On my cell at the dog run, I had the most unbelievable conversation I've had with a Housewife's husband in my seven years as an EP on the show. For twenty-five minutes he made insane, unrealistic demands and I said no. As I threw a ball to Wacha, I said no to renegotiating his wife's deal while the series was airing and no to giving his wife a bonus for her (very low) Q score and finally no to calling him in a week and letting him know what I'm going to do to make his wife feel more loved. Went to the gym; I am 165.

I shot an episode of Larry King's web show, because I figured it would be fun to be interviewed by a legend. We shot it at the Paramount Hotel and it was hot as Hades in there, which meant I was sweating on his show. Lovely. I showed him how to use Tinder and swiped on some Italian guy just to show Larry how it worked.

From Larry I went to host the Clio Awards for fashion and retail advertising at the Pierre, where SJP was being honored. I was tired but pleased to spend the evening across a table from her. I realized when I was onstage that I had only really read half the script in advance of the awards, so I saw an hour's worth as it was coming up on the teleprompter, and the second part was totally new as the words were appearing in front of me. I'm pretty proficient at prompter-reading, and so with the exception of an ad-libbed JonBenét joke, I think I did OK.

Raced from there to the show where we had Connie Chung and Maury Povich as guests. I'd been excited for them to be there but my expectations were low, which typically means the show winds up being excellent, and this one was. They were on fire and our elements were hilarious. Wacha came on at the end and snatched what I thought were Connie's reading glasses. I was furiously chasing him around as we were wrapping it up, when I discovered they were Maury's glasses and for some reason it seemed like less of a crime, so I gave up. He wound up pretty much destroying them. I gotta remember to tell the kids we need to buy Maury a new pair. I think Connie was pretty lit up by the end of the night. She looked vintage Connie Chung, by the way.

Eli came to the show tonight. He's now at Lifetime, but to celebrate old times at Bravo we did our classic post-show Cubbyhole/Corner Bistro late-night twofer, culminating in a juicy cheeseburger and fries at 2 a.m. Goodbye 165.

▦ THURSDAY, MAY 8, 2014

I saw a man on Gansevoort Street walking—actually propping up—his seventeen-year-old (I asked) skin-and-bones dog. I got teary at the sight, and was so obsessed with the dog that I was kind of dragging Wacha, until a woman said, "Excuse me, your dog is trying to go to the bathroom." I looked up and it was Brooke Shields, on poop patrol for Wacha. Thanks, Brooke!

We taped a show with Jon Hamm this morning. Sedaris was on with him and had assumed we were doing the show at 11 p.m., not a.m.—which makes sense—and completely overslept. I called her at ten-fifteen and she begged me to find someone else to fill in. I told her there was no one and that I would see her in twenty minutes. I don't know how she did it but she showered and was in the chair made up by eleven-ten. Lots of St. Louis talk with Jon Hamm, who was incredibly handsome and very nice. I asked him about the MLB event I was invited to in July (he's done it several times) and he said it's really fun and easy, that he would be there, and that I should *absolutely* do it. He talked me into it! I'm still scared, but doing it.

So now I'm in a conversation with that Italian on Tinder who I swiped just as an example on the Larry King web show, and Larry King keeps tweeting asking what's going on with the guy. It's like he thinks he is officiating my wedding to this guy.

Had dinner with Jason and Lauren and gossiped about everything, then did a great show with Ricki Lake and Jason Priestley. Ended the night with what I am pretty sure was a two-and-a-half-hour massage. I don't know what time I went to bed.

▦ FRIDAY, MAY 9, 2014

Worked out but was really sore from the massage, which seems sort of counterproductive.

Today was the day of Abby's first ever visit to New York City, and I met her and Em at their hotel as they arrived from the airport. We did what I guess you do with seven-year-old nieces, went directly to the American Girl Store, which is a tremendous racket. You just look around and picture everything floating in a garbage barge in twenty years. But she loves it, so I don't need to be living in Haterville. From there to a diner and then I dropped them at Serendipity 3 to run down to my place, where I was meeting Grac, Bruce, and Amanda to pre-game before the Cher concert. It took a whole hour (and some pot lollipops) for our collective attention spans to settle down and for us to get off our phones and out of our heads, and when we did, it was a magical night. Ray drove us and took us in that backstage car entrance at Barclays Center with the elevator that's like the *Star Wars* compactor room. Bill, who is also P!nk's tour manager, met us backstage and brought us into a big, mostly empty hospitality room, in the middle of which were gathered: Sandy, Brian Fox,

Michael Douglas, Catherine Zeta-Jones, Brian Williams and his great wife, Jane, and Ron Meyer. There was a woman with CZJ who was asking me all sorts of questions about *WWHL* in front of Miss CZJ, who I am pretty sure was looking at us like we were speaking Mandarin. She ultimately asked what I did in the hours before the show to kill time and I jokingly said "masturbate," but maybe that wasn't appropriate because did Michael Douglas have a masturbation issue? A sex thing? Brian Williams was nice and we joked about how obvious it was that I would be seeing *him* at a Cher concert. But I did wonder why I licked a pot lollipop before having to make small talk with Catherine Zeta-Jones and Brian Williams. At this moment of my life is this the reality of what it's like to go to a concert? Will I ever learn?

The show was so fun and amazing—another killer farewell tour, better than the last one, I think. There were a few long breaks for costume changes (the costumes are the only weak part; Bob Mackie didn't do them for I think the first time in Cher's existence and you could tell—we saw some bunched-up tights!) but who cares. She's sixty-eight, as she told us ("What's *your* nana doing tonight?"), and can do whatever the hell she wants. We took a lot of bad videos of the concert that we won't ever do anything with and then when all our phones go dead for good because of the impending takeover of the world, we will forget they ever existed.

We waited backstage for Cher and I ran into her best friend Paulette, who is a big reason why Cher did *WWHL* in the first place. Paulette is allegedly my biggest fan and forced Cher to do the show, so I will forever be grateful. We had hugs and photos and I met her husband and son and we talked a little baseball. When Cher came out she didn't know who I was at first, then it clicked in and she was great. We took a selfie and I just fawned all over her. On the way out her manager told me she was announcing additional dates at the Garden, the Izod Center, and somewhere else in the area next week. Awesome that she can sell out four arenas in the metro area still—at sixty-eight.

On the Manhattan Bridge heading back into the city, Grac read us some of the items on her "ideas list" she's been keeping for a few years and they were brilliant. One was pot suppositories and another was a Grateful Dead Nursing Home. I would invest in both. Ray was in hysterics and he hadn't even had a lollipop!

SATURDAY, MAY 10, 2014

I woke up with a hazy memory of Liza Minnelli at the Cher after party, and then spoke to Sandy, who said indeed Liza was there. How did I not pay more attention to *that*!?

Em, Bruce, and I had been plotting for weeks to put Ava and Abby together and today was the day. They are a year apart and even though it can be tricky forcing two little girls to bond, it worked from the word go. Pre-*Wicked* matinee, we all had lunch at the Palm. Coincidentally, Dave's family was there too and were all heading to the show, which I hadn't seen since opening night ten years ago. The witches still got it! The end of Act 1 will go down as one of the great act endings on Broadway, right? It has to. We took the girls backstage to meet the witches afterwards. I want to do an all-black version of *Wicked* called *Blicked*.

It was a monsoon outside and we got soaked leaving the theater, which Abby declared to be the best part of her visit to NYC. We ducked into Trattoria Dell'Arte and rosé'd it up in a corner booth.

This friend of Padma's has a beagle thing—hers passed away while she was on her honeymoon—and she asked if she could ever come hang out with Wacha. So she was at my apartment today for hours while I was at the show. He didn't have any burn marks on him or anything when I got home, so I am fairly certain there was no abuse. I didn't really think that, my mind just wandered to poor Penny on *Good Times*. (These are the things that fill my brain.)

SUNDAY, MAY 11, 2014

Perfect NYC day. It was like the day the Hobbits were freed, or whatever the hell happened at the end of *Lord of the Rings*. It felt like a party in the shire, 72 degrees and sunny. Wacha started the day in front of the mirror, barking at himself for twenty minutes. It was the first time he had noticed the mirror. He is a lil dumb, as discussed. Took him to the dog run and met Em and Abby at the Standard for brunch, where I completely stuffed myself: nova platter, scrambled eggs, turkey sausage, and then obviously I picked at Abby's fries. Teaching Abby to walk Wacha was priceless. I put

Em and Abby in a cab for LaGuardia and ran into Seth Meyers and his wife, Alexi; she and I engaged in a weird handshake/aborted kiss greeting, to which I demanded a do-over. I hate a weird greeting.

I met Joe on the Piers and we encountered an amazing forest ranger lady with a badonk of a booty who almost gave me a fifty-dollar citation for having Wacha on the lawn, but I made a plea that we weren't under Taliban rule and she let me off just this once. She was in a scooter with a sliding window that she used with great effect. It was like her own little portable DMV station.

It was one of those days when you just didn't want to go inside, ever. A sweet twink informed us we were listening to the strains of the great Ariana Grande coming from the next pier and we walked over, crashing some sort of fancy event that looked like a set for a White People Benefit for Africa on *Sex and the City*, with Samantha doing the PR. It was sparsely attended, as if with just enough background players to shoot a scene. We saw Donna Karan and some models and ate pizza, ice-cream sandwiches, and cookies, and I got a bag of candy to go. Wacha got recognized twice. We sat on a bench for an hour after the party and watched people. People don't cruise anymore. That's just over. The amount of cruising and pickups that happened on those piers for years and years and now no one even *looks* at each other that much anymore. I am from the generation of meeting on the street and connecting—there was nowhere else to do it, but Grindr and Tinder killed that. I still look at everybody. I dig eye contact!

We ran into more people, then I left Joe and sat on a bench in Abingdon Square and obsessed over Wacha's Instagram and showed this old lady next to me how to use her phone in what seemed like the unlikely event that she would choose to call her sister. She made it very clear with me that she did not actually care to call the sister—who does not own a cell phone—and had no future plans to do so either. She is scared of her iPhone and it's turning into a problem, she said. I did some good troubleshooting with her but I couldn't tell what was sticking. What did stick is that this old lady doesn't like her sister *one bit*. Every time I was talking about the phone she brought it back to the sister.

I take way too many pictures of Wacha. I think it is a potentially disturbing addiction, although certainly better than crack or even excessive masturbation, despite what I implied to Catherine Zeta-Jones the other night.

Tonight Simon Halls hosted dinner for Ryan Murphy and *The Normal Heart* at the Palm and I ate like a pig: steak, chicken parm, creamed spinach, repeat. Mark Ruffalo and I took a selfie and he is absolutely my doppelgänger. I have no problem with that, and he seems fine with it too. His wife, Sunny, says he will play me in a movie, which is unlikely but I'm glad there's an actor of his caliber ready to step in. While dinner was wrapping up I got a text from a random number that said, "Uncle Boons—a few weeks ago. Outside under the awning." It was the guy in the yellow raincoat that I'd cruised after dinner with Bill Persky. I knew he would find me! I replied: "What took you so long to find me?" (I thought that was a clever response.) We went back and forth and decided that fate had brought us together at the end of a perfect day and we simply must meet each other immediately for a drink so that we could plan the rest of our lives together. We didn't actually talk about fate or marriage but that was the ongoing subtext in my mind. I told Bruce what was up and he said, *"Go now!"* I went to Anfora and he was waiting, not exactly as I remembered him—Did he have a beard? Was he really that young? He wouldn't tell me his age, or how he'd gotten my number. After a few minutes, his suspected age was dropping precipitously because he had no frame of reference for any iteration of Cher (not even "Believe"). I don't know what age you have to be to have not been touched by Cher. I guess under twenty-five. Anyway, the longer we talked, the more I realized this was not going to be the person I spend the rest of my life with. He was coming from a Sunday of day-drinking, so he kinda needed a shower and maybe a nap, but he made it clear that he was up for a roll in the hay. I don't know if it was my deflated expectations, my full stomach, or what, but I settled for a peck in front of my apartment and sent him off, which I think surprised him. I don't think we'll see each other again.

MONDAY, MAY 12, 2014

This morning Wacha was taking a massive dump and who appears from thin air? Brooke Shields! Is she the prophet of Wacha's poop? I went to the gym knowing I'd gained weight, not planning to weigh myself. But Mark was there and egged me on to get on the scale. I *gained five fucking pounds*. I weigh 170. Of course I do after what I ate this weekend. Pigging off Abby's leftovers, gorging at the Standard, grazing at that White People Benefit for Africa, eating everything at the Palm—all while bragging to my sister what a health kick I'm on. I am a dejected pig.

Tonight was the premiere of *The Normal Heart*. It gutted me completely. I was sitting there sobbing between Kelly and Allison Levy, who were also sobbing. Everyone was. It is a story that needs telling. I can't stop thinking about these thousands of people who just disappeared in the most inhumane way possible, with all of society turning their backs on them. That this happened in my lifetime is a travesty. We are supposed to be a civilized society. This should go on Reagan's record in a more significant way. He let it happen.

TUESDAY, MAY 13, 2014

Martha Stewart sent me an incredible basket of dog products. Totally unrelated, I was in a horrible mood all day. My allergies were horrible, Ricky Martin's people were micromanaging our interview with him, there was irritating stuff I had to deal with at work, and I felt fat. I had an impossible workout boxing and kicking and still didn't get my aggression out of my system. I got out of my funk in time for the Ricky Martin taping. I honestly think they were worried I was going to gay him up—that was the undertone I was getting—and after seeing *Normal Heart* last night, it felt contrary to the whole point of being out of the closet and where we are in 2014. I'm the only gay host in late night—if you can't gay it up with me, where can you? But he was lovely, very warm and sweet and adorable. And because he was so disarming (did I misread the situation?) my upper lip was sweating and I was way, way too flirty with him on camera. I should've toned it down but he was so cute and I couldn't stop. I felt a little gross but he seemed fine. After the show I met with Bethenny and pitched her the Martha idea. She loved it. I think the next step is getting P. Diddy to do it.

Tonight Daniel Craig was being honored at the Spring Benefit at

MoMA and I was happy to be there with Bruce, Bryan, and Barkin. Somehow I wound up seated at Madonna's table, which was a great surprise and subsequently a total buzzkill since I had to leave for my show midway through dinner. She was chatty and funny. She hated the wine and texted her driver to go grab a bottle from her house and bring it back to her. I never found out what kind she was getting—she told me to wait and see. I couldn't. Motherfucker. What *kind* did Madonna get??? I was still in *Normal Heart* mode, thinking about an entire lost generation of gay men, so I quizzed her about Herb Ritts, Keith Haring, and Basquiat. She said she feels like all her contemporaries are dead, including Michael Jackson, who she said she wasn't great friends with but considered a contemporary. I asked if Whitney fell into that group and she said probably not because she didn't ever get to know her well.

I went from Madonna to Ramona, and the show was nutso. Stayed after and had drinks with Michael Davies for a couple hours. We're going to produce the Martha show together. I never did find out what kind of wine Madonna ordered. Now that I think about it, she might've said rosé, but *what kind*??

My Tinder match who saw me on the airplane said he saw me at the *Normal Heart* premiere but couldn't get to me to say hi. This is starting to feel very *Sliding Doors*; I love a romantic backstory.

WEDNESDAY, MAY 14, 2014

Woo-hoo, I am 164.6! Praise Him! It helps that I have eaten next to nothing for forty-eight hours and have had two insane workouts. I took my svelte, rock-hard frame straight from the gym to tape an episode of *The Soup* with Joel McHale, also guest-starring (do we say "guest-starring" in this situation?) Willie Geist. Joel and Willie are both around six-foot-four; in other words I looked elfin in between these two guys. I had never met Joel before and he was really warm. We did a quick run-through and it was really easy—Willie and I just popped into the frame (he shoots it all in front of a green screen and an audience of about seventy-five people) and read funny jokes off the prompter. Before the taping, the three of us went out to look for a Starbucks—we were way west in Hell's

Kitchen—and wound up wandering around for about a half hour. We got back and the entire production was in a panic, thinking Joel was pissed and revolting in some sort of talent walk-off. I guess he'd forgotten his cell phone, so what the hell did they know. We laughed.

Went from there to rehearsal for tomorrow's NBCUniversal Upfront, which is a huge production. I got permission (I think they had to take it to the president of E!) to make a joke about Kim Kardashian selling sponsorships to her wedding at the after party, so I felt subversive.

My Tinder made two matches by mistake in my pocket today. And both guys emailed me. It's like butt dialing with consequences and now I'm a dick if I don't respond. I haven't responded.

Tonight I went to the Friends In Deed benefit for the AIDS Walk. I met a bodyworker who said he is getting his body ready for the Ascension and I thought he meant the party in Fire Island in August, but I think he was talking about the Rising of Christ. I couldn't figure out why he would need to be in shape for the end of the world; it seemed like Jesus would be the one who would need to be worried about that, so I kept going on about Fire Island and he said that there would certainly be fire at the Ascension. And this went on for solidly three minutes because he also decided to violently loosen my shoulders in the midst of the conversation, which hurt—but in a good way. I finally explained what the Ascension party was and by that time I was too irritated to continue and feigned a trip to the bathroom. I also met a guy who told me he'd been with his partner for twenty years and he's more in love with his dog. He said he would choose the dog over the husband. My cab driver home was the Moroccan Dylan McDermott—he was steaming hot. I told him he looked like McDermott and he loved it. He got really bashful but wanted to hear more. I told him that I'd met the guy and so I was an authority on the subject. To my dismay, we were at my front door before it went any further. John Mayer and Ricky texted really late saying that they were coming over for dessert. I asked what kind of ice cream to get and John texted that Ricky wanted "Ben and Jerry's something, I don't know, something with crunch in it" and John wanted "something that will keep me aggressively thin." I wound up ordering Chunky Monkey and FroYo from the deli. I felt good about my choices. John met Wacha, dubbed him the perfect dog, and did a photo session with him for his Instagram (Wacha's, not John's).

John gave us the blow-by-blow of his (very positive) experience recording a duet with Barbra Streisand, from the recording studio to the barn, and it sounds like they loved each other. He was telling me about her house and the mall underneath with the wonder of a straight guy detailing the discovery of some strange new world—as though I hadn't watched, dissected, and obsessed over the episode of *Oprah* with her house tour. He even said, "You know there are only two 'A's' in her first name, right? Have you heard the story of why she did that?" I said, *"Who do you think you are talking to right now?"*

He recorded a version of the Beyoncé song "XO" and wanted to play it for me, but how do you play something in someone else's system? When did something so simple like playing a song become so complicated? What a drag. Eventually we played it on my Mini Jambox thing and it's great.

▦ THURSDAY, MAY 15, 2014

This morning I had an interview and photo shoot with Conan O'Brien for a special pre-Emmy issue of *Variety*. I was excited and a little apprehensive to be paired with Conan. The topic was, of course, late-night television. As I waited for him to show up at the Gramercy Park Hotel (he was stuck in massive Obama traffic), my consternation grew about his potential attitude towards me, since he has been doing this for twenty-something years versus my five. (For instance, was he going to walk in and ask, "Why exactly am I here with this douchebag?") When he arrived I was struck by three things: how short I was going to look in the photos, that I had forgotten to ask for makeup (he was beat down), and that once again, all late-night hosts roll deep and I need to start considering building a posse to run around with. I have the posse (assistant, publicist, agent, executive producer, other randoms) but I never think to bring them anywhere. To make everything less awkward, the photographer immediately had us get into a bed together so he could take pictures of us jokingly having pillow talk. So five minutes into meeting the guy, I am cheek-to-cheek in bed making funny faces for a camera. The photo shoot was mercifully short and I really enjoyed the interview. The journalist connected us by our commonality of coming from behind the scenes (he as a writer and I as a producer) before becoming late-night hosts. Conan said for years and years he felt like he didn't belong, and questioned what everyone thought of him; I asked when that would go away for me and he said never. Joy. I told him about my problem with not remembering people and he told me exactly how to say hi to people: Always assume you know everyone, and say "Good to see you," never "Nice to meet you." Apparently they will then slowly give you clues about how you actually know them and you just have to think carefully. You will figure out who they are within nineteen seconds, he says. I am definitely using this technique.

I had to be at the NBCUniversal Upfront at the Javits Center early in the afternoon; this year it was massive—all the cable channels were combined (Bravo, USA, E!, Syfy, Oxygen, Esquire). The red carpet was a scene, with E! doing *Live from the Red Carpet* and bleachers of screaming fans behind Giuliana Rancic. I saw DVF backstage and I think she was a little shell-shocked because she didn't recognize a soul. In the midst of the chaos I got a panicked message from Ramona telling me her car didn't show up and to hold the red carpet for her because she had put a lot of effort into her look. It was an amazing voicemail and I should've saved it for a rainy day. When I went onstage I realized Kim Kardashian was sitting directly in front of me. I totally pussed out about making the joke about her selling sponsorships to her wedding. Instead I said I was hoping to take a selfie with her ass. (I bet Conan would've told the original joke. I'm an imposter!) After my spiel I was seated with the Bravo posse, next to Jeff Lewis and Patti Stanger and in front of NeNe, who was on the aisle of the row of Housewives, two from each city. As I walked from the presentation to the party with DVF, I saw Khloé Kardashian, who said that she and Kim wanted to offer their asses for selfies with me. I stupidly said, "I'll see you in there," and never saw them again. That would've been a good selfie, damn it. I'm glad I changed the joke.

There were three thousand people at the party, most of them women, and many of them very sweet fans who wanted a selfie not with Kim's ass but with me. After seventy minutes of walking two steps, taking five pictures, seeing someone I wanted to say hi to, walking two steps towards them and watching them disappear as I took five more pictures, I hit the wall. For instance when a publicist rushed me with a photographer and a funny-looking dude, saying, "I have a *Preacher of LA*!" instead of saying, "Great, let's take a picture," I said, "Who cares, why is that my problem?" And when a girl—half chewing a crab cake—insisted that I kiss her on the lips for a selfie, instead of politely declining, I said, *"I am not doing that!! No way!"* Before it got any worse and I started alienating fans everywhere, I asked Ryan to remove me. I went home to walk the dog and to my great pleasure found the script for the first episode of *The Comeback* waiting for me. I had to delay meeting Jeff Lewis and posse for dinner and just sit down and read the damn thing. It was *perfect*. I couldn't be happier with it as a fan, and for how the *RHOBH* and I tie into the story. My bad attitude from the party was completely erased.

It was a Housewives cabal at Koi that started with Jeff Lewis, Gage, Jenni, and the new OC Housewife Shannon Beador, who I hadn't yet met. I don't think Vicki loved all the time I was giving Shannon. Then we were joined by Kyle and Mauricio, Melissa and Joe, NeNe and Gregg, Kandi, and Kim Richards. At my end of the table, I was codependently trying to get Kandi, Kim Richards, and Jeff to realize that they should actually be best friends. I am not sure they should but it was fun trying and even more fun having all the girls from other cities together at one table. Kandi told me that she and Ramona are friends, which surprised me—I can't picture it. Sonja showed up with a bang and wound up telling all of them that she's the richest woman in NYC and was imploring me to contact Elvis, which I agreed to but did not understand at all. I left and went to some after party where Jax from *Vanderpump Rules* explained exactly the nose job he is getting tomorrow and we compared notes about booty calls. When I got home I reread *The Comeback* script and went to bed with a smile.

⊞ FRIDAY, MAY 16, 2014

On the way to the dog run we walked by a Willy Wonka Ice Cream pop-up shop, and Wacha was completely flipped out by the Oompa Loompa in front. I took a pic of them, which was nearly impossible. My weight seems maintained at 165. Praise Him. Went to a meeting at CAA to go over new stuff. Hickey is back from Santa Fe (where he's shooting *Manhattan*) just for the weekend and I took Wacha over to see him. It was Barbara Walters's last day on *The View*—they did an amazing tribute. I feel bad all over again for offending her. I emailed Michael Patrick King and told him I was having a philosophical debate about whether I, Andy Cohen, would call Valerie Cherish "Val," as the script has me doing. He said, "Trust the writers—they know your character best." Ha! Massage, then drinks with Billy Eichner at Barracuda.

SATURDAY, MAY 17, 2014

Gorgeous day. Reread *The Comeback* and am practicing playing myself. Ran into Flotilla DeBarge and Lady Bunny on Twelfth Street, out of drag, which for me is always like seeing Oz in his sweatpants. Dinner at Blue Pearl with SJP and Hickey. We talked about everything—didn't shut up, actually. In speculating about Solange in that elevator, I realized that must've happened right around the time I got stuck in mine with Kristen Wiig and company. I got in the wrong car! Went home and ran through my *Comeback* scene with SJP playing Valerie Cherish. She said I was ad-libbing too much and needed to learn my lines exactly as written. Having worked with MPK all those years on *SATC*, she would know. So I shall. We all got on my bed (Wacha too) and watched the Barbara Walters ABC retrospective and it was phenomenal. It could've been another hour or two!

SUNDAY, MAY 18, 2014

The mean guy came to the dog run and had a *fit* when other dogs (thankfully not mine) were taking *his* ball, and then he stormed off because no one cared about his stupid fucking ball. It was amazing. Victory for the people! Troy and Jonah came over and we tried to figure out where the new staircase would go. Jonah is getting huge—he's taller than me. I still haven't hired an architect.

Had a doggy playdate in Central Park with Jackie, who knows of this great little fenced-in area where the cops won't bust you for having your dog off leash. There were straight couples everywhere holding hands. It didn't gross me out, even though I know some people find it disgusting. On the cab ride home, Hickey texted to meet him and Barkin at Morandi. It was lasagna night there, so that's how that went. Amazing. The show tonight was a total snooze. Stayed hanging out till two-thirty with John Jude, Deirdre, and Anthony.

MONDAY, MAY 19, 2014

I felt like such a working actor today, meaning I had absolutely nothing to do until my show. It was gorgeous out and after the gym I grabbed Wacha and had a two-hour lunch outside with Hickey, Victor Garber, and Rainer at that place Monument Lane across from Equinox on Twelfth Street. We just blabbed and blabbed. I got Liza's wedding invite and, habit, almost threw it out after I looked at it, but given that we have been waiting for this day to arrive, I kept it. It's a great invite, actually. Bryan and Bruce threw Billie a lovely graduation party tonight. Carrie Fisher was there but no Debbie Reynolds. I hope I meet her someday.

TUESDAY, MAY 20, 2014

Wacha was at doggy day care in Brooklyn all day, so I was just a solo unit doing my thing. I worked out, had lunch with Bruce outside at Good, and on my way home encountered the hottest beer delivery guy ever. He was a little thuggy, Puerto Rican I think, and just hot. Would life be so bad to be married to him? I would have a beer in hand and dinner on the table when he got home. We could talk about his route. I would have to watch my words, though, because he has a little bit of a short temper. I don't tell anybody this, but he hits me sometimes.

Usually it's no big deal, and never in the face, and I deserve it because I can be stupid. I don't think before I talk, is all. But I have had to lie about scars here and there.

OK, I just talked myself out of the beer delivery guy. Wacha got home at 6 p.m. completely exhausted from his day. When he's tired, I get tired.

⊞ WEDNESDAY, MAY 21, 2014

I am firmly, solidly at 165. My stomach still looks like it could lose a layer of fat, though. So I thought 165 was the pot of gold, but now I'm pretty sure it's 160. Or 158. It's all torture; I know that to be true. It feels like I do the same thing every day—schlep to the gym, go to Ready to Eat on Hudson and order either salmon with two sides (usually quinoa and brussels sprouts) or chicken and two sides (maybe sweet potato and broccoli). Even though I order essentially the same thing every day, the price is never the same. It's all over the place. I can't figure it out. I am too bored by the whole thing to ask.

We were taping Debbie Harry and Lea Michele this afternoon and beforehand I went back and read every mention of Debbie's name in *The Andy Warhol Diaries*. He seemed to be obsessed with her weight, is all I really learned. It was up and down and all over the place, kinda like mine. I asked her on the show if she thought Andy would've been pissed at the publication of the book after his death and she was sure he'd be thrilled about it, that he planned for it, actually. She is very cool but the energy of the show was a bit off; I was doing my normal "I'm gonna put :60 on the clock and pummel you with questions" and that's not her speed, so we got through two and a half questions in :60. I was entertained during the break watching Lea Michele leaf through pages of her new book for Debbie; the look on Debbie's face was somewhere between bemused and confused as Michele showed her pictures and narrated: "Here are my beauty tips. . . . These are my red-carpet looks. . . ." Stopped by Bruce's on the way home and Ava was just out of the tub and let me brush her hair. Give me a doll or a little girl and I will brush that hair like my life depends on it. I love it. I got out all the knots. Michael Patrick King emailed and said that my lunch companion on *The Come-*

back on Friday is going to be RuPaul, which thrills me for a hundred reasons, not least of which is I really enjoy shooting the shit with him and I'm sure we will have plenty of downtime. I'm glad he's doing it and a little surprised; he doesn't have any lines. Did they tell him that?

I guess Toni Braxton's lupus was acting up and she canceled around eight-thirty. I called Fredrik from *Million Dollar Listing NY*, who left his dinner at Bottino with his dreamy husband to come fill in for her, along with Ian Ziering and some Chippendales behind the bar. I found out one of them was gay on the after show and it sent me spinning with possibilities of getting his spray tan on my new comforter. Kidding.

After the show I had a Tinder date with the guy from the airplane and *Normal Heart*. I'd thought he was a big WASP but it turns out he's a nice Jewish boy in finance—maybe too young (twenty-eight)—and a seemingly good person. He wanted to talk about my hobbies. I am so bad with that question. My dog's Instagram—is that a hobby? The guy loves to cook and uses some service where they deliver the exact ingredients, measured out, everything you need for whatever dish you're cooking, which to me somehow defeats the purpose. It's like the Garanimals of cooking. He walked me home and we had a decent kiss in front of the building. I'll see him again.

THURSDAY, MAY 22, 2014—NYC–LOS ANGELES

There was a clip of Ricky Martin and me on a gay website this morning and the comments were brutal. For instance: It's disgusting the way I flirt with my guests, no one wants to see my dog on TV (shut the fuck up), I am a gross caricature—all the greatest hits of the take-downs I have received through the years. The dog comment, however, put me over the edge and I wrote what I thought was a pretty great response. I said how much I liked the site, how I was happy whenever they included clips from my show, and how I was immediately deflated when I read what vile things people have to say about me. I then listed all the nasty stuff and said that I want people to know that I love my show and I am having the most fun of my life. It was essentially a "sticks and stones . . ." kind of diatribe. I decided to go to the gym and burn off some steam before posting it. When I got home there were a few more nasty comments about how disgusting my flirting was, and I started to think this item may be the wrong one to post under because I kind of agreed that the flirting wasn't my best moment. So why fall on my sword defending a clip I didn't love? I decided to figure it out on the flight to LA. Ironically, the Internet wasn't working on the plane and you would've thought they said the *wings* weren't working by the near-riot around me. I wanted to shout at this man across from me that he would survive without his Facebook for six hours. I didn't, of course. And that also ended my fantasy of posting that comment. I'm glad I let it be. The flight attendant wanted to talk to me about *Fashion Police* and would not accept that I am not a part of that show. He just wouldn't believe me. So that was frustrating for both of us, I'm sure.

Checked into the Chateau and went directly to meet Lisa Vanderpump (and Ken and Giggy) and Lance Bass (and Michael) for dinner at her new place, Pump, which is kind of the gay version of Sur. I loved it—it's like a "Garden of Eden meets St. Tropez" vibe plunked down right on the corner of Santa Monica and Robertson. And the food is good, as it is at her other places. It was my first time seeing her since the reunion taping, and the subsequent flood of tweets saying I was tough on her, which she threw in my face in a gentle way. I threw them back in her face, though, because I really don't think I was tough. I kept saying, "I'm sorry I asked you so many *questions. How horrible and mean* of me!" She is dancing around not coming back to *RHOBH* next season but we want her and I can't see her leaving it behind. Today it went public that we didn't pick up Carlton and Joyce, so she's wondering who will join the group next season. I said nothing. Three rosés in, I split to get a decent night's sleep and ran into a fun group at the Chateau on my way in. The best laid plans . . .

FRIDAY, MAY 23, 2014—LOS ANGELES—NYC

I had a 5 a.m. pickup for *The Comeback*, which meant I got about two and a half hours of sleep before the shoot. I had dreamed of how hilarious it would be to be among the cast, and here's how playing myself on my favorite show actually went: I walk into a makeup trailer at five-fifteen and stop dead in my tracks at the sight of Lisa Kudrow in a wig cap. She thinks she scared me, that I wasn't prepared to see her in said wig cap, and keeps asking if I'm OK. I *am* OK! We get made up next to each other and gossip about the *Housewives* and I kvell over the script for the episode we're shooting today (it's the first one, which marks the big return of *The Comeback* after ten years). Lisa tells me about her shoot yesterday with Lisa Vanderpump at Villa Blanca—in which Valerie quits season one of *RHOBH*. (The premise of the rest of the episode is motivated by Valerie shooting a sizzle for me, and her impression that I want her to run around making scenes everywhere. She sees on Twitter that I'm having lunch at the Chateau with RuPaul and shows up to "run into" me and tell me about her sizzle.) Michael Patrick King had initially pitched it to me as akin to that classic *I Love Lucy* episode where she purposely "runs into" Bill Holden at the Brown Derby. (I *get* a *Lucy* analogy.) When Lisa emerges from the trailer with red wig as Valerie, it's like seeing a different person. A big light comes on within her and she's giggly and somewhat giddy, and so am I. I can't stop myself from trying to riff with her-as-Valerie, which is of course ridiculous. Michael Patrick King is also directing the episode and seeing him on set—Amy Harris by his side—makes me feel like it's 2007 and I'm visiting the *Sex and the City* set. Dan Bucatinsky arrives and tries to help me get tea, which is lovely and comical. We're all whispering, by the way, because it's the crack of dawn in the lobby of the Chateau and we can't wake anybody up with our racket. We begin shooting sometime after 7 a.m. and it's Ru and I at a table with half-eaten food (cheeseburger for me and beet salad for him). Every ten minutes or so Valerie comes out with the cameras and we do the scene, then MPK follows with really specific notes ("You seem too *happy* to see Valerie." "Now you seem like you *hate* Valerie!" "Wait two beats after she introduces herself to then let the audience know that you *do* recognize her." "Give me some kind of reaction after she leaves the scene." "Tell her, 'We tried to work together *a hundred years ago*' and see what she does"), and then we do it again—beyond surreal to be talking in a scene to Val, playing myself, and I love it. And in between takes, Ru and I do a deep catch-up. We talk about: Diana Ross (career of, favorite B-sides), NY vs. LA, people and their cameraphones (and lack of etiquette), his morning rituals (up at four-thirty, cardio, hike, meditation), politics within large entertainment companies, his show, *The RuPaul Show* (specifically, that time they reunited Bea Arthur and Esther Rolle and it came out that Bea was not on Esther's "favorite people" list, and the fact that Liza—*my Liza*—produced that reunion), my show, Oprah (early days of, her *WWHL* appearance, Kitty Kelley book), dogs, and—of course—Valerie Cherish! When it's all over I can barely tear myself away from talking about the show with the creative team. We're done by nine, so I grab the noon flight, but we get diverted to Philly because of weather and I wind up home after midnight. I don't sweat the delay because I shot *The Comeback* today! The pic I took of John Mayer and Wacha is in *People* magazine.

▦ SATURDAY, MAY 24, 2014—NYC–SAG HARBOR

Whenever I text Bruce a funny thing that's happened, he texts back #AHWAC, which means Anything Happens With Andy Cohen, and is also an anagram for "Wacha." He thinks it should be my brand. I love an anagram.

Drove to the beach. Invited myself to Mark and Kelly's for lunch. I have been inviting myself to people's house for lunch, specifically in the Hamptons, for as long as I can remember. I kind of decide where I want to eat and then make it happen. Obviously, you should never invite yourself somewhere that you know you're not wanted. And I can tell (I hope!) who wants me and who doesn't. My East End lunch circuit is essentially the Consueloses', Marci Klein's, the Perskys', Sandy's, and Amanda's. (I've been known to invite myself to the Seinfelds' for breakfast.)

Stopped by Bruce's and played catch with some straight guys in his backyard in preparation for the MLB thing in July. I lasted about four minutes. Dinner at Marci Klein's (she invited me this time). We talked about pool houses, architects, interior designers, 9/11, dogs, kids, fucking, spinning, skin cancer, cooks—Hamptons chatter. All night I was telling SJ and Matthew's twins that I was their younger brother; it was simultaneously confusing and entertaining to them.

Wacha's picture is in *Hamptons* magazine.

⊞ SUNDAY, MAY 25, 2014—SAG HARBOR

I am fairly certain that ice cream will be my undoing this summer. I was slurping it up like crack last night. And on that note, I ran three miles with Wacha this morning. Ice cream is going to win this battle, but I'm fighting. Fun lunch with Bruce and co., then brought Wacha over for a playdate with Gary Fallon and ate a jumbo bag of nacho cheese Doritos, which are going head to head with the ice cream to be the food to do me in. Went to Sandy Gallin's party, which for him was small, like seventy people. Or to measure it another way, there were only about five hundred votives lit, whereas at a typical party there could be twenty-five hundred. For real. Robbie Baitz asked me if I ever get "existentially exhausted." I think that's called being read by a playwright. It was a good line, though, and I think I *might* get existentially exhausted, so maybe he had a point. (Sometimes reads teach us something about ourselves!) Ingrid Sischy told me her whole history with Warhol and *Interview* magazine. Lorne Michaels showed up for dessert with the Fallons and was gregarious and very wise, distinguishing for me his take on what executives do and what "talent" does. Having been on both sides, I thought it was valuable insight. David Geffen mercilessly made fun of my Brooks Brothers sport coat, which was admittedly loud and a one-off, but he was wrong about it. Donna Karan was in what looked like the most comfortable shmatte—but not shmatte, maybe Villager outfit. I would've worn it in a second. Went deep with Janie Buffett, which is usually the sign that summer is officially here.

⊞ MONDAY, MAY 26, 2014—SAG HARBOR–NYC

Memorial Day. A classic Andy-at-the-beach day, which means that I went from house to house and grazed on food, jumped into pools, and socialized all day. Started with breakfast at Sandy's with SJP, which was very decadent. Fresh baked stuff, flagels, eggs, and French toast that tasted like buttered, fried candy. From there I went to the Seinfelds', where I thought I was stopping by for a WachaVisit but it turned out that the buffet was starting, so I jumped in the pool and had a hot dog (no bun), corn, and half a chicken dog. And a rosé. I talked to Jerry about having Joan Rivers on *Comedians in Cars*. I think she'd be great. Their house remains the centerpiece in Elegant Adventures in Semitic Living. Next I headed to Amanda and Jim's, where we hung out and took a walk to their private beach. We found four ticks on Amanda, one on Jim, two on me, and two on Wacha. So I keep checking and checking to make sure we found them all. Terrifying. Then I had to stop by Mark and Kelly's because they were hosting Albert and a gaggle of gays by the pool, which sounded delicious and it was, like a gay pool club with Kelly as Julie McCoy—very satisfying. More rosé. (I would just like to take a moment to mention that all of today's visits were by invitation.) Hung back at the house with the dog for a few hours chilling out, doing work. Listened to the Grateful Dead the entire car ride home: summertime on the highway with the Dead, marveling at how I used to be alone and now the dog is there, always by my side. It feels good. Turned on Howard 101 near the Midtown Tunnel and Greg Fitzsimmons was interviewing John Henson. I was trying to call in to say, "I went to college with John—I've known him since before *Talk Soup*!" but the phone just rang and rang. Must've been on tape.

When I got home the love affair with Wacha came to a screeching halt when I found a tick trying to burrow itself into a teeny crevice behind his back leg. I was pinching him and hurting him trying to get it out. I became possessed with urgency to remove the evil tick and ultimately got it with a strong pinch that must've really hurt, because he yelped and as a reaction bit towards my face. And he got me. It wasn't a deep bite but it quickly turned into what looked like a red lip print, with minor bleeding. He immediately knew he'd hurt me and ran into the living room, burying his head in his bed. I told him to come with me and he so sheepishly and sadly watched me clean my face and remained in a deep state of humility for the rest of the night. I was unhappy, he was miserable, and we slept as far as we possibly could from each other on the bed.

▦ TUESDAY, MAY 27, 2014

Wacha's trauma and shame were evident from the moment we looked at each other this morning. I was very indifferent towards him for an hour and then gave him a lot of hugs and took him to the dog run. He was clingy and still feeling bad, and he made it clear that he was done after a few minutes. I went to the gym, then took him to the vet, who checked us both out. All good.

We taped an early show with Willie Geist and Lacey Chabert. Wacha was so mellow he just came out and sat.

After the early show there was a dinner for Sandy's birthday at the brand-new Tribeca branch of Tutto il Giorno. It was a full cast call of people who love Sandy. I spent a lot of time with the people who'd just flown in from LA, like Stacey Winkler and Carole Bayer Sager. Donna Karan made a toast that was very DKNY and Carole Bayer Sager made one that was very CBS. So everyone was in character, I guess.

The live show was Radzi and Amar'e Stoudemire. In my endless quest to get my nephew to think I'm cool, I got his signature for Jeremy, but he just signed his name, so I don't know if that's gonna get me into the Uncle Hall of Fame. He lives around the corner from me. Lady Gaga's manager emailed that she's in a hotel without Bravo and she needs to see tonight's *RHONY*. I'm trying to get her a link or something. #FirstWorld Problems.

▦ WEDNESDAY, MAY 28, 2014

Who knew a day with realtors could be so dramatic? It was the *MDLNY* reunion and there were tears. Ryan was wearing so much makeup he looked like a hologram, but after an hour of staring at him I decided I needed to bump up my own bronzer, so I can't imagine how nuts I will look alongside him. Luis cried and was so emotional he made the rest of us cry; he was pontificating about love. We all cried at a reunion *of realtors*. During lunch I ran over to Seize sur Vingt and I have finally gotten to the tipping point where I actually have every single thing in the store that I want, which is a lot. I had a *TV Guide* interview about our fifth-year anniversary in the Clubhouse. These interviewers want specifics, they want names. This is the shit I can't pull out. I gotta think a little harder before I do another of these. Harry Hamlin and Lisa Rinna were on the show. We have been secretly talking to Lisa about joining *RHOBH* and I was terrified I was going to see her at the show and want to take the invitation back. I thankfully went deeper in the other direction, and we whispered about it during breaks. The big question right now is whether her husband can take part, which we need in order for her to join. He is droll and funny. Totally vamping, I said, "You and Susan Dey legendarily did *not* get along on *L.A. Law*," and he confirmed it and said maybe that was why their tension was so electric onscreen. But I was making it up, just talking shit, and he went with it! Funny for the forty-five-plus crowd! The bartender was a Cambodian sandwich maker whose name I fucked up, then I got it right but fucked up the name of his restaurant. So that was good. It was our last show till June 15 and even though I am going to be working my ass off the next few weeks I am so psyched to have nights off. Deirdre organized a cake for my birthday and we hung out and drank. The kids on staff tried to explain who Danity Kane is to me and also Demi Lovato, whom I realize I am supposed to know but I am too stuck talking about Susan Dey. I am very old, I guess? But I act like an idiot, so that balances it out.

THURSDAY, MAY 29, 2014

By the way, the dog-bite redness hasn't gone away and it looks like I have a lip imprint on my cheek. I am back to 166. Wacha went to doggy day care today and I had conference calls all day. I am still totally ignoring these proposals from the architects. Don't know what's blocking me from getting into it and making a decision. I think they're just confusing and expensive and irritating. I want it done but that's as much as I got right now. SJP got Bruce and me all hyped up about Manhattanhenge 2014, which from what I understand happens twice a year and is when the sunset matches up perfectly with the cross streets of the city. But I had to go to these parties for the Book Expo, so I couldn't see it. The first was at my publisher Steve Rubin's on the Upper West Side. I walked in and he said what do you want, we have everything, and I ordered rosé, which they didn't have. I had a light red, then changed to a really good white. I was introduced to Alan and Arlene Alda. In the day, my mom was obsessed with Alan Alda and loved him even more because his wife looked like a nice Jewish girl rather than a titsy movie star, which was a reflection of his good taste (i.e., my mom coulda been a contendah). Arlene wrote a book about the Bronx and Alan reaffirmed what I already knew: that people from the Bronx love to talk about the Bronx. (Kind of like people from St. Louis.) I was introduced to Dick Cavett; I was in awe. Carole Radziwill was there and she joined me at the *People* party at that Ink hotel rooftop. I thought I might catch the Henge but it didn't look like it was happening. I saw Willie Geist, Pat O'Brien, and Anjelica Huston, who all have new books coming out, and my old friends Jess Cagle, Rob Weisbach, and Bill Clegg. With no sign of the Henge, I split and headed to Añejo with John Hill, Bruce, Liza, Kelly, and Mark. Liza had just done a makeup test for her wedding and so that was what the celebration was about. To celebrate her makeup. I can think of much more ridiculous reasons for a party.

Got a two-hour massage from Adam. I was so tired that I almost asked him to stop when he was half done with my second side. I was asleep in my bed before he was packed up and gone.

FRIDAY, MAY 30, 2014—NYC—SAG HARBOR

Wacha puked in two neat piles sometime during the night. On the wood floor. So that's what I woke up to. Thankfully, it doesn't look like he tried to eat any of it. Spent an hour at a booth at the Book Expo, signing blank diaries, which was painless. The ratio of women to men was twenty to one. Somehow a trip to Google headquarters (I was shooting a video for them) triggered some kind of rage within me, as the kid who was bringing us to the studio gave us a tour of what has to be the coolest workspace around. Actually it is *someone's* idea of the coolest workspace but looked to me like a parody of a Silicon Valley hub of cool for Generation Next. There are kitchen pods everywhere with different themes and guest chefs, a big Lego station, meeting rooms that are made to look like everything from train cars to diner booths. I wanted to scream. It looked like a preschool. Is this the stimulation that this generation requires in a work environment? Can't they get some magnets to play with at their desk? I felt ninety years old. And the tour guide was so blasé about it. Oh, and there were scooters everywhere. Let me hop a *scooter* to the *train car* for our little meeting—and I'll grab some *Legos* on the way so we can build while we strategize.

I drove to Sag with Wacha and we went on a run when we arrived so that I could go directly to Sam's Pizza and devour a medium. On the run I looked for the Ghost of Esther Rolle. That bitch is gone for good. I was late for dinner with Sean Avery and Hilary Rhoda. The two of them did not finish a medium between them. So I felt great about my accomplishment of wolfing down an entire medium mushroom and onion in front of hot, thin people. (Fairly certain Sean was on his way to get donuts across the street when we parted, though.) Had talked to Nancy Fallon about coming over for a Fresquila but it was raining and I was in a food coma and needed to cuddle Wacha.

The word is that it was too cloudy last night for the Henge. I'm not clear on whether it's one of those things that will next happen in 2158 or in September.

▦ SATURDAY, MAY 31, 2014—SAG HARBOR

I am in love with a man I don't know. I was driving to Estia's to grab something to eat and I was stopped at the light in front of the Getty station, where I was blinded by a fireball of blond hair on top of a too-thin guy who looked like he'd been transported from 1982. And he wasn't a hip, cool guy trying to be ironic—this was his legit look. It was a thick head of hair, a bob version of the Farrah, bright blond (not dyed). He was tanned and thin and smoking a cigarette. In other words: *my type.* A type I have fetishized since 1982, actually. I thought he might've been a ghost. He was standing in front of the car vacuums and I contemplated pulling in, cleaning out my car, and starting a conversation with him. What deterred me was that I wanted to pull up and immediately start applauding his hair, and I knew that would be creepy. Why I didn't come up with an alternative, I will never know. I continued and went to Estia's. On the way home, he was gone. An hour later, on the way to Marci Klein's, I stopped for gas just to sniff around. Still gone. It was a fun, boozy birthday dinner with Amanda and Jim at Vine Street on Shelter Island, made weird by a drunken guy at the next table in a Superman T-shirt who would not stop staring at me, and I mean the man did not take his eyes off me for an entire hour. He sent me a drink and I crossed my eyes (worse than their resting cross) when I thanked him so that my eyeballs never really looked at his face.

Got home from dinner and watched the last hour of Game 6 of the 2011 World Series. The entire game is on YouTube! I cried. It does not and will not ever get better than that game.

SUMMER 2014

» IN WHICH . . .

» I AM PUBLICLY LYNCHED FOR BEING
  A SCHLOCKMONSTER,
» GET A PHONE CALL FROM CHER,
» SOAK UP THE AMALFI COAST,
» ATTEMPT TO HIT A BALL IN FRONT OF THIRTY-FIVE
  THOUSAND PEOPLE,
» AND GO DEEP ON FIRE ISLAND.

Happy June! My favorite month. It just seems happy to me, not just because it's my birthday month. Tried Tracy Anderson's band class this morning with Sean and was so happy I kept up. All the kicking and shit I've been doing at Willspace totally translated. I thought it would be an awful scene but it was actually mellow. Sean's nipples were erect the whole time; I don't know what that's about. He gave me a cool pair of sunglasses. Brought Wacha to Shelter Island for his first playdate with Sassy, Bill and Joanna's rescue pup, and it was a raging success. They did everything they were supposed to and Joanna made them homemade frozen yogurt treats, which Wacha loved and then puked up as a special hostess gift. Going to the Perskys' for me is like a trip to Disneyland—they ply me with deviled eggs the minute I walk in the door, I never have an empty glass of rosé, and each visit is topped off with Joanna's *incredible* homemade peppermint ice cream—my summer favorite. And they made a fuss over my birthday with a cake. Bill came up with a slogan for Entenmann's: "Who needs homemade when you have Entenmann's?" I thought that was pretty good. Saw Bethenny's new house, which is great. She got it for under $3 million and it has a lot of space, so I'm impressed (only in the Hamptons would this be considered a deal). She is in the middle of a *brutal* custody trial over Bryn, who seems oblivious and happy. I keep dropping hints about her returning to *Housewives*. Seems insane but there's something in the back of my head that says it's not an awful idea for her (I know it's a great one for us). Wacha chased and killed two flies in the house, which at last answered the question of his roach-killing capability. I crashed from the Tracy Anderson around five-thirty and then drove back to the city. Zachary Quinto and I share a birthday and he had a drinks thing at the Little Owl Catering Space, where I unfortunately turned into Valerie Cherish at midnight, when a cake came out and the birthday boy made a sweet toast to his friends. I was standing there—loaded—with a big grin on my face waiting to be called up or acknowledged or something and it didn't happen, which was a very Valerie moment. I was flirting with two guys, neither of whom was technically available, so I went and got my real boyfriend and brought him over. The group—specifically Jennifer Westfeldt—went wild for Wacha. Jason Weinberg wants to set me up with the same guy Allison Levy has been talking about for the last year.

Ann B. Davis died today and I was shocked she was still alive, so that was a double-edged sword. She was eighty-eight.

▦ MONDAY, JUNE 2, 2014

I woke up to a birthday tweet from Marie Osmond! Between that and Wacha, I don't need another gift. I certainly don't *feel* forty-six today. And I don't think I look forty-six, right? I hope? It's funny to see who wishes you happy birthday first thing in the morning, and you have to then question how they know it's your birthday. Is it Facebook? Which, by the way, has become the worst thing about birthdays. It's just too much. I don't actually know half my Facebook friends, so there's no way for me to find what my real friends have posted for my birthday, and so I wind up not looking at any of it because it's overwhelming. That being said, by the end of the day, I heard from essentially everyone I know and there's nothing not nice about that.

Because Solly and I have the same birthday, Jeanne and I are always looking for special ways her son and oldest friend can connect and celebrate—even though there are thirty-four years between us, it's always fun. This year she suggested taking a helicopter to a water park on Long Island or finding a pool to hang out at in Manhattan. I chose option two: the pool. So Daryn booked us a cabana at the Dream Hotel. I realized on my way out that I didn't have a gift for Solly, but the good Lord intervened when Surfin handed me a package from Cardinal outfielder Jon Jay that included two hats that were too small for me. Perfect. The Monday afternoon pool scene at the Dream in Chelsea was nuts: I saw Spike from *Top Chef*, a black dude in a mesh thong, two managers from Tao who gave me their cards, a whole lotta titsy ladies, and our waitress—who happens to deliver pot lollipops in my neighborhood. You have to wonder what Solly thought of it all—he's twelve. We ate like pigs, and Jeanne, Fred, and I drank plenty of rosé. I checked my Twitter at one point and saw that the sweet flood of birthday love had been decidedly interrupted by an uprising of people pissed that I would stoop so low as to produce a show called *I Slept with a Celebrity*. The idea, which we had collectively yet to even finish developing or pitch to anyone, got leaked, and the press was positioning me as the driving force behind it. And it was backfiring all over my birthday cake. I called my agent to discuss next steps, then made a conscious decision to let it drop and enjoy my birthday. And can we all agree that the song "Happy Birthday" sounds like a funeral march?

Brought Wacha to dinner at Morandi, where we sat outside with Bruce and Liza for a fun, low-key hang. Bruce saw *Chef* the other night, and at the theater, the guy next to him pulled out salami and started eating it. Can you imagine? Sarah Paulson walked up with none other than the guy Jason Weinberg and Allison both are trying to set me up with. He is handsome.

Wacha freaked when I went to the bathroom. I hope I am not turning him into an overly dependent, crazy dog. I think I am. It was a lovely birthday, even with being publicly shamed.

▦ TUESDAY, JUNE 3, 2014

Married to Medicine reunion tomorrow and I am having a hard time rallying. Went to the gym, where I think I did eighty squats. I am still 167.5 but something happened to my stomach that is positive—there are some new indentations—so if this is my weight, so be it. Had a pitch meeting with Joan Rivers and Michael Rourke and we all agreed on a concept for what could be a fun show for her called *What's Your Problem*, where she basically sits in judgment of people and solves their social problems, kinda like Judge Judy laying down verdicts on *Real Housewives*–type fights. I think it could sell. On that note, the *I Slept with a Celebrity* leak continues to be irritating, because I didn't have a chance to properly position it, and now everyone is just talking about how gross it is and I am. My production company has fifteen shows in development and this is the first one people have heard about and so now people think that my company is just going to do shit. I can't blame people because this is at the top of the schlock pile, but it's an unfortunate situation.

Eric Wattenberg got me a pair of Cardinals cuff links for my birthday, which I love. Agents give good gifts. Considering the amount of Snoopy, Cardinals, and Wacha gear I already have, I am virtually impossible to shop for. Had a bitch of a time getting to 30 Rock; my Uber canceled on me after I gave him a lil attitude for going to the wrong address. I felt like Carrie Bradshaw when Berger broke up with her on the Post-it: it's just not supposed to happen that way. Then I willingly allowed my cab to get jacked. I had all these bags but let two other people have my cab for some reason, then had intense residual anger towards them and debated giving them the finger when they drove off. I didn't. I got a gypsy cab for twenty-five bucks and the sky opened up the minute I got out.

I *thought* I loved New York in June, how about *you*?

I had drinks with Frances Berwick at Morell's and a girl came up and said she'd been in the audience of the *Tonight Show* taping and Jimmy mentioned *I Slept with a Celebrity*. I am going to become infamous for a show I never wind up producing. Mike Darnell called me at 9 p.m. EDT, which is the most classic LA move in the book. I was already deep into my evening and couldn't handle the conversation at that moment. Wacha was at doggy day care, but his Fitbit for dogs (his Whistle) says he only had ninety-seven minutes of exercise today, which is confounding because he will be under goal for the first time in the three weeks I have been obsessing over it. SMH, man. Maybe it was all that extra energy he had that then made him chew up the sunglasses Sean Avery gave me. I was furious, then he puked up his dinner and I felt bad for him. Roller coaster of emotion going on here, people. Kolten Wong got a grand slam tonight.

WEDNESDAY, JUNE 4, 2014

Early call for this *ferkakte* reunion and I woke up to an email from Gayle King saying *I Slept with a Celebrity* is a bad look for me. Apparently both the *Today* show and *Wendy Williams* were going to debate whether a show like this should be made today—but we managed to get the stories killed and by 9 a.m. I had told Eric to pull out of the deal. *Basta*, rasta.

For weeks a massive team of workmen has been grooming the triangular patch of grass and trees on the corner of Jane and Eighth Avenue;

it was un-fenced this morning and Wacha took a big dump in there. The last remaining workman flipped out. "This is expensive, man! No dogs!" he yelled at me. I told him he just created a dog poop park and that this was its destiny. He didn't want to hear that.

The *Married to Medicine* reunion was actually painless and enjoyable, partly because it was set up like a tea party and there were (real) cakes and pastries littering the table, so I spent all day putting my finger on the top of cupcakes and eating little dabs of frosting, which in retrospect is gross. Plus I can't imagine how fat I will be tomorrow. Dr. Heavenly kept saying she had a craving for crab legs, which tickled me for some reason.

Wacha and I had dinner with Mike and Elaine Goldman outside at Morandi, my new favorite summer doggy-dining experience. On the way home ran into Jerry O'Connell, who was looking extra-sinewy in a tee and Dodgers hat and wondering WTF had gotten into me producing a show about sleeping with celebrities. I spilled the tea, then we went deep under my awning for twenty minutes. Got a two-hour massage that was over at 2 a.m. and hobbled into bed. I am enjoying this two-week *WWHL*-free hiatus, but it's not resulting in any more sleep for me.

THURSDAY, JUNE 5, 2014

They talked about the fucking show I'm not doing on *The View* today. It. Won't. Die. I worked out and had a civilized lunch with Bruce at Good. Three months and counting until he moves to LA.

I had dinner with Sandra Bernhard and Sara Schaefer at Cookshop, where Sandy regaled me with stories of being a manicurist at 350 North Canon in the seventies for the likes of Dyan Cannon, Victoria Principal, and Diandra Douglas. From there it was Anfora for a second Tinder date with the finance guy, who was coming at me from every direction trying to figure out why I don't have a boyfriend, what I am looking for, and where a boyfriend would fit in my life. So he was keeping my brain churning hard. It was not light convo until he realized—thank God—that the girl sitting across from us had given him many (by his accounts amazing) blowjobs while he was at Columbia and she at Barnard. The relationship had ended poorly, so it was an apparently awkward run-in, which was fun for me. He said all the Barnard girls would go all the way with anybody and that they weren't the brightest bulbs. My ageist alarm bells were on a low buzz regarding the amount of college stories sprinkled into our conversation, but I like a college story and it was by then clear we weren't getting married, so what did I care? Then another couple of twenty-eight-year-olds gravitated to us with a round of tequila, and then another, and I was once again America's Oldest Teenager. We had a better goodbye than last time in front of my building and someone yelled "Get a room!" from a cab. We made plans to have dinner next week but I have a gut feeling we'll never see each other again.

ⵉⵉⵉⵉ FRIDAY, JUNE 6, 2014—NYC–SAG HARBOR

The NYPD or some jerk (*not* Chris Christie) made getting out of the city impossible today—West Twelfth Street closed, roadblocks, workmen, one lane at a time, blah blah blah—so getting to the Midtown Tunnel was treachery. Oh, and besides National Donut Day, it's First World Problem Day where I am allowed to bitch about traffic to the Hamptons. A fun, light lunch at Amanda's where we broke shit down. I had two conference calls with architects that got me motivated to get this thing going. Why did I put that off for so long? Dinner with Mark and Kelly and Michael Consuelos—he and I celebrated our birthday together (the culmination of my weeklong birthday festival)—and the Consueloses once again gave me a too-generous gift, ten workout sessions with Kelly's trainer and something else on the way.

The twink from the sunglass store left the price tag on my gift to Michael, so that was elegant.

I got home and was sucked into a YouTube vortex watching about fifteen of Sandra Bernhard's eighties Letterman appearances. You can't beat their chemistry. Lightning in a bottle.

There was a rustling on the deck this morning that I assumed to be Consuelos stopping by with coffee. I threw on my summer Gant robe, which is really short, and found two adorable Jehovah's Witnesses at my doorstep to try to convert me and Wacha. They engaged me on various topics: Is the suffering in the world what was intended by God? What is our purpose here? It was such a pretty morning and I was up for some deep talk with two hot, barely legal believers, so we chatted for twenty minutes. One was Asian and really jacked. I was like a fifties-era cougar when a hot plumber came over. They want to come back next week and talk some more! They left me with some literature. I love suburban livin'. My robe was way too short for a convo about God, by the way.

Lunch at Calvin's with Sandy and David Geffen. His house was just completed and is the most talked about out here. It took years and a lot of resources to build and is a minimalistic glass masterpiece that looks to me like the manifestation of the Calvin Klein lifestyle. Not a scrap of paper or knickknack in sight and views of the bay and ocean from both sides. Lunch was as good as the house. On the way home we talked about how expensive it is to go clubbing in Vegas and all agreed we'd split before dropping 30k for a night out with bottle service. Who says rich people don't know the value of a dollar? David may buy a basketball team. That's worth more than a night in Vegas, for sure. I got home to an email from Ramona wanting to know the schedule for Friday's *RHONY* reunion and a request that the room be 65 degrees. So now we can cross from our lists the question of where to set the thermostat on Friday.

I was a co-host for HMI's "School's Out" benefit. They do great work. It was a cavalcade of Hamptons gays in pastels, white pants, statement shoes, and SOTS (sweaters over the shirts, cashmere). The bartenders were all perfect 10s—straight dudes bused in from the city. I did the Conan thing of "Great to *see* you!" and it worked flawlessly. But every cute guy already had a boyfriend and I got depressed. I did meet a cute resident at Southampton Hospital. By the end I was scarfing brownies.

SUNDAY, JUNE 8, 2014—SAG HARBOR—NYC

One more thing about yesterday's visit from those darling Jehovah's Witnesses: like Dan Rather, they used my name very liberally in sentences, which, as I've said, I enjoy. "You know, Andy, the world is beautiful but there is a lot of suffering. Do you wonder why, Andy?" I forgot their names, so I couldn't return the favor. James? Todd? I don't know but they were go-getters. I look forward to our second date, and am one inch closer to converting. (Look how great it's worked out for the Jacksons!)

I went to Tracy Anderson and sweated my ass off working the bands. I met Tracy herself, who really is a sight in person: tits, tan, muscles . . . what you'd expect but even more blonde.

Joined Justin Tarquinio, George Kolasa, and co. at Two Mile Hollow Beach to officially kick off the summer. As beautiful as that gay beach is, the scene is kinda sad. There's nothing going on, certainly no hot guys. Two guys did come up to me, boyfriends, and one was attractive and we allegedly know each other (he got a "Good to *see* you!") and as we were talking I noticed that he had a third nipple, a lil mini-nip right under his left nipple. It was a baby nipple with an areola and everything. I was obsessed and staring and gratefully wearing my Oakleys, which completely mask my eyeballs. I wanted to tweak the #babynip but I refrained. I wonder if it's sensitive. How does that happen?

Meanwhile Mom had a realization during our Sunday Skype session: "You OBSESS about poop, pee, penises, and boobs. Do you realize how much that comes up in your conversations? Do you think that's UNUSUAL? What's wrong with you? Did WE DO THAT to you?"

MONDAY, JUNE 9, 2014

I shot a promotional video for a car company with Wacha and he was a total champ. I actually felt bad for him towards the end of the day because I thought they were asking too much of him. Of course none of the culpability could come back to *me* for prostituting my dog for a car company; I blamed the producer. Smart. I think he's earned back the cost of his hip surgery by now. There's a touch feature of the vehicle where you wave your arm like a wand and the motion sensor kicks in. The problem was that every time I waved like a wand, nothing happened. The producer kept screaming at me, "You need to *own your wand*!" I wanted to snap, "Oh, I *own my wand*, lady." But that would be bitchy, obviously.

We shot the whole thing in my neighborhood—on the far end of my block toward the river. So it was exactly in front of the building in which I lived from '91 to '96, and who comes out all these years later but my downstairs neighbor Dottie, the old lady with the dogs whom Grac and I dubbed the Gladys Kravitz of the meatpacking district—a real rabble-rouser and busybody before the area was cool. I haven't seen her in so many years, and had assumed she had passed away, but there she was: thin, old, with one of those old dogs still kicking with her. I was so happy to see her that I went right up to her and explained that I used to be her neighbor and fondly remember her and her husband, who worked for the MTA. She wasn't as happy to see me; in fact I think my energy, camera crew, and made-up face completely freaked her out. Her husband has passed away and she seemed frail. I'm a sentimental guy and this was not the reunion I hoped for. Later in the shooting, however, I ran into Eric Stonestreet and he seems like a really nice guy. I think he's from Missouri too.

We had a party for entertainment publicists on the roof of the Dream Hotel, celebrating *WWHL*'s fifth anniversary, which means that I schmoozed PR girls all night. We are targeting Katy Perry for the summer.

TUESDAY, JUNE 10, 2014—NYC–BOSTON

Every time I go from Manhattan to either Boston or DC, I endlessly ruminate about whether to take the train or the shuttle. I compare the timing, which often winds up being even either way, and usually make a bad decision. Today was one of those days, as Dave and I bet on the shuttle to get to Boston to shoot our College Roommate Quickfire on *Top Chef* and were delayed three hours at the airport because of weather that we'd be sailing through on the train. Joy.

We landed in time for a late dinner at Sportello, which we initially thought was too bright but won us over with its food and lesbian waitstaff. Some guy from our freshman-year dorm floor was at the bar and Dave remembered him and then reminded me I used to borrow his CD player and Genesis CDs. (I had an Early Genesis Moment freshman year of college, about which I feel no shame.) Our driver seemed to be in Boston for the first time in his life, so Dave and I knew more than he about getting around and we made him drive all around town on a quest to find the perfect bar. Boston remains charming, beautiful, and a perfect mini Americanization of London. Driving through the South End took me back to being head over heels in love for the first time as a college senior with a twenty-six-year-old who at the time seemed like an intellectual, but I now realize was perhaps a windbag. He was a sun-kissed blond trust-fund guy who lived in a loft, spoke several languages, and took me to nice dinners. I was young and in love, and it was all so foreign it felt like I lived in Paris.

Dave and I went to Toro for a drink, then got lost looking for a bear bar and wound up at Paradise in Cambridge, which had strippers and featured TV screens showing men doing things to each other that had never crossed Dave's mind, which I should point out he handled with great aplomb. At around midnight our trusty driver took a wrong turn and we were on a Boston University "campus" drive-by. The campus is as unimpressive now as it was when we were there all those years ago. But one of the reasons I went to BU was because Boston was its campus.

▦ WEDNESDAY, JUNE 11, 2014—BOSTON—NYC

On the front page of the *Boston Globe* is a story with the headline "Local Names Hard to Find in Clinton's Pages," about the dearth of Bostonians mentioned in Hillary Clinton's new book. The *Globe* feels that Boston's political relevancy is stronger than the number of mentions it got from Hillary, so it's a whole deal with a chart of how many mentions locals got (John Kerry led with twenty-one). Some would say this town has a massive insecurity complex, some maybe that it has a major chip on its shoulder, but I am a lover, not a fighter, so I like to think of it as Massachusetts's pride. Still—*this* is front-page news?

Top Chef was a blast. We judged a Ramen Noodle Quickfire, a classic dorm meal that Dave and I know all too well. After ten seasons as an EP on that show, it was wild to be in front of the camera, delivering and judging a challenge with Padma. And I saw Dave nervous for I think the first time in our thirty-year friendship—when we were running through the directions we had to give the chefs, his mouth was tensed in a whole new way. I was supportive, but put this moment in my back pocket to take out and rib him about later. Tasting the food was the best and giving the results was the worst. Dave thinks that I sexually harass Padma, and he may be right. Before announcing the winner of the Quickfire, I told the chefs that she and I had made sweet love while they were cooking. She is saucy. And knows about sauces. Ma-ha. We do have a very unique relationship; she has a fantastic sense of humor.

TSA at Logan is staffed by a League of Older Gentlemen Massholes who are very serious about inspecting licenses and everything. But there is something weird going on there. At the first checkpoint, a man snarled at my New York license and said, "You did one thing right, you got out of New York."

"Yeah, but I'm going back now," I said.

He wasn't happy. "Massachusetts is the *best state*, you know that." He was looking me in the eye, *deadly* serious.

"Yes, I know that," I agreed before he sent me to be cavity searched. The second man at the metal detector looked at me and said, "If you have a metal shank in your shoe, you'll need to take them off."

Yes, I figured that, sir, but thank you for the reminder about a metal shank being off-limits. And finally the guy sitting on the other end of the luggage conveyer—unsolicited—said, "Good for you for getting the hell out of Boston." So there's a weird mix of self-hate and self-love going on in the Delta terminal, which maybe shouldn't have surprised me after this morning's newspaper headline.

It took two shuttle experiences for me to once and for all agree with what Bruce has been saying for years: In the summer, if it's after 2 p.m., you always take the train from NYC to Boston or DC. We were delayed again three hours to LGA. I had two tequilas, Dave had three.

Wacha has a girlfriend in Brooklyn. Her name is Lola and she's a King Charles. Sherman says he's obsessed with her—he sent me pictures from doggy day care. She looks like she wears a weave and he appears shy and smitten in her presence. I don't want him to get hurt. I worked out with the Ninj—tons of core work on the floor and running around that ladder thing, then had lunch with Bruce at Good. Went to Three Lives bookstore and got Dad a bunch of books for Father's Day. I asked them why they don't carry *Most Talkative* but they didn't seem interested in that conversation. After consulting with Jeff Lewis and Nate Berkus, I finally pulled the trigger on hiring an architect. If I had a therapist, I might consider asking him what about the decision scared me. But I don't.

Skyped with Mom and Dad, and Blouse was there. She and Eddie love how I dress on *WWHL* but cannot get over how many commercials there are.

Tonight was Joey Walsh's eighth-grade graduation from Brooklyn Heights Montessori School. It was sweet and full of emotion for the parents and kids, but I blundered at the cookie and cheese reception afterwards when I asked for a glass of wine. I just assumed there would be wine, but I was very wrong. I was too embarrassed to tell Jeanne and Fred what I'd done but I had a feeling they'd get a report from the teacher later.

Stopped by the birthday party for Anthony from *WWHL* at Boxers and some dude next to me at the urinal was whistling that Lorde song so forcefully I wanted to whack him. Whistling is a massive pet peeve for me. Cannot bear it.

I'm actually looking forward to the *RHONY* reunion tomorrow.

FRIDAY, JUNE 13, 2014

It was a monsoon outside all day and in the Hammerstein Ballroom it was raining absurdity, my favorite kind of storm. The day was a wild dance with Ramona, and after doing six of these with her, I was ready for it. Before the show, she made me promise on my dog's life that I wouldn't go deep about what's going on in her marriage with Mario, but I wouldn't promise all the way. I told her to just listen closely to my questions—which were going to be more along the lines of "What did you *learn about yourself* from your marriage struggles?" rather than "Who cheated on who?" We had saved that section for the end of the day, and until then I kept her happy by telling her when the next break was, how many cards I had left to ask, how many packages were remaining—I have learned that as long as I keep her closely in the loop, she remains calm. For her. When I told her we might have enough content for three parts, she was ebullient and I got a really heartfelt emo moment of how appreciative she is of our relationship. Then the love ended when I did start asking the questions about her marriage—she kept saying, "Roll the next package!" and "Next question!" Then she asked me who *I* was planning on having sex with tonight, and I told her when I go on a reality show about my life I would be happy to tell her. It was a tug-of-war and I wound up getting nothing out of her. And she did herself no favors by evading every question. At the end of the day she told me to watch my dog. Did I *actually* swear on his life before the shoot? I was going to drive to the beach after we wrapped but it was still pouring and I wound up at Whitehall 10014 with Bruce and Bryan, where we downed margaritas. The city on a summer Friday night is a mellow delight.

▦ SATURDAY, JUNE 14, 2014—NYC–SAG HARBOR

I opened my eyes and realized with a flash I had a morning meeting with some Jehovah's Witnesses in Sag Harbor, so I hightailed it out to the beach and was on my couch by ten-thirty, exactly the time they showed up last week. I didn't know what to wear, so I figured sweats was the best look because I didn't want them to think I thought about it. I got stood up and headed to Shelter Island for lunch at the Perskys', where Joanna went absolutely nuts with the deviled eggs—I think she had two dozen for me. Which begs the question: What's the protocol when someone goes out of their way to make you a massive amount of something and you can't possibly eat it all? I made it through five. The peppermint ice cream was absurd. I had to stop myself from having more because I knew it was pizza for dinner tonight. We pondered Liza's age-old favorite topic: What one thing would you ask your dog? Bill said he would ask Sassy, "Who do you love more, me or Joanna?" Joanna said she would ask what one thing she could do to make Sassy's life better. For the life of me I can't decide what I would ask Wacha, which is odd considering I interview people for a living. Maybe I would ask him what he would ask *me*.

I ran with Wacha and thought he might have a heart attack near the end. And on that note, maybe I would ask him if he could come up with a clear sign for me before having cardiac arrest. Dinner at Sam's with Barry, Sandy, and Bryan Fox. We ordered Cokes and the waitress said they have Pepsi, which Barry, a member of the Coke board, couldn't understand. Graham, the owner, came over to the table and we broke down his relationship with Coke and Pepsi, and Barry took his name and number. Suffice to say I will guarantee Graham will be convinced to switch to Coke by the end of the summer.

Had a drink with the doctor I met at the gay pastel party last week who is so handsome but I think too young for me. A common theme?

SUNDAY, JUNE 15, 2014—SAG HARBOR—NYC

I am not a dad, but every Father's Day I get greetings and salutations from gay guys all over the place thinking I am a *daddy*. So that's weird. It is, right? And now dog lovers are wishing me well because of Wacha. I love this dog so much but I don't think I can embrace Father's Day as my own. Dad loved his books except he doesn't have an interest in the Hillary Clinton one. Tracy Anderson must be obsessed with hip flexors, because the whole workout was about lifting legs.

This isn't a new observation but, wow, does Wacha follow me everywhere. Like every step I take. And I know it's supposed to be "Father's Day" for "dog parents" but he is bugging the shit out of me. I went back to the city early for our first show in two weeks and didn't bring Wacha to the studio. I felt like we needed a few hours apart.

Recorded the voice-over for a *Married to Medicine* special and they had me say "tea," "shade," and "side eye" in every line I read. André Leon Talley had a little silver thing in his hand for the whole show; I asked what it was and he said an Elsa Peretti minaudière that he holds to calm his nerves. I asked him if it had pills in it and he said, "No pills, no coke!" On air. Love him.

Stayed after with John Hill and went deep. A late-night walk with Wacha got me vibing with him again. Danny from the Cubbyhole bartended on *WWHL* and then I wandered into him standing in front of the bar smoking a cig when we walked by—because I live in Mayberry—and he said he'd been very nervous on the show, which hadn't registered with me. Anderson went to Baghdad. I'm worried about him!

▦ MONDAY, JUNE 16, 2014

As we headed down the hallway for Wacha's morning walk, I heard the old lady down the hall screaming and crying on the phone with someone. It was heart wrenching. Wacha kept looking up at me while we waited for the elevator, both of us listening to her tearfully *pleading* for something. It was too much to bear and she was on my mind all day. What was wrong? Who was she pleading with and for what? And in other sad news, I read in the paper that Warhol muse Ultra Violet died.

Had conference calls about a new show I'm developing that we'll hopefully pitch to NBC sometime soon, screened an episode of *RHOC* and one of *RHONJ*, then Bruce took me to SoulCycle for a class with his favorite instructor, Marvin. It was a great workout and much less irritating than those classes usually are. As I mentioned, I can't handle getting screamed at about spirituality by sweaty lesbians in a dark room. But Marvin was great. And Bruce has completely transformed his body by spinning.

Interviewed David Lauren for the cover of *Hamptons* magazine, which was interesting because I am so passionate about his brand. He answers questions like a politician. Maybe he should run for something. I'd vote for him. Doggy playdate with Jackie in Central Park, and Wacha seemed overheated so we left after an hour. Ran into Lady Bunny on the way home and we talked about the intense word-patrolling of the gay community. Now "homosexual" is a bad word. And they're after the drag queens about half the things they've been saying for years. We're going to outlaw speech itself before it's all over.

Gabrielle Union and the new OC Housewife Shannon were on *WWHL* tonight. Before the show, Union's publicist said not to ask about Dwyane Wade and so we killed a whole thing where we'd put :30 on the clock to grill her about him, and then wound up talking about him a bunch anyway. That happens all the time.

Ultra Violet's passing had me up late flipping through the *Warhol Diaries*. The idea that Diana Ross comes to pick him up at his house to go chopper to Atlantic City to see Sinatra blows my mind. In the middle of the night I thought I saw a big bug on my sink but it was one of those bow-tie-y things from the dry cleaners.

▦ TUESDAY, JUNE 17, 2014

Lunch with Bill Owens at Morandi. Went deep about *60 Minutes* and CBS News.

Had a booking meeting at the studio. There are always so many politics involved with booking. For instance, suddenly Wendy Williams won't do *WWHL*. I don't know why. I thought we were buddies.

I did a signing of the paperback of *Most Talkative* at Club Monaco. Book signings make me feel overwhelmingly positive about humanity. Everybody's so nice to me, and people bring me very sweet things. I got three bags of Jolly Ranchers because I've recently been going on the air with colored tongues because of pre-show Jolly Ranchers, also a lot of treats for Wacha, a few business cards from guys looking for dude-on-dude intimacy, some résumés, a few sweaty handshakes, some good hugs, and a picture of myself. We did photos with 350 people in an hour—impressive. Oh, and two ancillary players from the *RHONY* showed up—Sonja's facialist and Harry. Randomosity!

Met Bruce, Ava, and a school-mom friend of his with her kid at Good. They were already a few vinos into the night when I arrived.

Patti LaBelle was on the show with Wanda Sykes, and I am reading between the lines here: I believe that Miss Patti *did* get dissed by Aretha at the White House. Patti wouldn't confirm it but I saw it on her face and she's my Gemini twin. Why the hell would Aretha dis Patti? I am racking my brain. Patti's hair stylist Norma was with her—she always is; I'd met them both when I did a profile for *48 Hours* in 1996 and have seen them together over the years. We played "Who's in the Cell with Patti LaBelle?" Classic.

I Googled "do dogs feel love." I discovered that a dog experiences all of the basic emotions: joy, fear, anger, disgust, and even love. But based on current research it seems likely that a dog will not have more complex emotions like guilt, pride, and shame. Benjamin and Pablo threw a Tall Night for people who like tall dudes at Atlas Social Club. What a good idea and why didn't I go? Been texting AC in Baghdad. To make matters worse for him, his Instagram is blocked. So I've been trying to give him a play-by-play of what he's "missing" from the people we follow to take his mind off his life being in peril.

▦ WEDNESDAY, JUNE 18, 2014

Like clockwork I got a request from *The Wendy Williams Show* to tape a fiftieth-birthday greeting. I told Ryan to ask the people who asked me to do it why Wendy won't do my show, and to tell them that I thought we were buddies. Why, Wendy? Why? I'll never find out the real reason. For some reason, the Sean Avery engagement rumors are back. I have been getting "Congratulations" tweets for the last two days.

I guess I wanted some attention, because I Instagrammed a muscly pic of myself at the gym. Seems kinda desperate in the rearview mirror but I'm in great shape—and terrified about gaining multitudes of weight in Europe over the July Fourth weekend. There's no way I won't be sloshing in wine and pasta. I got twenty-five thousand likes, so I guess that gave me some confidence for a few hours.

We taped JLo tonight for air tomorrow. Despite the many diva she-nanigan stories I've heard about her, she was completely graceful and drama-free: on time, no restrictions on the interview, no rider, and totally open and willing to go beyond my questions. She says she's a fan of the show. Not only was my Ninj in the audience, but Surfin was too and I think Liza came just because she knew Surf would be there. (They love each other.) It's always weird seeing people you know from one place in another ("Why is my *teacher* at McDonald's, Mommy!?"—I never said that but I am making a point) but having Surf in the Clubhouse felt just right and he'll be back. He couldn't believe how close he was sitting to JLo. There's not a show that gets you closer to the guest. JLo is probably the most beautiful woman I've ever seen. She is flawless. Benny Medina was with her and he's a lot of fun. We always talk about Motown and Diana Ross. He started out working for Berry Gordy, so he has a ton of great stories. I was posing for a picture during a commercial break and JLo noticed that thing I do with my leg—the Angelina Jolie extension—and I told her I had to do it because of how big my dick is. So clearly I felt comfortable with her.

The live show was 50 Cent and Jerry Ferrara. A caller asked how much cash each of them had and 50 pulled out ten grand (in hundreds) from his back pocket. I still can't get over it. The idea of him having sex with Chelsea Handler confuses me. He's really hot.

After the show we all partied like it was our birthday and I wound up bringing my glass with me in the car home. That's not messy. Joe was the night doorman and he said, "Oh, you brought your glass with you, huh?"

⬛ THURSDAY, JUNE 19, 2014—NYC–SAG HARBOR

I asked Anderson how much danger he's in and he said they have major security detail and are restricted in their movements. I suggested that he play Whoopi Goldberg saying "You in dangah, gurl" from *Ghost* over and over in his head so he wouldn't get lazy. The poor guy is trying to report on world news and this is what I'm telling him to do.

Lunch with LZ at Good. We talked about everything and of course the last topic, as it often is with us, is what's going on with my love life or lack thereof. I explained that I do *want* to be in love. But I am so happy right now, and unfortunately the older I get I am probably boxing myself more into my own lane and routine, which may not be helping the relationship cause. Though the dog opened me up, I remain concerned that Wacha falsely convinces me I already have enough love. And maybe I do have enough love, because I got an email from Bryant Gumbel entitled "What?" saying that someone told him that I got engaged.

I had a daytime massage before our Friends In Deed board meeting. I feel like we have some momentum on this board, new members and new energy for events we are planning in the next year.

Drove to the beach to see the doctor, because I have plans all weekend. Maybe the chat with LZ got me in the zone, because we had a great date, chilling until 3 a.m. He had to be at the hospital at 6. Beyond being incredibly delicious, he is a quality guy.

▦ FRIDAY, JUNE 20, 2014—SAG HARBOR

Ran into Hilary Rhoda at Tracy Anderson and told her that the engagement rumors are back. She didn't seem thrilled. Why *would* she be thrilled that her fiancé is rumored to be engaged to a dude? I shoulda kept my mouth shut. The class wasn't great. The instructor played "G.U.Y.," which I guess is my theme song because I'm in the video; Bruce's instructor at SoulCycle also played it for me last week.

Hung out at Bruce's. Bought three new diaries: Virginia Woolf, Noël Coward, and Alan Bennett.

Voted for myself for the Emmys. We won't get nominated. It is an impossible category with all the heavy hitters—the Jimmys, Colbert, *Daily Show*, etc.

Saw Sandra Bernhard at Guild Hall in East Hampton. Two of her doctors were in the crowd, which made sense given the venue, and she went off on a lot of WASPs. She was brilliant. Her "Wrecking Ball" rework is perfect. Went to the Palm after and some guy came up to Bruce and Bryan and me and told us about finding a son he never knew he had. After he left, we realized that this guy was a friend none of us ever knew *we* had. None of us knew him. So that was weird—hovering over us with seven minutes of personal baggage dumped on us while our food was served and we ate. Everybody wants to be heard!

The longest day of the year began with a gorgeous morning. I was sitting on the deck gossiping on the phone with Lynn when a van pulled up and my Jehovah's Witness buddies—dressed in vests and "slacks" (that expression makes my skin crawl but slacks they were)—came down the stairs, books in hand. I was happy to see them and they were cuter than I remembered, but I told them my call was urgent and we should speak another time. I'm not sure what the end game is at this point. I need to break it off when they come back.

Lunch with Amanda, Jim, Fred, and Jeanne, who were undercharged last night at Topping Rose. They told the waiter, but he came back and explained that the bill was correct. They knew they were right and yet paid the lower amount. So the ethical question is, did they do the right thing? I believe they did. Should they *argue* with the waiter to convince them they owe more? Wacha broke a glass. Amanda is questioning whether I have any control over the dog.

Left Wacha at Bruce's and went to the beach for a quick swim. The water is gorgeous. Driving around the beach listening to new and archived Howard Stern is my idea of bliss. The doctor came by for a hangout. Engagement party for Allison and Ricky at John and Lizzie Tisch's house, which is sick—very cool and mod with incredible contemporary art everywhere. I sat next to Brian Williams and we talked about his early years at WCBS, when I was working in the same building at CBS News. He said that when he was anchoring the local noon news, CBS told him they didn't see any future for him and then NBC offered him Brokaw's job. CBS always was horrible at spotting talent. We talked about the segmentation of the media, how there's no national platform anymore, nothing matters—my favorite conversation. He is into *The Bachelorette*. The food was great—they'd imported the chef from ABC Kitchen.

After dinner, doors were opened to reveal a massive table covered with every kind of candy you can imagine. And in the center a rainbow cake. A cake like you cannot believe. From Flour Shop in Brooklyn. Bruce and I ate so much of it.

Lunch at Sandy's. Ron Meyer was there and the two of them told us about a hilarious meeting they had with Michael Jackson. I don't know how Sandy managed him for eight years; I need to remember that he did that. It says something about a person's constitution to be able to deal with that kind of *unique* on a daily basis.

Great drive home with the top down, flipping all over Sirius, lots of Grateful Dead and endless Eric the Actor vs. Hanzi nonsense on *Howard Stern*, then I stumbled upon a Village People song on Studio 54 that I can't believe I never heard: "Ready for the 80s," which the Village Peeps most assuredly were! The song pretty much wrote itself as it went on, and I realized that the eighties were a totally irony-free moment for a song like that to come out with no problem. Although it clearly wasn't a hit, so maybe people were more aware than I'm giving them credit for. *Or maybe they weren't ready for the '80s.* Then the Sirius went out and I had a solid hour to kill, so I called Kristen Johnston for what Natasha would refer to as a "proper chat" (*definition*: that special kind of long chat where both parties are fully available to focus and meander until the catch-up is complete). We wound up our conversation as my car wound downtown, the sun setting over the city, bars crowded with World Cup watchers. Mom got to town yesterday with her bridge group—the "girls" leave Tuesday and Dad joins her. She was supposed to bartend tonight with Kandi and Mama Joyce but we bumped her; I think she's relieved. Last night they saw *A Gentleman's Guide to Love & Murder* and Evelyn Brantley (her *New York Times* theater-critic alter ego) did not love it. Tonight it was the Lyndon Johnson play with Bryan Cranston; she said it was the best she'd ever seen, so I expressed my sadness that Dad didn't get to see it. "He won't know what he missed," she replied.

MONDAY, JUNE 23, 2014

Last night I gave Cristiano Ronaldo the Jackhole for getting a stupid haircut, but the paper today says the cut was in tribute to a sick kid with cancer. So I look like an idiot. And the cover story in the *New York Times* is that Union Square Cafe is closing. Greedy landlord. Danny Meyer transforms Union Square into a destination and now he's forced out, probably for a Chipotle. I feel powerless to protect the city's integrity, which is small businesses. My Ninj didn't have a solution either, but we had a good workout nonetheless. Had lunch with Shari Levine at an outdoor café right by that church next to the Four Seasons Restaurant on Park Avenue. I never even knew this place existed. Mom came and met me for coffee. From there I went to a meeting at CAA and my cab driver was snoring while driving. Literally. I still can't figure out what was wrong. He was assuredly awake, I know that. But snoring. Maybe he was a pug mix?

I had to fill out a form for the MLB All-Star softball game in July—I said I want to play outfield or anywhere the ball won't come, and requested to be put on Jon Hamm's team. Also I put down small for all the clothes because sports clothes are usually huge. For guys with bellies. So we'll see what happens there. I want a fitted outfit!

Had dinner with Mom and the bridge group at that Italian place around the corner from the studio, then they came for their star-bartending tour. We put them in my office with Mya the makeup lady and left Mom in charge. She had specific ideas about who needed how much time with Mya. I was in the studio running through the show and we kept sending spies back to find out what the hell was going on back there. We played a game where the ladies read filthy names of strip clubs ("The Fuzzy Hole," "The Titty House") and Joe Manganiello had to figure out if they were real or fake.

Met Lance Bass and his friend Curtis for drinks at Barracuda and the night went way later than I'd planned. There is not a negative bone in that one's body. As for me . . . maybe this is something I need to work on?

⁜ TUESDAY, JUNE 24, 2014

Cher called today. But let me start from the beginning. I woke up feeling guilty about making the bridge ladies say such dirty things. We pushed it with a few of those.

Then I had my first real meeting with my architect. We wound up talking about Diana Ross for a long time. He once saw her apartment on the UES.

So he left and my phone rang; it was Liz Rosenberg, who told me to hold on, someone wanted to talk to me. "Andy!?!" It was Cher. Totally Cher, in fact. "Cher!" I said. "How are you, Cher?" She wanted to know how I recognized her voice. I told her that when Liz Rosenberg calls and hands the phone to someone who sounds like Cher, you know it's Cher. (Unless Madonna does a great Cher impersonation, I suppose. But in no world can I picture Madonna "doing" Cher.) We chatted back and forth about her show, what I was up to, and I asked if the Mackie costumes are in the show and she said they're slowly rolling out. She said he doesn't work from patterns, and then went into detail and worried that she was boring me. Which I disagreed with. She said they are all bored to hell in Canada right now, that's where she is. And the whole time I was sitting there trying to figure out the exact reason she was calling, but I think it was to say that her friend Paulette thought she'd offended me somehow by referencing the wrong team when we were talking about baseball backstage at Barclays last month. Because she knew I'm a Cardinals fan and she talked about the Phillies or something? I dunno, I couldn't figure out what the hell the issue was but I didn't care either. Cher said Paulette had a dossier on me and that she was sick to hell of hearing about me. I told her to use me to fuck with Paulette. She said she didn't need me to fuck with her, she could do it on her own. I said I would come see Paulette when Cher was at MSG and she said, "Hell, come see me, not her!" But the truth is that Paulette is the reason Cher did my show, so I am grateful to her best friend. She said please give my love to Anderson and I said we're going on vacation next week and she said I'm stuck on the road, will you please text me pictures of you guys on vacation? I asked for her email and she had no clue what it was. She said she doesn't know her address either and I said, "Cher, Carbon Beach, Malibu," and she said no, it's not Carbon Beach, she knows that. And then she again asked if I would text her. Yeah, I'll text you, Cher. She had someone get her cell phone number for her but she couldn't read it. It was a long process and while we were getting to the bottom of what the hell her cell number is, my parents showed up at my door. I kept trying to mouth to my mom

"It's *Cher*!" and she was pretending like she knew what I was saying. "OK! OK! We GET it!" she said in a loud non-whisper whisper. I told Cher I needed to know if the blond guy in her show was straight and Cher said he is, and that his hair is growing out and he looks like a romance novel guy. She lost me on the romance novel look but I guess it's hot in an eighties way. I hung up with her and as my mom tried to get me to explain why Cher was on the phone, Anderson texted and said, "I'm bored," and I said, "Well, join the club, because I am kinda bored and Cher's bored in Canada right now, so we're all bored I guess."

Rob Wiesenthal is starting a helicopter service to the Hamptons, and Nan Kane was doing a launch party; she said if I just stopped by the party I could get a free round trip to the Hamptons. I dragged Mom and Dad to the party, which was something of a pigfuck—lots of people in a small space. I asked if I could bring Wacha on the helicopter and they said whatever I want, but the truth is he will freak out (he's scared of the top going down in my car), so I think I'll never use the round trip—what am I gonna do with the dog?

We taped an episode with Tori Spelling and Jenny Garth that'll air on Sunday when I'm in Italy, and hilariously Tori did not want any questions about her marriage or personal life, *just weeks after the finale of her reality show which was set in couples counseling with her and her cheating husband*. So we said no way, and bless Jill Fritzo, who was trying to make all of us happy. (Being a publicist can be a thankless job.) I agreed to only asking her a few questions during a game, and then revised that during the show to include more. She was on a reality show about her personal life but didn't want to talk about her personal life! I just have to repeat that. WTF.

The live show was amazing—the dog was there, my parents were there, the *Today* show was there filming a piece about our fifth anniversary, and Sonja was there and, after all, she's the straw that stirs the cocktail. I was supposed to have a date with that actor that *two* people wanted to set me up with, but he totally blew me off, and it was okay because we all hung out after the show and John Oliver and I went deep about the psychology of hosting a talk show, about the mind fuckery that ensues when you have a bad show—or even a great one. I told him I never doubted myself until

I started the show. He's been doing stand-up for fifteen years and said he always can remember a worse audience, which helps him realize that whatever he just did wasn't so bad. He and his wife brought me presents from Jonathan Adler—a London needlepoint pillow and a Puppy Uppers jar. Also I told John that I thought it was amazing that Jon Stewart had the confidence to let him sub for him while he was directing a movie. No late-night hosts have guest hosts anymore. I don't think anybody wants someone to do it any better than they do it, and who can blame them? I allowed it one time, when I was scheduled to be at Liam's in the South of France three years ago. Jay Mohr, who'd been blogging about *RHONJ* for us, sat in one night. I woke up like a shot at 6 a.m. French time and checked Twitter to find a stream of "You should go on vacation more! This guy is hilarious!" and I realized I didn't care to leave my seat again.

So it was a motley crew and we partied late. My dad talked my director Rocco's ear off, Mom and Sonja somehow found things in common, then we debated whether it was an urban myth that someone had been attacked with excrement in Times Square sometime around 9/11. The team watched as over and over Siri misunderstood my mom's request for information on "Times Square FECES." We stayed until one-thirty—my poor parents. . . .

▦ WEDNESDAY, JUNE 25, 2014

World Cup fever has overtaken the city and it feels like Europe—you can hear the sound of games coming from bars, restaurants, dry cleaners, magazine stands. I love it. The architects are here measuring the apartments, which apparently takes two days.

Had an old-school dinner outside at Morandi with Bruce, Jess Cagle, who is now the editor of *People*, which totally blows me away after knowing him twenty years, and Chris Bagley, who has just moved back from France.

Joel McHale and Stanley Tucci were on the show. Mom and Dad were sitting in the front row and Mom thought McHale was a wiseass, which is exactly what he is but I like him. It was Chase's birthday and we had cake and somehow that turned into me getting Mom to do her runway walk for the staff. It didn't take much coaxing.

I had a date with this Croatian basketball player who used to play professionally in Turkey but when they all found out he was gay, he had to leave the country. Now he plays in a league here, and during Gay Pride Week a few weeks ago his entire team surprised him at the bar he was at wearing T-shirts that said "Equality." He said he was in tears—it was the happiest day of his life. I was in tears hearing about it.

THURSDAY, JUNE 26, 2014

Had the hardest workout—I think we did seven rounds of boxing and kicking. He let me freestyle on the punching bag for a minute each round and I was a total disaster at it. I've been doing sequences with the Ninj and Will for a few years and I couldn't come up with anything but a straight assault. Maybe that's all you need if you get in a fight.

I came home drenched and somehow hadn't gotten the memo that there was no water in the building until four. So I hung out sweaty and waited for a conference call with Martha Stewart and watched us get beaten by Germany in the Cup and then spent a while online trying to figure out how we lost but didn't get knocked out. The water wasn't on at four, so I had to shower at Equinox (I was in and out of there in six minutes) before going to the show for a meeting.

Brought Wacha by Bruce's, where he, Liza, and I continued our lament about more NYC institutions that are closing, specifically her deli, which for years has not only hidden her extra key but killed a mouse for her and basically guarded her life.

Met Mom and Dad at Morandi with Wacha. They had been at *Buyer & Cellar*, which she loved and he was lukewarm on. I was a dick to Mom for the first fifteen minutes of dinner, then she told me I was being an asshole and I broke it down and decided her energy was too intense for me to handle so I had turned on her. Once we talked it out, we were great for the rest of the meal. Then Mom announced that her favorite shoe repair store in the city is closing, so add *that* to the list, and who even knew my mom had a favorite shoe repair store in the city? Anthony from the show stopped by, then John Hill, then Liza on her way home from Bruce's. She told them about the deli and it was a big commiseration. Wacha was crying when I left to go to the bathroom, and Liza said her answer to her own question would be that she would ask a dog what they were so afraid of happening when you leave. I'm both concerned and flattered by his attachment to me.

Mark Ruffalo and Keira Knightley were on and we played a game about Mark and I being doppelgängers and then we got some tweets saying we look nothing alike, so who knows.

Before bed, Wacha was standing over something next to the bed, looking very quizzical—it was a dead bug lying on its back. I got rid of it with little incident.

FRIDAY, JUNE 27, 2014—NYC–ROME

This morning I found another bug in the exact same spot! Dead! I need a CSI!

I felt very mournful all day thinking about leaving Wacha, and it seemed like he was mirroring my energy. He was really snuggly and big-eyed. That being said, it was a lovely day. I took a walk with the Croatian basketball player and packed after a two-hour massage.

The big group I travel with is converging on Italy for Hamilton's birthday. If Bruce and Barkin were in charge, we would've left for the airport at noon for our 10 p.m. flight to Rome. Suffice to say we left at 6:30 and got there in record time and had plenty of time to debate whether Kendall Jenner would become a big star. One person suggested it was only possible if a nose job was in her future. I had no idea what she looks like, but disagreed on principle.

Before passing out on the plane, I re-realized Wacha is a dog and isn't thinking about anything deep—most especially he's not thinking about me when I'm not there. Why do I keep getting sucked into the guilt trap? It's been nine months already.

SATURDAY, JUNE 28, 2014—ROME–POSITANO

Thank you, pinot grigio and Ambien, for the full night's sleep on the plane. And thank you to our great host, Hamilton, for picking us up in two helicopters, which we took from Rome to Sorrento, landed on what looked like someone's backyard, then drove to Praiano, where we spent the whole day and night at Villa Lilly, which is gorgeous. Swam in the Med, played "Gay or Italian?" with a whole group of Speedo guys (I lean more towards Euro), napped, and watched Barkin unpack. Dinner was fresh fish, al dente pasta with spicy red sauce, light salad, eggplant. Bruce got furious at someone's suggestion that Brooklyn is past its prime, and just when the night started to have the potential to get messy, my water taxi arrived amidst lil anchovies jumping in the night water—and I hiked up that Positano hill to the Sirenuse.

SUNDAY, JUNE 29, 2014—POSITANO/CAPRI

I had my room as cold as a meat locker, so it was a good sleep. Woke up to a marching band playing in front of the church in the square. Sounds kind of unpleasant but since it's Italy it was exactly how you want to be woken up on your Sunday. Ate a massive breakfast on a terrace overlooking the Med. After forty-eight hours of food I feel like I haven't worked out in months. That's sobering. And so boring.

The Villa crew picked me up in a speedboat and we went to EOS and joined Barry and DVF for a hike/shop in Capri. Jason bought pink pants and Bruce got red shoes. Lunch on Barry's boat was epic: steak and lobster and beef carpaccio and a bunch of crazy summer salads. For dessert a Capri cake—torta Caprese—which is chocolate and almond. Mary South thought of a slogan for the Palm: "Let them eat steak." I don't know if Bruce will go for it but it's great. I was gossiping with the EOS crew on the bridge and our entire group was waiting for me on the tender without me knowing. I like the crew gossip, especially who is doing who, but ya never wanna leave ten people waiting. Especially this bunch.

Jeff Klein, John Goldwyn, and Cornelia Guest joined us for dinner. Of course I had to ask Cornelia about Warhol and she had some wild stories, like riding out a hurricane on a boat off Newport with Andy, one of the chicks from Sister Sledge, and Randy from the Village People (I mean!?). Also she told me about getting in a snowmobile accident with him in Aspen. She thinks he would've dug the Housewives but turned on them "when they started thinking they were Sophia Loren"—that's when the fifteen minutes would've been up. Interesting that she thinks he would've been turned off by their acting like stars, he liked them real. Very drunky, we schlepped up the 250 stairs to the road where we waited for a cab. I dropped them off at the San Pietro, realized I didn't have any euros, and Cornelia threw me a fifty. There were fireworks coming from Positano as the driver texted his way around the windy, treacherous Amalfi Coast. Comforting. I paid it forward, giving him the fifty on a thirty-euro fare, and got back to the Sirenuse in time to see a spectacular finale and hear sweet applause and whistles breaking out from various parts of the hillside village.

MONDAY, JUNE 30, 2014—POSITANO/AMALFI

The Amalfi Coast is one steep stairway after the next, but there's a pot of gold at the end of every one. My cab driver today said he's thirty-two years old—"So one quarter of my way through life." Um. Bruce and I hung out over the windy coast for a few hours, laying out, watching the boat traffic, swimming, and checking into Instagram. His face lights up when his SoulCycle schedule for the week comes in—he loves it!

Wandering around before dinner in Amalfi, I bought a blue straw hat (there is a graveyard somewhere full of the straw hats all of us have bought in Europe and discarded) and for some reason I also bought at least five pounds of hard candy. So that'll be fun to take home. We had dinner on the port and Barry and DVF joined us. We talked about the new Muslim superpower. Fun vacation talk. I got stracciatella and could've had three more servings.

░ TUESDAY, JULY 1, 2014—POSITANO

Ran into Radzi at the Sirenuse breakfast and we dissected the *RHONY* reunion while we watched boats come in on the pier. One of these things is not like the other. We went over to Barry's boat and then all swam to Rudolf Nureyev's island. What the hell went *on* on that island? is what I couldn't stop wondering. Were there rivers of lube rolling through the hills? Volcanoes of poppers? I have never wanted a time capsule so much as one that would transport me back forty years to see *that* bacchanalia off Positano. We went to a restaurant Barry and DVF said was the best in Italy, Lo Scoglio. It was phenomenal and by the second course I was stuffed. DVF said her new E! show isn't a reality show and I gleefully told her we're all swimming in the same dirty pool. It was a laugh all around. I do think her show will be a hit; she is a big, inspiring *character*—brilliant to listen to and women of all ages go nuts for her. After lunch I napped around and then had tea on my balcony. We had more pasta for dinner and I have officially lost the entirety of whatever momentum I had going for the last six months. My fear is that I am now careening into the second half of the year in a state of fatness. My back hurts. I'm old. I feel as if I'm eating for two, by the way. So it's no wonder.

After dinner I got Anderson to take a picture to send to Cher. It took us several—OK, *many*—tries to get one we liked. Taking that photo was as awkward and gay as the very idea of taking a picture from your vacation to text to Cher because she asked for one.

Watched World Cup at an outdoor café and it went into overtime. The gingy from Belgium not only scored a goal against us but kicked one of our hottest guys in the face. Bruce and I simultaneously marveled aloud at the endurance of the part in one player's hair. This is what he and I think about; great minds . . . Barkin was in love with the goalie with Tourette's and who wouldn't be? We lost in overtime. So we're completely out.

░ WEDNESDAY, JULY 2, 2014—POSITANO

I dreamt that I threw a lemon at a computer and Dan Rather appeared and had a stern chat with me about my anger issues. *I* have *anger issues?*

I was surprised about this even in my dream but I was enjoying the fatherly chat so much that I didn't fight it with Dan. I quit analyzing the dream when I grabbed my phone and found a couple happy texts from Cher saying "You boys look ADORABLE" with an emoji of a one-eyed ghost (a pirate ghost, perhaps?). In her world, are we "boys"? Also she told us to have a blast, accompanied by an emoji of a smiley face with heart eyes. So all in all, the awkward photo did the trick. Finally had pizza today—after five days in Italy—and it was fantastic. We all did water activities, showered, then Anderson, Ben, and I took a water taxi to Hamilton's birthday dinner at San Pietro. We sent Cher another pic on the way. I decided that sending Cher vacation pictures is never not fun. The dinner was spectacular—on a patch of grass at the bottom of a stone canyon right on the Med with yachts bobbing in the distance. Lee Radziwill looking flawless smoking superthin cigarettes was all the punctuation anyone needed to confirm that this was a special occasion. I sat between Cornelia Guest and Jessica Yellin, former White House correspondent for CNN and ABC News. Guest and I talked about her years with Sylvester Stallone—she was only eighteen and he was the biggest star in the world—and now I need to cross-reference what Warhol said about them. Apparently they went to the White House and Nancy Reagan said she and Cornelia *needed to talk*; presumably Nancy was going to set her straight about dating Sly. (Unclear if that chat ever happened, but Sly and Guest wound up breaking off their engagement.) Yellin and I discussed my favorite topic—the death of network news. Networks are laying off more and more people and paying for stories by licensing footage, and now reenactments are commonplace on the prime-time news magazines (not *60 Minutes*). It's the *Daily Mail* on TV, basically. There were sweet wonderful toasts to the sweet wonderful birthday boy, which made Hamilton very uncomfortable, and five courses of cheese and cheese and more cheese. I am going to have a rough transition back to the Ninj. I was asleep by two.

THURSDAY, JULY 3, 2014—POSITANO—OUTSIDE ST. TROPEZ

Woke up to a text from Cher—liberally sprinkled with emojis—saying she wishes she was here but she is doing what she was born to do in this life—"come out in ridiculous costumes, sing, be fabulous and make people happy." At least she knows her place in the world! She said Bob Mackie's new costumes are great and I will "pass out." And she said, "P.S. I'm dyslexic, so if you're expecting spelling OR grammar, you've come to the WRONG ICON." I don't actually come to my icons for spelling *or* grammar, and for the record hers was perfect.

Getting from the Amalfi Coast to Nice turns out to be a pain in the ass. Jason and Lauren Blum and I were in a car, and we gave ourselves several hours of pad in case the traffic was bad, and asked the driver to stop at a restaurant along the way; he said there were absolutely *no restaurants* in all of Italy between Positano and Rome. Cornelia had gotten a list for me, but he said they were too far, and that there were just *none*, so that added a contentious layer of tension to the drive. And thus I had plenty of time to sit and read Twitter, and find a nasty article about me in the *Daily News* saying my office has been downsized and I have nowhere to hang my prized possessions: pictures of myself. I actually got a kick out of that one. And somewhere along the way our driver turned to me and said, "What is 'schlep'?" I guess I had used the word once or twice or fifteen times.

Jason and Lauren fell asleep in the car and my heart turned heavy as I thought about the journey at hand—returning to the magical place Natasha welcomed us for all those years, where every year summer came alive with her essence—her deep throaty laugh, her cooking, her theatricality, unique turn of a phrase, and devilish sense of humor. We all met there for the first time over a decade ago—she introduced us disparate souls, brought us together by her design in the centuries-old hamlet tucked into a valley in the South of France—and today all our lives are interwoven because of all those summers. "Natasha" is the answer to a question I get all the time—"How do you know X, Y, or Z?" Forty years ago her father, Tony Richardson, was the ringmaster—Jagger partied there, Hockney painted by the pool, and little Natasha and Joely put on plays for the guests after dinner. Today Liam would be welcoming us back for our first visit in three years. It was a reunion of part of the old gang—Danny will be there, Ralph too, and Tom Hollander comes tomorrow.

Hours later, we finally stepped onto that magical *terrazzo* at sunset and it was like time had stopped, but it was all happy. We immediately started in on the "French Water," and soon we were having a great meal under the string of twinkly lights and then games and more laughs back on the *terrazzo*. Late into the night, the evening turned into a Rolling Stones dance party and I felt at peace. Somehow, she is here and I think she loves that we are too.

FRIDAY, JULY 4, 2014—OUTSIDE ST. TROPEZ

The French are charmless. Completely. Not headline news, and a nasty generalization, but such a stark contrast to the Italians a couple hundred miles away. We took a two-hour hike through some vineyards. Then we had a July Fourth BBQ back at the house, prepared by a French chef who gave us her interpretation of American food, which translated sweetly with burgers and beans. Watched an episode of Tom Hollander's UK show *Rev.*, which was great. Took half an Ambien at 11 p.m. and went to bed with a smile as *le mistral* whipped around outside.

SATURDAY, JULY 5, 2014—OUTSIDE ST. TROPEZ

For sure *le mistral* was fucking with all of us last night, because everyone had crazy dreams. Mine involved Bruce, Howard Stern, and SJ. It was the perfect day. Jason and I spent a fair amount of time trying to pose for an Instagram picture re-creating Hockney's *Portrait of an Artist (Pool with Two Figures)*, which he'd painted here at this pool in 1971. A tree has grown in the background, blocking the view of the valley, but we did pretty well. Jason has a connection to Hockney and is going to mail the side-by-sides to him; I am sure David Hockney, at this moment in his life and career, is anxious to see what we came up with. Also we had a plank contest (I folded after a minute, Ralph won) and a long lunch, so long that the sun moved and drove us from the table to the terrace; anyway it was full of laughs and felt like the old days. If I had a therapist, I might ask why I am forever trying to reclaim the "old days." I happen to like the current days a lot.

Jason, Lauren, and Tom woke up to send me off. I felt a little melancholy, walking away wondering if I'll ever return to this special spot again, and feeling incredibly fat. Six months of hard work down the drain for one carb-filled week in Europe. Even my humorless French flight attendant knew I shouldn't eat anything on the endless flight home. Every time I asked a specific question about the food, he would hand me the menu from the seat pocket in front of me. ("What kind of soup is it again?" *"It's yellow,"* he said, and handed me the menu.) He wound up knocking my entire tray of food off my table, and a pat of butter flew onto my foot. Watching him disdainfully wipe the butter off my foot was neither amusing nor satisfying.

Got home and had a hilarious night with Bruce at some outdoor gay place in Midtown. Freshly back from Italy, we ended the night cramming New York pizza into our mouths. Welcome home.

MONDAY, JULY 7, 2014

Woke up at the crack of dawn. Wacha was still in doggy day care.

Grac is in Kauai for three weeks and she described it as Vietnam meets Topanga Canyon meets Montauk, which I think is brilliant. Went up to 30 Rock to pitch NBC syndication the show Michael and I want to produce for Joan Rivers. There's a big Jeff Koons flower sculpture in front of the building called *Split Rocker*. I didn't love it; it's two doggy heads split in half. I tried to take a great Instagram of it but realized I couldn't because the piece itself isn't great. (Am I Jerry Saltz all of a sudden?) Ran into Seth Meyers in the lobby and he said, "You gotta come on my show soon," and then it was a little awkward, because when you run into a talk-show host and they say that you should come on, you don't know if they mean it. It's never not weird, even when I'm the host in the encounter doling out the meaningless pleasantries. And then there was Joan, fresh from walking off her CNN interview (she's selling a book) and all dolled up in black and white—she's always dolled up. She'd gotten a private tour of the Koons retrospective at the Whitney. She told me that when she wants to see an exhibit she calls in advance and says, "I'm stopping by and maybe someone could show me around *if you could . . ."* And they do. So she said the story of the sculpture is that Koons was so upset he was losing custody of his kid, he split his toy in half. Doesn't make me like the sculpture any more. She also said there are ninety thousand flowers in it. Now you have my attention.

After the pitch, I went down to *WWHL* for an interview with Willie Geist for our fifth anniversary, which we are celebrating next week. Of course when I got home I realized a bunch of stuff I should've said. Wacha was really hyper returning from Brooklyn. And sheddy.

The live show was Heather Dubrow and Caroline from *Ladies of London*. For the anniversary next week, we're doing the Andy Awards, celebrating achievements in I don't know what, and the award is a Ken doll (literally), dipped in gold glitter and holding a *WWHL* note card. It looks nothing like me. Why should it? It's a Ken doll. Meanwhile we have a new straight PA, a big tall guy, who left *Letterman* to work at *WWHL*. I nicknamed him "Straight Pat." I hope he doesn't mind.

At the end of the night, I got an offer to be the lead guest on Seth Meyers tomorrow night, so I guess he meant what he said in the lobby. Now I gotta think of something to talk about.

▦ TUESDAY, JULY 8, 2014

Found out Jon Hamm is not doing the MLB Celeb All-Star thing this weekend, so now I don't even have a *fake* friend to do this with. At the dog run a guy explained how to tell if your dog is overheated and I still don't totally get it. They sweat through their tongues? Had a horrible workout with the Ninj today, possibly the worst ever. *I* was overheated. Also overweight, overtired, and overindulged after all that time away. I didn't dare go on the scale. Even my egg rolls stunk. I *excel* at egg rolls! Here I go again.

Did phone interviews promoting *WWHL* all day. Some people are horrible interviewers and I wonder why they do it. It made me think back to when I was twenty-four and on the phone with celebrities. I am sure I was alternately charming and super awkward. So I should check myself with my strong opinions.

Gary Oldman had canceled on Seth Meyers so I was the fill-in. Dave met me there to keep me company. He has lost seventeen pounds this year (Dave, not Seth), which made me feel even fatter! Who was in the dressing room next to me but Jeff Koons. He was in there alone, so I went in and said hi and had a fairly awkward conversation with him. "I was talking about your show with Joan Rivers yesterday," I stammered. He shot back, "Who the fuck are you and why are you dropping Joan Rivers's name to me? Are you trying to impress me? I could buy and sell you!" Of course he said none of that, but the vibe was off. I told him I tried to get a good Instagram of his piece, but as I was talking I could remember neither the name of the piece nor whether you call it a sculpture or what. He filled in the blank and said the name, *Split Rocker*. Then I taped my bit (I brought an Andy Award to make fun of and we talked about my anxiety about the MLB thing this weekend) and afterwards Koons came out and said, "Oh, you were great," and was really sweet. I wanted to take a selfie but I didn't have the guts. Of course it's a sculpture, by the way.

We had Rachel Maddow and Nicole Richie as guests tonight and during the run-through Straight Pat was sitting in for Maddow and inadvertently revealed he knows nothing about the Housewives—I asked him to name one and he said "Nay-Nay." Couldn't even pronounce the great Linnethia Leakes's *name*! I roasted him. Straight guys! A lady in the audience gave me a cake. Like a really nice frosted cake. The unspoken rule is not to eat food presented by total strangers—but I made the staff scarf it with me. At least we could all go down together in a Jonestown moment. Kolten Wong got a walk-off home run to win the Cardinals game tonight. I tweeted a salutation and he retweeted it.

WEDNESDAY, JULY 9, 2014

Did I mention that the talk backstage at Seth Meyers is all about how nice the dressing rooms are? It's all everybody is talking about up there—the first thing out of their mouths is "Can you believe the dressing rooms?"—four separate people! For some reason I got on a soapbox, furious about how much money they spent on them. (Okay, maybe it's because we don't really *have* dressing rooms at my show.)

Did a cardio and core workout with the Ninj and I am inching back. Also inching towards puking. My back hurts. From there I went to Morandi for a lunch with two lovely people who donated a lot of money to Friends In Deed for the distinct pleasure of lunch with me. Their names were Aviva and Pete and they were great. I was overly gesticulating to them early in the conversation about some overblown theory I have about how working women can take on an innumerable number of projects, when the woman at the table next to me chastised my loud volume. Smacked down! In public! It hurt. Ran into Mickey Drexler, who at first I didn't recognize until I saw he had a monogram on his shirt and I figured out who he was mid-convo by his initials. I wish everyone had monograms. Or name tags.

Went to the batting cage with Mike Bell from the gym. I didn't do horribly, but the longer I did it, the worse I got. I was overthinking it. Mike's advice was:

» Wait for it, don't lunge.
» Start with weight on back leg, then shift to front.
» Follow through.
» Don't swing at bad pitches.
» Don't turn my head.

Oy vey. This thing is gonna be televised on ESPN.

Coming home from the dog run, I saw two separate girls who were either going out for the night or legit prostitutes. You never see real whores on the street anymore. I also ran into Joe Mantello, then Matt Bomer.

We taped a show with Taye Diggs and John Legend that was really fun. They were perfect together and Jon and Tommy Alter were in the audience. I am gonna play myself on Jon's show *Alpha House*.

The live show was Steve Guttenberg with Leah Remini, who brought JLo. I went into her dressing room (to clarify—we *call* it a dressing room but it's actually a conference room and nobody's bragging about how gorgeous it is) before the show and was careful to pay more attention to Leah because she was the guest and JLo was the friend. The three of us talked about dating guys who are not conventionally handsome in the face but otherwise sexy. I asked JLo if she would consider walking onto the show to bring the shotski out, unannounced, and she agreed. She is still presenting herself to me as Miss Low-Key Easygoing Non-Demanding Un-Diva; maybe she *is* just Jenny from the Block! I really liked Leah.

The whole audience—besides JLo—was the Mets wives I'd met at that game in April. That hot catcher's wife is pregnant, so that's good for her. And I asked whose husband was the last to hit a homer and of course David Wright's wife, who is the Melissa Gorga of the group, raised her hand.

Hung out late listening to music in my office with the team. Wacha left my office and came back twenty minutes later wearing a Pucci scarf. (Thank you, Ryan.)

▦ THURSDAY, JULY 10, 2014—NYC–SAG HARBOR

Woke up with Wacha, who was snuggling up to me, still wearing the Pucci scarf, which in the light of day made him look more like Angela Lansbury than the office mascot—hysterical! Emmy nominations came out today and Bravo got four nominations. Zilch for *WWHL*. Under what circumstance could we get nominated? None. Before I worked out with the Ninj we had a weigh-in, and lo and behold I am exactly 165. I almost fainted. Hallelujah. I felt like I didn't need to work out after that, but we boxed. I was on the phone the whole drive to the beach. We have four scenarios for the next season of *RHONY* and each involves layoffs and rehires. It makes me excited to see the possibility in each one. I pitched Martha Stewart creative for the show we will take out; she was in a car on her way to a tree farm on Long Island to get some maple trees. Maybe some other kind I can't remember. I'm sure it was something more exotic now that I think about it.

Met SJ and Matthew for dinner at some new overpriced sushi place, Shuko, that says online is in Water Mill but it's in Wainscott, so I went to the wrong place and got there in a huff and SJ said, "OK, *Evelyn*, calm down." Ha! She was right. Matthew told some horror stories about playing right field in a charity softball game for Puffy, and made me rethink that position. Would second base be a crazy idea? SJ said to protect my face. She looked very Carrie Bradshaw, tan and summery, hair blonde from the sun. She just bought a big red 1976 Ford Country Squire station wagon and gave me a lil ride in it; it's sweet and sentimental—glass everywhere, crazy roomy with only AM radio. And it smells like 1976 in a bottle.

▦ FRIDAY, JULY 11, 2014—SAG HARBOR

My cousin Dave emailed me this morning: "You asked Shaq how big his dick is but you're terrified of a softball game? I don't think you get it: you're *supposed* to screw up, so if you do it's kinda expected. If you don't, that's fine too. It's a no-lose situation!" He is so right. Then I got a text from Anthony at *WWHL*, who reports that Straight Pat is *actually gay*. WTF! I'm shocked. And embarrassed. Now is he going to have to come out to everyone because I falsely accused him of being straight? I overstep with PAs! Bethenny made me lunch at her house—she has Skinnygirl products for everything, it's amazing. She wanted to pitch me doing *Bethenny Starting Over*, but I had my own ideas, and turned the discussion into the (seemingly insane at first but makes sense the longer you talk about it) idea of her coming back to *RHONY*; and I can't believe it, but I think it worked. I made a lot of compelling arguments (good money, ensemble show, she knows what she's getting into, it would certainly be a success ratings-wise vs. this season). She is seriously considering it, and I left feeling upbeat. It would be huge for that show to get her back. Huge!!!

Hung out with the doctor. He's a real person. I invited him to the show next week.

Met Amanda and Jim at Bell & Anchor, which was very crowded. Here's what I watched on YouTube when I got home: a Writers Guild interview with Michael Patrick King and Lisa Kudrow about *The Comeback*, a really long interview with Marla Gibbs about her time on *Jeffersons* and *227*, Isabel Sanford winning her Emmy, Lucy on *The Tonight Show* and Barbara Walters, and Lucy winning an Emmy. Asleep by midnight. Who says the Hamptons aren't glamorous?

Texted with Jason Motte about tomorrow and he said, "The key to hitting and fielding is to watch the ball. Seems simple. But very helpful." I hate watching the ball!

Had a gorgeous lunch at Marci's in her chic new pool house.

Drove back to the city early and when I got home read three articles online about how to be a better softball player, then watched clips of last year's game and what I saw made my face burn red and I completely lost my appetite. It's a night game with bright lights and you can hear the players talking. I am so glad Eli is going with me; he is calming and positive. He was my behind-the-scenes sidekick for the first few years of *WWHL* and he's the perfect accomplice for this affair. Liza came over for some rosé after her dinner and said, "Why don't you just *see* if you can have *fun*?—an elemental suggestion I had never considered. *Have fun?*

Lying on my bed scrolling through Instagram, I felt something on my leg. It was my worst nightmare: a water bug. I was alone for once—Wacha was going to town on a Kong in his dog bed—and I didn't have time to think. I shook my leg, it went flying, and I realized if I didn't kill it at that moment I would legit have to move into my extra bedroom for the rest of the summer. (I am not kidding.) I grabbed a shoe and killed it. My freaking canine protector was zero help, just wandered in after it was all over and smelled the spot where the beast had lived and died. Thanks for nothing, Wacha. But I took it as a sign—from God or from the ghost of Stan Musial (or Esther Rolle)—that I am stronger than I think. I will have *fun* at this game tomorrow.

Surfin took one look at my face as I stumbled out of the building early this morning and knew exactly what day it was: "You ready?" he tentatively queried. I told him I'd barely slept and was terrified. But he was bullish: "You're gonna go one for three."

"I'll take that!" I said. I was a nervous Nellie, though, and spilled tea all over myself in the car to LaGuardia.

I sat behind Derek Jeter's parents on the plane, and across the aisle from—I think—his sister. When I landed, my phone rang and mine was on the other end having just heard startling news.

"Are you really playing a *game*?????? An *actual game*?" Em was as exasperated as I've heard her.

"*Why* did they ask you? Do they know . . ." Her voice trailed off before she could state the obvious. I told her they asked because I am a known fan, thank you very much.

"Well, *I'm* a fan *but I can't play the game*!!" She was starting to sound like another woman we both know who lives in St. Louis. *"Oh boy."* She sighed. I told her this was exactly the call I did not need to be getting right now. "I'm just trying to understand. I didn't know you were actually *playing.*" Yes, we've established that. "Well, at least it's all celebrities—there aren't any actual baseball players, right?" There are. Ozzie Smith. Mike Piazza. Dwight Gooden. She stopped me. "Well. It's just a game." She said I was going into convulsions over throwing the first pitch a few years ago, so she didn't know how I was going to get through this. I changed the subject and asked about Aspen, from where she just returned and where our mother is now. She reported that Mom is charging around town with a fanny pack everywhere she goes. "It's a *town.* And she's wearing a *fanny pack.*" That image took my mind off my troubles.

I hung up with Em and here's how it all played out from there:

In the lobby of the W in Minneapolis a tall blonde woman introduces herself and says we'll be playing together. She says she's done it before and it's a lot of fun. I ask her if, like me, she is wondering what to even do with a softball. She says she's OK at softball. I find out an hour later that she is Jennie Finch, who is only *the most famous softball player of all time*—she won the freaking gold medal at the '04 Olympics. So I get an early jump on offending people to their faces. Eli arrives from Los Angeles and is shocked at how nervous I am; he can't believe that after all the live TV we've done together, a softball game is what's brought out my nerves. I try to explain that my exact skill set is hosting live TV, which is why it doesn't make me nervous. We go to a meet-up with all the other players and I tell Andrew Zimmern and Minnesota Vikings running back (and *very* hot dude) Adrian Peterson that Jon Hamm talked me into this whole thing and wound up canceling. "Me too! He got me into it too!" a blonde woman next to us says. On the bus to Target Field, the blonde sits next to us and I introduce myself. "I'm January," she purrs. How had I not recognized Betty Draper?

We walk into the press room at the stadium and there waiting is a roomful of All-Stars and Hall of Famers. Eli's face lights up and he becomes Gary from *Veep*, whispering in my ear names of the people around us: Rollie Fingers, Rickey Henderson, Arizona Cardinals wide receiver Larry Fitzgerald. The two team captains read their rosters and positions; mine is John Smoltz, who says I'm playing for the National League repping the Cardinals, playing outfield. January is playing catcher for the American League—intimidating! I talk to Sway and Fat Joe from MTV, who claim they suck, Charlie McDermott from *The Middle* on ABC, who is as wide-eyed as I am, and a really nice All-Star, Fred Lynn, who says his wife loves my show.

Then we're told to leave our guests behind and we go with our teammates to the locker room to get suited up. My locker is between Ozzie Smith and Andre Dawson, and Piazza is on the other side of Dawson. As I stare at this locker overflowing with gear (it's all there: pants, shoes, underwear, socks, a bat, glove, hat—the whole thing—and I know what I'll be wearing for Halloween next year) I realize I am on a *team* with these guys (locker room inspiration!), I have to not only play for the crowd but I have to play in front of *them*. More importantly, I have no clue whether I have to strip down and wear the Under Armour underwear they gave me, or if I can keep mine on. Maybe their undies give you extra warmth or something, what the hell do I know? Conscious of being the only gay guy in the locker room, I don't want to actually make eye contact with anyone below the waist to find out the answer to my question. Finally I sheepishly ask Ozzie if we have to wear the undies or what. He says it's a personal choice based on comfort. Crisis averted, I decide that nothing comes between me and my Calvins. I keep talking to Charlie in the locker room, mulling over whether to wear long shorts instead of baseball pants (Piazza does, we don't), whether or not to tuck pants into our high socks (Ozzie says don't, so we don't), and what we bring to batting practice (Glove? Yes, to break it in. Bat? They'll have bats there. Phone? Yes.) and how to wear our hats (low). I love my outfit—I mean *uniform*—but I wish I could've gotten my pants taken in a little in the crotch, especially when I see January in hers. "Did you have a fitting in LA before the game?" I joke but I am not joking. I really think she did. She laments her cameltoe. The grass isn't always greener.

Eli says I look like an actual baseball player, which is all I need to hear. We all get on the bus to BP at FanFest, where I am going to have to attempt to hit balls in front of my teammates. I go to the furthest cage with Charlie, Adrian Peterson, and two wounded warriors from Iraq—one with one leg and another with one arm—who pound the ball. I step up and pretend I'm with Mike back in NYC and guess what—I hit *every single ball*. When it's done, Fred says I did great and gives me a couple tips, which I promptly forget and then vow not to step back into the cage because I don't want to ruin my streak. Problem is Eli didn't see me bat, so I step back in and hit every single ball *again*.

We head back to the ballpark and in the bus I ask January Jones if she feels like we already kind of did it and should be allowed to go home. Why do we actually have to play the game? We do and we have ninety minutes to kill. We sit with Andre Dawson at dinner, who seems to not want to have a thing to do with us and the behind-the-scenes-of-*RHONY* stories I'm laying on Eli. They bring in a group of Make-A-Wish kids and my heart explodes watching the baseball players sign autographs for them. I'm pulled out to go say hi to the owners of the Twins—it's one big family that owns the team and they're all in this gorgeous box eating way better food than we are downstairs ("Isn't that how it should be?" one of the wives crows when I comment on it) and I'm shocked to get my first look at the field and realize there are already thirty-five thousand people watching the Futures Game before ours. I thought it was going to be half empty.

I am really crashing, all the energy from the speculation over the last twenty-four hours and especially at batting practice has evaporated and I feel finished, but suddenly they're telling me to go to the field. I do and immediately get another rush of adrenaline. I see the other team throwing balls and realize that I have yet to actually catch a softball in my glove. I grab Charlie for a game of catch. One hundred feet away, Panic at the Disco is doing a quick concert with pyrotechnics and I am sweating like a whore in church. Thankfully I'm sitting next to Charlie on the bench and we watch and learn as the other players are introduced—hat off, shake teammates' hands, get your place in line, wave to the crowd—until it's our turn. Fist-pumping and high-fiving my team on the way out makes me feel like a dude.

Game on and we get a couple runs right off the bat. I head to right field and, luckily, Charlie is in center. So we're outfield buddies too. I am teleported back to Little League, standing in the outfield praying the ball won't come to me. One does—well, more to Charlie, I barely even run for it and he doesn't get the play and I apologize if it was actually my play to get. He says it was his to get. When it's my turn to bat, I am halfway to the plate and realize I don't have my gloves on (so much *gear!*) and scramble to put them on. My at-bat music is the theme from *Real Housewives of Orange County*—sure to intimidate all in the field. January tries to trash-talk me (*did Betty Draper just call me a "pussy"!?*) and I take my first swing in a game since losing the game for us at the end of my humiliating six-year run in Little League thirty-five years ago.

It's a hit! A line drive actually! I am beaming! I am leading off first base and get called back by the announcer. The lady NBA star playing first has some fun with me. I have some fun back. (*It's all fun*, right?) Charlie bats after me and pops up. I think someone catches the ball, but screws up the throw to first and Charlie is still running, so I run too. Then they're all telling me to go back to the last base because he's out, but I think that's the third out so I'm kind of like a frozen idiot and get tagged out. And yet again *I wasn't paying attention!* Nelly ribs me but I am so grateful to have gotten a hit I am just excited. And at my next at bat I get another hit! *I'm two for two!* This time I don't screw up on the bases. Ozzie Smith gets me home. I am so elated about my two hits I feel like I could conquer the world. Even better, I'm subbed out of the outfield for the rest of the game. We kill the American League 15–4. Lots of high fives and fist pumps as fireworks blast over Target Field.

In the locker room people are taking showers, but I just put my clothes on and go home dirty. We shower at the hotel and head to the Nelly/MLB party at Epic, which is the whitest club on earth, literally Nelly and six hundred white people. They put us in an area with Matt Carpenter from the Cardinals, whose wife I met at *WWHL*. I ask who his best friend on the team is and he says Wainwright. I love that. My best friend on *my* team is Charlie, but I don't tell him. As we're leaving the Nelly show (early), there are eight cops out front and I ask them, "Officer, can you tell me where the strip club is?" They direct us to one a few blocks away on Washington, and as we're walking there we run into a guy with dreads who questions our choice of venue. He tells us we need to go to Rick's Cabaret downtown and so we get in a cab. We get to Rick's and almost immediately, as happens, a random stripper comes and sits down with us. She starts telling us about the night before, when a pro hockey player came into the champagne room and whipped out his dick and got kicked out. This after he asked for the menu for sexual favors—how much for hand job, blowjob, etc. She said that's off the menu. (They do serve food, by the way, and I am so hungry I almost order some, but who gets food at a strip club?) We ask her who the most crazy athletes are and she immediately says hockey players, because they're Russian and Canadian and drink insane amounts. A group of hockey players spent 40k on booze the night before. Later, she's going to a party at our hotel with some minor leaguers who played in the earlier game tonight and as she tells us I wonder how I can get into that party. She tells me she is from the South and travels to cities for big sporting events like the All-Star Game and NBA playoffs. She asks me to buy her a martini and I do. She tells me how much she loves Vicki Gunvalson as I stare at her face wondering if she is Right or Ratchet. I think she may be Ratchet.

On the way home we get a cabby who is unmarried (at sixty-five) and tells incredibly misogynistic jokes about women, kind of exactly what you'd expect from the guy that trolls outside the strip club at 2 a.m. But shocking, still. When I get home I realize I've been looking at my watch all night, which is on East Coast time so actually I should still be out. I don't care, though, because I feel like a hero. *I went two for two.*

▦ MONDAY, JULY 14, 2014—MINNEAPOLIS-NYC

I couldn't wait to get home to tell Surfin the big news. His face lit up. I could see the pride in his eyes. Em emailed and said that once again I had proven the whole family wrong. I also heard from Uncle Robert (I'm sending him my MLB softball glove), who was quite impressed, and Jim Edmonds loved the pic I sent him. (My arms are *cut*, it's undeniable!) Anderson is shocked at the sight of me in a baseball uniform, in a good way.

▦ TUESDAY, JULY 15, 2014

Bethenny is indeed interested in coming back to *RHONY*. This is a bombshell for the show, so we are gonna see if we can make a deal. If it doesn't work out, we move on. On that note, I met with Bethenny, Martha Stewart, and Michael this morning about the show we're developing to pitch. It was fascinating to watch those two women together in a meeting. They're more similar than either probably would want to admit. Bethenny mentioned that people would be interested in the tension between them—which added an overlay of tension, or intensity, to the meeting itself. Martha pulled out her camera and started taking pictures of us all. Michael just returned from five weeks in Brazil doing *Men in Blazers* for the World Cup. He agrees that the service in Brazil leaves much to be desired and said, "It's as bad as the Soho House," which is officially the funniest and most true thing I've heard all day.

Worked out with the Ninj and did *not* weigh myself. I am two for two, what the hell do I need with a scale?

We taped our fifth anniversary show early this evening and I had more fun than I've had on TV in a long time. The whole thing was a surprise orchestrated by the rest of the staff—all I knew was that Jeff Lewis would be there and that I just had to read what was in the teleprompter. I figured there would be doorbells ringing and people coming in throughout—and there were. I *love* a doorbell. The surprises were: Snoopy appearing as the bartender, wearing a Cardinals jersey, NeNe coming in the door (I was so happy to see her and touched she'd flown from LA just for this), Martha Stewart ringing the doorbell to steal NeNe's Andy Award, Jimmy accepting his Andy Award for Greatest Addition to the Clubhouse (the shotski), a taped message from SJ and James Wilkie and another from my parents (my dad said, "We can't believe the show is still going, frankly") and one from Jackée accepting her award for Special Achievement in Clubhouse Drunkenness. And at the end Wacha came in with the Gay Shark and flipped out at the sight of Snoopy; it was so freaking cute. Dave, Liza, and Bruce came and I was thrilled they did.

The live show was Anderson and Kelly. I'd indulged myself by drinking Whispering Angel during the anniversary show even though I never drink before the live show, so I was feeling no pain. The three of us probably shouldn't be allowed to be on TV together anymore, for our own sakes, because we are now trying to shock each other by seeing how far we will go on air. Kelly asked Anderson if he's circumcised, I told Anderson his fly looked like it was down and he said it was because he was straining his zipper, and the poll question was a setup for me to be embarrassed: "Who do you want to see reveal a secret about me? Anderson or Kelly?" Anderson won and revealed that I am a top. So there was that. *And* Cher was our mystery caller and said that Anderson and I had sent her lovely pictures from Italy. Anderson said you have no idea how many we took in order to get just those, to which Cher responded that that was incredibly gay of us. The hot doctor from Southampton was at the show and we hung out after. He is nineteen years younger than me. Does that matter? I can't see how it doesn't. After the show Cher and I were texting back and forth. Now, *that* is a diva who loves an emoji. And I give them right back to her because I feel that's how she communicates.

WEDNESDAY, JULY 16, 2014—NYC–LOS ANGELES

Surfin calls me Slugger now. I love it. Willie did a great piece on *Today* about *WWHL*—I mean like the best ever. Also all the other interviews I've been doing about the show hit this morning—*USA Today*, the *Post*, BuzzFeed, *Us* magazine, blah blah blah. Seeing all the articles together made me feel like we've achieved something. Before heading to LA for the *RHOOC* reunion, I pre-taped Liv Tyler and Common and, wow, are those two lovely people. We all exchanged emails after the show and Liv Instagrammed a picture of me and Common sitting across my desk from each other pretending to have a meeting. Best Friends Forever!

After an uneventful flight to LA, the people at the Tower put me in the penthouse and I tried to keep my voice down because Renée Zellweger was across the hall. Voices carry. Especially mine.

THURSDAY, JULY 17, 2014—LOS ANGELES

While I was reuniting the OC Hens the drama wasn't contained to the soundstage—during the breaks I kept turning on my phone to incoming hysterics coming at me from all cities. Teresa has a crisis manager who seems to bring on a fair amount of crisis herself. Plus two of the NY ladies are mad at me. The reunion was solid. We'll get two parts out of it. Tamra goes off the rails at the reunion. Heather was thoughtful and deliberate. Lizzie left crying. I felt horrible for her.

Afterwards I met Bruce and Bryan at Pump and chatted with Lisa for a bit. Great reaction to our anniversary show, especially Snoopy and Wacha together at last. Anderson's revelation that I'm a top is getting picked up on all the gay blogs. I can't even look at the comments.

FRIDAY, JULY 18, 2014—LOS ANGELES—SAG HARBOR

I had a panic attack on the plane, convincing myself we were going to crash, this after reading every word in the *New York Times* about the Malaysia Airlines tragedy. If you really sit there and think about hurtling through the sky, powerless, in a tube, you can really lose your shit. Needless to say, we made it, and I had poor Daryn pick up Wacha and my car and meet me at 6 p.m. at JFK, where she handed me my keys and took my driver back to the city, thereby saving me several hours and getting me out to the beach in two hours at peak travel time. Now I'm suddenly *that guy* who sends his assistant with his dog and car to get him at the airport? I guess I am and I like it! But I'll tell you what guy I will never be—I don't have her place my calls. I am decidedly not *that* guy. By the way, everybody *else* is that guy, because I am the only one on either coast placing my own calls. Went over to Jimmy and Nancy's for nosh and Fresquila; I swear when I pull up in the driveway Nancy has the best Pavlovian response—she pours a jumbo bag of nacho cheese Doritos in a bowl and I go to town for hours as we talk. Wacha and Gary Fallon are in *love* but I think their roughhousing completely freaks Jimmy out. This from a man who loves roughhousing himself, but Jimmy encourages them to have little time-outs. We talked about TV and music for four hours and I went home and slept like a baby.

SATURDAY, JULY 19, 2014—SAG HARBOR

Cloudy day. Went to breakfast at Sandy's, then wandered around East Hampton and bought a new pair of shoes and two terry-cloth hoody sweatshirts at Scoop. I am obsessed with them and wore one out of the store. Terry cloth is so seventies beachy.

On Skype with my parents, my dad said, "Who knew that you would turn into a ballplayer?" I said that was an overstatement and my mom put it more simply: "Oh, get a GRIP, LOU!" The subject changed to "Did the WORLD need Anderson to tell them you're a TOP?"

Hung out with Dr. Kyle.

Mark and Kelly picked me up for dinner at Janie Buffett's (Jimmy was singing in Boston). Janie—the coolest woman on Long Island—told me she's in Warhol's diary. Will Arnett and I talked about late night TV for a long time. He said he and Letterman always wind up talking about sobriety when he's on that show, and I told him about my chip line falling flat last December. He and Amy Poehler have uncoupled perfectly. And he showed me his underwear (just the top) because I wanted to know if *he* was still rocking the Björn Borgs. (Affirmative.) Molly Sims was there—she's cool. There was fantastic vaporizer action floating around at the Buffetts', so it was that kinda night.

SUNDAY, JULY 20, 2014—SAG HARBOR—NYC

Worked out at Tracy Anderson—my hip flexors will never be the same. Ow.

Met Kelly's parents for the first time after all these years. It's always a trip seeing your friends in the light of their parents. I loved how Kelly's dad talked about her. We took a helicopter back to the city and I was terrified that Wacha would jump out the window. I tried in vain to put the headphones on him and succeeded at the end, but he didn't need them—he was an absolute champ! I fell a little bit more in love with him.

Hickey is back from purgatory (shooting *Manhattan* in Santa Fe) for exactly twenty-four hours and we had a quick dinner at Good. I showed him the plans for my apartment and decided that right now they're designed too much for resale value, and I need to make them more about me.

Before I left for the show I looked for Janie Buffett in the *Warhol Diaries*, and there she is, hosting yearly New Year's Eve parties in Aspen that people like Barry, Diana Ross, Jack Nicholson, and Angelica were at. Warhol chose Janie's party over Cathy Lee Crosby's fete for Sonny Bono's wedding, which seems smart given it *wasn't* to Cher. And because Janie throws a great party.

MONDAY, JULY 21, 2014

Felt happy, grateful, and lucky all day—spurred on by a morning meeting with Eric Hughes to go over plans for my apartment. He had some great ideas and it was the first time I could totally visualize the new place. From there it was seven rounds of boxing and kicking with the Ninj, a quick lunch with Bruce, screening *RHONJ*, two conference calls, a nap, and two shows. Took Wacha for a walk before work, and the restaurant that used to be Focaccia (with the incredible Christmas tree during the holidays), then became Tremont (not so great), is now a diner-type place with a soda fountain. I think it'll be a big success. You won't be able to get in on weekends. How they'll pay their astronomical rent serving burgers I don't know, but I am praying they make it. Mxyplyzyk is still vacant, by the way, over a year later. So that's a greedy landlord with a large helping of karma. On the walk some woman was pretending not to be taking pictures of me picking up Wacha's poop, but she was. Benny Medina invited me to a dinner for JLo's birthday Thursday night in the Hamptons. Random. I'm there.

My aunt Gisela was at the show tonight and she keeps saying she hates to impose on me for tickets, and I keep trying to explain that there's no such thing as imposing on me for tickets to my own show. It's always so fun to see her. We taped Kate Hudson and Zach Braff; she was wearing a midriff and has great abs (Kate, not my aunt Gisela). She said it was the most fun she's had on a show. She had a high pony and answered a ton of Goldie questions exactly as you'd want her to.

My heart wasn't in it for tonight's live show. It was one of the Americans from *Ladies of London* and Lizzie from *RHOOC* but I was checked out, so much so that I went into the control room during commercial breaks, which has happened on only one other show. But the first time was for a reason—to give John Jude shit for giving me exasperated time cues during the show that are tantamount to him whispering in my ear, "*Ugh*—3:30 left in the act . . . [*sigh*] . . . I can barely stay awake. . . . *The control room is bored.*" The good news is that some woman in the audience brought me a bag of gifts that included a first-edition copy of the *I Love Lucy* book that I repeatedly checked out of the local library growing up, and was probably my mom's first sign that I might be gay. The woman had read about it in *Most Talkative* and brought me the book. And dog treats. And whiskey. Very thoughtful. After the show I got an email from SJ and Matthew, out at the beach, saying "Tell me the truth, could you concentrate on tonight's guests?" So I guess the gig was up. And Evelyn's text came in a minute later: "Don't like this show. No energy." So she got that right.

▦ TUESDAY, JULY 22, 2014

Woke up wondering what in the hell I bring JLo as a birthday present. Got a text from Bethenny saying she was pleasantly surprised with Bravo's offer after fighting with us about money for so many years. This thing is either going to close quickly or not at all.

Did weights with the Ninj today. I feel fat again—gonna weigh myself tomorrow. Went and spoke to NBCUniversal's summer interns—I do this every year because I believe that children are our future—teach them well and let them lead the way. OK, I am half serious, half paying tribute to Whitney. I do it because I figure if these kids are the chosen few that have managed to get these coveted internships, I owe it to them to pay it forward and give them whatever advice that might help them along—it's an incredibly competitive job market for these kids. But the questions ranged from "What's your favorite snack?" (dark chocolate, Doritos) to

"What's one thing we wouldn't know about you from looking on the Internet?" (I said that I'm a stoner, but that's probably online and I am sure the Comcast HR people were *thrilled* I shared that)—so all in all I am not sure what I was able to impart to them in terms of wisdom.

I somehow said yes to a spread in Rachael Ray's magazine that I thought was just a Q&A but it turned out to require me to actually *cook* something, which ain't going to happen, so I made Daryn come over and do the cooking and then take pictures of me posing with the ingredients. It was orange glazed salmon over spinach and it was delicious. I took credit for it after I ate it. Am I *that guy* too? It was, after all, my kitchen. Two points for that?

We taped Gayle King and Kristin Chenoweth and it was perfect. We got talking about the swirl, and Gayle says she's never been with a white guy, and Kristin has never been with a black guy. (I said I'm the UN.) They were taking pictures together after and Gayle said they look like Michael Strahan and Kelly, which was both hilarious and true. Met Bruce and Liza for dinner at Morandi—Wacha joined too—and it was our last meal with Liza as a single girl—she gets married in ten days. We gotta write our toast! I feel like she's famous right now (on account of being a bride) and everybody wants to get to her. Michael and Wes showed up and were seated at the table next to us with Nate Berkus and his husband, Jeremiah. I got snippy, we went to the show, which was on in prime time tonight, and for a variety of reasons there was chaos until we went on. It was #legGate night and Aviva's leg flying through Le Cirque seemed to dominate Twitter. I hope the ratings are great. Bruce bartended and I plugged his Instagram. Liza, Bryan, and Hammy were in the audience, and after we went next door to the Ear Inn and sat outside. Bruce said he ran into Martha Stewart the other night and she told him I sent her black flowers and she was wondering if there was something she should be reading into that. I thought I sent her a white orchid to thank her for surprising me on my anniversary show. Gotta ask Daryn what we sent! (Black flowers do sound super-chic, though.)

I've been listening to inordinate amounts of Bob Marley lately. I am back on the reggae train and highly recommend it.

Bruce got two thousand followers overnight. He's at 10k. Meanwhile Wacha is at 59k. They both got juice.

Got robocalled *again* by Newt Gingrich. I keep telling them to lose my damn number. I stayed on the line after Newt's important message about America's future and told the lady—again—to lose my number. I said, "Didn't he cheat on his wife and lie about it?" and she said, "What man in America hasn't?" and hung up on me. Lovely. Went to the Ninj and hit the scale—165. My new normal. I see a medium Sam's pizza in my future.

Hung out with Jackie for a couple hours, met Liza to help her finalize placement for her wedding tables.

I was the inaugural speaker at PMK's new series for their employees, spearheaded by Cindi Berger. They're a huge PR firm and I want all their clients on *WWHL*, so maybe this speaking gig will help. She interviewed me about my career, and when it was over gave me an incredible gift bag. (I will say I have received so many Beats by Dre headsets in the last few months that I could open a Beats franchise out of my apartment.) They also gave me an Audi with a driver for the day (way cooler than the headphones) and I got chummy with the man behind the wheel—Jay—who was a NYFD fireman at one time. He confirmed that there are plenty of gay firemen. I told him to get to work for me. We went to pick up Jeremy, who was in town looking at colleges. I'd gotten intel that he might like to go to Clyde Frazier's restaurant and on the way I revealed to him that I don't actually know who Mr. Frazier is, which became a big "let's laugh at Andy's stupidity" moment between him and Jay the driver. I'm happy to give my nephew the opportunity to laugh at me. And I might add that the fajitas at Mr. Frazier's suck. The basketball court is cool, though.

WWHL was the *Million Dollar Listing: Miami* people. I made it through fine. I finally had a moment with Straight Pat before the show and said I was glad to hear he is actually Gay Pat and that I'm a little embarrassed to have been calling him Straight Pat and am sorry if I caused him any trauma. He was cool. The artist Mr. Brainwash was the bartender. He was the subject of the Banksy doc *Exit Through the Gift Shop* and we told people that he'd be painting live on the show, but it turned out that he couldn't because his painting is actually spray painting and the fumes and the cameras' aversion to spray paint made that impossible so it was kind of a bust, but he did make me a few prints that combined me with Warhol's image of Marilyn. It's scary and cool and derivative and weird all at once. I read some stuff on the Internet after the show that says he's a total fraud and doesn't do his own stuff at all, so now I'm wondering what the real story is, and need to find out if it's actually worth anything.

After the show I had a Tinder date, my first in a while, with someone completely age inappropriate. I can't even write the number down because I will hate myself while I type it. He is very handsome but laughs quite loudly at the end of sixty-five percent of his sentences. (That's a high rate of shrill laughter per sentence.) But two drinks in we were having a lively conversation about trends in fitness (Barry's, SoulCycle, Tracy Anderson, CrossFit—2014 is an exciting time for fitness!) and we had an intense goodbye on the street. Even so, unclear if we shall ever meet again.

▦ THURSDAY, JULY 24, 2014—NYC–SAG HARBOR

The Bethenny deal is closed. I can't believe it. We're trying to keep a lid on it for as long as possible. We'll see how long that lasts. As of right now, only five people at Bravo know. Page Six says this dinner for JLo tonight is not a dinner, but a party at a restaurant. So that means you don't bring a gift, right?

My weeklong speaking tour about my career continued with a morning stop at the RCA Records off-site. I did it because they represent half the music industry and I also want their clients on *WWHL.*

Got booked on Jimmy for next week. Need to think of some stories.

Lunch with Bruce at Good. Trying to figure out where to go for Christmas. He thinks West Coast Christmas, then Cabo or Hawaii. I am intrigued, but also excited by Trancoso in Brazil.

Got another ride to the beach from Kelly and gave Wacha a few Happy Travelers for the helicopter because I was terrified he'd have the fit I thought he was going to have last week, but he was perfect. Went with Mark and Kelly to the JLo birthday thing and it turned out to be a lot of fun. (No one brought gifts, it wasn't that kind of party. I had decided, though, that were I to bring her gifts, I would've gotten her books because who is buying JLo books? *JLo needs books!*) I probed Benny Medina for even more Diana Ross/Berry Gordy stories and he told me about the night he was working for Berry when he was in the studio mixing "Love Hangover"— that was the only thing I needed to hear all night. JLo was in white pants and a white kind of bra/bustier thing and her hair was super eighties. She said she was doing a Cindy Crawford homage and I said it was very *Fair Game* and she said she auditioned for that and wanted the part more than anything, and I said I heard that Cindy felt the same way about JLo's part in *Gigli*. Laughs all around. She said it would take a strong woman to survive *Gigli*. Kristin Chenoweth was there and it was her birthday too, and our show was airing tonight so we were extra bonded. Rachel Zoe was in a black jumpsuit and her hair had a braid that she said her nanny did. Leah Remini told me some good backstage stuff about *The Talk*. She loves Julie. I also chatted with Elaine Goldsmith-Thomas, Darren Star, Tracy Anderson, and Aaron Rosenberg. Met Bethenny's branding agent, who was very verbal about *RHONY,* and I said keep a lid on it, fella. No way this will not leak. And Tony Dovolani from *Dancing with the Stars* showed up at the end and said he does get put with all the difficult ladies. He survived Kate Gosselin. I need to hear that story but we had to go because Mark had an early call for *Alpha House* and my car was at their house and I was exactly at the point where I could still legally drive. Saw Khloé Kardashian on the way out and I sensed an initial cold front coming from her. Her ass—I don't even know how to describe it. It was so bulbous and extended and shelflike and badonka-donkulous. I asked her if her ass had always been like that or if I was looking at something different or what. She said she was wearing special Spanx that lift it. JLo said Spanx usually flatten your ass so these must be a new kind. I got home and realized I have been shit-talking Kanye a lot on the show and maybe Kim a little too so I deserved some Kar-dashiShade.

FRIDAY, JULY 25, 2014—SAG HARBOR

Woke up feeling blah and canceled my Tracy Anderson. Hung out all day at Amanda's pool with Graciela, planning our yearly Fire Island getaway. We talked about: the Upper East Side, prescription meds, Botox, Israel vs. Palestine, marriage, Hamptons real estate, *The Real Housewives of New York City*, anal sex, our parents, ex-boyfriends, tits, and Wacha. Got a little work done, then had a date night with my long-term lover, me. (The doctor has been working overnights and our momentum is challenged.) We went to see *Boyhood* in East Hampton and it was the type of thing that felt a little plodding, then totally hit me in the end. An incredible achievement in filmmaking, says Andy Cohen. Went to Sam's and killed a medium mushroom and onion pizza at the bar. Graham said that the lady from Coke was at his door the Monday after my dinner with Barry last month, and they've been back. I filled in some blanks for him about how this turned into a matter of importance for Coke. I think he's going to make the change.

SATURDAY, JULY 26, 2014—SAG HARBOR

At Tracy Anderson there was a guy working out in full tennis whites. Of course I was watching him instead of the teacher. I zoned out several times trying to think of a great toast for Liza's wedding. Bruce wants it to be a Smothers Brothers kind of deal where he is the quiet one who gives one-word answers and I do most of the talking. Could be cute.

Winnie Fallon's birthday party was like Christina Crawford's without the matching mom-daughter dresses, or the intense physical and psychological abuse. And Winnie wasn't adopted. OK, this comparison doesn't work at all but I'm trying to say they had a bouncy house, balloons, pizza truck, a pony named Keebler, swimming, and endless food; it was really colorful and festive. I was sitting with Alec Baldwin, who said that his MSNBC show reminded him of me because we'd talked a lot about it socially before it launched. I asked him to refresh my memory about what got him fired, in one word. "TMZ," he said. I thought about it and remembered the whole story, but if he'd said the word "faggot" I would've caught on quicker. Oy. What a thing for me to be asking him to re-explain. I do not think he is homophobic, by the way, at all. He loves hanging out with gay people. Seeing him, Lorne Michaels, Marci, and Jimmy together was like the Mount Rushmore of NBC comedy. I ate like a pig—tons of mini hot dogs, a long hot dog, turkey burger, mac and cheese, ribs, and pizza. And a Popsicle. And candy. And rosé. Jimmy's parents are hilarious. Gonna go out on a limb and say Wacha was as popular with the kids as Keebler.

Ninety minutes later Mark and Kelly were at my door picking me up for Rocco from Gant's birthday beach party in Amagansett. It was sublime—spectacular music, tikis, bonfire, everyone in Grecian leaf wreaths (mine looked like a cabbage tree on my head; everyone else's made them look exponentially hotter). The beach is perfect. In retrospect we wound up leaving too early.

SUNDAY, JULY 27, 2014—SAG HARBOR–NYC

I do wake up occasionally and wonder where those go-getting Jesus freaks are and why they never came back.

Today was blah. I was blue. Overcast. I dove for my bed at the end of day.

MONDAY, JULY 28, 2014

I remembered today that Wacha's name was at one point Ron Swanson and at another Norman Reedus—and so I called him by both. He didn't respond to Ron but he gave me a crazy look—like he was having a West Virginia flashback—when I called him Norman Reedus. I did it a few times through the day and he would quickly look at me with a suspicious face. I felt guilty for Shirley MacLaine–ing him (it's a verb—look it up) back to the hill country. Or wherever. I'm going to stop with the Norman Reedus, though it is a crazy temptation.

The show was Zoe Saldana and Laverne Cox. I got a quick primer on what not to say to a trans icon (i.e., "How did you pick the name Laverne?") and Zoe (not allowed to ask if she is pregnant even though her pregnant belly is sticking out), so I said, "Congratulations on *everything* you are *beaming*." I thought that was smart.

⠿ TUESDAY, JULY 29, 2014

Woke up to a big article in the *NY Post* entitled " 'Real' Boring: How the 'Housewives' Franchise Spiraled into Dullsville"—proclaiming that the whole goose is cooked. Not a fun read. I, of course, disagree, but we have work to do in a few cities. We rebooted *Jersey* this season because there was an overwhelming outcry from viewers for new women and new stories, but now ratings are down and there's an outcry to bring the old women back. So, um . . . What to do?

Worked out with the Ninj and I weighed in at 163.4; I was thrilled, but I ate barely nothing yesterday, so I won't get used to it.

Conference calls all afternoon. When I was walking the dog, Johnny Iuzzini ran out of that Little Owl catering spot where he was doing some kind of event promoting éclairs (do éclairs need promotion?) and insisted I eat one and it was beeswax and sugar and honey and I didn't really want one and then a photographer appeared and I was in a tank top and it was awkward. I love Johnny, though. I took a bite and it was amazing. Jeanne texted—she and Fred were at Grahame Fowler—so I walked there and they were kid-less and decided to meet me at the show later.

I had a two-hour massage—my first in a month because, and this is what happens in life—I have recommended Adam to every single person I know and gifted him for Christmas to people and now of course he has built up his clientele to the point where *I* can't get a fucking appointment. *Can a white man get a break?* For the first hour (the on-your-back portion) I was on a conference call about *RHONY* casting and pickups and showrunner and all the rest. I am so crazily pumped for Plan B. The producers had dinner with her last night and are really excited too. I was speaking in code in front of Adam because I don't want it to leak. For the second hour I gave him shit about my being at the bottom of his client totem pole. But it was a great massage, so I will be back for more ASAP.

Tonight's show was a potential disaster. Joan Rivers arrived about twenty minutes before air, and there was a lot to discuss. I wanted her to do a little *Fashion Police* thing on the *RHONY* because we were coming out of the reunion; I could tell immediately when I pitched it to her that she wasn't a Housewives fan ("I'll just say they all look like whores" was my first clue). Michael Rourke was there, and we wanted to go through the new creative for the show we're pitching with Joan, and she said it was fine but we had to figure out a role for Melissa. This was new information to us, and a little concerning because we hadn't initially conceived this as a vehicle for them both, but I walked away admiring her for wanting to help her only child. (*And is Melissa Rivers now an EP on my show?*)

I went to say hi to Maksim Chmerkovskiy, and he was not the warmest; I guess that's his reputation? I don't watch *DWTS*, so what do I know, but I guess Joan Rivers had a similar experience, because she marched into the Clubhouse and all signs pointed to her eviscerating him on live TV. I told Jeanne and Fred that the shit was about to go down and I had a pit in my stomach. Their chemistry was tense for the first act (indeed she trashed the *RHONY* but I walked right into that one), and then during commercial break they started talking about Israel and once Joan heard he is on her side she totally fell for him. Crisis averted.

After Sadat and Begin worked out their issue, and just before we came back on air, I asked her if she had any new Helen Keller jokes (Joan is the last person alive still telling them, and the only one who could get away with it) and she thought for a second and gave me a nod as we came back. I asked her if she was still friends with Helen Keller and she went right into a shtick about how boring Helen was, how all she talked about was "the water, the water!" Not that funny in print, but she killed it. During the next break, Maxim turned to her and asked how she could get away with saying terrible things about people. She said it's because she's eighty-one. I told her it's because she's Joan Rivers. Legends get a free pass.

We still don't have a toast for Liza's wedding. My parents and Lynn get in tomorrow—so nice that she included my folks. Oh, I keep wanting to shout "Norman Reedus!" at Wacha to see if he will run to me, but I have controlled myself; I am fascinated and irritated that he has past-life memories. I feel like I'm living with Goldie Hawn in *Overboard*.

After a mostly sleepless night, I boxed six rounds with the Ninj. Didn't weigh myself. Was trying to wrangle a cab with Wacha over to Jackie's while on my headset with the Fallon producer for our pre-interview and was interrupted by a sweet gay guy who needed to tell me at that very moment that his life is fabulous and he needs a show on Bravo. I told him I was on the phone and he said he would wait for me to get off. I said I'm getting in a cab and he should find a production company to partner with and then bring it to Bravo. He did *not* like that answer and stormed off. I felt bad. Short of an eight-episode pickup on the spot, there was no pleasing her (I mean *him*, but he was acting like a chick). Millennials! They want it *all* and they think they deserve it *now*. Little Monsters is right. I should've told him to go check out the Legos at Google HQ. Uptown after Jackie's, Wacha was frothing at the bit to get me to take him into Central Park. I didn't. Poor guy. He is Norman Reedus from Tree Country of West Virginia—and I put him in a cab to his concrete dog run on Little West Twelfth instead. Torture.

Mom and Dad got to town and we had dinner at Morandi with Wacha. They are once again sharing a hotel with a boy band—they can't remember which—and my mom is on a tear about the fans. "They're in CAGES outside on the street! They have them in CAGES! SCREAMING! At NOTHING!" My dad corrected her, "They're behind *barricades*, Evelyn, not in cages." "Whatever—they're in HYSTERICS!" My mom told some fans they'd seen One Direction when they stayed in the same hotel in Toronto last year. "It wasn't TOTALLY true, but the girls screamed anyway."

Lynn was waiting for me at home, she's staying with me for the wedding, and we hung for a while and then crashed really early. I was exhausted.

Woke up to an email from Dave saying he'd crushed graham crackers in a bowl and put some milk in it, and that I needed to try it ASAP. Sounds revolutionary; skip the middleman! Took Wacha to get dry-cleaned because

CBS Sunday Morning was coming over to start shooting a profile of me. He was *furious*! He knows exactly where Canine Styles is and tries to pull me in any other direction. Am I *sure* he only has the comprehension of a two-year-old? (I don't know a baby that knows where things are in the West Village, I'm just saying.) Worked out with the Ninj—a lot of abs— and Ben McKenzie from *The OC* was at Willspace; it was fun to have someone new to look at for an hour. Erin Moriarty and Jay Kernis come to my apartment with their CBS News crew. Twenty-five years ago I was interning for Erin, Jay, and Lynn, who happens to be staying in the guest room, so this is the definition of a full-circle moment.

Here are some things Erin wanted to know:

» Why don't I have a boyfriend? (I went through all the reasons and tried to keep it positive because there was a sadness in her voice.)
» Do the Housewives feel pressure to get plastic surgery? (I said it's really fillers and injections we're looking at and they might feel pressure from each other.)
» Is it hard firing them? (I said sometimes yes, sometimes no.)
» Did you always want to be a celebrity? (I said I always wanted to be myself on TV.)
» Is this the happiest I've ever been? (I told her I am by nature a happy person, so it's hard to assess. But that I'm pretty damn happy.)
» She asked if being around narcissistic famous people all the time feeds into my own narcissism. (I said I'm around narcissistic non-famous people all the time too. So, no.)

They shot me walking Wacha and getting dressed for *The Tonight Show*. When I got to 30 Rock I schmoozed with Marcy Engleman and Julia Roberts in her dressing room in attempt number three to get her on *WWHL*. As we were talking, Daryn was leading my parents into my dressing room and I called them in and suddenly they were face-to-face with a huge movie star. "This is more than I bargained for," my dad said in his best approximation of a former President. My mom was perky, then five minutes later announced in the safety of my own dressing room that she thought Barkin was better in *The Normal Heart* onstage than Roberts was in the film. Thank you for keeping it real, Evelyn. Oh, and she figured out who the boy band is at their hotel: "It's FIVE DEGREES OF SUMMER!" She meant, of course, 5 Seconds of Summer but who cares. Nancy Fallon redid Jimmy's dressing rooms and they are phenomenal. Dave, my parents, Daryn, Ryan, and Anthony from *WWHL* were all with me in the Adirondack Room. No one was carrying on about them, but *these* are the best dressing rooms in late night, and I wasn't envious because I just was happy to *finally* be rolling deep with a large posse. I left an Andy bobblehead on the faux fireplace as a housewarming gift for the dressing room. Jimmy came in and was sweet to my parents. I'd say my performance on the show was fair, but I was ebullient that they played the *What's Happening* theme song as my intro music. I wasn't bad, I just wasn't too great. And Jimmy was super nice about *WWHL* and plugging all m'crap. Generous. Julia called me back into her room again after we were both done and said she was nervous to go on Jimmy as she is usually a Dave girl. I said, "Will you please do my show?" and she said yes, next time. I believe it. (I'm always on the hunt, which can make me feel like a whore.) I raced downtown and met Hickey, who is finally back for good from shooting *Manhattan*, and who did we run into on the street but that catcher for the Mets that Bruce and I ogled from behind home plate a few months ago, Anthony Vito Recker! He is impossibly hot in person. Took pics of him and Wacha but Wacha wanted nothing to do with him. He's a Cardinals fan, what do we expect? Bruce and I had dinner at Good, then joined Liza's rehearsal dinner at the Palm for dessert—we were the late-night cameo. "Ricki Lake's husband turned me into a POTHEAD!" was how my mom greeted me. Apparently she got an earful about the uses of cannabis at dinner. It's about time she came to the dark side, although it'll never happen. She let everyone know that Dad would be wearing his "Box Suit" at the wedding tomorrow—a comment which is grotesque to all who hear it. Bruce put Liza's Brian up on the wall of the Palm and I gave her the wedding greeting from Valerie Cherish—both cherries on top of their best night ever, until tomorrow. Came home and hung with Lynn and Wacha and was in bed early. Well, 1 a.m., which ain't bad.

Liza's wedding day! Hickey and I took Wacha to the dog run and he couldn't be bothered with his friends. He was handing out side eye and general indifference to all. Meanwhile, Mom and Dad raided Uniqlo for the third time this year—they think because everything is so cheap that they need to buy it all. Their fascination with that place knows no bounds.

Met Surfin's brother from Ohio; his name is also Surfin! Watch, I'll forget that. Em told me there's been much chatter in St. Louis about the fact that I didn't know who Clyde Frazier was when I took Jeremy to that restaurant, so I texted my nephew and asked him to name two Madonna songs. A couple hours later he texted back, "Like a Prayer and Holiday," and I replied with several over-the-top emoticons. I was genuinely excited that he knew them! SJ's mani-pedi lady, Gina, texted me that she was in my neighborhood (I later found out she was servicing the paws of Miss Liv Tyler) in case I wanted some buffin' on my nails. I did and while I was soaking in it, Bruce and I hashed out our toast for tonight. We built on Bruce's Smothers Brothers idea, where he is my shy brother and I keep setting him up for one-word answers. It's either gonna be great or sink, like so many things. Lynn got home and we got dressed in a flurry. Liza—consummate producer—had warned everyone that traffic on a Friday to Thirty-first Street and Twelfth Avenue would be rotten and she was right. Everyone arrived acting as though they had to travel through Afghanistan to get there. I hadn't expected to get emotional during the ceremony, but the sight of my friend of twenty years—a friend who in my mind has been perennially stuck at age seventeen (in the best way)—walking down the aisle calmly looking her guests in the eye with all the composure of, dare I say, *a grown woman*, just did me in. Waterworks. The sobbing was paused by the divine Mary Matthews, who led the ceremony and began with a nod to Liza and her culty Web series: "Welcome to the finale of *39 Second Single*, brought to you by Match.com"—laughs! (They indeed met on Match.com.) They wrote their own vows and they were lovely, especially Brian's. I thought Jamie was going to faint but if I was Liza's twin I would've too. Hell, I'm not her twin and I felt a little faint. I didn't expect it all to touch me so much. During cocktail hour I brought my mom over to Joan Rivers and facilitated an open mic during which I threw out topics and Joan went to town about Streisand (so many stories about coming up together—she imitated her waving with a finger across a room), Heidi Abromowitz (a fictional name based on a real person), Woody Allen (she loves him, but still tells Soon-Yi jokes), Nancy Reagan (will forever be grateful she sent a plane to pick up Edgar after he committed suicide), and Barbara Bush (Joan confirmed she and Nancy hated each other). Two topics on which they did *not* need my help were Israel (they both were going *off* on what's going on there) and Bill Maher. Joan agrees with my mom that I shouldn't do the show. She says she doesn't know if *she* would do it because it's very serious and you gotta know your stuff. So it's official: if they ever *do* call, I'm out. I took a pic of Joan and my mom that's a perfect juxtaposition of a natural and unnatural face. Joan and I were talking about the *Warhol Diaries* and I told her about my own. She said that I better include some good dirt and told me that her good friend Roddy McDowall had incredible diaries but made a stupid decision: in his will he says they can't be published until 2050. "My grandson will be sixty then and *he* won't even care! Who's gonna care about Danny Kaye's sex life in 2050!?" So true. And how do I get ahold of those diaries?

Old friends everywhere: Ricki had great hair, Amanda was in fine form and her chemistry with my dad was off the charts as always (stepmother Amanda? Oy!), Troy looked amazing—vintage Troy from 1990—Bill was the perfect proud dad, Joanna was gorgeous, and most importantly Liza, who has the most consistently positive and celebratory energy of anyone I know, was present, poised, and so in love with Brian. Our toast killed. (It was surreal doing a *routine* in front of Joan.) Near the end of dinner, Joan—seated across from me—took an empty Ziploc from her purse and tidily filled it with meat for her dogs. At some point in the night Alexandra ran over to everyone and glitterbombed them, which would be irritating at anyone's wedding but Liza's, who is the Queen of Glitter. (Liza keeps the glitter industry robust.) So we all had faces full of it. Dancing with Kelly to a fifteen-minute version of "Last Dance" was a top three moment of our friendship. If there has ever been a moment when two people were feeling a song, it was then. Oh, and I danced with my mom to "I like big butts and I cannot lie" and that Icona Pop song "I Love It." Bruce's shirt came off on the dance floor, which is just what happens at this point. Someone took Hickey's suit jacket and so he left wearing a stranger's suit jacket. Went to Barracuda for a nightcap with Mark, Kelly, Hickey, and Bruce and ran into Keith Kuhl, who was the one who'd taken Hickey's jacket by mistake! As mentioned, I live in Mayberry. Bruce, Hickey, and I stumbled—and I mean stumbled home—down Eighth Avenue and it was one of those New York City nights where everyone on the street is a supermodel. In front of my building Bruce drunkenly convinced me to bag going to Sag tomorrow. The countdown is on for his move back to LA and we need to maximize our time together. As I was going to bed, I saw that I had a message. It was from the bride, she just wanted me to know she was wearing a Mazel thong under her wedding dress. All was right with the world. Good night, NYC.

⬚ SATURDAY, AUGUST 2, 2014

Woke up to rain, wondering in bed if Jeremy really knew the names of those Madonna songs. He could've Googled them. Or asked someone. Chilled out with Lynn and wedding debriefed.

Bill Persky called and we had a lovefest. He said, "I love the friendship you have with your mom—it's a relationship but also a friendship. And your dad is so elegant and just lets it happen. But you need to play catch with the man once in a while." The *Daily Mail*'s online site, not a reputable source for much of anything, cobbled together my and Kelly and Mark's Instagram pics from the wedding and did a breathless piece about Kelly at her "best friend's" wedding, claiming that *Bruce* was the groom. Went with Bruce and Ava to Liza and Brian's roof for more wedding debriefing. Mary Matthews says the *Daily Mail* is "Instagram journalism"—I like it! Billy Eichner came and we shared an Uber home with the dog. Got in bed so early it was a record—ten-thirty—and checked into a *Designing Women* marathon. It's so 1990: they all look like drag queens, first of all, and they just sit around spouting about feminism. I was transfixed by Julia Sugarbaker's enormous eyeglasses. Each half hour is like a play. They could do it now and call it *Golden Designing Women*. I still got it.

Bruce says *Designing Women* was kinda *Housewives*-esque and that's an interesting concept. Anderson is heading to Israel. Poor guy. Mellow day. Did work at home and got sucked into *The Wiz* on HBO Family. It's simultaneously awful and kinda great, featuring every huge black star from 1978 and Diana Ross—at thirty-four—playing Dorothy; the acting is, um, not amazing. It's sporadically inventive, though, and feels huge, and when Diana sings "Home" at the end, all is completely forgiven. It's worth it for that song and "Ease on Down the Road" and the scene where they kill Mabel King the wicked witch *by pulling the fire alarm.*

Brought Wacha over to Bruce's, where Barkin was cooking spaghetti and meatballs, and ran into Isaac Mizrahi in front of the building. He was wearing all black on an August summer day and was ready with a (good) show idea for us to produce together and a proclamation about his new "most chic Housewife" (Shannon Beador). I love him. The daft doorman wasn't there and the sub knew who I was and sent me right up. Makes a difference! Barkin put me in a food coma with her spaghetti. We were live tonight at nine and after that dinner, I was schlumped in the backseat of Ray's car on the way to the studio. It was Melissa and Joe, so I didn't have to work too hard, but the audience was dead and I literally forgot what I was going to say mid-sentence at one point, which is never a pretty look on live TV and feels like forever even though it's only a few seconds. I was in bed by eleven-thirty. Breaking a lot of early-bedtime records this week.

⠿ MONDAY, AUGUST 4, 2014

The *Sunday Morning* crew came to shoot me boxing with the Ninj this morning. I was kind of showing off for them and coming out of the gate hitting really hard and by the time they left, after three rounds, I was completely pooped. I limped through three more. Met Bruce and Liza at his house (temp doorman, sent me right up) and had our final wedding rehash (the three of us can rehash endlessly) before sending Liza off for her Hawaii honeymoon. The next big goodbye is going to be to Bruce in a couple weeks and I almost can't handle it already. Come fall my life is going to be a whole lot lonelier. (Maybe that will push me into a boy-friend situation?) The show was *RHOOC* Shannon and Elisabeth Moss. I was stumbling all over words, but completely sober. Mom texted after we went off air: "Pretty good."

▦ TUESDAY, AUGUST 5, 2014

Liza called from her Hawaiian Airlines plane, excited to be in first class. I had an incredibly boring (almost fell asleep midway through it) work-out today and wandered home feeling trapped in a web of monotony, feel-ing like I do the same thing every day and just blah. My languid spell was broken when I walked into my lobby and the sweet elderly lady from down the hall (who I overheard crying and pleading on the phone a few weeks ago) approached me. She was shaky, in a state. *"I need a witness,"* she almost begged, holding out a piece of paper. I agreed immediately and we walked over to Surfin's perch, where I saw that I was about to sign her living will. My mind was racing, wondering what brought about this suddenly urgent situation. The moment felt simultaneously so personal yet completely anonymous. She looked on helplessly, and in the flash of a pen, it was over and I was in the elevator as Surfin provided her second signature. I had a quiet lunch in my apartment thinking about time, how fleeting it is. You see people in your building every day. You watch them age, their kids grow, change, and you see little things start to hap-pen to us all. Then they are gone. You don't see them again. The wonder-ful Italian couple down the hall who loved each other so much. He went first; she held on a few years, then disappeared. Now there's a cute young couple in there. My current apartment belonged to a beloved woman who lived in this building for thirty years. Now I'm here, and I'm expanding into the apartment of the man upstairs, whom I never knew but was here for half a lifetime. Apartment living is at once intimate and impersonal, with moments like today that you can't forget. Sometimes I wish I was Wacha.

Went in to 30 Rock and schmoozed around Bravo for a couple hours, doing my thing. The Koons flower sculpture in front is in full bloom and now I love it. Shari and I had a productive *Housewives* catch-up. Sounds like *RHOA* is going great. Viewers aren't thrilled with our *Jersey* reboot. We booked Kim Kardashian for next week and she wants to be perceived as a businesswoman now, so I said WTF are we going to ask during "Plead the Fifth" and our booker Robyn said, "How about 'What has been your favorite business venture?'" We LOL'd. The live show was Tyra and Derek Hough and I guess Tyra likes to spotlight that she went to Harvard and is a businesswoman. So everyone wants to be known as a businesslady.

▦ WEDNESDAY, AUGUST 6, 2014

You know what is not my favorite way to spend a day? Recording an audiobook. It is torturous reading back your words, and this is meta that I'm *writing* in my book about *recording* my book, but it is what it is. A minute after I Instagrammed a pic of me recording, I got an email from Nicole Richie saying, "NOTHING is worse than recording an audiobook! I didn't even finish when I was supposed to do mine. I was also twenty-two and on pills, so don't follow my lead." She's hilarious. The best part of the day was the cheeseburgers the producer, audio guy, and I ordered out from 5 Napkin Burger. Mine tasted like candy. I got home and Skyped with my mom, who made me promise I'm not an alcoholic. Also she kept telling me I had blood on my face, an accusation of which I was highly dismissive. Wacha went after a fly that was buzzing around and ate it out of the air. Impressive! He's a hunter. The day *will* come when he kills a big water bug for me. I know it. Oh, and I found out today that he's nominated for *InStyle* magazine's "Super Stylish Pet" award, but he's losing to Zooey Deschanel's dogs Zelda and Dot. I am upset on his behalf. I want him to win but should I publicly solicit for votes?

Dinner with Bruce, SJP, and Matthew at RedFarm downtown and after our hellos they asked what the red mark on my cheek was. Turns out I have been walking around with *ketchup on my face since 2 p.m.* I have been in contact with about twenty-five people since 2 p.m., and I couldn't figure out that I had ketchup on my face? Bruce was fascinated that I don't look in the mirror to check myself out in the course of the day. I really don't until I go on the air. Maybe I'm not as narcissistic as I think I am.

They'd all just seen the Lance Armstrong documentary and filled me in. Sounds like he actually is a more horrible person than I'd ever imagined. Every two or three years the tabloids print that SJ and Matthew are getting divorced, and I guess a whole new round of articles just came out. It's nuts. I wish they would sue but that winds up being a huge time and money suck. I had to leave at nine-fifteen to go change and do the show, which turned out to be spontaneous and fun—Mel B and Mark-Paul Gosselaar were the guests.

THURSDAY, AUGUST 7, 2014

New York City is so weird without Liza in it. She never travels, so she's always here. And I don't watch the weather, I just ask her what it's going to be. So now I have no clue what the forecast is. Fucking honeymoon. Meanwhile I *do* know the forecast where she is: there is a tropical storm *and* hurricane headed for Hawaii! *And* Liza emailed that the New York City Empress of Weather, Janice Huff, just started following her on Instagram. Coincidence? I don't *think* so. . . . Does Janice Huff rely on Liza for her weather reports too? Is she following Liza for info on the hurricane? Met this morning with Gordon the architect and Eric my designer—we're on our third set of plans and though I'm incredibly excited, all I could think as we went over each room is how broke I am going to be when this is all over. At the gym, I convinced myself that Jeremy Googled the names of those Madonna songs. I took a break and texted him and he said, "I really knew." I have never been prouder of my nephew. By the way, the kid is a straight-A student and excels at everything he touches but it took him spitting two Madonna song titles at me for me to give him respect. It's too late for *me* to get my priorities in order but I am thrilled he's on the right track.

Bruce and I saw the Imelda musical *Here Lies Love* at the Public, where we ran into Radzi and her friend, the guy who is dating Susan Sarandon. She said he has a new reality show coming on and he said it's not a reality show, it's a "docu-series," and that's a pretty way of saying "reality show." It's what I say all the time and it's what Oprah said when she launched OWN. It makes people who are on the shows feel better about being on a reality show. The musical was incredible—super-inventive staging, great score. It's like a moving theater piece where the audience is a part of it (usually I hate that but it worked here). And Imelda was just as horrible a person as you remember—and to think that the Reagans had them airlifted out of the Philippines to live in Hawaii for the rest of their lives! The U.S. had to *help* them?

My show was Daniel Radcliffe and Rebecca Romijn. Daniel Radcliffe's security guy is crazily handsome—in the same league as Lady Gaga's. Bruce and I had a mini going-away night for him, just the two of us, at the Copacabana, which is gay and isn't the original Copacabana, just some-place that uses that same name. The roof is retractable, though, so that's a bonus.

FRIDAY, AUGUST 8, 2014—NYC-SAG HARBOR

Drove out with Bruce. Had to go straight to East Hampton and endure that tragic stretch from Southampton on 27. Hung out with Bruce and Ava in the pool and Ava got even cuter. Went by the Countess LuAnn's new place in Sag Harbor to discuss her role on *RHONY* next season. She asked if I would consider bringing Jill back and then as an aside mentioned that there was no way Bethenny would ever come back. I agreed. Went to the Palm for Jonah's sixteenth-birthday dinner with Troy, Bruce, and Ava. I will never forget first meeting Jonah ten years ago right when Troy brought him back from Africa. Bruce and I taught him how to play baseball in Bruce's lush backyard as a helicopter flew above us and Jonah freaked out wondering what the hell he was seeing in the sky. He has grown into an amazing young man. People who eat at the Palm are my people, but that East Hampton branch is essentially full of barbarians. The noise level is unprecedented—it's people just yelling at the top of their lungs at each other. Rachel Zoe came by the table and gushed over Ava's J.Crew sequined hot pants and top. I heard that Jill Zarin was on the porch but I didn't see her. When I got home I looked up Imelda Marcos in the *Warhol Diaries* and besides commenting about how fat she got, Warhol wrote that after partying with her on Malcolm Forbes's yacht in 1984, "Every-body said that once Imelda gets started partying you can't stop her, that she's always the last to leave, and it was true, she was going strong." Apparently she had a mic and sang about twelve songs on the boat. I solicited for votes for Wacha on Twitter for the stupid *InStyle* award and now he's beating Zooey Deschanel's dogs. Meanwhile he is perfectly content running around trying to eat flies out of the air, so why am I bothering? Oh, and he has 65k Instagram followers.

⣿ SATURDAY, AUGUST 9, 2014—SAG HARBOR

Gorgeous day! No humidity and in the eighties. Mark and Kelly picked Wacha and me up to go to the Perskys' on their boat. It was his first boat ride and he just chased shadows and reflections on the floor the whole time. The Perskys were in full summer gear with incredible meatloaf sandwiches, topped off by Joanna's peppermint ice cream, of which I had two helpings. I couldn't help it. When I got home I had a great nap, then Wacha fell asleep on my shoulder and the cuteness of it was too much to bear. I decided if he didn't wake up I'd have to cancel my plans. He did wake up and Mark and Kelly picked me up again, this time for the Seinfelds' dinner party. (Having the Consueloses down the street makes for an incredibly convenient designated-driver solution on nights when we're invited to the same places.) The Ninj was fighting tonight in Atlantic City and on the way over Mark and I worried about him. The party was outside and beautiful. Nacho Figueras got interrupted midway through telling me his polo-playing schedule for the rest of the year by a call on his phone from Aspen. "It's Aspen," he said. I want Aspen to call me! (Was it Goldie?) Cameron Diaz told Bruce and me about her new apartment. She is digging Restoration Hardware and I think I need to take a deeper dive into their essentials, like couches. A lot of people at the beach are digging Resto Hardware. Gwyneth Paltrow was there and so was Rachel Zoe. We were seated next to Kourtney Kardashian and Scott Disick, but I didn't believe it was Kourtney. (I am really bad with Kardashians because I don't watch that show.) It was her, though. We talked about NY vs. LA in the summer. Scintillating. They left very early. There was dancing. Bruce spilled rosé all over Kelly. Home by one-fifteen.

SUNDAY, AUGUST 10, 2014—SAG HARBOR—NYC

Unfortunately, the fight did not go the Ninj's way last night. Went by Jimmy's so Wacha and Gary Fallon could run around. Had a forty-five-minute debrief with him and Nancy in the pool while the dogs ran around like maniacs, then Jimmy took his Vespa and followed me over to Marci's, where I had lunch and pool time. The water in the ocean was blissful. I picked up Bruce and we drove back to the city. He fell asleep in the car and so did Wacha, which almost put me to sleep. I was not looking forward to the live show, just not in the headspace, but I'd forgotten how adorable David Arquette is. His energy is flawless. Met Hickey after the show at the Cubbyhole for a quick drink.

MONDAY, AUGUST 11, 2014

Wore my Ninj T-shirt to the gym to support the fallen fighter, but his attitude is so good he didn't need the boost. Recorded that damn audiobook all afternoon and I was quite exasperated about it. Went straight from there to tape Kim Kardashian. Contrary to what I'd surmised, there were no restrictions on the interview. I had killed some Kris Humphries and Ray J questions that were on the "Plead the Fifth" list out of respect, then when she told me she was expecting much worse, I instantly regretted it. Am I getting soft? I took a selfie with her ass. So that was exciting. Also, Caisse had referred to North as a girl in the prompter and during the show I kept changing it to a gender-neutral reference (i.e., "baby") because I was quite positive that North was a boy. My team couldn't believe I didn't know the sex of this freaking baby. I could've told them I didn't know who Barack Obama was and gotten the same reaction. Right before the show, we learned that Robin Williams had died. Instant sadness. When I was in my first year as a desk assistant at CBS News, Lynn was set to interview him for a piece she was doing about Julliard and decided to let me interview him myself. I was horrible, stepping on everything he was saying, not listening and just sticking to my question list. He was so lovely and took care to make sure my horrible skills didn't sink the whole interview—something he didn't have to do. Anyway, I guess he was tortured and sad. It's all really upsetting. The live show was Terry and Heather Dubrow.

⁝⁝⁝⁝ TUESDAY, AUGUST 12, 2014

On Tinder this morning, I swiped right on someone who is . . . drumroll please . . . wait for it . . . age appropriate! Forty-two, to be exact. But now that it's a match I don't know what clever bon mot to throw at him to begin a dialogue. Hmmm. Booked Radzi to dogsit for the day since I am trapped in audiobook hell. We had played a game with Kim Kardashian where she had to guess retail prices of things rich people don't know about and thereby save Kris from peril. The graphic of Kris in peril kind of looked like she was hanging herself. So we had to change it of course because it turns out Robin Williams hung himself. This is the danger of pre-taping a show. Things will happen that make you look totally insensitive. Willie Geist challenged me to the Ice Bucket Challenge. I'm gonna do it on tomorrow's show. And Lauren Bacall died tonight. So sad. I met her a few times at Natasha's house. Now all the big legends are gone.

I had a date with this guy tonight who did not ask me one question. It was fascinating, and exhausting. There were periods of (for me) long silences! Long silences completely freak me out. (Ask my last therapist.) After about an hour I just retreated into my phone because the Kim K. *WWHL* was airing and I wanted to see what people were saying. My Twitter feed was blowing up with people saying "How dare you have her on, she's not famous for anything," but I am the guy who has Housewives on all the time, so I don't get the big difference. I think it's fascinating that people are drawing a line between the Kardashians and the Housewives. *I like it* that they're drawing a line, but it's confounding to me. And the selfie of me and her ass is like a wildfire on Twitter. People are fascinated by that ass! Got a text from Mom after the show: "Dad likes Kim K. I don't get it but she does have a huge ass."

Surfin is very pumped about my #belfie with Kim Kardashian. Last work-out with the Ninj before my summer break. Who knows in what shape I'll be when I return to him in September? Long call with Kenya to talk about next season. Ramona is now apologizing for stonewalling me at the reunion. I finally thought of something to say to the age-appropriate guy, and it was, "Hey there, how's it going?" Had two shows tonight—the first with Demi Lovato and Jessica Alba. Loved Demi; she reminded me of Lisa Marie Presley—strong and vulnerable all at once. Had dinner at Bottino with my old crew from CBS News—Diane, Mary, Mo, Josh Gelman, and Lynn joined us as a surprise. The live show was Kim Zolciak with Bruce bartending. The two of them competed in Bravowood Squares and Bruce completely lost the plot when it was his turn to guess a square—he picked a star—Billy Eichner, not a square that would block Kim's X. It was such a Chrissy Snow moment. I died. Kim even said, "We're playing tic-tac-toe, honey!" He put his hand over his face. It was, as I said on the show, a battle of the brainiacs. I did the Ice Bucket Challenge. Guess what—it was cold. Did it raise money for ALS? I dunno. I gave. We have a ton of huge guests coming in the fall (and are working hard on getting Streisand—OMG) but I have to admit it felt great to end the show and break for three weeks. We had a *WWHL* wrap party at Amy Sacco's club, No. 8. Man, does my team know how to have fun at a party. And they *love* to pose for pics. I think I set the tone on that one. Walked Wacha at 4 a.m. around the Village. There wasn't a hell of a lot going on out there.

THURSDAY, AUGUST 14, 2014—NYC–SAG HARBOR

Weight of the world lifted! This is my summer vacation! Two weeks of absolutely nothing to do and I couldn't be happier to be staying local. Drove to beach. Wacha chased shadows. Heard back from the age-appropriate guy on Tinder, who said, "Hey Andy! Doing well, thanks! How are things?" This conversation is turning serious so fast! I can't believe we are opening up to each other so quickly. Amanda and I hadn't been to Beacon all year and decided to give it a shot—in the midst of an August sunset—only to walk into a ninety-minute wait. So what little celebrity I have is meaningless towards getting a table at the Beacon. We went to the Dockside, which always seems more low key than most places out here. There was a seventy-minute wait but the nice lesbians in front found one for us inside fast, which we jumped all over. So I have juice at the Dockside. Turns out we were surrounded by Daughters of Bilitis inside. A hive of them. My food was good and I got in the Lebanese vibe by ordering all-veggie. Amanda had paella, which was served in a taco bowl. Odd. We skipped dessert and went directly into the center of the Sag Harbor FroYo sensation of the summer: BuddhaBerry. It was bedlam—teeming with my Jewish brothers and sisters on an absolute *tear* to get artificially sugared to oblivion with their favorite flavors/toppings/extras. It took me a couple hours to come down from the whole BuddhaBerry experience. I need to take a Xanax before I go in that joint again.

FRIDAY, AUGUST 15, 2014—SAG HARBOR

I sleepwalked through a Tracy Anderson class, then grabbed the dog and spent the day at Marci's beach club. There was a great lunch whose highlight was a dill-heavy egg salad. Marci is deep into the Gwyneth cookbook. Long talk with Ramona that was meant to be about her future with *RHONY* but devolved into a treatise (hers) on the state of affairs with Mario: not good. I put a pin in it till early next week, although I realize now I will be on Fire Island and even more zoned out. Skyped with my parents. Mom and her two friends Lynn and Barbara took food to Ferguson, Missouri, which is where the rioting and tear gas has been all week over what looks like the callously unjust killing of an unarmed black kid a week away from starting college. They bonded with the ladies of the neighborhood. My mom can be counted on for community building, and I love her for it. Spectacular dinner at Tutto il Giorno with Bruce, Bryan, Billie, Max, and Ava. We saw Grace Hightower and Marshall Rose and Candice Bergen—at different tables. Then got ice cream. I could eat an endless amount of chocolate chip ice cream if given the chance.

Happy birthday, Madonna! At Tracy Anderson they played a ton of Britney, so I don't know if that was a dis, a tribute, or completely unrelated. Katie Lee Joel was working out in front of me. Now I know how she got her body. Ran a bunch of errands to get ready for Fire Island, which essentially has nothing but a general store and a lot of alcohol. Went to BookHampton to stock up on books but it was on Secret Service lockdown because Hillary was coming in a couple hours. They sweetly ran inside and got me a few beach books and charged them to my account. It felt old school. Got a waffle long-sleeve thing at Double RL and some bones for the WachStar. Went by Jeanne and Fred's and saw their divine new pool. On the way home for my massage I stopped by Sandy's and walked into the remains of what was a major lunch: two #PowerBabs—Walters and Streisand. Gave Barbara Walters a kiss, though not sure her cheek was receiving. She left. Shook Miss Streisand's hand and James Brolin told me he loved my (Gant, bordering on hot pants) bathing suit, and I could tell he meant it. (Mr. Brolin is one stone-cold silver fox.) Wacha was running around and I could tell that Streisand was worried that he was going to eat her little puffball Sammie, but he *mercifully* left it alone. I told Barbra I was obsessed with her Instagram and she said she doesn't get it *at all*, and doesn't see the *need*. I explained the concept of sharing bits of her inspiration with her fans and she said she *still* didn't see the need. I got the sense she approves the photos and someone else does the posting and stuff. We talked about how amazing John Mayer is. She sang in the studio with only him, her son, and Michael Bublé; the other partners on her duets album sang to a track of her. I asked if she sang live with Sinatra when she did *his* duets album and she said hers was to a track. It came up that I was seeing Jimmy later and she said she was desperate to meet him because she was doing his show. That was my big opening, and I took it. "You know we are desperately trying to get you to do *my* show?" I said, too cheerfully. "I know but I'm only doing a couple things and I *hate* doing press," she said quickly. *It ain't happening.* Not even a sliver of a chance. "I feel like the album *is the thing.* Why do I have to do another thing about the thing??" I got what she was saying. Then she told me a story about doing Mike Wallace when she was nineteen. He asked her questions about herself and then when she answered, he told her she was vain. Honestly I think she would hate my show. It's not her thing. Oh, and neither is Instagram, because we started talking about that again and she still didn't get why she needed to share anything.

The massage I got later from Adam was fantastic. As good as the medium mushroom-and-onion pizza I had with Hickey at Sam's. (Graham is meeting with the Coke people in September, so we'll see.) Hickey and SJP are coming to Fire Island for the weekend—I'm excited. Went by Nancy and Jimmy's on the way home and gorged on Doritos. He won an Emmy tonight (at the Schmemmys) for hosting *SNL*. They lent me an amazing portable crate for Wacha—it's light as a feather, like a little mini Pack'N Play for the dog. Wacha smelled Gary Fallon all over me when I got home and completely lost his shit.

▦ SUNDAY, AUGUST 17, 2014—SAG HARBOR–THE PINES, FIRE ISLAND

"I may be a bottom but I'm working my way to the top!" I'd only been at Gay Beach Camp (Fire Island Pines) for a half hour before I'd heard my first gay *Housewives* tagline. I like it! Rented the same great house that I did the last couple years—right smack on the ocean, clean, two bedrooms with a pool and Jacuzzi. Fire Island is an untouched jewel that to me feels like Malibu in the seventies meets Studio 54—no cars and little boardwalks connecting groovy wooden and glass treehouses; the energy is sexy and free. There's naked yoga on the beach at any hour of the day, classic disco wafting, a hint of poppers blowing through the air from down yonder, every house door left open, dogs off leash (except mine, are you kidding? He will run the hell away from me), lesbians, gay guys, the people who love them, and in 2014, more kids than you would've ever imagined possible. Oh, and people here are *so nice*. Wacha had a bad first experience with the Gary Fallon Pack'N Play—he was crying like a motherfucker when I left for the store and I didn't latch it right so when I got home it was a bad scene—he was basically trapped in an overturned, undone, pee-stained (his, not Gary's) pup tent. He was upset, poor fella. Ran into Sam Champion and husband; they are staying in a gorgeous house two doors down from me. Met Michael, Wes, and little Beckett on the beach and brought Wacha down to watch the Ascension party, which essentially involves a couple thousand very muscular gay guys dancing to heavy bass on the beach high out of their minds, probably on Molly. They unfortunately look the opposite (run ragged from a weekend of partying) of how they feel (euphoric/perfect). It sure was fun watching and judging, though. (When is watching and judging *not* fun?) Walking to dinner at the Powell-Rourkes', I met a super-handsome Clark Kent-y shirtless guy leaving the party with someone who wanted a selfie and I was happy to oblige, if only to get closer to Mr. Kent. They had just met and were leaving together, i.e., *true love in the Pines*. After dinner Michael and I went to the Sip n Twirl, and Lina was on the porch spinning deep disco under the stars. This transcontinental, transcendental mocha diva rules that porch, weaving music that from her is magic and electric—the vibe is gay *Alice in Wonderland*. We met Bill and Chris there and they were giving me the 411 on all the mess and drama around the dance floor. They are like the mayors of Fire Island and spin the lore while Lina spins the tunes. There was plenty to keep me entertained. I met a very hot Latino trainer who I quickly figured out is the ex-boyfriend of the doctor in Southampton. So I backed away slowly from that potential disaster and made my way home. And on another note, is there anything better than going to sleep to the sound of the ocean?

MONDAY, AUGUST 18, 2014—THE PINES, FIRE ISLAND

Is there anything better than *waking up* to the sound of the ocean? I'm not sure my stereo will be getting much use, because it can't compete with the lulling, which is like therapy for me. I've been here a day and I feel like I am taking deeper breaths and completely letting go of all the stress of the last year. I will be Jell-O within no time. Gillian came by first thing to go over a huge stack of photos that we had to edit down to put in the middle of this book. I walked her back to the ferry and it was like *Night of the Living Dead* seeing the hordes of hungover Ascension tribes going back to the city. (They call the Monday ferries the "blood buckets"—an apt title.) On that note, after surveying the locals last night, I've surmised that the drugs at the Ascension party were: Molly, meth, and GHB. I am proud to say I have never once done meth (highly addictive and ruins your life) or GHB (if you dose it wrong, you die), and "proud" would not be the correct word, but maybe I can say I am happy to say that I *have* experienced Molly and it is phenomenal, euphoric, wondrous, mystifying, and memorable—an experience I *would* wish for everyone to have once, if it weren't dangerous and illegal and, if you get the wrong stuff, lethal. Mark and Kelly arrived on the one-thirty ferry with a double magnum of Domaines Ott. Never seen a bottle so big! We got back to the house and I made flank steak and tomatoes and mozzarella. *All I ever do is cook!!!* Kidding. We took a long walk on the beach, poked around the deck of Jenna Lyons's (gorgeous) house, which may or may not be for sale, ran into the Sam Champions and had rosé in their luxe (and very warm) pool, Jacuzzi time, and the Consueloses may or may not have had private adult time. (Those two are like bunnies. Or newlyweds. Or newlywed bunnies.) Then we all went to low tea (high tea, low tea, whatever, it's all just an excuse to drink), where we danced to disco on a dance floor that was empty at first and then packed soon enough. Had a long talk with Clark Kent, who, as it happens, is also a super-handsome lawyer. (Things didn't work out so great between him and his new friend from last night at the party.) I got his digits. Mark and Kelly took a 10 p.m. water taxi out of here—he had to go back to the city for a 5 a.m. call on *Alpha House* and she went to the kids in the Hamptons.

TUESDAY, AUGUST 19, 2014—THE PINES, FIRE ISLAND

Have I mentioned that Gay Beach Camp is essentially clothing optional? Well, not really, but kind of. No one wears shirts anywhere, and I am the guy who says I'm not gonna be the guy who doesn't wear a shirt anywhere and then I turn into a hippie after day one and I am walking around barefoot in my swimming trunks. I dig it! By the way—for years I also was the guy who disparaged Fire Island because it seemed too much for me: too gay, too much partying, too skeevy. It turns out that my younger self was a know-it-all idiot (See: my hair pre-2000). Now, at the end of an exhausting year, I am so grateful to be able to have such a complete escape from reality without having to go through security at an airport. It is another world.

I finally removed a pair of my stockpile of Beats headphones from its (complicated and intricate) packaging and took a magic-hour beach trek with Wacha with some intense sound pumping through my ears. Sure, they are good headphones, but they were really squeezing my head after about an hour. Glad I have seventeen more pairs. Wacha's long leash has its benefits—I can strategically steer him to go right up to hot guys—and drawbacks—I swear he was going straight for guys' dicks in the nake-o section by Cherry Grove. Saw Clark Kent Lawyer on the walk and we talked in the waves for a good hour. I invited him over for a drink before tea. I took a nake-o Jacuzzi at sunset and there were a bunch of twinks on the beach I didn't notice until I heard them giving me a round of applause. I guess that's better than boos? Clark Kent Lawyer texted that he was too tired to have a drink, so that was a complete buzzkill. It was too good to be true. Ten minutes later he texted that he was making coffee, showering, and coming over. Rally time! He did come over and it was a river of words at home and then tea and then back home again. A fun date! I told Clark Kent Lawyer I was keeping this diary and he wanted to know what I did on September 15—his birthday; I looked and there ain't no record anywhere of September 15. I skipped it! The only day of the entire year. Hmmm. I got an email from Mom when I got home tonight: "Glad you are having fun. Find a husband."

WEDNESDAY, AUGUST 20, 2014—THE PINES, FIRE ISLAND

I dreamed I shot the pilot with Joan Rivers and she said to never give her any notes, ever. Hmmm. Clark Kent Lawyer went back to the city and it turned into a mellow day. I asked Daryn to find out anything she could about what I did on September 15; it was a Sunday, and she said Andrew Dice Clay and Kathy Wakile were on my show that night. I give up. I read a lot and took Wacha for a very long walk on the beach this afternoon with those headclasps pounding music in my ear. He hates water of any kind, which thrills me not only because I don't have to dry him off but also he doesn't bring wet sand home, and even better, the way he runs away from the water is so cute. He's cute when he's scared. I wandered by a fun group of fashion people, got to chatting, and joined them for some sunset rosé. Two Brazilians were on mushrooms and one had a tattoo that looked like either a state (California? New Hampshire?) or maybe a bust of George Washington. He of the mystery tattoo had a lot of personality and flair, shall we say, and kept declaring, "It's *obvious*, it's waiting for you to figure it out *right in front of your face!*" I tried to guess what the tattoo was for about fifteen minutes as his friends hysterically egged the situation on (*"No one can ever tell what it is and he is trying to make it happen!!"*). There was a very sane and cool Hawaiian guy there who was trying to give me clues but I finally gave up. "It's *Grace Jones*! *Obviously!!*" In no universe did that tattoo look like Grace Jones. Walking around with a tattoo that nobody gets can't be fun, except if you're on drugs and it turns into a parlor game. Mellow night—I actually made myself dinner (barbequed chicken and a salad) and watched a link of the new Kristen Wiig movie *The Skeleton Twins*. I was deep into it when the dog started barking and I heard a pounding at my door that I inferred to mean this tinderbox of an island was finally ablaze and it was time to get my wallet and head for the ocean. Instead it was my neighbor Michael Carl and his housemates, who were in a desperate state. *"Do you have vegetable bouillon cubes?? We only need a few!"* An emergency on Fire Island is unlike those elsewhere. We raided my kitchen and found none. I hate to disappoint.

⠿ THURSDAY, AUGUST 21, 2014—THE PINES, FIRE ISLAND

Cloudy morning. Read a bunch of that Ann Patchett book *State of Wonder* that Jeanne lent me. I'm into it. Hung out on the beach with the Hawaiian who I met yesterday with the not-Grace-Jones-tattoo guy. He's cool. Saw this guy on the beach who I had a thing with from around 2004 to 2007 and he's in *Sleep No More* now and was with his boyfriend and we were all in our bathing suits and the conversation seemed loaded and weird to me. Oh, and it was their anniversary. What's more awkward, running into someone you had a years-long fool-around thing with or someone you dated for years? I think fool-around. What do you even call it when it was never anything official?

There's a pair of binoculars in the house, and I sit on the deck and grab them when something interesting is coming down the beach. It's better than an opera. At tea ran into Sam Champion and team—it's their last night here. He is a very nice person, as you would expect. Two people at tea told me their maids here are also their pot dealers. How efficient! Also an Israeli guy was peeing next to me at tea and casually told me that his pee smells stronger on Fire Island because he only drinks alcohol while here, which was further reminder to hold my breath and hydrate. Really fun dinner party at Michael and Wes's with Josh Wood, Chris Nelson, and Jason Moore, who just directed the new Tina Fey–Amy Poehler movie. We had what I hope is my last conversation of the summer about Ice Bucket Challenges. When I took mine eight days ago, my *WWHL* team already thought it felt old. They're still happening! And the new ones are horrible. Is it un-PC to say "We got it, let's stop now?" I took Wacha on a midnight beach walk and back at home watched Madonna's first Carson appearance, which was amazing on several levels—there's a whole daddy/daughter thing happening, or is it a daddy/sexy-girl thing? Plus it's over fifteen minutes long, and she is so brazen and flirty and ambitious. Blonde Ambition.

FRIDAY, AUGUST 22, 2014—THE PINES, FIRE ISLAND

Amy Sedaris was on *Fallon* last night and she told me that in the Adirondack Room she saw my bobblehead and stole an owl. She says she's gonna give it back when she is on the show again. So there's stuff coming in and stuff going out. I love that. I was walking Wacha on the beach this morning and when I looked back up at my deck I realized that people can see me checking them out with binoculars. It's not like I'm miles away up there. Great. Hickey arrived for what has become our new tradition of a weekend in Fire Island feeling fun and free and gay and groovy. We puttered around the island and everywhere we went people asked us if we were going to the night's marquee attraction: the underwear party on Cherry Grove. We certainly had not planned to go to an *underwear party*, which doesn't even sound hot—right? But the longer you discuss any idea, the more not-crazy it sounds, and on our beach walk with the just-back-from-the-city mayors of Fire Island, Bill and Chris, during which Chris gave us his yearly Fire Island Beach Home tour ("there's the *Normal Heart* house; that's where Calvin used to be; that's Robin Byrd's house"), it became clear that they wouldn't rest until we were all in Cherry Grove surrounded by underwear. After further discussion, we discovered that if we *did* go we did not have to actually walk around in our underwear. That sold it. Saw Fredrik Eklund at low tea in a beachy hoody; that is one realtor who can pull off a beachy-cozy look. After, on the porch at Sip n Twirl, a dude came up to me and told me that he's decorating Joan Rivers's bedroom and that he had seen Joan on my show, which he'd never seen before and about which he now had plenty of judgment: he really wanted me to know that I don't get too deep with anybody. But he wanted to make it clear that he wasn't insulting me, and the more he explained it, the more insulting it sounded. Bill and Chris explicated the schedule of events on this nuthouse island and it's insane—it's low tea (in straight terms, "tea" means *happy hour*), then Sip n Twirl, then you eat, *then* you go out! So Hickey and I were distressed to learn that after the magic of Lina we had to go *kill time* before the underwear party, which didn't start until around midnight. We did so by hitting our YouTube at home and vibing on some classic duets—highlights were Kenny and Dolly singing "We've Got Tonight" live—just check her out walking into the arena mid-song like the country thoroughbred she is—and Lionel and Diana singing "Endless Love" at the Oscars, which is magic despite the fact that she seems to be barely looking at her singing partner. The underwear party was a zillion guys checking their clothes as they walked in, and Hickey and I hanging with the clothed people with restricted access on the porch. We could *watch* the people on the dance floor in their undies, but we couldn't partake. You know what, that was just fine with us. There were people of all shapes and sizes and I will tell you there are many varieties of underwear these days. I spent much of the night talking to an insurance lawyer wearing a leash and collar. So many nuances to Obamacare! We walked back from Cherry Grove via the beach around three, glad we went.

SJP's arrival on the ferry was the closest thing I've seen to Dolly Levi returning to the Harmonia Gardens—boys carrying her luggage, others handing her flyers, kisses blown, photos taken—for real I thought a song-and-dance number was gonna break out and the kids passing out flyers by the ferry were going to thrust her into the air. As the sun set over the ocean outside, Hickey made incredible steaks; she made some corn and a salad (I watched and refreshed drinks). SJP has a thing for grocery stores—she feels like when you travel, the local stores tell you a lot about where you are. She was fascinated—a lot of visitors are—about how an island with no cars and no (good) restaurants functions, and what kind of grocery store must service such a place. So after dinner we took a walk to town and went into the Pines Pantry so she could investigate. She walked through that Pantry with the wonder of a child visiting Disney World for the first time. *"Look at the beautiful butcher section! Here's the hardware! A Crock-Pot!"* and the people working in the store reacted to her with the same wonder, so it was like the animals in the zoo watching the visitors. We wound up on the porch at Sip n Twirl, having a drink and listening to music. And when I say that, I should point out that we were right next to the speakers, which didn't stop this kid from coming over and telling SJ that he would be honored to sing her a song. Ever gracious, she acted as though it was purely natural when he sang the entirety of John Legend's "All of Me" in full *American Idol* audition mode while ABBA *blasted* from the speakers five feet away. I was in hysterics, I might add. And we became obsessed by the mechanics (or lack of) of an incredibly drunk girl who seemed like she was going to topple over at any time. We ran into a ton of Broadway Boys who either knew SJ, Hickey, or me—so there was a lot of catching up and one of them said a big theater critic for the *New York Times* was at the underwear party last night and that really levels the playing field between critic and actor, when everyone is in their undies. Right?

We saw the super-drunk girl on the beach today! "I am so sorry," she screamed to us as we walked. SJ told her she was just happy she made it out alive. She looked different coherent and in a bathing suit, although I am fairly certain she had a cocktail in her hand. It was blazing sun all day and we took advantage of every second. We became fascinated with the choices people make regarding their swimsuits. So many options! Speedos in every shape and cut, some G-strings, not a lot of board shorts, and for me, what I would consider to be trunks that border on hot pants. And may I remind you that Mr. James Brolin complemented my almost-hot pants not eight days ago. Hickey wore board shorts. The Clark Kent Lawyer made an impression on me the other day in his square-cut Speedo with a lot of junk in the trunk. Sam Champion's suits resonated with me even after he left, because he seems to enjoy several manifestations of a sunset motif on a square-cut Speedo. It was a special joy walking through the nudie section with SJ and seeing her react to the varietals of penis and testes splayed out for display. For a lady who starred in a TV show with "Sex" in the title, her level of innocence is surprising. Hickey and SJP are here for thirty-six hours total and the amount of food they have brought into my kitchen is astounding. I am not used to having so much food in the house. Hickey made an incredibly robust breakfast and lunch. I had a mini breakdown because Wacha spent roughly six hours chasing his shadow—on the deck, on a long walk. . . . I Googled "compulsive shadow chasing" and it could turn into a real disorder. I felt a weight on me for the first time since I got to the island. We took SJ back to Sip n Twirl before her 9 p.m. ferry and sat on the railing listening to music as twinks 'n gays of all shapes and sizes testified at her feet. One gentleman presented her with something of a modern dance that you might consider in the vogue family. Guess who else was there? The high-ponytailed hype-lady from James Wilkie's October birthday party! What are the chances? She freaked me out again, so at least she's consistent. Hickey and I got SJ on the ferry and danced the night away. It was a great one.

Years ago Grac and I came up with a phrase that we decided to say to each other in the event that one of us suspected that the other's body had been overtaken by aliens. This phrase would be proof of whether or not we were still us. The problem is that we keep forgetting the exact phrase, and today spent ten minutes in the pool hashing it out. And as I write this I am realizing that maybe Grac is in fact an alien. She (or her shell inhabited by an alien) and Amanda came on the noon ferry. I walked there barefoot in wet bathing suit and nothing else; my inner island self is almost fully realized here, I may never leave. (Actually, I tried to extend a couple days but they rented the house to someone starting Thursday.) Hickey and I had a sentimental goodbye at the 10 a.m. ferry and ran into Robin Byrd. A guy came to the house to record narration for two Bravo shows and it was hilarious recording lines about Vicki Gunvalson on a closet floor in a wet bathing suit. Bill and Chris took the day off to hang out with the girls. While I was scoping out this guy in a traditional-cut blue Speedo who was parked in front of our house reading a magazine, Grac had another idea for her ideas list—an app for binoculars. I think it's genius. It probably exists. She made a special Fire Island Pines 2014 playlist featuring Samantha Fox, Boston, Run-DMC, Milli Vanilli (Grac and Amanda were Fab and Rob for Halloween one year), and six more hours of perfect music that was the soundtrack of our day. Bill said he sweats pot at the gym. Grac got him a Hawaiian necklace with a bone on it that he's gonna wear like a choker. Oh, and there were pot lollipops. We all tried to point out our livers—another new parlor game!—I don't think any of us got it right. I kept debating going and talking to the blue Speedo guy and didn't. I didn't see him at low tea, either, but there was a flag dancer making a rainbow in the sky to the tune of "Take Me Home"—he's a member of the local flag-dancing group the Flaggots, of course. We had dinner at Bill's, though it was cut short when they ran out of pot and tequila. I was so glad I remembered Blouse's birthday before the night was over—I left her a long message, which made me wonder where the hell Blouse was late on a Monday night in St. Louis. It was no easy feat stumbling home across the island on endless boardwalks in the pitch-black night, but the smell of meat-filled barbeques wafting through the air and the perennial sound of the waves made it all better. We were in bed by eleven-thirty and Grac was doing a character who was rating every wave after it hit the beach (CRASH—"Yeah, yeah, that was good." CRASH—"No—that one stunk . . ." CRASH—"OK, fair."), which was funnier than it sounds here.

▦ TUESDAY, AUGUST 26, 2014—THE PINES, FIRE ISLAND

After nine days here I think my motor skills are deteriorating. Thankfully, Wacha has not lost his; he was a normal dog on his morning beach walk. Amanda had diagnosed him with anxiety and compulsiveness that may have to do with past trauma. Joy. I gave Grac the Beats by Dre headphones for Sam. I figure they can't crush his head like a vise in the same way as mine since he's under ten. Grac suggested to Bruce that he buck the LA trends and get himself a muscle car. And yesterday he did, a Dodge Charger. He texted wanting to know what he should name it and Grac said it needs to be "something like Carmen, something with a good edge, *West Side Story* meets Marisa Tomei meets a maraschino cherry." Bruce agrees but doesn't like Carmen or Carmine. So he's thinking. After I put the girls on the ferry, my last day here evaporated into thin air like the mist over the ocean. (Was that cheesy? But it's true!) Andrew Rannells and Mike Doyle dropped by in their swimsuits with roadies. We killed my last bottle of Whispering Angel—they made wine spritzers (which Mike thinks get you more drunk because of the bubbles), and we talked and talked while taking sun, jumping in the ocean, looking at people from my deck with my not-obvious binoculars, and jumping in the pool. Those guys are a cute couple and—even though this aired like fifteen years ago—I can't get the image of Mike Doyle dressed in a miniskirt and lipstick as the *Oz* prison bitch out of my mind. Wacha ran right up to this creepy scene happening on the beach, which was a Thai massage, but a shady one, and he was trying to jump up on the guy getting the massage. Wacha loves massage lotion, which is a constant battle for me during my weekly Adam massages. Then Adam showed up and *I* got one (but not creepy), for ninety minutes. I told him he is looking more like a man and less like a twink and he said I have been saying that to him for almost a year, which

I forgot at the time but now vaguely remember. At one point I got up to go to the bathroom and the blue Speedo guy was back, in the same spot. I decided to definitely go talk to him after the massage but at that point he was gone. At tea I got invited to an "It's a Madge Madge Madge Madge World" party, which I'm told will be the largest-ever gathering of people dressed as Madonna (a rep from Guinness is coming to map it out) and I momentarily considered finding another house to stay in for the next few nights so I can attend. The host is going as "Live to Tell" Madonna; he has a huge cross he's going to schlep around. We wondered who we would be. I am all over the map about my *Madentity*, but I think "Hung Up" Madonna. Guess who came up to me at tea—Blue Speedo Guy! He said he'd been hanging near my house because of the incredible music (Grac's six-hour playlist). He is from San Francisco and he's a twin. We made plans to see each other later but I had dinner at Wes and Michael's (they don't eat buns and they got hamburger buns just for me) and was so tired after, I canceled. Not exactly making great use of my last night on Fire Island but Daddy is tired.

▦ WEDNESDAY, AUGUST 27, 2014—FIRE ISLAND– SAG HARBOR

Blue Speedo Guy came by the house to say goodbye while I was packing, which was sweet and very Fire Island. We don't have one thing to say to each other. Took the ferry with Andrew and Mike and discussed our Madonnas. Andrew says he would be "Borderline" Madonna and Mike seems to think he'd be in the "Holiday" outfit from the "Blonde Ambition" tour but then he said he wants to be her when she's hairy. So I don't know. Then they both went back to "Like a Prayer" Madonna and I don't even know what that means. Drove straight to Amanda's in Sag Harbor for lunch with Jim and Hickey, and Amanda got stung by a bee on her ass, then stood up and broke a glass of wine, so it was very dramatic. I FaceTimed with Bruce, who was in the Dodge Charger. He thinks he might name it Roxie but I think it needs a man's name. He doesn't disagree. Then I Skyped with my parents and my mom announced, "The FIFTH DIMENSION is in town and EVERYBODY'S talking about it! People are going NUTS!!" I paused to think and my dad cleared it up. "No, Evelyn—it's *One Direction*." Aha! Wacha seems over his compulsive shadow- and reflection-chasing now that we're home. There are a ton of parties this weekend and everybody's out here but I am purposefully trying to be open and play the weekend by ear. Met Sandy and Elaine Wynn at Sam's and had a little Vegas open mic with her; I asked about her favorite casinos and the Vegas club scene and then I realized I should be talking to her about Siegfried and Roy, who of course she has known for years. Watched some Dolly Parton stuff on YouTube, then got on to old Teri Garr appearances on *Letterman*. The chemistry between them! Magic! I found what is regarded as her last TV appearance (on his show in June of 2008) and read something published recently saying she's really ill. It made me so sad. Life goes by in a blip. Trite but true: One day you're the toast of the town and the next . . .

THURSDAY, AUGUST 28, 2014—SAG HARBOR

I am often the guy trying to keep the party alive when everyone's leaving, and that's kind of how I felt today as the carefree excesses of the Pines were strangled by reality. Next week is a bear, so Daryn had a lot of scheduling questions plus I had several phone interviews, a conference call about casting the next season of *RHONY*, and on and on. Boring. We're not back on for another nine days, but sitting on the phone all morning, I felt like my vacation was over. Then Liza emailed me that TMZ was saying Joan Rivers had stopped breathing. *Stopped breathing?* I was stunned. And upset. And this has nothing to do with the show we're pitching, it boils down to something simple that Liza said: *I don't want to live in a world without Joan Rivers*. I was on edge all day, and reached out to my rabbi, Bill Persky, for a little therapy over a hamburger at LT Burger. He was full of classic Bill wit and advice, and I was so glad he ordered onion rings, because there's no greater delicacy. The service at LT was all out of whack, though. I was texting with Anderson and he said that people at CNN heard that Joan was in bad shape, and with Liza and with Michael, with whom I am scheduled to continue pitching our show in the next few weeks. I took Wacha out for a long walk on the bay. He is back to normal now, all obsessive-compulsiveness gone. Then I got to find out what it's like to be a doctor's wife. I had a date with Dr. Kyle but he texted at seven-thirty that after a thirteen-hour day, the ER was full and he would be late. I realized at nine that I probably shouldn't count on going out to dinner and I was fucked, with no food in my house other than a Sam's pizza in the freezer. So Sam's it was, second night in a row, and I felt a little pathetic. I texted Anderson a picture of Wacha chewing on his bone with his back to the TV, *AC360* on the screen, then tweeted it but didn't realize that the bone was placed where my dick would be, so then everybody started saying how filthy I am. Then Anderson joined in and tweeted, "Is that a bone?" and I started watching *Project Runway*, which I haven't seen since I was one of its EPs at Bravo about five years ago, and was horrified to see the makeup is sponsored by Mary Kay Cosmetics and the accessories are Aldo. Low rent! So I sent a tweet about Mary Kay . . . and then immediately deleted it. This is what would happen to me if I was always staying home at night left to my own devices! The doc showed up at ten-thirty and I was very supportive. I wonder what would be worse, being married to a doctor or to a late-night talk-show host?

▦ FRIDAY, AUGUST 29, 2014—SAG HARBOR

Still no news about Joan Rivers. Liza sent a clip of a 2006 pilot—one of my big on-air breaks—called *Straight Talk*, starring Joan and four gay guys, one of them me. She was so kind to me then and never stopped. (And she begged me to get Botox—I didn't.) It was such a big deal for me to be sitting next to her on that show, just as it is now when she's on mine. Feeling sad. Did more scheduling stuff for September. It's going to be a bear, is all. I just have to get over the stress and enjoy the next few days because this bliss is about to evaporate.

Went by Sandy's; Barry and DVF are staying there. They analyzed Wacha's shadow chasing, which was in full effect. DVF follows him on Instagram, which amuses me. Sandy is having two hundred people Sunday night, which he said really means two hundred and fifty with houseguests (OK, maybe three hundred), so there were lawn mowers, delivery men, a masseuse, pool guy, caterers, a chef, and Sandy's houseguests all milling around. Controlled chaos. Stopped by the Fallons', where a birthday party for Cameron Diaz was in effect—Nancy really knows how to put on a birthday party—and I took a Jacuzzi in their deep, 1970s-style wooden tub that smells very "Rocky Mountain High." Also Jimmy set up a full karaoke thing with these microphones that have sound effects on them and some guitar lyric program on his iPad. I, of course, got deep into Fresquilas and Doritos. Rashida Jones said that Wacha looks really big and I said he photographs smaller than he is and she said, "You dick, I've *met him*. I'm not *a fan*." So I have officially gone nuts. Came home, fed Wacha, and went to Jeanne and Fred's for dinner. Fred just got an enormous job with the New York City Department of Education and we all toasted to him. Then to the 1.2 million kids starting school in the city public schools next week. Then to Joan Rivers. Then to great old friends. Actually, I think we toasted to great old friends first. Bruce texted me potential car names for the Dodge Charger: Vito, Monty, Rocky, Sly, Carlo, or Tony. I would like Carlo the best if there wasn't a Monte Carlo already in existence. We are discussing tomorrow because I have thoughts on the others too. You can't keep a car for too long without naming it. Come to think of it, mine doesn't have one, so what do I know?

▦ SATURDAY, AUGUST 30, 2014—SAG HARBOR

Perfect Hamptons beach day. Walked Wacha on Long Beach for an hour and chatted with Em and Bruce, who feels like the car name has gotta be Monty. I was mostly leaning towards Carlo, so I think we're on the same page. (Although thinking more about Carlo, I'm just getting the pun of a *car* named *Carlo*. Cute!) I will support Monty, though. It was a drama-packed day at Beach Lane Beach Club, i.e., Marci's house. After a gorgeous lunch (cold salads and smoked gravlax), we had a big beach hang and her friend Joe somehow dislocated his shoulder and it needed to be snapped back into place. Snapping a shoulder back into place is not in any of our skill sets, so Marci (flowing blonde hair over flowing Dior-gray beach dress that come to think of it was maybe actually a gown) and

I ran around the beach asking every clump of people if anyone was a doctor. Marci (she cast *SNL* for years and years, so she's great at casting) found the most typecast-looking Hamptons doctor (tall, gray hair, some kind of golf hat—Alan Alda-y), who told him to get to the emergency room. So off a group of them went and I realized that I happen to know someone at the ER at this very moment who might be able to help. I told them to look for a soap-opera-looking doctor with an intensely full head of hair and then texted Dr. Kyle, who I have come to realize looks just like that guy who played Grant Putnam on *GH* in the day. They hooked up and the shoulder got snapped into place. In the meantime there were doobies on the beach, and I had long chats with Adam Glassman, who I tried to get on Tinder, and ScottStuff, who just returned from surfing in Malibu and told me all about the beach scene there vs. what we were looking at today. The difference seemed to come down to more fake tits in Malibu, but maybe I'm oversimplifying. Hickey had a dinner party at his incredibly groovy rental in the Springs overlooking the Sound. My highlight of the night was hanging with Ron and Iva Rifkin—together forty-five years this week—who were endlessly entertaining. I coaxed Iva not only to tell me all about her early days as a chorus girl with Valerie Harper, but to take her (always in a bun) hair down. Fun! I drove home in the hot night with the top down listening to the Grateful Dead under the stars, which is what summer is all about.

⊞ SUNDAY, AUGUST 31, 2014—SAG HARBOR

You think the last weekend of the summer is going to be a sun-kissed dream, but the reality is you wake up and it's overcast and Joan Rivers is on life support and you have a September of obligations looming and you have to reevaluate everything. Blundered around all morning. FaceTimed with Bruce, who was in the middle of his own morning of blahs in Los Angeles. Invited myself for lunch at Mark and Kelly's and I arrived just as David Muir left, which was upsetting because I would've liked to have seen the hair up close. (It's a newsy masterpiece!) Then back at my house Adam appeared and my mood turned around on the table. I started feeling really grateful for everything—a two-hour massage will do that. For

Sandy's party, I took the opportunity of the last night of summer to throw on a white sport coat while my designated driver, Mark Consuelos, waited by the road. On the way, Mark and I decided to do some variation of Sober September—it may be weekdays. We have to figure out the logistics tomorrow. It was raining in Sag Harbor but East Hampton was clear and the thousands of votives in the yard lit up everybody known to have ever set foot in the Hamptons: Martha Stewart, Lorne Michaels, Jon Bon Jovi (amazing hair), DVF nursing a bee sting, Donna Karan just back from Bali, Roger Waters (of whom I am in awe), Michael Eisner and family—the son is making a Grateful Dead documentary and I wanted to take out my credit card and invest—Les Moonves and the very sweet Chenbot, and on and on. It was fun, but Hickey and I were fantasizing about what could be happening at Sip n Twirl. In that spirit, I connected with a guy who appeared out of nowhere and after twenty minutes I decided was *the one* until he asked, "What do you think of Brits?" clueing me in that he was actually interested in the third member of our conversation, who'd gone off to get a drink. I told him that normally I love a Brit, but that for some reason this Brit was not passing muster for me. I fled the conversation soon thereafter. Janie Buffett and I had a great hang in one of the outdoor couch areas after dinner and were joined by Anjelica Huston, who told me she recently was sucked in by *The Real Housewives of Melbourne* and, on a separate but similar note, is very sympathetic to Teresa's plight.

Towards the end of the night, SJP, Matthew, and I were talking about Joan Rivers. We'd all seen her at various points this summer, and she was now all the proof needed that life, as the saying goes, can change in the blink of an eye. With that, SJ offered a toast to the end of summer of 2014, and as we raised our glasses and drank, she saw that I was sad. She began to offer a toast to the future, but Matthew jumped on my lamenting bandwagon, listing our current ills: "Isis, Putin, China taking over the world . . ." I began throwing some of my own in: "Israel, our vanishing Manhattan . . ." but she would not hear it and cut us both off. "*Both of you—raise your glasses.* Here's to the fall—which holds great promise for each of us here. There is good to come for us all. . . . It will be great." We drank to that, and in that moment, we all believed it.

Labor Day. Unofficially the last day of it all. It's been almost a year since I began this diary and in some respects I'm back where I started. Fashion Week is upon us, next week I'm heading to the DVF show and the U.S. Open (Mom and Dad are going on a tour of Nazi hot spots and can't make it), and I feel kinda fat (but that's for the Ninj and me to deal with this week). I'm still single but there are prospects, and this morning I called Surfin to make sure my apartment hadn't burned down in the last few weeks. Before we hung up, I asked him about that guy Brandon from the tenth floor who was on the flight with Madonna. "He moved out last month, Andy, back to LA," Surfin informed me. *"You were too slow!"* Why is Surfin always right?

Slow start to the day. Jeanne and Fred stopped by and Jeanne gave me some great notes about the architectural plans to my new Barbie Manhattan Dream Pad. (Hmmm, why do I go right to Barbie? Wouldn't it be a *Ken* Dream Pad?) With luck, a year from now I'll be almost ready to move in. Met Hickey at SJP and Matthew's beach. We had some amazing ocean time while Wacha chased reflections; I swear that dog might be on the spectrum. Hickey told me my phrase of the summer has been "A hundred percent"—that's been my response to him all summer. Who knew? As magic hour approached, Marc Shaiman and Scott Wittman arrived with the ashes of their beloved dog Wally Woo, who passed almost a year ago after fifteen years, much of that spent swimming at this very beach. Rainer had painted a beautiful picture of Wally, which he brought along, and Victor, Bridget Everett, Matthew, and I all watched from the edge of the water while Marc and Scott scattered Wally's ashes in the surf. For all the iconic music those two have created for the stage and screen, I think Wally might have been their greatest source of joy. Marc was in tears putting the dog back where he loved the most, and then we all were too. Standing there watching Marc end his time with Wally Woo, with Wacha at my feet, filled me with love for what is, I hope, the beginning of fifteen years of our togetherness. As for Wacha, I *wanted* him to experience some of the poignant moment but he was so self-involved I could've killed him.

I came home to a message from Nancy and Jimmy to meet them at the American Hotel for some end-of-summer caviar. You don't have to ask me twice. Many toasts to the end of the beach season, and we moved on to Sen and some sake. Rashida Jones joined in progress. We all walked to BuddhaBerry, the FroYo craze of the summer of 2014, where they had locked the doors a couple minutes before and the Nordic lady in charge would make no exceptions. We felt defeated—*how can we end the summer without FroYo?!?* As we stood dwelling in our misfortune, a Real Housewife of I don't know where (hell?) approached. She was tall, mid-fifties, fake blonde and fake boobs in a black tank top that said "Never Never Never"—we told her it was closed and she got into a long thing with Jimmy, who is the mayor of everywhere and has the unique ability to talk to anybody anywhere about anything without hitting a wall. (I do not have this gift.) She left and we stayed hanging out like teenagers with nowhere to go, pondering the "Never Never Never" shirt. *What did that mean?* I will never *sleep with you*? I will never *marry you*? (We think she would've gone all the way. . . .) Twenty minutes later the "Never Never Never" lady returned with a big bag of FroYo (from the inferior place down the street) in her bountiful bosom! We were thrilled—what a gift! It hit the spot, and we stayed laughing and loitering on the empty street for about an hour. Came home and watched old Dick Cavett interviews on YouTube while Wacha endlessly licked my face. Back to the city—and real life—tomorrow.

ABOUT THE AUTHOR

Andy Cohen is the host and executive producer of *Watch What Happens Live,* Bravo's late-night live interactive talk show. He also serves as executive producer of *The Real Housewives* franchise and hosts the network's highly rated reunion specials. He recently launched Radio Andy, a 24/7 entertainment channel on Sirius XM. He's won an Emmy and two Peabody Awards for his work, and lives in New York City with his dog, Wacha.